Public Sector Ethics

Public Sector Ethics: Compliance, Integrity, and Comparison presents a comprehensive treatment of the subject of ethics in the public sector. What structural elements are necessary and how to create organizations that make ethics their priority are the questions that this edited book addresses. It focuses on ethics management in public organizations and includes national case studies from select low- to middle-income countries.

Taken together, the chapters in this book cover the mechanisms, activities, and approaches that public organizations employ in ethics management. These are of utmost importance because the actions of public organizations affect citizens' lives, liberties, and property, and their ethical character affects citizens' faith in government. Numerous factors are at play in each instance of ethics management in public organizations, and controlling ethical behavior is difficult. This book suggests that effective ethics management requires a comprehensive approach. Traditional approaches such as ethics codes, policies and legislation, training, incentives, sanctions, monitoring, and compliance reviews are tools to achieve ethical conformity. Yet, they are effective only if leadership, values, and cultural transformation support them. This edited volume is a cohesive treatment of the subject, covering traditional approaches to ethics management, such as monitoring and compliance, and more contemporary approaches, like integrity building through ethical leadership and organizational values, as well as how to skillfully and effectively combine them to change organizational ethical contexts.

This book exposes readers to new approaches and emerging issues in public sector ethics, aids in understanding the challenges of creating ethical organizations, and helps to develop a deeper understanding of ethics management in government organizations. It will be of interest to researchers, academics, and advanced students in the fields of business ethics, public administration and management, leadership, and organizational studies.

Christopher Reddick is a professor in the Department of Public Administration at the University of Texas at San Antonio (UTSA), USA.

Tansu Demir is an associate professor in the Department of Public Administration at the University of Texas at San Antonio (UTSA), USA.

Bruce J. Perlman is Regents' Professor in the School of Public Administration at the University of New Mexico, USA.

Routledge Critical Studies in Public Management
Series editor: Stephen Osborne

The study and practice of public management has undergone profound changes across the world. Over the last quarter century, we have seen

- increasing criticism of public administration as the over-arching framework for the provision of public services,
- the rise (and critical appraisal) of the 'New Public Management as an emergent paradigm for the provision of public services,
- the transformation of the 'public sector' into the cross-sectoral provision of public services, and
- the growth of the governance of inter-organizational relationship as an essential element in the provision of public services.

In reality these trends have not so much replaced each other as elided or co-existed together—the public policy processes has not gone away as a legitimate topic of study, intra-organizational management continue to be essential to the efficient provision of public services, whilst the governance of inter-organizational and inter-sectoral relationships is now essential to the effective provision of these services.

Further, whilst the study of public management has been enriched by contribution of a range of insights from the 'mainstream' management literature it has also contributed to this literature in such areas as networks and inter-organizational collaboration, innovation and stakeholder theory.

This series is dedicated to presenting and critiquing this important body of theory and empirical study. It will publish books that both explore and evaluate the emergent and developing nature of public administration, management and governance (in theory and practice) and examine the relationship with and contribution to the over-arching disciplines of management and organizational sociology.

Books in the series will be of interest to academics and researchers in this field, students undertaking advanced studies of it as part of their undergraduate or postgraduate degree and reflective policy makers and practitioners.

Public Value and the Post-Pandemic Society
Usman W. Chohan

Social Equity and Public Management Theory
A Global Outlook
Kimberly Wiley, Sarah Young and Denita Cepiku

Public Sector Ethics
Compliance, Integrity, and Comparison
Edited by Christopher Reddick, Tansu Demir, and Bruce J. Perlman

For more information about this series, please visit: www.routledge.com/Routledge-Critical-Studies-in-Public-Management/book-series/RSPM

Public Sector Ethics

Compliance, Integrity, and Comparison

**Edited by Christopher Reddick,
Tansu Demir, and Bruce J. Perlman**

NEW YORK AND LONDON

First published 2025
by Routledge
605 Third Avenue, New York, NY 10158

and by Routledge
4 Park Square, Milton Park, Abingdon, Oxon, OX14 4RN

Routledge is an imprint of the Taylor & Francis Group, an informa business

ISBN: 978-1-032-72728-8 (hbk)
ISBN: 978-1-032-72730-1 (pbk)
ISBN: 978-1-003-41625-8 (ebk)

DOI: 10.4324/9781003416258

Typeset in Times New Roman
by Apex CoVantage, LLC

Contents

List of Figures   *vii*
List of Tables   *viii*
List of Contributors   *ix*

Introduction   1
CHRISTOPHER REDDICK, TANSU DEMIR, AND BRUCE J. PERLMAN

1 **What Is Compliance? The Coercive Approach to Ethics
   Management**   14
   DANNY NATHANIEL CARR

2 **Ethics Codes, Codes of Conduct: Definitions, Applications,
   and Effectiveness**   28
   DIANE L. ODEH AND JESSICA HOMER

3 **Ethics Training and Employee Development**   49
   BRETT S. SHARP

4 **Sanctions and Incentives in Public Ethics Management**   72
   NEVBAHAR ERTAS

5 **Comparing and Bridging Ethics Management Approaches**   92
   EDGAR KARSSING AND ALAIN HOEKSTRA

6 **Does Leadership Matter? Why and How?**   111
   RUSI SUN AND YAHONG ZHANG

7 The Power of Organizational Values: Communication,
    Conflict, and Alignment in Shaping Employee Behavior
    and Decision-Making   127
    CHEVANESE SAMMS BROWN AND KAREN D. SWEETING

8 Public Sector Ethics in the Americas: The Brazilian Public
    Ethics Management Case Study   146
    TEMÍSTOCLES MURILO DE OLIVEIRA JÚNIOR AND
    JOAQUIM MANUEL CROCA CAEIRO

9 Preconditions for Anti-Corruption Reform: The Post-1989
    Italian Experience and Lessons   169
    DANIEL L. FELDMAN AND JASON D. RIVERA

10 Public Integrity Compliance in Thailand   187
    AMPORN TAMRONGLAK, PATTHARA LIMSIRA, AND TASS PONGPISIT

11 Political Leadership and Public Sector Ethics in Africa:
    A Comparative Study of Ghana and Rwanda   217
    GEORGE BABINGTON AMEGAVI AND ZECHARIAH LANGNEL

    Index   *236*

Figures

6.1	The Chapter Structure and the Main Findings	113
7.1	How Organizational Values May Be Communicated	130
10.1	Social Media's Effect on Whistleblowing Intention Model	209
11.1	Corruption Perception Index for Ghana and Rwanda, 2013–2023	224
11.2	World Governance Indicators, Control of Corruption in Ghana and Rwanda	224

Tables

3.1 Differentiated Ethics Training for Public Sector Roles   68
5.1 The Main Characteristics of the Compliance Approach and the Integrity Approach   97
7.1 Key Organizational Value Types and Their Associated Behavioral Drivers   132
7.2 Shifting Value Paradigms   138
10.1 Thai Anti-Corruption Agencies' Duties   191
10.2 Summary of Anti-Corruption Theories in Research   196
10.3 Examples of Good Governance Principles–Related Laws and Significance in Thailand   199
10.4 Summary of Big Six Strategies, Its Pros and Cons   201
10.5 Summary of Whistleblowing Studies   207
10.6 Goodness of Fit Result   210
10.7 Structural Model Results   210

Contributors

George Babington Amegavi, Industry Skills and Advisory Council, Australia

Chevanese Samms Brown, Savannah State University, U.S.

Joaquim Manuel Croca Caeiro, University of Lisbon, Portugal

Danny Nathaniel Carr, University of the West Indies, Trinidad and Tobago

Nevbahar Ertas, University of Alabama at Birmingham, U.S.

Daniel L. Feldman, John Jay College of Criminal Justice, U.S.

Alain Hoekstra, Integrity Consultant, the Netherlands

Jessica Homer, Florida Licensed Attorney, U.S.

Edgar Karssing, Nyenrode Business Universiteit, the Netherlands

Zechariah Langnel, University of Education, Winneba, Ghana

Patthara Limsira, Thammasat University, Bangkok, Thailand

Diane L. Odeh, Portland State University, U.S.

Temístocles Murilo de Oliveira Júnior, University of Lisbon, Portugal

Tass Pongpisit, Thammasat University, Bangkok, Thailand

Jason D. Rivera, John Jay College of Criminal Justice, U.S.

Brett S. Sharp, University of Central Oklahoma, U.S.

Rusi Sun, University of Michigan–Dearborn, U.S.

Karen D. Sweeting, University of Rhode Island, U.S.

Amporn Tamronglak, Thammasat University, Bangkok, Thailand

Yahong Zhang, Rutgers University, U.S.

Introduction

Christopher Reddick, Tansu Demir,
and Bruce J. Perlman

This book focuses on public sector ethics management. Ethics is the study of what is right, fair, and just (Amundsen & Andrade, 2009). In the context of public administration, it is the discovery and application of society's normative standards to the official conduct of public servants in public organizations. How to make ethical decisions, how to prevent ethical misconduct, and, more importantly, how to create organizations that make ethics their priority are the questions that this edited volume addresses. Why a book that focuses on ethics in the public sector? An answer to this question involves two related but distinct challenges for public sector organizations: commitment and corruption.

Importance of Ethics in the Public Sector

Public employees' commitment to their jobs, organizations, and public service depends on their ethics. On the one hand, their professional ethics underpins the felt obligation to safeguard the public. Their professional ethics commit them to act in the public interest rather than in their own, as whistleblowers have been shown to do (Brewer & Selden, 1998), or altruistically at the risk of lives to save others as part of their as firefighters have been seen to do (Lee & Olshfski, 2002). On the other hand, commitment fosters the work ethic of public administrators. Commitment is a key determinant of their motivation to work (Liou & Nyhan, 1994). Effective public administration rests on the assumption that government employees will carry out their duties competently and enthusiastically. Yet, they are often characterized as overly bureaucratic and inefficient, giving public organizations a reputation for lacking the efficiency and effectiveness of business organizations. A 2019 Gallup poll found that 60 percent of Americans agreed with the statement that, in general, businesses can do things more efficiently than the government. A 2014 Gallup poll found that nearly 90 percent (89 percent) of Americans believed that federal tax dollars were wasted. Though the perception of waste for state and local governments was better, still 83 percent and 77 percent agreed, respectively. These numbers suggest that public employees are closely scrutinized by citizens who are skeptical of their commitment to performance.

DOI: 10.4324/9781003416258-1

Corruption in the public bureaucracy has been a grave worry for low- and middle-income countries since the modern study of public administration (Dwivedi, 1967). In these systems, unethical public employees may augment meager pay and pocket public funds using mechanisms that range from keeping tax collections to charging citizens for public services (Graycar, 2020). In higher-income nations, public employees and officials often enter the public sector for job security or prestige rather than to enrich themselves. Moreover, the opportunities for self-enrichment in the public sector in developed countries have meager payoffs. For example, among the charges of receiving illegal campaign finance contributions against New York Mayor Eric Adams, the accusation of self-enrichment boils down to soliciting "free and heavily discounted luxury travel" valued at $100,000 in exchange for political favors (Barron, 2024). This is nothing compared to the private sector, where top-level executives can be paid millions, and self-dealing, fraud, and embezzlement can yield mega-millions. For example, former CEO Joseph Nacchio is estimated to have used insider trading fraud to gain $52 million in the Qwest Communications scandal.

Nevertheless, even in the United States, the public sector still suffers from a high risk of corruption and misbehavior by officials in public agencies. For example, the US Department of Justice's (DOJ's) Public Integrity section compiles data regarding public corruption convictions in each state. DOJ's report shows that high rates of misconduct continue to be an issue in government and need to be addressed. According to Transparency International, which measures experts' perceptions of corruption worldwide, the United States has done little to improve in its battle against public sector corruption. In 2023, out of 180 countries and territories, the United States ranked 24th for the second year. The United States scored 69 out of 100 on the group's 2023 Corruption Perceptions Index, the same score as the previous year and only a two-point improvement from its 2020 and 2021 scores. In developing nations, corruption is even more pervasive due in large part to environments more conducive to ethical misconduct. The Transparency International Index indicates dramatically low scores and concomitant rankings for developing nations. Corruption has forced many governments to renew their emphasis on, and take action to, promoting ethical conduct in public organizations (Beeri et al., 2013).

Ethical behavior in a nation's public administration is essential to establish or maintain the legitimacy of government (Frederickson & Ghere, 2014). Public administration is the face of government most familiar to its citizens, and it is evidenced in its public institutions. Public institutions play a key role in the lives of a nation's citizens as service providers, order-keepers, and regulators. The decisions and actions of public organizations affect citizens' lives, liberties, and property, and thus, their ethical character underpins citizens' faith in government. The consequences of ethical violations and lapses in public organizations are costly. Widespread ethical weakness of public organizations damages the reputation of public administration and reduces citizens' confidence in government. They erode government management capacity and worsen declining trust in the public sector (Lee & Liu, 2022). Declining trust makes citizens less willing to contribute to their governments and encourages them to engage in damaging behaviors such as tax evasion or white-collar crime. A lack of respect for public administration may result in a flagging interest in filling public sector jobs and political pressure for alternatives to the public delivery of services (Dodek, 2018).

Traditional Approaches to Ethics in the Public Sector

Whether it is important to study ethics has long been an area for debate in public administration. Some practitioners dismiss the study of ethics as irrelevant to their work and rely on laws, personnel manuals, and job descriptions to define the limits of their public responsibilities. However, the view of public administrators as possessing neutral expertise has been augmented by an understanding of the discretion they exercise in their work and how it affects others (Amundsen & Andrade, 2009).

Most of the traditional literature on ethics in the public sector is abstract and philosophical. It focuses on conceptual dichotomies, such as Rohr's famous "high or low" roads, but has not focused much on empirical research (Menzel, 2015). It privileges a theory-driven approach to writing about public sector ethics. Overall, there is less empirical than theoretical work. There is even less work that derives theories or tests them empirically (Perlman et al., 2021).

Public Sector Values for Public Organizations

Some of the most important contributions to the ethics literature center on the question of what values are most appropriate for public administration (Ekhator, 2012). The debate about whether public sector ethics should be based on business-inspired entrepreneurial or traditional public service values is ongoing and has deep roots in public administration (Goss, 1996). Some, like John Rohr (1998), advocate a tight fit between existing constitutional values and public sector ethics. The challenge for this approach is to have practicing public administrators consciously and knowledgeably reflect these values in their actions, decisions, and conduct on a day-to-day basis. Others, like Gawthorp (1998), have urged a rediscovery of the spirit of democracy to discover values that make public administrators into public servants by combining them with utilitarian values like efficiency and effectiveness. The heavy lift for this view is how to mesh values with the measurement and calculation that are the *sine qua non* of modern metric-driven government agencies. Still, others like Van Wart (1998) have noted that public sector values are always changing and that choosing among them to reflect sociopolitical consensus and establish norms for public administration is the key task of public sector ethics. The difficulty with this undertaking is that developing a notional framework in which choice is ultimately not merely ideological or idiosyncratic may be a bridge too far.

Attempts to reconcile these ideas by combining the entrepreneurship of the New Public Management with the traditional values of public administration into a New Public Service ethic have not been wholly successful (Rauh, 2018). They suffer from some of the same shortcomings as more traditional approaches. They are mostly theoretical and do not reveal what concrete actions keep public employees effectively ethical and committed. They are primarily ideological and rely on prescribing the values inherent in a public service ethic. Ultimately, they do not tie these values to the ethical issues inherent in the coproduction mechanisms essential to the New Public Management. One difficulty is engendering a commitment in public administrators to use their expertise and act as genuine public servants in coproduction with citizens. Another is addressing the self-interested incentives for rent-seeking among citizens in those same endeavors.

Ethics Management in Public Organizations

There is a well-known early debate in public administration between Carl Friedrich and Herman Finer over whether the promotion of accountability is achieved best through the inculcation of internal mores or by promulgating external norms (Cooper, 2006). The so-called Friedrich-Finer debate pits the idea that public servants are best made responsible for professional, ethical norms through their felt integrity against the notion that this is done most effectively by externally constraining them to comply. Most approaches to managing ethics in public organizations rely on just one of these approaches to public sector ethics: ethical behavior in public organizations results from either internal or external forces. Typically, an approach to ethics in public organizations focuses on just one of these views of ethics management, either building integrity or forcing compliance, prescribing one model over empirical practice.

Traditional approaches to implementing ethics management in public organizations include adopting ethics codes, policies, and legislation; utilizing training programs, incentives, or sanctions; and monitoring compliance. As indicated earlier, ethics programs based on conformance to norms (compliance) versus commitment to values (integrity) have different theoretical foundations.

After World War II, a new focus on ethics and responsibility in public organizations emerged in the study of public administration. Yet, research on managing ethics in public organizations has continued to point out significant limitations. Despite increasing awareness and targeted efforts such as comprehensive ethics legislation and training programs at all levels of government, researchers noted that certain issues still plagued the effectiveness of those initiatives. Problems such as emphasizing the role of individual factors over contextual factors in ethical behavior, reactive approaches to unethical behavior, a lack of consistency, and an overly legalistic focus mitigated against the full realization of the potential public sector organizational benefits of ethics undertakings (Treviño & Weaver, 2001; Bowman & Knox, 2008).

Research suggests that to be successful, ethics programs in public organizations should involve more than just the refinement of organizational structures such as roles, rules, procedures, hierarchies, divisions, and departments. Also, they must strengthen the system of core principles, symbols, and rituals around shared values, that is, the organizational culture (Theobald, 1997). Demir et al. (2023) proposed an ethics infrastructure model consisting of four building blocks: awareness and knowledge, incentives and reinforcement, enforcement, and policy support. The authors argued that ethics programs should be comprehensive in both scope and application for them to effectively change behaviors.

Leadership plays a key role in promoting ethical organizations. Brown et al. (2005) define ethical leadership as the "demonstration of normatively appropriate conduct through personal actions and interpersonal relationships, and the promotion of such conduct to followers through two-way communication, reinforcement, and decision-making" (p. 120). Ethics programs are effective only when leaders support them. They should demonstrate commitment to action, display integrity as role models, and employ their organizational resources to incentivize ethical conduct. They should promote integrity throughout the organization by setting examples as moral persons and managers.

Research links ethics to building strong ethical cultures through value development, and leaders are champions of the processes that build consensus around ethical values. Culture is a reasonably stable, value-based, and often profession- or sector-specific outcome of symbolic interaction between individuals and environments that marks an organization and parts of its environment (Raile, 2013, p. 254). Comprehensive ethics programs are effective in the long run when the culture of organizations supports them. Public sector organizations increasingly try to create strong cultures through training programs. These programs promote values such as integrity, transparency, democracy, public interest, social equity, professional excellence, virtue, and accountability (Svara, 2014). Evidence shows that strong and well-implemented programs, combined with the critical support of organizational leaders as role models and enforcers, can drive a strong ethics culture in organizations (Bowman & Knox, 2008; Hassan et al., 2014). Also, it links ethical organizations to greater levels of innovation, productivity, positive organizational climate, and organizational citizenship behavior. In summary, ethical behavior is important for both legal-compliance reasons and higher organizational performance.

The Compliance-Integrity Framework for Ethics in the Public Sector

All ethics programs seek to influence the ethical conduct of individuals. A key distinction between them is whether that influence is thought to be achieved largely by internal or external checks on individual conduct. Internal checks result from inculcating individuals with ethical values and principles so that they control their conduct by choice. External checks result from the operation of recognized frameworks of rules and attendant reinforcements that regulate individual conduct.

A values-based approach to ethics rests on the ideas of social exchange theory (Blau, 1964). This theory argues that when an organization supports and cares about its employees' goals and well-being, this, in return, creates a perceived employee obligation to support the organization's goals. It is a reciprocal relationship that encourages ethical behavior without the force of strict rules and the threat of sanctions. The organization emphasizes activities that help employees in decision-making, provides them with honest advice and counseling, and supports the development of a consensus about what is considered ethical.

A norms-based approach to ethics is grounded in contractual exchange theory (Homans, 1961). Expectations for employee behavior are clearly defined in ethical norms, obedience to which is behaviorally monitored, and deviations from which are sanctioned. Those norms are imposed on employees from the top-down rather than resulting from values all employees identify, and fear of punishment enforces ethical conduct. This suggests a distrust of employees. The lack of trust and reliance on fear suggest that employees respond to organizational ethics programs in a calculating and self-interested way. As Weaver and Trevino (1999) offer, the threat of discipline for violations of ethical norms makes ethical issues salient to employees, heightening their awareness of circumstances that might risk moral failure.

Public service ethics is unique in that it is shaped by the social and political context rather than just professional standards. Public servants must react to environmental constraints and set standards following them (Kyarimpa & Garcia-Zamor, 2006). Cultural, political, and social environments are crucial for understanding ethical conduct in the public sector. On the one hand, public servants encounter bureaucratic discretion in performing their roles and serving the public interest. On the other hand, public scrutiny confronts them with a high degree of accountability and responsiveness to the citizenry and elected officials (Reddick et al., 2020). Accordingly, public service organizations have complex bureaucratic processes to keep employees ethical. This is why compliance has been a focus of many efforts to raise awareness of ethics in the public sector.

These key ideas from the literature suggest that effective ethical performance of public sector organizations requires individuals with awareness and willingness to act ethically, organizational systems that promote integrity, leadership that sets the moral tone, and a political environment that demands accountability. Promoting ethical behavior is difficult because any single instance has many factors at play. Traditional approaches such as adopting ethics codes, policies, and legislation; utilizing training programs, incentives, or sanctions; and monitoring compliance are important, yet insufficient. They must be supported by organizational leadership, shared values, and cultural transformation to be successful.

In other words, the literature on ethics management features both compliance-oriented and integrity-oriented activities in public organizations. A similar distinction has been introduced in the business literature by Paine (1994), who examined "compliance-based" and "integrity-based" corporate ethics programs. Compliance-based programs are motivated by the need to "prevent, detect, and punish legal violations." Integrity-based efforts combine a concern for law with organizational values, which develop a corporate ethos that supports self-governing conduct. In the former approach, the key objective is to prevent misconduct, and in the latter, it is to enable responsibility. These closely mirror the distinction made in the public sector literature.

Nevertheless, this position begs the question of whether these key ideas found in the literature for both sectors are worked out in practice in public sector organizations. As mentioned earlier, observational research is a less robust area in the public administration literature on ethics management than is the theoretical. However, in their work, the editors of this volume have found empirical support for both the existence of these ideas in public organizations and the efficacy of combining them into a comprehensive Compliance-Integrity Framework (Perlman et al., 2023). Their confirmatory factor analysis showed that both approaches are separate and distinct, are highly correlated, are used in practice, and should be used together to understand ethics management properly. Their results challenge existing literature focusing on one dominant approach and show that both ethics management systems are essential.

Therefore, ethics management needs a comprehensive approach for public sector organizations and research about ethics in the public sector. Compliance and integrity must be understood as necessary parts of organizational ethics management. Values support employee conduct and vice versa. There is neither a high nor a low road, but a road to successful ethics management in the public sector. This comprehensive approach suggests a practical Compliance-Integrity Framework. Ethics management should link leadership through social exchange to values and norms in a robust organizational ethics culture that achieves internal inculcation of values and external conformance with rules (Perlman et al., 2024).

Comparison in Public Sector Ethics

The study of public administration has tended to concentrate research on the administrative systems of individual nation-states. Although such parochialism has been criticized, this is particularly characteristic of the discipline as it evolved and gained recognition in the United States. There have been occasional efforts to broaden the horizon of attention, but only during the last few decades have these efforts produced substantial results (Heady et al., 2005, p. 606). Nevertheless, from the beginning of the field, some students and practitioners of public administration have shown an interest in the administrative experiences of other contemporary political systems (Riggs, 1976).

Numerous comparative issues have been identified as crucial for the study of comparative public administration. These include the major trends and prospects for developing administrative capabilities in national public administration systems. To do this, the public organizations that make up these systems must play an instrumental role in them: they have to serve as institutional agents, responding to political leadership outside its ranks in the choice of public policy objectives and the citizenry in their implementation (Heady et al., 2005 p. 616). Strong public sector ethics in the organizations of a national system helps to guarantee this instrumentality.

A background question for this and similar points of view is a lasting one in public administration: on what basis to compare national governmental and bureaucratic contexts? Some, like Heady (1996), have taken a structural-functional approach to issues in comparison. Others, like Riggs, have used culture and practice as a basis for comparison (Riggs, 1964). Some others have focused on similar organizational positions (Baker, 1994) or conceptions of merit-based civil service (Bekke et al., 1996) or developed democracies (Rowat, 1988) across national contexts. In addition, questions have been raised about the ability of any single approach to cope with new considerations raised by government action from homeland security to diversity and inclusion (Heady et al., 2005). A problem for settling on an appropriate comparative method or approach for the study of Public Affairs and Administration is how to make cross-national situations similar enough for meaningful comparisons. Often, when articles mention other national contexts at all—usually the United States—it is to show what is lacking in a national system, government, institutions, or public organizations and how standards can be met or potential improvements made.

An area that lacks concerted comparative study in the public sector is organizational ethics and ethics management. Reviews of masters-level educational curricula from a comparative perspective do not turn up ethics as a study topic from a national or transnational perspective. The addition of several chapters on countries other than the United States in this book is an attempt to use the Compliance-Integrity Framework to bridge this gap. The studies in this volume are most appropriately classified as national rather than transnational studies because they consider one country or national arena over others rather than proportional consideration to more than one country or national context in a balanced way, whether bi-lateral, multi-lateral, or regional.

The Purpose and Plan of This Book

This edited volume is an integrated treatment of the subject of ethics in the public sector, covering compliance and integrity approaches to ethics management and how to apply them skillfully and effectively in changing organizational contexts and cultures. It presents a comprehensive treatment of the subject of ethics in the public sector, including some national case studies from low- to middle-income countries. It covers traditional approaches to ethics management, such as monitoring and compliance, and more contemporary approaches, like integrity building through ethical leadership and organizational values. Applying compliance and integrity approaches in the context of modern and complex organizations is a challenge that requires meticulous planning, commitment to implementation, constant feedback, and adaptation to emerging issues.

By reading this edited volume, readers will be exposed to new approaches and emerging issues of ethics management, will be able to understand the distinctive challenges of creating ethical organizations in the public sector, and will be able to develop a deeper understanding of integrated ethics management in government. It brings together accomplished scholars to contribute to presenting a fresh approach to understanding the complexities of ethics management and long-term solutions to ethical misconduct. It is a timely, comprehensive, and integrated study of public sector ethics in a global era.

This book comprises 11 chapters that deal with important issues of ethics management. It focuses on integrity and compliance, but it includes some chapters on ethical issues in national contexts for country comparisons. Our first chapter is by Carr, who identifies two key approaches to managing ethics in the public sector: the compliance-based and integrity-based approaches. His focus is on the compliance-based approach, which stems from choice theory. These theories assume that people are inherently self-interested and need to be coerced into ethical behavior through punishment. For coercion to be effective, punishment must be certain, swift, and severe, necessitating innovative monitoring and disciplinary processes. Carr explores these processes and highlights the role of punishment in enforcing ethical behavior in the public sector.

In Chapter 2, Odeh and Homer examine the role of ethical codes in the public sector, highlighting their purpose as guiding documents for operationalizing organizational values. They differentiate between codes of ethics, which provide aspirational principles, and codes of conduct, which prescribe specific behaviors. The chapter outlines the challenges of codes being either too compliance-focused or too aspirational to implement. To address this, the authors recommend clear writing, stakeholder engagement, and leadership support to create effective codes that encourage proactive ethical behavior.

Sharp, in Chapter 3, emphasizes the importance of ethics training in public organizations, given the accountability expected from government agencies. Citizens demand transparency and ethical behavior, as they cannot easily disengage from public services. This chapter explores the design and impact of ethics training programs, including the use of case studies and simulations to enhance moral awareness. Sharp also discusses the influence of emotion on decision-making and how new technologies present both challenges and opportunities for promoting ethical behavior.

In Chapter 4, Ertas advocates for a dual approach to ethics management in the public sector, combining compliance-based strategies with value-based incentives. Sanctions, including penalties for violations, and incentives, such as rewards for ethical behavior, both play a role in shaping behavior. However, the chapter warns of the limitations of these approaches, such as their short-term effects and potential misalignment with intrinsic motivations. Ertas emphasizes the need for a balanced system that aligns organizational values with public service goals.

In Chapter 5, Karssing and Hoekstra contrast the compliance-based and integrity-based approaches to ethics management, tracing their origins to the Friedrich-Finer debate. While compliance focuses on external controls and rule-following, integrity emphasizes internal self-governance guided by moral princi-ples. The chapter argues for a hybrid approach, integrating both compliance and integrity to effectively manage ethics. The authors discuss how public organiza-tions can foster moral character and bridge the gap between external and internal controls through an integral systems approach.

In Chapter 6, Sun and Zhang explore the strategies leaders can use to promote ethics within their organizations, including role modeling, reinforcement, and fostering ethical communication. They examine the complexities of leadership in multi-agency collaborations and how differing roles and expectations influence ethics management. The chapter concludes by recommending ethics as a key factor in leadership hiring and promotion decisions, along with ethics training for leaders to cultivate an ethical work environment.

In Chapter 7, Samms Brown and Sweeting highlight the centrality of organi-zational values in shaping ethical behavior and decision-making. They intro-duce nine primary value types that influence leadership and employee actions, discussing the challenges of value alignment in the context of various public administration paradigms. The chapter advocates for value-based management as a driver of ethical behavior and concludes by proposing an integrated frame-work that weaves integrity and value congruence into organizational systems.

In Chapter 8, Oliveira Júnior and Croca Caeiro present Brazil's ethics manage-ment system as a case study, focusing on the challenges posed by the centraliza-tion of power and ambiguities in reform efforts. Using institutional analysis and development perspectives, the chapter identifies power dynamics and international influence as key factors in the fragmentation of Brazil's ethics management. The authors propose a causal mechanism to explain these challenges and suggest that their findings can be adapted to study ethics management in other regions.

In Chapter 9, Feldman and Rivera examine Italy's efforts to combat corrup-tion from 1945 to 1989, exploring the historical, political, and cultural factors that hindered reform. They discuss the persistence of local power structures and tolerance for corruption during the Cold War. The chapter also reviews the pro-gress made after 1989, following major scandals and the fall of the Iron Curtain. It concludes by considering how Italy's experience can inform anti-corruption efforts in other European nations, with references to Armenia's velvet revolution.

In Chapter 10, Tamronglak, Limsira, and Pongpisit analyze the corruption chal-lenges in Thailand, where cultural norms, institutional inefficiencies, and weak enforcement undermine efforts to promote public integrity. Despite a robust legal framework, corruption persists in forms such as bribery and power abuse. The chapter proposes extending the Theory of Planned Behavior (TPB) to include social media as a tool for grassroots anti-corruption efforts, emphasizing the need for a comprehensive approach that includes policy reforms and societal transformation.

Finally, in Chapter 11, Amegavi and Langnel explore the role of political leadership in shaping ethics management in Africa, with a focus on Ghana and Rwanda. The chapter contrasts the weak political leadership in Ghana, which hinders ethical reforms, with Rwanda's more successful efforts due to strong political commitment. The authors highlight the importance of sustained political leadership in implementing ethics reforms, drawing lessons from Rwanda's experience for other developing countries seeking to promote an ethical public sector.

References

Amundsen, I. & Andrade, V. (2009). *Introduction to public sector ethics*. Compendium for teaching at the Catholic University of Angola (UCAN). Luanda, Uganda. Retrieved from https://www.agora-parl.org/resources/library/public-sector-ethics

Baker, R. (1994). *Comparative public management: Putting U.S. public policy and implementation in context*. Praeger.

Barron, J. (2024, September 27). The charges against Mayor Adams. *The New York Times*. Retrieved from www.nytimes.com/2024/09/27/nyregion/the-charges-against-mayor-adams.html

Beeri, I., Dayan, R., Vigoda-Gadot, E., & Werner, S. B. (2013). Advancing ethics in public organizations: The impact of an ethics program on employees' perceptions and behaviors in a regional council. *Journal of Business Ethics*, *112*(1), 59–78.

Bekke, A. J. G. M., Perry, J. L., & Toonen, T. A. J. (1996). *Civil service systems in comparative perspective*. Indiana University Press.

Blau, P. M. (1964). *Exchange and power in social life*. Wiley.

Bowman, J. S., & Knox, C. C. (2008). Ethics in government: No matter how long and dark the night. *Public Administration Review*, *68*(4), 627–639.

Brewer, G. A., & Selden, S. C. (1998). Whistle blowers in the federal civil service: New evidence of the public service ethic. *Journal of Public Administration Research and Theory: J-PART*, *8*(3), 413–439. Retrieved from https://libproxy.unm.edu/login?url=https://search.ebscohost.com/login.aspx?direct=true&db=edsjsr&AN=edsjsr.1181863&site=eds-live&scope=site

Brown, M. E., Trevino, L. K., & Harrison, D. A. (2005). Ethical leadership: A social learning perspective for construct development and testing. *Organizational Behavior and Human Decision Processes*, *97*(2), 117–134.

Cooper, T. L. (2006). *The responsible administrator: An approach to ethics for the administrative role*. Jossey-Bass.

Demir, T., Reddick, C. G., & Perlman, B. J. (2023). In search of ethics infrastructure in U.S. local governments: Building blocks or dead end? *Administration & Society*, *55*(10), 1866–1892.

Dodek, A. (2018). What lies ahead for public sector ethics? *Canadian Public Administration*, *61*, 102–113.

Dwivedi, O. P. (1967). Bureaucratic corruption in developing countries. *Asian Survey*, 245–253.

Ekhator, E. O. (2012). Public sector ethics in the United Kingdom. *Journal of Humanities and Social Sciences*, *4*(2), 91–100.

Frederickson, H. G., & Ghere, R. K. (2014). *Ethics in public management*. Routledge.

Gawthorp, L. C. (1998). *Public service and democracy: Ethical imperatives for the 21st century*. Chatham House Publishers of Seven Bridges Press.

Goss, R. P. (1996). A distinct public administration ethics? *Journal of Public Administration Research and Theory*, *6*(4), 573–597.

Graycar, A. (2020). Chapter 1: Corruption and public administration. In A. Graycar (ed.), *Handbook on corruption, ethics and integrity in public administration*. Edward Elgar Publishing.

Hassan, S., Wright, B. E., & Yukl, G. (2014). Does ethical leadership matter in government? Effects on organizational commitment, absenteeism, and willingness to report ethical problems. *Public Administration Review*, *74*(3), 333–343.

Heady, F. (1996). *Public administration: A comparative perspective*. M. Dekker.

Heady, F., Perlman, B. J., & Rivera, M. A. (2005). Issues in comparative and international administration. In J. Rabin (Ed.), *Handbook of public administration* (3rd ed., pp. 605–626). Marcel Dekker.

Homans, G. C. (1961). *Social behavior: Its elementary forms*. Harcourt Brace.

Kyarimpa, G. E., & Garcia-Zamor, J. C. (2006). The quest for public service ethics: Individual conscience and organizational constraints. *Public Money and Management*, *26*(1), 31–38.

Lee, J., & Liu, C. (2022). Public corruption and government management capacity. *Public Performance & Management Review*, *45*(2), 397–427.

Lee, S. H., & Olshfski, D. (2002). Employee commitment and firefighters: It's my job. *Public Administration Review*, *62*(s1), 108–114. https://doi.org/10.1111/1540-6210.62.s1.19

Liou, K. T., & Nyhan, R. C. (1994). Dimensions of organizational commitment in the public sector: An empirical assessment. *Public Administration Quarterly*, *18*, 99.

Menzel, D. C. (2015). Research on ethics and integrity in public administration: Moving forward, looking back. *Public Integrity*, *17*(4), 343–370. https://doi.org/10.1080/1099 9922.2015.1060824

Paine, L. S. (1994, March-April). Managing for organizational integrity. *Harvard Business Review*, *72*(2), 106–117.

Perlman, B. J., Reddick, C., & Demir, T. (2023). A compliance—integrity framework for ethics management: An empirical analysis of local government practice. *Public Administration Review*, *83*(4), 823–837. https://doi.org/10.1111/puar.13610

Perlman, B. J., Reddick, C. G., & Demir, T. (2024). Toward an organizational ethics culture framework: An analysis of survey data from local government managers. *Public Integrity*, 1–16. https://doi.org/10.1080/10999922.2023.2295643

Perlman, B. J., Reddick, C. G., Demir, T., & Ogilby, S. M. (2021). What do local governments teach about in ethics training? Compliance versus integrity. *Journal of Public Affairs Education*, 1–18. https://doi.org/10.1080/15236803.2021.1972742

Raile, E. D. (2013). Building ethical capital: Perceptions of ethical climate in the public sector. *Public Administration Review*, *73*(2), 253–262.

Rauh, J. (2018). Ethics problems in the new public service: Back to a service ethic? *Public Integrity*, *20*(3), 234–256.

Reddick, C. G., Demir, T., & Perlman, B. (2020). Horizontal, vertical, and hybrid: An empirical look at the forms of accountability. *Administration & Society*, https://doi.org/10.1177/0095399720912553

Riggs, F. W. (1964). *Administration in developing countries: The theory of prismatic society*. Houghton Mifflin.

Riggs, F. W. (1976). The Group and the Movement: Notes on Comparative and Development Administration. *Public Administration Review*, *36*(6), 648–654. doi:10.2307/975058

Rohr, J. A. (1998). *Public service, ethics, and constitutional practice*. University Press of Kansas.

Rowat, D. C. (1988). *Public administration in developed democracies: A comparative study*. M. Dekker.

Svara, J. (2014). Who are the keepers of the code? Articulating and upholding ethical standards in the field of public administration. *Public Administration Review*, *74*(5), 561–569.

Theobald, R. (1997). Enhancing public service ethics: More culture, less bureaucracy? *Administration & Society*, *29*(4), 490–504.

Transparency International. (2023). *Corruption perceptions index*. Retrieved October 10, 2024, from https://www.transparency.org/en/cpi/2023

Treviño, L. K., & Weaver, G. R. (2001). Organizational justice and ethics program follow-through: Influences on employees' harmful and helpful behavior. *Business Ethics Quarterly*, *11*, 651–671.

Van Wart, M. (1998). *Changing public sector values*. Garland Publishing, Inc.

Weaver, G. R., & Trevino, L. K. (1999). Compliance and value-oriented ethics programs: Influences on employees' attitudes and behaviors. *Business Ethics Quarterly*, *9*(2), 315–335.

1 What Is Compliance? The Coercive Approach to Ethics Management

Danny Nathaniel Carr

Introduction

Compliance refers to all the policies, procedures, and systems that an organization adopts to coerce employees into behavior deemed to be right, good, or appropriate. Compliance is one of two approaches to ethics management in the public sector (Lartey, 2021). Ethics management aims to maximize the number of public servants who conduct themselves in accordance with normative standards and minimize the number of those who don't. But this is often difficult to achieve. The compliance-based approach to ethics management focuses on law, codes of conduct, monitoring systems, and punishment. It is based on theories that assume that people are inherently bad.

Further, the compliance-based approach to ethics management stands in contrast to the integrity-based approach. Some key differences are that compliance-based ethics is extrinsically driven, relies on rules and punishment systems, and ignores the development of individual ethics. By contrast, integrity-based ethics is intrinsically driven, avoids focusing on rules and punishment systems, and aims to develop individual ethics by focusing on ethical values (Lartey, 2021; Perlman et al., 2023).

This chapter briefly discusses ethics management before discussing the compliance-based approach to ethics management in the public sector. Next, a discussion of the theoretical framework of the compliance approach is provided. The theoretical framework examines the main assumptions of choice theory, the Principle-Agent-Client (PAC) model, and the economic calculus that have informed the compliance approach. It will be argued that a key feature of this theoretical framework is the assumption that people are inherently bad. Inherently bad people will only act as per ethical standards if they are deterred from wrongdoing through punishment. The discussion then moves to the historical context that shaped the development of the compliance approach. The components of the compliance approach are then discussed with particular attention paid to codes of ethics. A critical assessment of the effectiveness of the compliance approach in the public sector is then presented. As will be seen, the question of effectiveness

DOI: 10.4324/9781003416258-2

has troubled researchers, and empirical evidence to answer this question is scant and lacks methodological rigor (Khaltar & Moon, 2020; Meine & Dunn, 2013; Pelletier & Bligh, 2006). The chapter then closes by summarizing key points and making recommendations for future research.

Ethics Management

The meaning of ethics in the public sector has been regularly discussed (Carr, 2023; Huberts, 2018; Rose & Heywood, 2013). Ethics is a set of widely accepted principles that provides the framework for individuals to judge behavior as right or wrong (Lawton et al., 2013) and motivates them to align their behavior with conduct judged to be correct (Carr, 2023; Haidt, 2003). Therefore, ethics management in the public sector involves providing an ethical framework that promotes ethical judgment and behavior (Khaltar & Moon, 2020). For example, Khaltar and Moon (2020) define ethics management as creating and maintaining an ethical environment so that ethics pervade all organizational activities. Ethics management is also defined as organizational control mechanisms that aim to stop fraud and corruption (Demir et al., 2023). Therefore, ethics management in the public sector involves guiding and controlling behavior to suit what has been deemed good or right.

The Compliance Approach

The dictionary meaning of the verb 'to comply' is to act in accordance with the wishes, desires, requests, or demands of another (Oxford English Dictionary. Oxford: Clarendon Press, 1989). This definition suggests that it is an external entity making the wish, desire, request, or demand. Therefore, 'to comply' carries the notion that the person complying is conceding to, fulfilling, or acting in accordance with the wishes of another, not his wish. Within the public sector, compliance can be seen as a power struggle between the organization that sets a law, rule, or standard and individuals who do not agree with those laws or standards but must obey them. Gelderman et al. (2006) agree with this view in their brief discussion of compliance. They note that compliance has a negative connotation that speaks to a power imbalance between someone giving a directive and the person receiving it. In those situations, people may comply with a directive because of the power imbalance and not because they agree with the directive. Therefore, compliance produces a half-hearted effort based on coercion. For this reason, compliance is referred to as the low-road approach to ethics management (Perlman et al., 2023).

Theoretical Foundations of the Compliance Approach

Several authors have defined the compliance approach as a control system or a coercive system (Huberts, 2014; Maesschalck, 2004; Tremblay et al., 2017) that aims to force individuals to behave ethically because it is believed that they are not intrinsically motivated to do so. Consequently, it can be argued that the compliance approach assumes that people are inherently bad. The notion that people are inherently bad and will act in their self-interest to the detriment of the public good has been one of the dominant ideas in public sector ethics management, if not the most dominant idea. It has its support in popular social theorizing dating back to the 1800s. Popular theories that assume that people are inherently bad include choice theory, deterrence theory, the economic calculus, and the PAC model.

Choice Theory

Choice theory, as posited by Cesare Beccaria, assumes that people are hedonistic, always seeking pleasure and trying to avoid pain (Siegel, 2011). According to this view, the most effective way to control human behavior toward doing the right thing is to punish. Punishment helps to ensure that the pain of engaging in wrongdoing is more than the pleasure derived from it (Siegel, 2011). Deterrence theory, which is a popular offshoot of choice theory, focuses on the notion of punishment as a general and specific deterrent to wrongdoing. It argues that when people are under the threat of punishment, or when they are punished, they can be deterred from future wrongdoing. This is referred to as specific deterrence. Deterrence theory further argues that when people see others being punished for wrongdoing, they can be deterred from engaging in similar wrongdoing. This is referred to as general deterrence. Therefore, the compliance approach is based on deterrence theory (Paine, 1994) as well. Furthermore, Becker (1976) used the same assumptions of choice theory and deterrence theory in his book *The Economic Approach to Human Behavior*. This book was influential in shaping the compliance approach in the public sector.

Choice theory also argues that for punishment to be effective, it must be certain, severe, and swift (Siegel, 2011). Certainty of punishment requires good monitoring, investigations, whistleblowing, and punishment systems, while swift punishment depends on good administrative/disciplinary processes. Concerning the severity of punishment, choice theory posits that the punishment should match the seriousness of the wrongdoing. Punishment that amounts to a slap on the wrist is unlikely to have a deterrent effect, while punishment that is seen as too severe may create other problems. For example, a recent study by Carr and Forde (2024) on the causes of corruption in the Trinidad and Tobago Police Service found that many supervisors and managers were unwilling to initiate disciplinary action because they perceived that the punishment was too severe for the offending officer. Therefore, while choice theory posits that the effectiveness of punishment depends on the certainty, severity, and swiftness of punishment, punishment in the public sector seldom achieves these theoretical ideals. This is so even though the compliance approach includes structures that aim to increase the certainty and swiftness of punishment, such as investigations, monitoring systems, accountability systems, and whistleblowing procedures (Kaptein, 2015).

Principal Agent Client (PAC) Model

According to the PAC model, agents are self-interested pleasure seekers motivated to maximize their benefits and minimize costs (Rose-Ackerman, 1978). The model assumes that the principal and the agent have different interests. When the agent is faced with pursuing the principal's interest versus deviating from it for self-interest, he will choose the option that provides him with the highest net benefit (Klitgaard, 1988; Rose-Ackerman, 1978). Generally, an agent acts on behalf of another (the principal) in a specific domain of decision-making (Ross, 1973). In the context of the public sector, an agent refers to a public service employee who has been entrusted with power by a principal to provide a good or service to a client, usually members of the public (Rose-Ackerman & Palifka, 2016; Shapiro, 2005) in accordance with rules provided by the principal (Lambsdorff, 2007). An agent is corrupt or engaging in wrongdoing if he abuses that 'entrusted power' for private gain. For example, a public transport officer who accepts a bribe from a citizen to provide a driver's license in breach of the rules and guidelines set out by the principal is engaging in wrongdoing.

Like choice theory, the PAC model assumes that the agent is inherently bad and will always act in his self-interest when his self-interest conflicts with the principal's interest. Further, because it is both difficult and costly to monitor the agent, agents can often deviate from the principal's interest without detection (Rose-Ackerman, 1978). Therefore, proponents of the PAC model suggest that government agencies must find innovative ways to improve monitoring.

The assumptions of choice theory and its offshoots can be more clearly seen in the criminal justice system in the developed and developing world. The criminal justice system, a public sector institution, is very punishment-oriented. The public has become accustomed to retributive justice. It should be no surprise, therefore, that ethics management in the public sector, at least in theory, also relies on retributive justice as a means of communicating to the public that wrongdoing will not be tolerated. From a choice perspective, the costs of crime must outweigh the benefits to achieve specific and general deterrence. Therefore, crimes such as taking a bribe, engaging in a conflict of interest, or embezzling funds which are common in the public sector, must be adequately punished. In this way, individuals can be deterred from engaging in unethical conduct, thus maintaining organizational integrity.

Since choice theory has been the dominant view for understanding human behavior relating to wrongdoing, many of the scandals of the 1800s and 1900s that were related to corruption in government and ethical violations in the public sector were interpreted from a choice perspective. Observers perceived that corruption in government occurred because those involved were bad (unethical persons) and lacked public service ethos (Roberts, 2009). Consequently, the responses were compliance-oriented (e.g., more rules, stricter rules, more punishment, harsher punishment).

Development of the Compliance Approach in US Public Administration

Political/Social Context

According to Roberts (2009), who discussed the rise of the compliance approach in the United States, four factors led to the explosion of the use of the compliance approach. These four factors were external pressure on the government of the United States to regulate financial conflicts of interest between 1950 and 1980, strong criticism of the government concerning massive wastage and fraud during the 1970s and 1980s, the Watergate scandal, and the expansion of the use of contractors to perform government services during the 1990s. His discussion clearly shows that these factors were interpreted as evidence that public servants lacked public ethos and should not be trusted. In other words, public servants were seen as inherently bad.

Hijal-Moghrabi and Sabharwal (2018) also track the evolution of ethics management in public administration in America, starting in the late 1800s and continuing to the present. They divided the evolution of ethics management in America into six stages. According to them, stage 1 was the Pre-progressive Era. They argue that this period was from the late 1800s to early 1900s, also known as the Jacksonian Era. They note that this Era was characterized by a strong desire to fight corruption and public service ethics was tied to efficiency, effectiveness, and economy. Public servants were considered ethical if they efficiently did what they were told (Menzel, 1997). The second stage was the New Deal Era (1930s–1950s), which was characterized by Weberian bureaucracy that gave supremacy to rules as the main tool for governing and regulating behavior. This produced a revival of duty ethics, but by the end of World War II, scholars were rejecting the idea of duty ethics in administration. The iconic debate between Finer and Fredrich in the early 1940s and the debate between Simon and Waldo in the late 1940s helped to highlight the difference between internal and external drivers of ethical behavior. Internal drivers were identified as the ideal; however, as noted earlier, many felt that public servants lacked an internal drive and were therefore intrinsically unethical.

During the Civil Rights Era, the third stage identified by Hijal-Mogharabi and Sabharwal (2018), there was an attempt to push public administration from being rational to being more responsive to the needs of different segments of American society. This Era saw the birth of New Public Administration, which brought the idea that ethics should be at the heart of public administration. The fourth stage was the post-Watergate Era, which saw the introduction of the Ethics in Government Act. The Ethics in Government Act paved the way for subjecting federal employees to behavior that aligns with a set of moral standards. Further, an ethics code was adopted by the American Society for Public Administration to promote public service ethics. The fifth stage was the Reinventing Government Era (1990s–2000). This Era was marked by the New Public Management (NPM).

NPM emphasized transparency and accountability. Other researchers have also argued that NPM helped to shape the compliance approach to ethics management in the public sector (Glor, 2001; Maesschalck, 2004).

The sixth and final stage identified by Hijal-Moghrabi and Sabharwal (2018) is the New Governance era in which the boundaries between the public and private sectors have been further blurred. The New Governance ethos means promoting a higher level of collaboration between the public sector and NGOs, businesses, and the general public. It was hoped that this higher level of partnership would help to increase transparency and keep public servants in check.

Legal Context

Researchers have noted the role that legislation in the United States played in shaping the compliance approach. For example, the Foreign Corrupt Practices Act (FCPA) of 1977 was very influential in promoting the compliance approach to ethics management in the public sector. It helped to carve the way for today's international anti-bribery movement because it influenced the formation and structure of the Organization for Economic Cooperation and Development (OECD) convention against bribery of foreign officials. This convention, in turn, has influenced the domestic laws of signatories. The OECD convention, along with other factors, helped to usher in the United Nations Convention Against Corruption, which has global reach.

The 1991 US sentencing guidelines also influenced the compliance approach in the public sector (Jackson & Grilli, 2014). According to Stuke (2014), the 1991 US sentencing guidelines led to the explosion of compliance as a big business. Lartey (2021) identifies the 2002 Sarbanes-Oxley Act and the 2010 Dodd-Frank Act as exerting notable influence on the compliance approach in the public sector. While the 2002 Sarbanes-Oxley Act and the 2010 Dodd-Frank Act targeted the private sector, they triggered a series of events that later influenced compliance in the public sector.

Scope of the Compliance Approach

The belief in punishment as a deterrent, and the idea that it needs to be certain, severe, and swift, has influenced the scope of the compliance approach in the public sector. The scope of the compliance approach refers to the range of measures incorporated into it (Kaptein, 2015; Weaver & Treviño, 1999). The scope of the compliance approach should be broad (Kaptein, 2015); however, in many public organizations it is quite narrow. Kaptein (2015) found that compliance programs can include any or all of the following: pre-employment screening, codes of conduct, accountability policies, monitoring and auditing systems, investigations and corrections policies, and incentive policies.

This brings the discussion to the effectiveness of the compliance approach in engendering ethical conduct in the public sector. It is important to note here that this question is not often phrased this way in the literature. In the literature, the question is phrased as though compliance (rule-following) is synonymous with being an ethical person. However, it has been argued earlier that they are not synonymous. For example, avoiding bribery to escape punishment is not the same as avoiding bribery because one believes it is morally wrong.

Therefore, Kaptein's use of the concept of 'moral competence' seems useful (Kaptein, 2015). Moral competence can be defined as understanding and applying guidelines of codes, rules, and policies (Eriksson et al., 2007). Moral competence does not denote agreement with codes, rules, and policies, or the values on which they are based. Therefore, a morally competent person (external drivers) can be distinguished from an ethical person (internal drivers). Such a distinction allows for a clearer assessment of the effectiveness of the compliance approach. The compliance approach seeks to produce morally competent persons, not ethical persons. However, the compliance approach is often criticized for failing to produce the latter, which it never set out to do.

The question of the extent to which the compliance approach is effective in producing ethical competence in the public sector can now be addressed. This question is best approached by examining each component of the compliance approach individually because it is rare to find studies that examine multiple components (Kaptein, 2015). The examination will start with the most popular tool in the compliance arsenal, codes of ethics, which will be followed by a discussion of the other compliance measures.

Effectiveness of the Compliance Approach

There is a dearth of literature that addresses the effectiveness of the compliance approach in the public sector (Meine & Dunn, 2013; Pelletier & Bligh, 2006). Some of the studies that are concerned with effectiveness examine the effectiveness of ethics programs. Such examinations usually include both the compliance approach and the integrity approach. In those cases, it is not possible to isolate the effectiveness of the compliance approach. Further, none of the studies that examined the effectiveness of the compliance approach only used an experimental design. Finally, studies that examined the effectiveness of the compliance approach have focused mainly on codes of conduct. Thus, one can conclude that the state of empirical work on the effectiveness of the compliance approach in the public sector is in its infancy.

The Effectiveness of Codes of Ethics

Ethics codes can be traced to ancient Athens (Meine & Dunn, 2013), and their use in the public sector to regulate conduct is widespread (Downe et al., 2016; Meine & Dunn, 2013). The use of codes of ethics in the public sector exploded in the 1980s (Downe et al., 2016). A code of ethics may be defined as a written organizational framework that identifies conduct deemed good or appropriate (Downe et al., 2016). A code of ethics may also be defined as a formal document that outlines and explains the ethical rules (and sometimes, the values on which they are based) that employees are expected to follow (Beeri et al., 2013). Since codes usually form part of the compliance approach, they should be accompanied by punishment (Downe et al., 2016). From a choice perspective, certain, swift, and severe punishment is needed to produce deterrence. However, it is often the case that codes of conduct in the public sector are not accompanied by punishment mechanisms (Svara, 2014). Thus, from a theoretical perspective, codes without an efficient punishment system will be ineffective in deterring unethical conduct in the public service.

Notwithstanding, codes are effective in producing ethical competency (Belle & Cantarelli, 2017; Bing et al., 2012; Gino et al., 2009; Meine & Dunn, 2013; Svara, 2014). Belle and Cantarelli (2017) found that a code of ethics can remind individuals about the moral standards expected of them and this reminder can effectively reduce unethical behavior. They concluded that since moral reminders are useful in preventing unethical behavior, and that moral reminders are effectively achieved through codes of ethics; codes of ethics can promote ethical conduct in public organizations. However, they note that more needs to be done to study the conditions under which codes serve as good moral reminders, for example, whether codes should emphasize positive or negative behaviors.

Pattison and Wainwright (2010) also found that codes are effective. However, unlike Belle and Cantarelli (2017), Pattison and Wainwright (2010) found that codes are effective when accompanied by an enforcement mechanism. The findings of Pattison and Wainwright (2010) align with those of Trevino and Ball (1992). Trevino and Ball (1992) found that only the harshest punishment influences ethical outcomes. The finding of Trevino and Ball (1992) should be approached with caution for three reasons. First, they conducted an experiment using college students and no attempt has been made to replicate the study using public servants. Second, harsh punishment can sometimes create a toxic work environment, which can eventually lead to an increase in ethical violations. Third, harsh punishment can discourage supervisors and managers from initiating the disciplinary process if they perceive the punishment as too severe (Carr & Forde, 2024).

Codes effectively communicate expected standards of behavior (Bazerman & Tenbrunsel, 2011; Beeri et al., 2013; Eskridge et al., 2012). Codes can also effectively raise employee awareness about the standards of behaviors expected of them (Eskridge et al., 2012). Also, Palidauskaite (2006) found that codes in transitional democracies helped to introduce traditional public service values to public servants. However, the effectiveness of codes in communicating expected standards and values depends on the clarity of the codes (Kontogeorga, 2017). For example, Kontogeorga (2017) found that the main reason for the non-compliance of public entities to budgetary laws and regulations was the ambiguity and complexity of the law rather than deliberate intention. She concluded, therefore, that coercive enforcement would not be effective.

The ability of codes to communicate expected standards should not be taken lightly. This is an important task because ethical standards often vary from person to person (Atkinson, 2015). Managers of public institutions are faced with the difficult task of managing individuals who disagree about the standards of right and wrong in a range of circumstances. Consequently, it is up to managers to set the standard for expected behavior. These expected standards must be effectively communicated to employees and potential employees. Thus, in some sense, a code of ethics is a statement of expectation.

Kaptein (2015) found that accountability policies were the most effective at reducing unethical behavior in organizations compared to other measures. He also found that a code of ethics, monitoring and auditing, and investigation and correction policies were also effective at reducing unethical behavior even though they were not as effective as accountability policies. He defined an accountability policy as a policy that raises employee awareness of their ethical responsibility to the organization and encourages them to act ethically.

The Effectiveness of Monitoring

Studies have found that monitoring is an effective means to reduce unethical behavior in the public sector (Belle & Cantarelli, 2017; Kaptein, 2015). Belle and Cantarelli (2017), in their meta-analysis to synthesize 137 experiments in 73 articles on causes of ethical behavior, found that monitoring decreased unethical behavior. Before the findings of Kaptein (2015) and Belle and Cantarelli (2017), Welsh and Ordonez (2014) and Mazar and Aggarwal (2011) had argued that monitoring works because it increases the perception that wrongdoing would be detected and punished. This reasoning is consistent with choice theory, which posits that punishment must be certain. It can also be argued that monitoring encourages ethical self-awareness (Alge et al., 2006; Welsh & Ordóñez, 2014) because of its potential to convey that punishment is certain. Consequently, Belle and Cantarelli (2017) concluded that the evidence produced by their meta-analysis supports the view that government initiatives that increase monitoring in the public sector can effectively reduce unethical behavior.

In the literature on political corruption, it has also been found that increased monitoring can reduce corruption (Barr et al., 2009; Di Tella & Schargrodsky, 2003; Olken, 2007). For example, in a well-read study conducted by Olken (2007), a randomized field experiment was used to examine the effect that transparency and grass-root monitoring had on corruption in road projects in Indonesia. Corruption was measured as missing expenditures, while the transparency measure was simply announcing that a government audit was likely. The author found that announcing that an audit would be conducted had a statistically significant, negative effect on missing values of road projects. Di Tella and Schargrodsky (2003) found similar results when they examined audit intensity and prices paid for hospital supplies in Buenos Aires, Argentina. Furthermore, a study by Barr et al. (2009) found that corruption in the form of expropriating behavior of nursing students was significantly reduced when monitoring and the ability to monitor were high. However, monitoring has been criticized for its tendency to be ineffective and expensive and because agents can circumvent monitoring and incentive programs (Banerjee et al., 2008; Rose-Ackerman, 1978).

While the studies discussed earlier have found that codes of ethics and other compliance tools can be effective, many researchers agree that the evidence is not yet sufficient. For example, Beeri et al. (2013), Downe et al. (2016), and Jensen et al. (2009) argue that there has not been sufficient analysis to determine the effectiveness of codes of ethics. Additionally, the effectiveness of codes might depend on several factors including the presence and effectiveness of regulatory institutions that seek to enforce compliance (Svara, 2014).

Others have argued that codes replace self-regulation, which eventually leads to an increase in ethical violations (Atkinson, 2015). From a choice perspective, this is an unfair criticism. Codes do not aim to replace self-regulation. The use of codes is based on the assumption that there is no self-regulation because people are inherently bad and self-serving. Another unfair criticism of codes is that they can promote rule dodging (Menzel, 2015). Codes do not promote rule dodging. From a PAC perspective, agents dodge rules because they are primarily self-interested. Consequently, if there is any conflict between their interest and that of the public good, the agent will find ways to pursue their interest irrespective of the existence or non-existence of formal rules. Hence, from a PAC perspective, the problem of rule dodging does not emanate from rules, but from bad people.

Another criticism of codes is that they can never be broad enough to capture every decision that should be made in the wide tapestry of behaviors and contexts within a public institution. Hence, rules must always be interpreted and re-interpreted when ethical issues arise (Downe et al., 2016; Jensen et al., 2009; West & Davis, 2011). The constant interpretation and re-interpretation of rules increase ambiguity. As Kontogeorga (2017) illustrated, ambiguity can render codes ineffective.

Conclusion

The compliance approach to ethics management responds to the demand for public servants to conduct their duties by established ethical standards. Ethics management in the public sector aims to maximize the number of public servants who conduct themselves in accordance with normative standards and minimize the number of those who don't. The compliance-based approach has emerged as one of the approaches to ethics management and stands in contrast to the integrity-based approach. The main theoretical assumptions of the compliance-based approach can be found in choice theory (and its offshoots) and the PAC model. These theories assume that people are inherently bad (self-seeking, self-interested, hedonistic) and would only act according to ethical standards if they are coerced to do so. People can be coerced to behave ethically through punishment. However, the punishment must be certain, swift, and severe. For punishment to be certain, swift, and severe, innovative methods for monitoring, investigations, whistleblowing, and disciplinary processes are required.

The compliance approach has been shaped by events of the early, mid-, and late 20th-century American society. Roberts (2009) identified four major factors including the Watergate scandal. On the other hand, Hijal-Moghrabi and Sabharwal (2018) identified six stages in the evolution of the compliance approach to ethics management in the public sector. In both accounts of Roberts (2009) and Hijal-Moghrabi and Sabharwal (2018), one can deduce that the choice perspective served as the primary perspective to explain wrongdoing. Therefore, it followed that coercion through enforceable rules became the driving force of the compliance approach.

The scope of the compliance approach and its effectiveness were also discussed. However, due to limited research on its effectiveness in the public sector, it was difficult to say the extent to which the compliance approach is effective. Even so, the few studies that were done have produced mixed results. Codes effectively produce ethical competency (Belle & Cantarelli, 2017; Bing et al., 2012; Svara, 2014). Punishment is an important factor affecting the effectiveness of the compliance approach (Pattison & Wainwright, 2010; Trevino & Ball, 1992). Further, codes were found to be effective in communicating expected standards of behavior (Beeri et al., 2013). Monitoring was also found to have some success (Bell & Cantarelli, 2017). The effectiveness of codes and monitoring can be explained from a choice perspective.

Other studies have heavily criticized the compliance approach for being ineffective and coercive. On the issue of effectiveness, authors seem to expect that the compliance approach should develop ethical persons. However, it was argued that from a choice theory perspective, the compliance approach was not designed to produce ethical persons. Instead, the compliance approach assumes that people are inherently bad. It argues that hedonistic people must be coerced through punishment, to follow rules. Therefore, it does not attempt to produce ethical persons but morally competent persons. Other criticisms of the compliance approach (see Atkinson, 2015), especially criticisms of codes of ethics, also seem unfounded. The compliance approach was not designed to produce moral persons. It was developed to punish into compliance people who are believed to be lacking moral acumen.

Future Research

The compliance-based approach to ethics management in the public sector can benefit from an exponential increase in empirical studies. As Menzel (2015) and many others have pointed out, the state of public administration research on ethics in government is scant at best. This paucity of research on ethics and integrity in the public sector can be contrasted with research on ethics management in business, economics, management, and psychology where there has been a robust and growing literature (Belle & Cantarelli, 2017; Moore & Gino, 2015). Furthermore, from a methodological standpoint, studies on ethics in the public sector do not use the experimental design, but almost exclusively use observational designs (Belle & Cantarelli, 2017). The experimental design is the most powerful research design. Studies that use the experimental design are more poised to shed light on the effectiveness of the compliance approach. Hence, future research should use the experimental design as much as possible.

Additionally, more needs to be done to study the conditions under which codes serve as good moral reminders, for example, are codes better when positive or negative behavior is emphasized (Belle & Cantarelli, 2017)? Some argue that using aspirational codes that emphasize positive behavior is more effective. However, there is not much research on the topic. Thus, future research can address this gap. Finally, future research should examine whether the findings of Kaptein (2015) can be replicated. His notion that the sequence in which the measures of an ethics program are implemented can improve the effectiveness of those measures should not be ignored. If there is indeed a 'correct' sequence for implementing a compliance program, then this is likely to be revolutionary.

References

Alge, B. J., Greenberg, J., & Brinsfield, C. T. (2006). An identity-based model of organizational monitoring: Integrating information privacy and organizational justice. In *Research in personnel and human resources management* (pp. 71–135). Emerald Group Publishing Limited.

Atkinson, C. L. (2015). New York city's conflicts of interest law: Compliance versus ethical capacity. *Public Integrity, 17*(3), 227–241.

Banerjee, A. V., Duflo, E., & Glennerster, R. (2008). Putting a band-aid on a corpse: Incentives of nurses in the Indian public health care system. *Journal of the European Economic Association, 6*(2–3), 487–500.

Barr, A., Lindelow, M., & Serneels, P. (2009). Corruption in public service delivery: An experimental analysis. *Journal of Economic Behavior and Organization, 72*(1), 225–239.

Bazerman, M. H., & Tenbrunsel, A. E. (2011). *Blind spots: Why we fail to do what's right and what to do about it.* Princeton University Press.

Becker, G. S. (1976). *The economic approach to human behavior* (Vol. 803). University of Chicago Press.

Beeri, I., Dayan, R., Vigoda-Gadot, E., & Werner, S. B. (2013). Advancing ethics in public organizations: The impact of an ethics program on employees' perceptions and behaviors in a regional council. *Journal of Business Ethics, 112*, 59–78.

Belle, N., & Cantarelli, P. (2017). What causes unethical behavior? A meta-analysis to set an agenda for public administration research. *Public Administration Review, 77*(3), 327–339.

Bing, M. N., Davison, H. K., Vitell, S. J., Ammeter, A. P., Garner, B. L., & Novicevic, M. M. (2012). An experimental investigation of an interactive model of academic cheating among business school students. *Academy of Management Learning & Education, 11*(1), 28–48.

Carr, D. N. (2023). Interpreting integrity: A qualitative approach. *Public Integrity, 25*(2), 234–244.

Carr, D. N., & Forde, T. (2024). Explaining corruption in the Trinidad and Tobago police service: A case study of organizational culture and police corruption. In *The Palgrave Handbook of Caribbean Criminology* (pp. 351–368). Springer International Publishing.

Demir, T., Reddick, C. G., & Perlman, B. J. (2023). In search of ethics infrastructure in US local governments: Building blocks or dead end? *Administration & Society, 55*(10), 1866–1892.

Di Tella, R., & Schargrodsky, E. (2003). The role of wages and auditing during a crackdown on corruption in the city of Buenos Aires. *The Journal of Law and Economics, 46*(1), 269–292.

Downe, J., Cowell, R., & Morgan, K. (2016). What determines ethical behavior in public organizations: Is it rules or leadership? *Public Administration Review, 76*(6), 898–909.

Eriksson, S., Helgesson, G., & Höglund, A. T. (2007). Being, doing, and knowing: Developing ethical competence in health care. *Journal of Academic Ethics, 5*, 207–216.

Eskridge, R. D., French, P. E., & McThomas, M. (2012). The international City/County Management Association Code of ethics: An analysis of violations. *Public Integrity, 14*(2), 127–150.

Gelderman, C. J., Ghijsen, P. W. T., & Brugman, M. J. (2006). Public procurement and EU tendering directives–explaining non-compliance. *International Journal of Public Sector Management, 19*(7), 702–714.

Gino, F., Ayal, S., & Ariely, D. (2009). Contagion and differentiation in unethical behavior: The effect of one bad apple on the barrel. *Psychological Science, 20*(3), 393–398.

Glor, E. (2001). Codes of conduct and generations of public servants. *International Review of Administrative Sciences, 67*(3), 525–541.

Haidt, J. (2003). The moral emotions. *Handbook of Affective Sciences, 11*(2003), 852–870.

Hijal-Moghrabi, I., & Sabharwal, M. (2018). Ethics in American public administration: A response to a changing reality. *Public Integrity, 20*(5), 459–477.

Huberts, L. (2014). *The integrity of governance: What it is, what we know, what is done and where to go.* Springer International Publishing.

Huberts, L. W. (2018). Integrity: What it is and why it is important. *Public Integrity, 20*(supp 1), S18–S32.

Jackson, K. B., & Grilli, K. C. (2014). Carrot and stick philosophy: The history of the organizational sentencing guidelines and the emergence of effective compliance and ethics program. In *The complete compliance and ethics manual* (pp. 23–251). United States Sentencing Commission.

Jensen, T., Sandström, J., & Helin, S. (2009). Corporate codes of ethics and the bending of moral space. *Organization, 16*(4), 529–545.

Kaptein, M. (2015). The effectiveness of ethics programs: The role of scope, composition, and sequence. *Journal of Business Ethics, 132*, 415–431.

Khaltar, O., & Moon, M. J. (2020). Effects of ethics and performance management on organizational performance in the public sector. *Public Integrity, 22*(4), 372–394.

Klitgaard, R. (1988). *Controlling corruption.* University of California Press.

Kontogeorga, G. N. (2017). Does (better) regulation really matter? Examining public financial management legislation in Greece. *European Journal of Law and Economics, 43*, 153–166.

Lambsdorff, J. (2007). *The institutional economics of corruption and reform: Theory, evidence, and policy.* Cambridge University Press

Lartey, F. M. (2021). Integrity-based and Compliance-based ethics programs: A critical analysis of key differences. *International Journal of Economics, Business and Management Research, 5*(5), 43–53.

Lawton, A., Rayner, J., & Lasthuizen, K. (2013). *Ethics and management in the public sector.* Routledge.

Maesschalck, J. (2004). Approaches to ethics management in the public sector: A proposed extension of the compliance-integrity continuum. *Public Integrity, 7*(1), 20–41.

Mazar, N., & Aggarwal, P. (2011). Greasing the palm: Can collectivism promote bribery? *Psychological Science, 22*(7), 843–848.

Meine, M. F., & Dunn, T. P. (2013). The search for ethical competency: Do ethics codes matter? *Public Integrity*, *15*(2), 149–166.

Menzel, D. C. (1997). Teaching ethics and values in public administration: Are we making a difference? *Public Administration Review*, 224–230.

Menzel, D. C. (2015). Research on ethics and integrity in public administration: Moving forward, looking back. *Public Integrity*, *17*(4), 343–370.

Moore, C., & Gino, F. (2015). Approach, ability, aftermath: A psychological process framework of unethical behavior at work. *The Academy of Management Annals*, *9*(1), 235–289.

Olken, B. A. (2007). Monitoring corruption: Evidence from a field experiment in Indonesia. *Journal of Political Economy*, *115*(2), 200–249.

Paine, L. S. (1994). Managing for organizational integrity. *Harvard Business Review*, *72*(2), 106–117.

Palidauskaite, J. (2006). Codes of ethics in transitional democracies: A comparative perspective. *Public Integrity*, *8*(1), 35–48.

Pattison, S., & Wainwright, P. (2010). Is the 2008 NMC Code ethical? *Nursing Ethics*, *17*(1), 9–18.

Pelletier, K. L., & Bligh, M. C. (2006). Rebounding from corruption: Perceptions of ethics program effectiveness in a public sector organization. *Journal of Business Ethics*, *67*, 359–374.

Perlman, B. J., Reddick, C., & Demir, T. (2023). A compliance—integrity framework for ethics management: An empirical analysis of local government practice. *Public Administration Review*, *83*(4), 823–837.

Roberts, R. (2009). The rise of compliance-based ethics management: Implications for organizational ethics. *Public Integrity*, *11*(3), 261–278.

Rose, J., & Heywood, P. M. (2013). Political science approaches to integrity and corruption. *Human Affairs*, *23*, 148–159.

Rose-Ackerman, S. (1978). *Corruption: A study in political economy*. Academic Press.

Rose-Ackerman, S., & Palifka, B. J. (2016). *Corruption and government: Causes, consequences, and reform*. Cambridge University Press.

Ross, S. A. (1973). The economic theory of agency: The principal's problem. *The American Economic Review*, *63*(2), 134–139.

Shapiro, S. P. (2005). Agency theory. *Annual Review of Sociology*, *31*(1), 263–284.

Siegel, L. (2011). *Criminology: The core* (4th ed.). Wadsworth.

Simpson, J. A., & Weiner, E. S. C. (Eds.). (1989). *Oxford English dictionary* (3rd ed.). Oxford University Press.

Stuke, M. E. (2014). In search of effective ethics & compliance programs. *Journal of Corporation Law, 39*, 769.

Svara, J. H. (2014). Who are the keepers of the code? Articulating and upholding ethical standards in the field of public administration. *Public Administration Review*, *74*(5), 561–569.

Tremblay, M., Martineau, J. T., & Pauchant, T. C. (2017). Managing organizational ethics in the public sector: A pluralist contingency approach as an alternative to the integrity management framework. *Public Integrity*, *19*(3), 219–233.

Trevino, L. K., & Ball, G. A. (1992). The social implications of punishing unethical behavior: Observers' cognitive and affective reactions. *Journal of Management*, *18*(4), 751–768.

Weaver, G. R., & Treviño, L. K. (1999). Compliance and values-oriented ethics programs: Influences on employees' attitudes and behavior. *Business Ethics Quarterly*, *9*(2), 315–335.

Welsh, D. T., & Ordóñez, L. D. (2014). Conscience without cognition: The effects of subconscious priming on ethical behavior. *Academy of Management Journal*, *57*(3), 723–742.

West, K., & Davis, P. (2011). What is the public value of government action? Towards a (New) pragmatic approach to values questions in public endeavors. *Public Administration*, *89*(2), 226–241.

2 Ethics Codes, Codes of Conduct

Definitions, Applications, and Effectiveness

Diane L. Odeh and Jessica Homer

Legal Ethical Standards, Codes of Ethics, and Codes of Conduct: Knowing the Difference

While they are often used interchangeably, legal ethical standards, codes of ethics, and codes of conduct have different intentions and expected outcomes. This chapter serves to create an understanding of the best way to create a code of ethics and their complementary codes of conduct; however, to do so first requires delineating the difference between types of codes that rule our public ethics space.

Legal Ethical Standards

Legal ethics are specifically applied to those who engage in the practice of law, are included in the rules for professional responsibility for each state, and often use the Model Rules of Professional Responsibility created by the American Bar Association as a resource. Legal ethics are different from the expectations of public sector employees—unless that employee is also an attorney acting as an attorney for the organization. Every state will have a code of ethics which can serve as an organization's starting point. Remember that the law is a bar, and oftentimes, a low bar. An organization can choose to have a standard that allows more rights for the members of their community, and more accountability of their public entity to the members of the community which may include higher standards of reporting and more strict conflict of interest rules.

While it is always important for the legal office within a public entity to be highly involved in the compliance plan, their ethical needs differ considerably. Specifically, an attorney's highest commitment is loyalty to the client, including confidentiality and zealous advocacy. That certainly includes compliance, but what happens when compliance choices and client protection conflict? Take the following simple scenario as a way there can be conflicts between legal ethics and a well-drafted code of ethics.

DOI: 10.4324/9781003416258-3

City X had a music festival that was advertised as "accessible" for everyone. Even though Title II requires all public events to be accessible, Stacey has been wary of participating in City events because they are in a motorized wheelchair. However, since the event was advertised, they attended. At the event, Stacey was unable to get to food, water, or shady spaces and the day was hot. Stacey has filed an Americans with Disabilities Act (ADA) complaint via the City X grievance process.

The Code contains a robust grievance and investigative processes, which go above the minimum requirements of the ADA. However, the City also has their legal office overseeing compliance with the Code. After an investigation, it was clear that the City violated Stacey's rights under the Code and the ADA.

Stacey would like a copy of her report, but if legal is the office in charge of investigating, there is a problem. If they admit fault in their analysis to Stacey, they may be violating their responsibilities to protect their client from liability. If they do not, they violate their own Code.

This is why it is imperative for an organization to not solely rely on legal to create and maintain codes of ethics, but to think broadly about the ways codes are developed. Laws are generally written to prevent behavior such as "discretionary abuse" (Gilman, 2005).

Codes of Ethics

Codes of ethics are defined as a set of guidelines intended to govern an individual's decisions and actions (Coughlan, 2005). In contrast to legal standards, codes of ethics are meant to promote principles that challenge an individual to be self-reflective about the best course of action in their decision-making (Gilman, 2005). Codes of ethics are presumed to provide individuals with a roadmap on how to make ethical decisions in environments with competing values (Grundstein-Amato, 2001; Kinchin, 2007; Rohr, 1976; Safitri & Hapsah, 2020).

The existence of codes of ethics in the public sector precedes the scholarly study of public sector ethics. Ethics as a scholarly discipline in public administration proliferated in the 1970s (Cooper, 2004). A commonly held belief is that the first code of ethics related to good governance was created in 5th century BC when Pericles wrote the Athenian Oath (Lewis & Gilman, 2005; Jørgensen & Sørensen, 2012; Svara, 2021). Codes of ethics related to public sector work in the United States have been created as early as the 19th century when the US Postmaster General released a code for postal workers (Lewis & Gilman, 2005). Codes of ethics related to government work proliferated in the United

States in the 1960s (Kernaghan, 2003). In 1961, President Kennedy introduced the codification of ethical values in federal employment by introducing conflict-of-interest statutes (Lewis & Gilman, 2005). By 1978, the federal government further formalized the role of codes and ethics and conduct via passage of the Ethics in Government Act, which established "standards of behavior" for government employees (Fuertes, 2021). Throughout the mid-century, there was a significant focus on compliance and behaviors related to what not to do in lieu of the promotion of public service values (Kernaghan, 2003). By 2004, over 90% of government employees reported that they were operating under an ethical code (Lewis & Gilman, 2005).

Professional associations that are salient to public sector work have released ethical standards that are expected of members since the early 20th century. For example, the International City/County Management Association (ICMA) Code of Ethics has existed since 1924 (Svara, 2021). The International Association of Chiefs of Police (IACP) created theirs in 1957 (International Association of Chiefs of Police, 2024). The American Society for Public Administration (ASPA) developed their first code in 1984 (Fuertes, 2021). The American Institute of Certified Planners initiated their first code in 2006.

Codes of ethics have varied functions within an organization. They have a symbolic function in that they are a declaration of the values an organization would like to promote (Grundstein-Amato, 2001; Coughlan, 2005; Gilman, 2005). In the public sector, the symbolic presence of integrity can build trust with the community (Moon et al., 2023). The existence of a code of ethics is also used to signal professionalism in the workplace (Adams et al., 2001). Codes of ethics also have a practical aspect to them. They can be used to sanction employees who do not behave in accordance with the standards put for by the codes (Adams et al., 2001). They can also provide benchmarks from which to compare ethicality across other institutions and jurisdictions (Moon et al., 2023).

Codes of Conduct

Codes of conduct differ slightly from a code of ethics. While codes of ethics focus primarily on value statements that should be incorporated into decision-making processes, codes of conduct offer specific behavioral expectations to be followed by individuals (Moon et al., 2023). They are generally more prescriptive than codes of ethics in that they contain specific guidelines on what to do and what not to do. Codes of ethics and codes of conduct often work in tandem with each other as part of an ethical landscape (Somers, 2001).

Common Values in Public Sector Codes

The majority of public sector employees operate under at least one code of ethics. In many cases, they can be exposed to many different codes of ethics: one for the organization, one for the jurisdiction, and those released by professional associations. This underscores the importance in ensuring a level of consistency within codes that serve the public. This section will discuss common values inherent in public sector codes of ethics.

Mosher (1938) argued that a code of ethics for public service at large should include the following elements: pursuit of the public interest, maintaining relationships with elected officials and community members, the promotion of personal integrity, and a commitment to serve the "whole" public impartially.

Pursuit of the Public Interest

Pursuit of the public interest is widely regarded as a normative value in public sector codes of ethics (Cooper, 2004; Lewis & Gilman, 2005; McCandless & Ronquillo, 2020). It was the first element, Mosher (1938) asserted, a code of ethics for public service at large should incorporate. In a comparative study of seven professional association codes of ethics, Odeh (2024) confirmed that all of them made a reference to the public interest. Although it is a normative value, the meaning of what pursuit of the "public interest" entails varied into two broad categories: (1) stewardship of resources and (2) promoting the "public good" (Odeh, 2024). Stewardship of resources mainly referred to actions related to maintaining fidelity of how taxpayer money is spent. Promotion of the public good refers to more general promotion of what's best for society. Many references to serving the "public good" also entailed the value of ensuring trustworthiness among citizens. The Government Finance Officers Association (GFOA) uses the concept of "trustworthiness" as its primary underlying value (Government Finance Officers Association, 2019).

Social Equity

Social equity has been considered a normative element of contemporary codes of ethics. In public administration research, the concept of "social equity" was a departure from the value of "equality" set forth in the US Constitution (Gooden, 2015). Gooden (2015) defines social equity as being aligned with the democratic value of "fairness." Marini (1971) more specifically aligns social equity in public administration as being based in John Rawls's conception of justice as fairness. Gooden (2015) states that the term social equity is distinct from that of equity because it incorporates an understanding of historical, political, social, and economic factors that contribute to structural conditions that impact access, opportunity, and outcomes. McCandless and Ronquillo (2020) analyzed ten codes of ethics that pertain to public sector work with the goal of understanding to what extent they promote social equity. They found that seven of the codes mentioned the value of "fairness" a total of 12 times. At the time, the concept of "equity" was mentioned in four codes a total of ten times. Six of the codes mentioned the concept of "respect." Since 2020, the explicit mention of "social equity" or "diversity, equity, and inclusion" (DEI) has become increasingly more common in public sector codes of ethics. For example, following the death of George Floyd, ICMA focused their codes of ethics review specifically on incorporating more elements of DEI (ICMA, 2023). Some codes, such as the American Evaluation Association (AEA) code of ethics, specifically mention the need to acknowledge historical events that harmed communities (McCandless & Ronquillo, 2020).

Prior to the proliferation of social equity as a field of study in public administration, scholars such as Mosher (1938) implied it by stating that practitioners should endeavor to treat community members "impartially" and without favor for one group or individual over another.

Regime Values

Codes of ethics can be a tool for expressing the values of public service, and subsequently, the values of a democracy (Gilman, 2005). Public administrators are the primary instruments of carrying out the constitutional values of a regime (Burke, 1988; Cooper, 2004). In an analysis of 14 codes of ethics across the globe, Jørgensen and Sørensen (2012) found that regime values are an overlapping component. Regime values are the values that the polity seeks to promote. Generally, regime values refer to the "spirit" of the constitution (Rohr, 1989). Rohr (1989) identified three primary regime values: freedom, equality, and property. Jørgensen and Sørensen (2012) found that codes of ethics that reference regime values assign specific behaviors such as upholding the dignity of the regime. Despite regime values being a common element in global codes, Svara (2014) found that they are not always explicitly mentioned in codes.

Promoting Virtue

Ethical codes are laden with values that they expect practitioners to uphold. This implies the importance of personal characteristics in carrying out behaviors conducive with the values. In his speech announcing ethics regulations in 1961, President Kennedy stated as follows:

> The ultimate answer to ethical problems in government is honest people in a good ethical environment. No web of statute or regulation, however intricately conceived, can hope to deal with the myriad possible challenges to a man's integrity or his devotion to the public interest.
>
> (Lewis & Gilman, 2005)

A vein of public sector ethics scholarship focuses on the role of individual virtue. To Cooper (1987), promoting virtue in individuals contributes to beneficence for the community, justice, a commitment to due process, and organizational excellence. In analyses of codes of ethics, Svara (2021) and Odeh (2024) found that the codes studied underscored the importance of virtue as a personal characteristic of practitioners.

The extent to which virtue is promoted in codes varies. For example, both ICMA and ASPA state that public service employees should demonstrate personal integrity (ICMA, 2023; ASPA, 2024). In both codes, the integrity of the administrator is directly tied to confidence in public service as a whole. GFOA also ties personal virtue to building trust in the community (GFOA, 2019). Public safety codes of ethics such as those from the National Society of Executive Fire Officers (NSEFO) and the International Association of Chiefs of Police (IACP) take the role of personal virtue further by stating that officers must conduct themselves virtuously on- and off-duty (NSEFO, n.d.; IACP, n.d.).

Elements That Promote Ethical Conduct

Despite the proliferation of codes of ethics and conduct in the 21st century, the extent to how well they promote ethical conduct has been debated. Codes that focus too much on what not to do can promote a culture of coercion (Lewis & Gilman, 2005). They can also promote what scholars call the "low road," or "hygiene" form of ethical decision-making. In low road or "hygiene" ethical decision-making, practitioners are focused on complying with formalized rules (Rohr, 1989; Lewis & Gilman, 2005; McCandless & Ronquillo, 2020; Morgan et al., 2021). The downside of a compliance approach occurs when practitioners hyperfocus on avoiding repercussions for violating rules instead of seeking ways to promote an ethical environment.

Conversely, codes that promote the "high road" of ethics incorporate principles that are aspirational at the expense of being implementable (McCandless & Ronquillo, 2020). They are often vague in nature and do not explicitly define what the principles mean. For example, many codes of ethics focus on emphasizing the principle of "personal integrity," but what that looks like in practice is vague. This becomes an issue because ethical principles are open to the way an individual interprets it (Kinchin, 2007). Codes of ethics are not effective tools if an individual does not know how to internalize them in a way that can be incorporated into daily decision-making (Grundstein-Amato, 2001).

When it comes to what promotes ethical conduct, codes should be written in a way that promotes a "middle road" way of thinking (Odeh, 2024). The following are elements that should be incorporated in codes.

Allow for discretion: codes of ethics and conduct that are too prescriptive run the risk of promoting a top-down, compliance-oriented workplace (Lewis & Gilman, 2005; Morgan et al., 2021). It's important to allow for broad discretion in how a practitioner is able to carry forth the principles in codes (Rohr, 1989). Calder (2020) found that employees who view codes of ethics as guidelines to promote ethical conduct will exercise more discretion than those who view codes of ethics as rules to be carried out neutrally.

Consider the ethical context: Morgan et al. (2021) promoted a "role-centered" approach to ethics that considers the profession that a public administrator is working within. Odeh (2024) found that codes of ethics emphasize different principles depending on the profession type. Some industries, such as a highly regulated and technical position, may require a high level of rule compliance (Morgan, 1987). For example, public procurement professionals have specific guidelines to follow related to making purchases with taxpayer funds. Other roles, such as those that work with the public environment in complex environments, may not require so much behavioral oversight. For these reasons, codes should be written with the specific profession and roles occupied in mind.

Provide examples and clarity: Codes work best when values are explicitly defined, leaving little to interpretation (Kernaghan, 2003). Grundstein-Amato (2001) identified clarity as one of two elements that contribute to the effectiveness of ethical codes. When writing codes, it's best to focus on how to be clear and communicate the principles well (Gilman, 2005). Additionally, examples of what the principle looks like in practice can serve as a roadmap for practitioners who are seeking guidance.

Process of Writing Ethical Codes

Now that the elements that good ethics codes should incorporate have been discussed, the question remains: how does one engage in the process of making ethics codes? The most effective codes are created with the involvement of many in a democratic process (Grundstein-Amado, 2001). The following section will offer guidelines on the process of writing your organization's ethical code.

Engage your audience: Prior to engaging in the act of writing, there is considerable groundwork that must be accomplished. The first step in writing codes of ethics and conduct will be establishing the target audience. Is this a code to instruct the behavior of all employees? Elected officials? Both? Is the proposed code issue specific (i.e., address the wrongs of a specific issue within that public organization) or general for behavior of your chosen audience?

Involving organizational players that the code directly impacts upon increases the likelihood they understand, and thereby can follow the rules. Involving the public who benefit from a well-established ethics code gives them the opportunity to understand the principles, debate the importance of the principles, and most importantly, hold their officials accountable when appropriate.

Establish ruling authority: Each state will have a public ethics code that gives a practical blueprint for the start of the organizational document. The law is designed to create a bar, not a ceiling, of the rights of the public from an overstepping government: your organization may hold yourself to a higher standard, but cannot dip below the bar. States vary greatly in how explicitly their ethics codes address issues and to whom. For example, the Washington State Code of Ethics for Municipal officers does not require each public entity to have a code, so long as the Revised Codes of Washington (RCW) is followed. RCW 42.23.10 covers municipal officers duties under contracts:

> It is the purpose and intent of this chapter to revise and make uniform the laws of this state concerning the transaction of business by municipal officers, as defined in chapter 268, Laws of 1961, in conflict with the proper performance of their duties in the public interest; and to promote the efficiency of local government by prohibiting certain instances and areas of conflict while at the same time sanctioning, under sufficient controls, certain other instances and areas of conflict wherein the private interest of the municipal officer is deemed to be only remote, to the end that, without sacrificing necessary public responsibility and enforceability in areas of significant and clearly conflicting interests, the selection of municipal officers may be made from a wider group of responsible citizens of the communities which they are called upon to serve.

From this code, we understand that those considered municipal officers have strong responsibilities under the code. However, in Rhode Island's Title 520, Ethics Commission, similar code applications apply to not only all employees, but many also apply to members of their families.

Consider the skill level of the reader: Of note, readers with advanced knowledge of public administration may catch that the Washington code above applies to "municipal officers" which are defined in RCW 42.23.020 as: "all elected and appointed officers of a municipality, together with all deputies and assistance of such an officer, and all persons exercising or undertraining to exercise any of the powers or functions of a municipal officer." However, even the advanced reader sees some room for interpretation. As a code is implemented, consider readability. Many codes are designed with legal writing, full of complex sentence structure and words the general public would need to look up to understand. According to the Organization for Economic Development (OECD), "Four in five U.S. adults (79 percent) have English literacy skills sufficient to complete tasks that require comparing and contrasting information, paraphrasing, or making low-level inferences" (OECD, 2019). As such, writing complex codes that disengage 20% results in further inequities (OECD, 2019).

While the code actions will not apply to the public to which your institution serves, it is the responsibility of the organization to provide the public tools whereby the public can hold the entity responsible. To do so, the organization must create accessible documents, which includes ADA compliance but also should be easily translated and digestible. Consider how principles of Universal Design can be implemented in your documents (https://universaldesign.org). In summation, applying Universal Design means you are making your program most effective for the person who needs the most assistance.

Avoid conflicts with other ethical authorities by engaging in intentional practices: The primary aim of ethical codes is to give guidance on how to balance competing values in the public sector environment. Scanning other codes is a best practice when creating your own (Lewis & Gilman, 2005). Professional planners, engineers, attorneys, city managers, educators, librarians, and more have their own professional ethics codes or professional codes of conduct. Understanding these codes has two particular benefits: (1) You do not have to reinvent the wheel! Well-developed codes can give you great advice on how to proceed in your own organization; and (2) while you are not obligated to use all the principles of each professional organization, and in fact many parts of industry or license-specific codes would not apply, it is imperative to not create a conflict of interest for your organizational participants.

For example, at the time of this writing, many states are calling plans for equity "divisive" and systematically destroying attempts at DEI. In 2022, the state of Florida enacted a flurry of bills including the Individual Freedom Act (aka Stop WOKE Act), a comprehensive law designed to end DEI programing in education and business, public and private. Among the requirements of the law, employers could not require "any individual, as a condition of employment," to "training, instruction, or any other required activity that espouses, promotes, advances, inculcates, or compels" (Honeyfund.com, Inc v. Governor, Florida, 2024). The American Planners Association's (APA) American Institute of Certified Planners (AICP) code states: "People who participate in the planning process shall work to achieve economic, social and racial equity" by "creat[ing] plans that ensure equitable access to resources and opportunities which, in turn, structure prospects for upward economic mobility, a sense of belonging, and an enhanced quality of life" (APA, n.d.). How would a planner, then, create plans about tackling historic patterns of inequity, without also recognizing that a workplace discussion may make folks uncomfortable? The planner is then made to choose: violate state law, which may get them fired, or violate their certification status. The more intentionality an organization puts into the creation of the code, the more likely the code will broadly apply to the organization.

Determining who creates and who reviews. The code should be treated like any other ordinance, minimally in compliance with all other entity code processes for writing, review, revision, public comment where applicable, and submittal. However, much like the law promotes low road decision-making, codes of ethics may benefit from more than basic processes. Grundstein-Amado (2001) argues codes often fail because they are not self-critical.

Code Implementation and Sustainability

Thus far, this chapter has spent considerable attention on how to create effective codes of ethics and conduct. However, the presence of a well-written code is only part of the process of promoting an ethical environment. Practitioners need to know how to adopt and implement codes within their organizations. Studies have shown that the presence of a code of ethics isn't enough to ensure ethical behavior. Ash (2010) found that nurses' inability to understand and implement codes of ethics resulted in elder abuse. Scholars argue that humans are subjected to the concept of bounded ethicality, which is the theory that individuals do not have the cognitive ability to make decisions in accordance with stated ethical principles or beliefs (Kernaghan, 1980; Coughlan, 2005; Kim et al., 2015). Codes of ethics and conduct often require a high level of internalization in order to be carried out (Ash, 2010; Safitri & Hapsah, 2020). This points to the importance of cultivating an environment where codes of ethics and conduct are embedded in an organization's culture. This section will discuss best practices of implementation and sustainability of ethical codes.

Code Implementation

In the process of internalization, individual members must fully understand the ethics concepts and understand how to apply them to everyday scenarios (Grundstein-Amado, 2001). This is why it is imperative that, in the preceding section, you align your code of ethics with a behavioral model. You may make these documents together or separate, so long as the members of your organization can easily understand them.

Educating and Training

Demir et al. (2023) identified ethical codes as one element of what is needed to create an ethical environment. Another crucial element is the implementation of initiatives to raise awareness and create knowledge about the expected ethical behavior (Demir et al., 2023). Gilman (2005) states that ethical code implementation should emphasize education. Even the most simple codes also need educational tools to ensure proper understanding of a code. This is often overlooked in many organizations. Many people operate under the "I know it when I see it" approach to decide whether something is ethical or not, and fail to think to refer back to the code unless they are drawn to it explicitly by the organization. In addition, many assume others have the same understanding of concepts as one another. Perform your own experiment in your organization by just asking everyone to define a word like "equity." There will be astonishing variations, without an intervening standard definition in your organizations. Gilman also notes that others find training more precise and exacting, "those supporting this approach would argue that familiarity with regulations would allow public employees to know what is expected of them, and where to look up the rules if they are unclear" (Gilman, 2005). Each method has its own benefits, and organizational purpose should be used to choose the best method. The following guidelines should be considered when implementing a training program:

1. Leadership must enthusiastically support a learning environment for the codes created. Leadership has been found to impact the ethical norms of an organization, and are critical to buy-in of staff (Bowman & Williams, 1997).
2. Consult with experts in the field. There are a plethora of trainers who can offer presentations and/or create training modules. Call upon them when you need to.
3. Remove as many barriers as possible by providing multiple learning modalities. All modalities should include options to both hear and read the information. Provide options relevant to your workforce: if you have a high Spanish-speaking population, for example, have a Spanish translation version of the session. If you have a test at the end, consider removing time limits so those with processing disorders are not left behind.
4. Once everyone is on the same page with the materials, continue providing the same options for new employees, and create a "refresher" for other employees on a regular basis (suggested, annually).

Ensuring Ethical Programs Support Ethical Codes

Many organizations, particularly governmental organizations, work from a place of distrust both internally and externally. Employees believe the organization will side with the managers, and the public may not trust the government is working in everyone's best interest. To mitigate this distrust, a formal ethics training program should be implemented alongside a code of ethics. J. Patrick Dobel (1999) asserted that "strong institutional support" is critical to ensuring an ethical environment. Members of the Public Service Research Group at the School of Business in the University of New South Wales, Canberra, state "direct links exist between perceptions of low integrity of public officials and lack of public trust . . . likewise integrity has been shown to aid in the performance of public sector organizations" (Moon et al., 2023). One way to ensure this support is by having a robust reporting system for people who perceive violations of ethical codes. Schwartz (2013) named the integration of a formal ethics training program as a key element in promoting an ethical environment. Strong compliance programs assist with the promotion integrity, so long as they are properly applied. Common forms of compliance programs include training, a designated ethics officer, and the implementation of an ethics hotline to report ethical code violations (Schwartz, 2013). There is a misperception that a good code of ethics will result in less ethical complaints. Rather, successful implementation of a code plus education will likely lead to increased complaints.

When ensuring compliance with the code, it is important to respond effectively to complaints, regardless of who has been accused of wrongdoing. According to Lewis and Gilman (2005), holding managers to the same standards as subordinates promotes legitimacy of the ethical codes. There is also an equity dimension to ensuring the same standards are applied across the organization, as women and other historically marginalized groups are more likely to face harsher repercussions when found in misconduct (Egan et al., 2022).

Sustaining Ethical Codes

Ensuring that codes continue to be implemented requires considerations of how to sustain them. Ethical codes should be viewed as "living documents" within an organization (van Wart, 2003). Because of this, codes of ethics and conduct should be created alongside a plan for how to sustain them. This happens primarily by ensuring values are embedded throughout the organization, and by engaging in a commitment to continuous revision and refinement.

Embedding the values expressed in the ethical codes throughout the organization is the first method of ensuring its sustainability (Schwartz, 2013). The more ethical codes are practiced and become organizational norms, the more likely they will continue to be implemented within an organization (Moberg, 2006; Elango et al., 2010; Mitchell et al., 2020).

Codes of ethics and conduct should undergo a periodic revision process (van Wart, 1996; Perlman et al., 2023). A commitment to continuous improvement continues to refine and enhance organizational functionality. Many governmental and professional organizations have revised their ethical codes (Kernaghan, 1980; ICMA, 2020). Organizations across many industries have adopted some sort of continuous enhancement policy mechanism to write, implement, and revise work as needed (Moynihan, 2005). Organizations have the capacity to choose which type of plan they model; however, the important piece to this work is the ability to revise as appropriate. While you have read throughout this chapter that consistency is important, it is also imperative the organization has a process in place to address outdated codes or add what is needed when implementation shows a gap. By creating adaptable planning using these or any other models, organizations can enhance their efficacy and ensure their program continues.

Examples of Well-Written Codes

Thus far, this chapter has offered guidance on what constitutes effective code of ethics and conduct. It's important to evaluate what this looks like in the practical sense. Although there is no "perfect" code of ethics and conduct, this section will offer examples that demonstrate the best practice described in the preceding sections. It is not meant to be an exhaustive list of examples, but rather demonstrate how practitioners can incorporate elements discussed in the previous sections.

ASPA Code of Ethics

The ASPA code of ethics was created in 1974. It has undergone revisions in 1984, 1994, and 2013. The ASPA code consists of eight principles:

1. Advance the Public Interest: Promote the interests of the public and put service to the public above service to oneself.
2. Uphold the Constitution and the Law: Respect and support government constitutions and laws, while seeking to improve laws and policies to promote the public good.
3. Promote democratic participation: Inform the public and encourage active engagement in governance. Be open, transparent and responsive, and respect and assist all persons in their dealings with public organizations.
4. Strengthen social equity: Treat all persons with fairness, justice, and equality and respect individual differences, rights, and freedoms. Promote affirmative action and other initiatives to reduce unfairness, injustice, and inequality in society.
5. Fully inform and advise: Provide accurate, honest, comprehensive, and timely information and advice to elected and appointed officials and governing board members, and to staff members in your organization.
6. Demonstrate personal integrity: Adhere to the highest standards of conduct to inspire public confidence and trust in public service.
7. Promote ethical organizations: Strive to attain the highest standards of ethics, stewardship, and public service in organizations that serve the public.
8. Advance professional excellence: Strengthen personal capabilities to act competently and ethically and encourage the professional development of others.

These principles follow the best practice of being clear and succinct. Grundstein-Amado (2001) found that codes work best when the principles are clearly communicated. Beyond the eight principles, ASPA incorporates many elements that align well with the guidance set forth in this chapter. The code is reviewed approximately every ten years (ASPA, 2013b). This review happens via a process in which a committee reviews the code and makes revisions on an as-needed basis in a democratic process that includes several stakeholders. Additionally, other public sector codes of ethics were reviewed in order to ensure consistency (ASPA, 2013b). At first glance, the principles run the risk of promoting unattainable "high road" thinking. Indeed, the revisionists in 2013 aimed at making the principles aspirational (ASPA, 2013b). In addition to these goals, ASPA provides examples of what specific practices will promote each principle. One element that makes ASPA's code unique is the creation of a supplemental guidebook intended to give guidance to public practitioners. In this guidebook, the principles are further defined and contextualized. Practitioners are encouraged to assess the context they exist within via self-reflective questions. For example, a question related to advancing the public interest asks "With what individual residents or groups do I have a direct service relationship? Do I treat all with the same respect and regard?" (ASPA, 2015).

ICMA Code of Ethics

The ICMA code of ethics is regarded as being the first professional association code of ethics pertaining to public service (Svara, 2021). It was created in 1924. As of 2024, the code consists of the following 12 tenets:

Tenet 1. We believe professional management is essential to effective, efficient, equitable, and democratic local government.

Tenet 2. Affirm the dignity and worth of local government services and maintain a deep sense of social responsibility as a trusted public servant.

Tenet 3. Demonstrate by word and action the highest standards of ethical conduct and integrity in all public, professional, and personal relationships in order that the member may merit the trust and respect of the elected and appointed officials, employees, and the public.

Tenet 4. Serve the best interests of all community members.

Tenet 5. Submit policy proposals to elected officials; provide them with facts, and technical and professional advice about policy options; and collaborate with them in setting goals for the community and organization.

Tenet 6. Recognize that elected representatives are accountable to their community for the decisions they make; members are responsible for implementing those decisions.

Tenet 7. Refrain from all political activities which undermine public confidence in professional administrators. Refrain from participation in the election of the members of the employing legislative body.

Tenet 8. Make it a duty continually to improve the member's professional ability and to develop the competence of associates in the use of management techniques.

Tenet 9. Keep the community informed on local government affairs. Encourage and facilitate active engagement and constructive communication between community members and all local government officials.

Tenet 10. Resist any encroachment on professional responsibilities, believing the member should be free to carry out official policies without interference, and handle each problem without discrimination on the basis of principle and justice.

Tenet 11. Manage all personnel matters with fairness and impartiality.

Tenet 12. Public office is a public trust. A member shall not leverage his or her position for personal gain or benefit.

This code has undergone several iterations over the past decade. Its most recent iterations occurred in 2017, 2018, 2019, and 2023. The most recent review and revision started in May 2021 in response to racial reckoning in the United States in 2020 (ICMA, n.d.). The ICMA code of ethics embodies what it means to be a living document due to its continuous review and revision process. The code contains a mixture of compliance-related and aspirational tenets. In the past, ICMA tenets have promoted anti-discrimination before the US government did: in 1938, the code was revised to ban discriminatory practices in personnel decisions—three years before President Franklin Delano Roosevelt made a similar declaration in Executive Order 8802. This provides an example of how codes of ethics can be used to promote ethical conduct when there are ethical gaps in policy. Since 1972, the tenets have been published alongside guidelines that give examples of what each tenet means (ICMA, 2023).

GFOA Code of Ethics

GFOA offers a short and simple code:

1. Integrity and honesty are the foundation on which trustworthiness is built. I, as a member of a public finance office, am in a unique position where my influence over the allocation of limited resources and the fiscal future of my community requires the highest standard of integrity and honesty. It means people can believe what I say, I act in accordance with my deepest values, I put principle ahead of my own ego, and I do the right thing even when it is hard.
2. Public finance offices have an important job. Doing that job well honors the trust the public has placed in me. When I show I am well informed and knowledgeable and can produce the results my community expects, I build trust.
3. Local governments depend on trusting relationships between people. If people feel unfairly treated, relationships break down, and they may withhold their support from my local government. This makes it more difficult for my local government to maintain a strong financial foundation. Therefore, I will treat people fairly and develop processes and procedures that are fair.
4. Communities across the country are constantly changing. Embracing diversity and fostering inclusiveness helps finance offices cultivate organizations and promote policies that reflect the communities they serve. When people feel included, they will see that I am concerned for their wellbeing, and that shows I am worthy of their trust.
5. When others can count on me, I prove my trustworthiness. When I consistently apply my standards—especially to myself—I honor my commitment to the community I serve and make it easier to do the right thing even when faced with challenging circumstances.

These principles are noteworthy because they clarify exactly why each value matters to good governance. It also details the implications on legitimacy if an individual does not follow through on their ethical commitments. The GFOA code also offers a set of specific behaviors that serve as examples of what the principle looks like when implemented. For example, one results-related behavior was listed as "Hon[ing] my expertise. Continually refining my knowledge, skills, and abilities assures people that I can produce results for my community now and in the future" (GFOA, 2019).

The GFOA code underwent an extensive revision process in 2018. The revisionists consulted experts and best practice literature during this time (Kavanagh & Gibson, 2018). A goal of the code was to promote tangible, proactive steps to promoting ethics in lieu of focusing on "low road" thinking. The code also comes alongside a companion training module to help members internalize the principles.

Public Sector Codes of Ethics and Conduct: Unique Challenges

In both the private and public sectors, codes of ethics and conduct are tools that encourage ethical behavior among employees. Best practices of writing such codes are similar across fields. However, there are some considerations that make the promotion of ethics in the public sector distinct from its private counterparts.

Capacity Issues

Ethical culture in an organization begins with the establishment of an infrastructure that promulgates ethical behavior (Demir et al., 2023). Earlier, it was established that in order for codes of ethics and conduct to work as intended, a robust training program, institutional support, and dedicated resources aimed at holding people accountable are needed. Public sector organizations often lack the ability to proactively ensure ethical behavior due to financial and staffing challenges. Private sector businesses, by contrast, have the resources and flexibility to create new positions quickly.

Contrasting Layers of Administrative Rules, Legislation, and Policy

As demonstrated at the beginning of this chapter, codes of ethics and conduct are only one element of the ethical terrain that an individual must navigate. Most public sector employees are beholden to layers of legislation, administrative rules, and policy that often supersede organization or professional codes of ethics. Some legislation, especially when created with political aims in mind, run in direct tension to public sector codes of ethics. For example, although "social equity" is a primary value found in ethical codes, state-level legislation has banned discussions of "diversity, equity, and inclusion" in public organizations (Kratz, 2024). Although private sector businesses are also beholden to legal standards, they often entail less scrutiny than public agencies that are dependent on resources provided by taxpayers—especially in situations where a reduction of funding is used as a sanctioning tool. In the case of promoting equity, private sector businesses are positioned to have less roadblocks than its public sector counterparts (Kratz, 2024).

Public versus Private Interest

Private sector companies are mostly concerned with shareholder interests. This means that their codes of ethics and conduct can focus on very niche goals such as profit accrual (Fuertes, 2021). This is in contrast to the goals of public service, which is to serve the multitude of stakeholders that constitute the *whole public*. This becomes further complicated because there are many ways the "public interest" can be defined in codes of ethics and conduct (Odeh, 2024). Due to the need for consideration of a broad community, public codes of ethics have been critiqued for not being specific enough. This is in contrast to private codes of ethics that often offer specific and strategic guidelines to promote business and leadership goals (Teubner, 2011).

Transparency and Accountability

A core value of public service is that of transparency (Lewis & Gilman, 2005). Many codes of ethics specifically name this as an important element to the profession. This runs counter to the private sector where "trade secrets" and other personnel matters are kept confidential. Transparency is paradoxical to public service because although it adds a layer of accountability, it can also negatively affect perceptions of an organization's integrity when a violation of codes of ethics and conduct is publicized (Kernaghan, 1980). The pressure to avoid negative perceptions results in codes of ethics functioning more as a public relations tool to retain legitimacy (Lichtenberg, 1996). It also encourages the blaming of individuals for unethical acts instead of looking at systemic ethical issues (Metcalf, 2014).

Emerging Issues and Conclusion

Moving forward, there are emerging issues that scholars and practitioners alike will need to consider as they create and implement codes of ethics and conduct. In an era of political polarization, legislation aimed at promoting a political agenda can be in tension with values found in codes of ethics and conduct. As private-public partnerships become commonplace in governance, questions remain about how to promote ethical behavior in industries that aren't beholden to the same normative ethical expectations as public organizations, which further complicates the efficacy of public sector codes of ethics and conduct. An issue that urgently needs attention has to do with how quickly technology changes. Scholars and practitioners are tasked with ensuring ethical conduct in a time when e-government has become more prevalent. Codes of ethics and conduct remain underdeveloped as individuals seek guidance related to the ethical use of AI, data governance, and cybersecurity. A commitment to periodic review and revisions will go far in mitigating these concerns.

This chapter has endeavored to describe codes of ethics and conduct as they pertain to the public sector. Through an overview of the history of ethical codes in the United States, it was demonstrated that the majority of public practitioners operate under at least one ethical code. The difference between codes of ethics and codes of conduct was outlined. The former offers principles that employees should endeavor to fulfill, while the latter offers prescriptive behaviors that are consistent with organizational values. The values inherent within ethical codes include pursuit of the public interest, social equity, and personal virtue. Issues with codes of ethics and conduct pertain primarily to being too compliance-focused, or too aspirational that they are not implementable. Guidance on how to overcome these issues was offered. If codes are written in clear ways that underscore proactivity regarding ethics, they are more likely to be effective. When writing codes of ethics, it is important to facilitate a democratic process that engages stakeholders who are expected to carry out the code. Leadership buy-in and support is also critical. To sustain codes of ethics and conduct, a commitment to embedding the stated values within the organization in addition to continuous improvement is paramount. Finally, it's important to scan other codes when creating your own. The codes of ethics for ASPA, ICMA, and GFOA were analyzed for the key lessons with the hopes that practitioners will mimic their best practices in the future. Finally, challenges faced by the public sector context were outlined.

References

Adams, J. S., Taschian, A., & Shore, T. H. (2001). Codes of ethics as signals for ethical behavior. *Journal of Business Ethics*, *29*, 199–211.

American Planning Association (APA). (n.d.). *AICP Code of ethics and professional conduct*. Retrieved from www.planning.org/ethics/ethicscode/

American Society for Public Administration (ASPA). (2013a, March 16). *Practices to promote the ASPA Code of Ethics*. ASPANET. Retrieved from www.aspanet.org/Common/Uploaded%20files/ASPADocs/Practices%20with%20revisions.pdf

American Society for Public Administration (ASPA). (2013b, March 24). *Developing the Revised ASPA Code of Ethics*. ASPANET. Retrieved from www.aspanet.org/Common/Uploaded%20files/ASPADocs/Revision%20Process%202013-03-24.pdf

American Society for Public Administration (ASPA). (2015). *Implementing the ASPA Code of Ethics: Workbook and Assessment Guide*. ASPANET. Retrieved from https://www.aspanet.org/Common/Uploaded%20files/ASPADocs/Membership/Ethics_Assessment_Guide.pdf

American Society for Public Administration (ASPA). (2024). *ASPA Code of Ethics*. ASPANET. Retrieved from www.aspanet.org/ASPA/ASPA/Code-of-Ethics/Code-of-Ethics.aspx?hkey=5b8f046b-dcbd-416d-87cd-0b8fcfacb5e7

Ash, A. (2010). Ethics and the street-level bureaucrat: Implementing policy to protect elders from abuse. *Ethics and Social Welfare*, *4*(2), 201–209.

Bowman, J. B., & Williams, R. L. (1997). Ethics in government: From a winter of despair to a spring of hope. *Public Administration Review*, 517–526.

Burke, J. P. (1988). *Bureaucratic responsibility*. John Hopkins University Press.

Calder, G. (2020). Discretion as ethical practice. *Discretion and the Quest for Controlled Freedom*, 393–407.

Code of Ethics for Municipal Officers, Contract Interests 42.23.10 RCW 1961 c 268 § 3. Retrieved from https://apps.leg.wa.gov/rcw/default.aspx?cite=42.23&full=true

Cooper, T. L. (1987). Hierarchy, virtue, and the practice of public administration: A perspective for normative ethics. *Public Administration Review*, 320–328.

Cooper, T. L. (2004). Big questions in administrative ethics: A need for focused, collaborative effort. *Public Administration Review*, *64*(4), 395–407.

Coughlan, R. (2005). Codes, values and justifications in the ethical decision-making process. *Journal of Business Ethics*, *59*, 45–53.

Demir, T., Reddick, C. G., & Perlman, B. J. (2023). In search of ethics infrastructure in US local governments: Building Blocks or dead end? *Administration & Society*, *55*(10), 1866–1892.

Dobel, J. P. (1999). The ethics of resigning. *Journal of Policy Analysis & Management*, *18*(2), 245–263.

Egan, M., Matvos, G., & Seru, A. (2022). When Harry fired Sally: The double standard in punishing misconduct. *Journal of Political Economy*, *130*(5), 1184–1248.

Elango, B., Paul, K., Kundu, S. K., & Paudel, S. K. (2010). Organizational ethics, individual ethics, and ethical intentions in international decision-making. *Journal of Business Ethics*, *97*, 543–561.

Ethics Commission, Definitions Title 520 R.I. Gen. Laws § 36-14-2. Retrieved from https://ethics.ri.gov/code-ethics

Fuertes, V. (2021). The rationale for embedding ethics and public value in public administration programmes. *Teaching Public Administration*, *39*(3), 252–269.

Gilman, S. C. (2005). Ethics codes and codes of conduct as tools for promoting an ethical and professional public service: Comparative successes and lessons. *Prepared for the PREM, the World Bank*. Retrieved from https://www.insightsonindia.com/wp-content/uploads/2013/09/codes-of-ethics-oecd-good-one.pdf

Gooden, S. T. (2015). From equality to social equity. In *Public administration evolving*. Routledge.

Government Finance Officers Association (GFOA). (2019). *Code of ethics*. GFOA. Retrieved from www.gfoa.org/ethics

Grundstein-Amado, R. (2001). A strategy for formulation and implementation of codes of ethics in public service organizations. *International Journal of Public Administration*, *24*(5), 461–478.

Honeyfund.com Inc., et al. v. Governor, State of Florida et al. (2024, March 4). *U.S. Ct. of Apps, 11th Circuit No. 22-13135*. Retrieved from https://media.ca11.uscourts.gov/opinions/pub/files/202213135.pdf

International Association of Chiefs of Police (IACP). (n.d.). *Law enforcement Code of ethics*. IACP. Retrieved from www.theiacp.org/resources/law-enforcement-code-of-ethics

International City/County Management Association (ICMA). (2020, March 1). *Timeline of the ICMA Code of ethics*. ICMA. Retrieved from https://icma.org/articles/pm-magazine/timeline-icma-code-ethics

International City/County Management Association (ICMA). (2023, June 2). *ICMA Code of ethics*. ICMA. Retrieved from https://icma.org/documents/icma-code-ethics-amended-june-2023

International City/County Management Association (ICMA). (n.d.). *ICMA Code of ethics review focusing on diversity, equity, and inclusion*. ICMA.org. Retrieved from https://icma.org/page/icma-code-ethics-review-focusing-diversity-equity-and-inclusion

Jørgensen, T. B., & Sørensen, D. L. (2012). Codes of good governance: National or global public values? *Public Integrity*, *15*(1), 71–96.

Kavanagh, S., & Gibson, S. (2018). *GFOA reinvents our profession's approach to ethics.* GFOA.

Kernaghan, K. (1980). Codes of ethics and public administration: Progress, problems and prospects. *Public Administration*, *58*(2).

Kernaghan, K. (2003). Integrating values into public service: The values statement as centerpiece. *Public Administration Review*, *63*(6), 711–719.

Kim, T. W., Monge, R., & Strudler, A. (2015). Bounded ethicality and the principle that "ought" implies "can". *Business Ethics Quarterly*, *25*(3), 341–361.

Kinchin, N. (2007). More than writing on a wall: Evaluating the role that codes of ethics play in securing accountability of public sector decision-makers. *Australian Journal of Public Administration*, *66*(1), 112–120.

Kratz, J. (2024, June 18). *Anti-DEI legislation: How we got here with tips to combat it. Forbes.* Retrieved from www.forbes.com/sites/juliekratz/2024/06/09/anti-dei-legislation-how-we-got-here-with-tips-to-combat-it/

Lewis, C. W., & Gilman, S. C. (2005). *The ethics challenge in public service: A problem-solving guide.* John Wiley & Sons.

Lichtenberg, J. (1996). What are codes of ethics for? In M. Coady & S. Block (Eds.), *Codes of ethics and the professions.* Melbourne University Press.

Marini, F. (1971). *Toward a new public administration.* Chandler Publishing Company.

McCandless, S., & Ronquillo, J. C. (2020). Social equity in professional codes of ethics. *Public Integrity*, *22*(5), 470–484.

Metcalf, J. (2014). Ethics codes: History, context, and challenges. *Council for Big Data, Ethics, and Society*, 1–15.

Mitchell, M. S., Reynolds, S. J., & Treviño, L. K. (2020). The study of behavioral ethics within organizations: A special issue introduction. *Personnel Psychology*, *73*(1), 5–17.

Moberg, D. J. (2006). Ethics blind spots in organizations: How systematic errors in person perception undermine moral agency. *Organization Studies*, *27*(3), 413–428.

Moon, K., Brunoro, D., Connor, J., Dickinson, H., & Huybers, T. (2023). Exploring integrity in Australian public services: A method to benchmark public service codes of conduct. *Australian Journal of Public Administration*, *83*(4), 1–13.

Morgan, D. F. (1987). Varieties of administrative abuse: Some reflections on ethics and discretion. *Administration & Society*, *19*(3), 267–284.

Morgan, D. F., Green, R. T., Shinn, C. W., Robinson, K. S., & Banyan, M. E. (2021). *Foundations of public service: E pluribus unum.* Routledge.

Mosher, W. E. (1938). Public administration: The profession of public service. *American Political Science Review*, *32*(2), 332–342.

Moynihan, D. P. (2005). Goal-based learning and the future of performance management. *Public Administration Review*, *65*(2), 203–216.

National Society of Executive Fire Officers. (n.d.). *Firefighter Code of ethics.* Retrieved from www.usfa.fema.gov/downloads/pdf/code_of_ethics.pdf

Odeh, D. L. (2024). Professional codes of ethics for public administrators: What are they really telling us? *Public Integrity*, *26*(2), 143–155.

Organization for Economic Cooperation and Development (OECD). (2013). *OECD skills outlook 2013: First results from the survey of adult skills.* OECD Publishing. Retrieved from http://dx.doi.org/10.1787/9789264204256-en

Perlman, B. J., Reddick, C., & Demir, T. (2023). A compliance—integrity framework for ethics management: An empirical analysis of local government practice. *Public Administration Review*, *83*(4), 823–837.

Rohr, J. (1989). *Ethics for bureaucrats: An essay on law and values.* Routledge.

Rohr, J. A. (1976). The study of ethics in the P. A. curriculum. *Public Administration Review*, *36*(4), 398–406.

Safitri, I., & Hapsah, H. (2020). Nurses attitude toward patients as a translating of nursing code of ethics in universitas hasanuddin hospital. *Indonesian Contemporary Nursing Journal*, *4*(2), 83–92. https://doi.org/10.20956/icon.v4i2.9120

Schwartz, M. S. (2013). Developing and sustaining an ethical corporate culture: The core elements. *Business Horizons*, *56*(1), 39–50.

Somers, M. J. (2001). Ethical codes of conduct and organizational context: A study of the relationship between codes of conduct, employee behavior and organizational values. *Journal of Business Ethics*, *30*, 185–195.

Svara, J. H. (2014). Who are the keepers of the code? Articulating and upholding ethical standards in the field of public administration. *Public Administration Review*, *74*(5), 561–569.

Svara, J. H. (2021). *The ethics primer for public administrators in government and nonprofit organizations*. Jones & Bartlett Learning.

Teubner, G. (2011). Self-constitutionalizing TNCs? On the linkage of "private" and "public" corporate codes of conduct. *Indiana Journal of Global Legal Studies*, *18*(2), 617–638.

van Wart, M. (1996). The sources of ethical decision making for individuals in the public sector. *Public Administration Review*, 525–533.

van Wart, M. (2003). Codes of ethics as living documents: The case of the American society for public administration. *Public Integrity*, *5*(4), 331–346.

3 Ethics Training and Employee Development

Brett S. Sharp

Introduction

Encouraging ethical behavior in public organizations is paramount. Citizens imbue their public servants with great trust to care for the most vulnerable among us, secure justice and equity, promote an equal playing field in the marketplace, protect the environment, and manage public assets and resources in a fiduciary manner. Citizens are rightfully invested in how their government performs. *Customers* can usually discontinue their relationship with a business that engages in questionable ethical behavior. But *citizens* rarely have a similar opportunity to escape the authority of a governmental jurisdiction. They therefore demand a higher degree of accountability and transparency from public sector agencies. For these reasons, instilling ethical awareness and knowledge in public sector organizations is imperative. A primary question for cultivating and preserving an ethical culture in public organizations revolves around possible intervention with human resource development strategies—of which training is the most common. In short, can training help ensure ethical behavior?

This chapter explores the role of ethics training in public administration, focusing on its design, delivery, and effectiveness in promoting ethical decision-making. It begins by examining ethical frameworks and principles that provide a foundation for ethical conduct in the public sector. The discussion then turns to the purpose of ethics training and its impact on employee development, including how ethics training can go beyond rule adherence to foster genuine moral reasoning and ethical analysis.

The chapter addresses the practical aspects of designing and delivering ethics training. It examines various methods of training, such as classroom-based learning, online modules, and interactive workshops, with a particular focus on how to influence the cognition of lower-level decision-makers. It also considers whether there should be differentiated training approaches for elected officials, top administrators, and lower-level employees, given their varying responsibilities and roles.

Furthermore, the chapter provides innovative examples of training and development that aim to equip employees with ethical analysis skills, highlighting

DOI: 10.4324/9781003416258-4

how the integration of new information technologies has transformed ethics learning and training effectiveness. These examples include case studies and the use of online and blended learning models to create interactive and engaging training experiences.

The final section of the chapter discusses strategies for fostering a strong ethical culture within public organizations, emphasizing the importance of leadership, policy clarity, and recognition of ethical behavior. By blending theory with practice, this chapter aims to provide public administrators with a comprehensive understanding of how to implement and benefit from ethics training, ultimately supporting a culture of accountability, transparency, and ethical excellence in public service.

Advancing Beyond the Minimum of Ethical Compliance

Organizational training in ethical behavior exhibits a range of approaches. Perhaps most ethics training focuses on fostering awareness of moral and legal obligations. It can be a powerful tool for initiating employees to at least understand minimum expectations and responsibilities. Such training can also decrease legal liability for the organization. Even so, this chapter argues that such a minimalist approach is insufficient for authentic promotion of morality in the workplace. The central idea is that training simply advancing *awareness* of laws, rules, and regulations with regard to proper compliance in the workplace is not enough to instill true ethical behavior. First, laws and rules can—in themselves—create true injustices on occasion. Public administrators need to work on finding ways to change or responsibly get around those rules in such situations. In most cases, it's fairly easy to modify "standard operating procedures" as a form of course correction that still maintains consistency for future applications. Appeals can also be made up through the chain of command. That is, public executives are responsible for serving as circuit breakers when agency rules seem inapplicable or inappropriate for new situations. Of course, changing an unjust law is a much greater hurdle.

The practice of ethics goes well beyond mere adherence to rules and laws. Sometimes there are no laws to govern certain situations, or laws may actually contradict one another. Workers should develop a set of skills and abilities to appropriately navigate situations in which there may be no immediately apparent set of applicable guidelines. These gray areas are where ethical analysis is most useful. For example, embezzlement is obviously wrong in almost all cases. You don't need real ethical analysis to come to that conclusion. Long-standing laws and norms govern the adjudication of such a crime anyway. But, frontline public service workers often enter into new unforeseen circumstances that require the exercise of some ethical muscle. Initially though, they may be unaware that they have entered into a true ethical situation. Administrative evil (Balfour et al., 2020) and groupthink (Janis, 1971) are just a couple of concepts that dramatically demonstrate that many public employees can be blind to their involvement in unethical practices. Familiarity with routine standard operating procedures and compliance with bureaucratic norms and rules is usually a good thing. However, public employees who are comfortable with such routine may also be more hesitant to question the morality of expected behaviors. Ethics training should encourage public workers to be watchful for morally questionable circumstances. They should be trained to recognize when they enter situations fraught with ethical implications. Ethics training should encourage public workers to then take the extra step and apply proper ethical analysis.

There's a marked difference between training and education. Proper education in ethics entails in-depth review of the major ethical theories and concepts going back to the ancient Greek philosophers up through their modern successors. Public administration requires a more applied approach. While training in practical ethics must by necessity forego deep dives into philosophical theory, reviewing some of the major precepts is helpful for guiding public decision-making and crafting of public policy. Selectively borrowing concepts, frameworks, and typologies from long-standing philosophical theories as well as contemporary research literature is the best approach.

In public policy, for example, the application of a utilitarian approach which maximizes the greatest good for the most number of citizens has obvious intuitive appeal. The concept of Pareto improvement is another useful criterion upon which to measure the effectiveness and fairness of public policy. In this context, a public policy has achieved Pareto improvement if it has increased the overall quality of life in a given society without negatively affecting any member of that society (Ehrenberg & Smith, 2012, p. 49). As one familiar example, take the Affordable Care Act (ACA), otherwise known as Obamacare. Since its passage, on the one hand, the ACA has succeeded in ensuring minimum standards and increasing health insurance coverage significantly across the American population (Sullivan et al., 2024). Therefore, the ACA passes the utilitarian criterion since it maximized its good parts for a greater percentage of the population. On the other hand, since the ACA has forced insurance companies to "provide a wider range of benefits and cover people with preexisting conditions," it has also increased the premiums paid by many people who previously had health insurance (Roland, 2019). So as a public policy, the ACA fails the Pareto improvement criterion. In reality, to achieve true Pareto improvement in a given policy often requires compensation for those individuals or groups that are negatively affected. Evaluating a policy using contrasting approaches might still come down reasonably on one particular side. Such is the case of the ACA which firmly justifies itself in the utilitarian camp.

Exposure to these concepts coupled with discussion and deliberation about similar cases in public policy or public decision-making is a wonderful starting point for effective training in ethics. In fact, case analysis has been a mainstay for ethical training for decades. Herzog and Claunch (1997) claim that through case analysis, "administrators can improve services, interactions with citizens, and the operation of their agencies" (p. 374). One problem with this strategy, however, is that it can be time-consuming and expensive. The trend over the past several years is to move more and more training online in order to save money. The rise of digital-based training is astounding, with 90% of organizations now taking advantage of the technology "compared to just 4 percent in 1995" (Association of Talent Development, 2021). This pedagogical mode is a very efficient tool for gaining widespread coverage of an organization's workforce. It very effectively documents employee involvement which in turn can protect the organization against legal liability. Organizational responses to the 1998 Supreme Court Case *Faragher v. City of Boca Raton* illustrate the appeal of online training. The Court held against the City because it had failed to disseminate its policy against sexual harassment, especially among employees in remote locations. Subsequently, U.S. employers responded by initiating and publicizing formal mechanisms for employees to report instances of sexual abuse. These reporting options became a regular part of the onboarding process for most large, contemporary organizations. The enormous appeal for online training to blanket all existing and incoming employees with such vital information is certainly understandable. Furthermore, the process documents that employees received such information and as a result, it provides employers with an affirmative defense should one of its supervisors engage in sexual harassment. A question remains: Is something being lost with this understandable move to online training?

Most online training takes place as a self-paced process by an individual employee. Its inherent asynchronous nature makes online training super convenient for the employee and less disruptive to the workplace. Unlike more personal forms of training, it probably can't create a sense of camaraderie or instill group cohesion that would help foster teamwork and organizational culture. To be clear, this chapter is not arguing against online training, but rather pointing to the virtues attained by synchronous training whether conducted in-person or virtually. The real-time deliberation that occurs among employees as they wrestle through a variety of ethical dilemmas presented in the training setting is valuable in its own right. Participants must confront the vastly different perspectives presented by others and learn to work through the often murky mazes of ethical analysis. Moreover, the person-to-person contact fostered through the dynamic discussions in such a training mode creates a valuable network across organizational divisions and agencies. If a participant encounters an ethically troubling situation later in their career, they can avail themselves of a ready-made list of contacts who would also be prepared to discuss the issues of the case at hand.

Through his research on the link between emotions and rational decision-making, famed neuroscientist Antonio Damasio (1994, 1999, 2003, 2010, and 2018) suggests important considerations for ethics training. Despite conventional wisdom otherwise, he argues that emotions are *not* obstacles to good decision-making, but are in fact essential. His findings suggest that ethics training should focus on understanding and managing emotions. The basis for effective ethical analysis depends on our ability to empathize, experience guilt, and intuitively navigate moral dilemmas. Damasio points out that some of these abilities arise from complex neural processes that depend on relatively slow chemical signaling in the body. The contemporary workplace often demands fast-paced problem-solving skills of the technical variety. Aided by technological advances, humans have shown an extraordinary ability to engage in the quick cognitive reasoning that helps solve the onrush of such technical problems. However, ethical awareness and wisdom develop over time as a form of maturation based on the stress responses of the organic body itself. Damasio notes,

> The system that encodes the stream of consciousness with value works more slowly than the system that feeds it data to encode. It stands to reason that we're going to have fewer and fewer chances to have appropriate somatic markers, which means we're going to have more and more events—particularly in our early years—that go by without the emotional grounding. Which means that you could potentially become ethically less grounded.
>
> (Johnson, 2004, p, 49)

The brain learns from external stimuli and creates simulated versions of emotional responses. As these associations build up over time, the brain will link certain triggers in the frontal lobe or basal forebrain and activate specific regions to mimic the body's emotional signals (Johnson, 2004, p. 48). In other words, quick exposure to codes of ethics, regulatory responsibilities, and legal obligations—while important—are no substitute for the kind of experiences that help individuals progress morally. According to the work of Kappes and Morewedge (2016), training based on analysis and deliberation of select case studies does yield similar results in the brain as to actually living through those experiences. This represents important validation of the tried-and-true case study method for ethical training.

Another consideration is the structure of government itself. Despite a worldwide movement among many developed democracies to decentralize human capital services, Witesman and Wise (2008) in their research on civil service reform found "that centralized government structure significantly increases the odds of receiving both anticorruption training and policy skills training" (p. 116). However, even in a decentralized environment, a near-universal mandate to require ethics training customized for implementation at the localized level of agency or department would be enormously helpful.

Training in the Fundamental Principle of Ethical Analysis

An under-appreciated classic of ethics training is an article by ethicist Kenneth Kipnis (1987) based on his follow-up debriefing about the results of a large-scale survey of professionals concerning ethical problems in early childhood education (Feeney & Kipnis, 1985). Kipnis offers one of the most succinct and helpful articulations of ethical analysis: "Ethical dilemmas characteristically involve conflict between two or more core values" (1987, p. 28). This elegant expression is remarkably helpful for encouraging thoughtful deliberation in a training setting. Participants can engage in a series of exercises to help them identify and define the conflicting values in a given situation. Wrestling with professional and their own core personal values along with engaging the perspectives of others is exactly the training method that yields the most useful takeaways for participants. The process helps prepare public workers to include a worthwhile moral dimension to real-life decision-making. It represents the heart of best practices in ethics training. Once this elemental principle is delineated, the effective trainer can move on to some of the ethical frameworks and concepts most useful for application to the public sector.

Setting the Stage for Ethics Training in the Public Sector

Despite the negative reputation, bureaucracies are incredibly successful technologies of social organization. Make your own short list of humanity's greatest achievements (e.g., landing on the moon, splitting the atom, eradicating smallpox), and you will quickly see that bureaucracy was key to organizing a vast array of professionals to tackle monumental challenges. In the training setting, presenting a quick primer on what constitutes a "bureaucracy" prepares learners to contemplate both the virtues and deficiencies of their own bureaucratic organizations. In terms of ethical considerations, practitioners usually enjoy recognizing the common bureaucratic pathologies evident in their own settings. While not an exhaustive list, the common bureaucratic pathologies include alienation (Marx, 1844/1992; Weber, 1919/2004; Hummel, 2008), bureaucratic infantilism (Argyris, 1960), continuous turnover of political leadership, the centralization/decentralization cycle of administrative reform, empire building, goal displacement (Huizinga & de Bree, 2021), groupthink (Janis, 1971), mission creep, political unresponsiveness, over-politicization, red tape, regulatory capture, working in silos, and the professionals versus democracy paradox (Stewart, 1985).

Perhaps the greatest indictment of the harmful effects of bureaucracy lies in the efficiencies obtained through its reliance on the specialization of labor. As neo-Weberian Ralph Hummel explains,

> Bureaucracy is an efficient means for handling large numbers of people—"efficient" in its own terms. It would be impossible to handle large numbers of people in their full depth and complexity. As a result, only those facts in the complex lives of individuals that are relevant to the task at hand are taken up by the organization. To achieve this simplification, the modern bureaucrat

has invented the "case." At the intake level, individual personalities are converted into cases. Only if a person can qualify as a case is he or she allowed treatment. More accurately, a bureaucracy is never set up to treat or deal with persons: It "processes" only "cases."

(Hummel, 2008, pp. 27–28)

Here, Hummel has diagnosed the source of what has troubled many scholars critical of bureaucracy—namely, its propensity for *dehumanization*. Along with technical language (e.g., "bureaucratese") and a continuous encroachment of rationalization, the bureaucracy becomes fertile ground for dehumanization. If a bureaucracy slowed down sufficiently to be able to deal with individuals in their full humanity, it would necessarily lose its special power of handling large numbers of "cases" so efficiently. As the proverbial cogs in the machine, bureaucrats become increasingly unable to see the bigger picture. This lack of awareness gives rise to "administrative evil" that, as explained by Balfour et al. (2020), occurs when public administrators buried deep within their bureaucratic systems commit morally reprehensible actions. Since these bureaucrats appear to adhere to legitimate procedures and norms, they are completely unaware of their own role in perpetrating evil. Balfour et al. (2020) initially explain their concept of administrative evil in the context of how the German civil service through its values of political responsiveness and neutrality cooperated to implement the Holocaust (pp. 43–60).

Although taking place more recently in a private-sector bureaucracy, the case of the Ford Pinto is equally illustrative of administrative evil. In the 1970s, Ford Motor Company's executives and engineers—in order to save on costs and expedite production—knowingly approved an automobile design that had a significant risk of causing the gas tank to explode during rear-end collisions. Despite internal memos acknowledging the dangers, the company decided against implementing a safer design because the cost of lawsuits from potential accidents was calculated to be less than the cost of the redesign. This decision exemplifies administrative evil as it demonstrates how bureaucratic processes and cost-benefit analyses can lead to harmful outcomes while maintaining an appearance of rational decision-making. In other words, the numerous professional employees employed by Ford at the time (accountants, attorneys, engineers, etc.) were so caught up in the metrics of production and sales that they completely missed the true costs of human fatalities caused by the Pinto's design flaw. The point of an effective ethics training program is to encourage employees to look outside their separate silos and see how their work impacts other humans (for a wonderful overview of the use of the Pinto case study in a seminar setting, see Strother, 2018). Other public sector cases that illustrate administrative evil include the Tuskegee Syphilis Study, Japanese Internment, Centralia Mine Disaster (Martin, 1948), the Space Shuttle disasters, Abu Ghraib tortures (Pfiffner, 2005), and the Flint Michigan Water Crisis (Balfour et al., 2020, pp. 111–130).

Cooper offers an important antidote to these dire diagnoses of dehumanization: "Regularly confronting live human beings who expect things from government is a healthy reminder of our service obligation and the sovereignty of the people in a democracy" (Cooper, 2006, p. 213). In-person training can in and of itself be an opportunity for public administrators to interact with other professionals at a human level. It's also an opportunity to encourage public service workers to get out and engage directly with the communities they serve.

Ethical Concepts and Frameworks Useful for the Training Setting

Trainers should play to their strengths and interests. A trainer's own enthusiasm and passion for the subject matter covered can be contagious among adult learners. Necessarily, a good trainer will cull down a subject as broad as ethics in order to convey a meaningful experience for training participants. As has been shown, contrasting utilitarianism with Pareto improvement as a means to evaluate policy alternatives reveals valuable insights into their ethical implications. Offered here is a practical series of other topics that can be covered selectively in a fully developed one-day training for ethics in a public organization.

Engaging the Hypothetical

A really good opener for a training workshop that involves planned discussion about moral dilemmas is the Ted Talk by James Flynn (2013). In his 18-minute explanation for why there has been a continuously measured increase in IQ scores from generation to generation, Flynn traces an evolution from very concrete thinking to a more advanced willingness to contemplate hypothetical scenarios. He states, "Over the last century, in developed nations like America, moral debate has escalated because we take the hypothetical seriously, and we also take universals seriously and look for logical connections." When Flynn speaks of engaging the "hypothetical" seriously, he is specifically referring to using a scenario such as might be presented in an ethical case study to more fully analyze its wider implications. Previous generations, he observes, were more "fixed in the concrete mores and attitudes they had inherited" and "would not take the hypothetical seriously, and without the hypothetical, it's very difficult to get moral argument off the ground."

This shift means that contemporary individuals are more capable of serious moral debate, considering universals and logical connections. For ethics training, this implies the importance of incorporating complex, hypothetical case studies to foster deeper moral reasoning and ethical analysis. Training programs should leverage this evolved cognitive ability by presenting scenarios that challenge participants to think beyond conventional attitudes. This approach not only enhances critical thinking but also prepares individuals to navigate the nuanced ethical dilemmas they may face in their professional lives.

Absolutists versus Relativists

Opening up a dialogue about ethical dilemmas means that an effective trainer will set some ground rules. Kipnis (1987) criticizes two extreme positions in ethics: Absolutists, who believe in unchallengeable moral truths binding on everyone, and relativists, who see morality as subjective and equally valid across differing opinions. He argues that both perspectives undermine meaningful ethical discussion. Absolutists are closed to debate, while Relativists deny the existence of any true answers. Kipnis asserts that for productive ethical conversations, participants must avoid dogmatism and maintain an open mind, willing to change when justified. However, they should also recognize that not all moral judgments are equally valid, as some arguments may be flawed or irrelevant. Ethical responsibility lies between these extremes. It requires balanced and thoughtful consideration (p. 26).

Moral Reasoning Components

James Rest, in his book *Moral Development* (1994), outlines four psychological processes essential for ethical decision-making: moral intent, moral awareness, moral reasoning, and moral behaviors. Moral motivation (intent) refers to prioritizing a moral choice over other values, emphasizing the commitment to ethical decisions. Moral sensitivity (awareness) involves recognizing that a situation possesses an ethical issue, understanding that actions can impact others positively or negatively. Moral judgment (reasoning) involves assessing and justifying potential solutions to a moral issue, requiring reasoned analysis to determine ethical choices and their consequences. Finally, the individual engaged in ethical decision-making must act (behavior) on the ethical course of action indicated.

Moral reasoning involves applying a set of moral standards to a factual situation, rendering a moral judgment, and then acting on that judgment. The moral standards used must be consistent and applied uniformly across similar situations. Effective moral reasoning requires accurate, relevant, and complete factual evidence. Logical reasoning ensures that conclusions follow rationally from the premises, and accurate information ensures that decisions are based on a true understanding of the situation. Several factors can mitigate moral responsibility, including uncertainty, difficulty of avoidance, minimal involvement, not being part of officially assigned duties, and the seriousness of the wrong or injury. These factors recognize that in some situations, individuals may have limited control or knowledge that reduces their moral culpability for the outcomes of their actions. Ignorance or inability can excuse individuals from moral blame if they were unaware of their actions' implications or unable to act differently. However, deliberately remaining ignorant to avoid responsibility or failing to inform oneself about important matters does not excuse moral responsibility. These exceptions ensure that individuals cannot escape accountability through willful ignorance or negligence.

Wicked Problems

Typically, the kinds of policy challenges confronting public administrators are messy and complex. Rittel and Webber (1973) characterize these as "wicked problems." Stakeholders lack even fundamental agreement on how a problem should be defined in the first place. Proposed solutions are judged as better or worse, not simply as right or wrong, and there is no straightforward test for their effectiveness. Each solution attempt is crucial as there is little room for trial and error, and potential solutions and operations are neither finite nor exhaustively describable. Wicked problems are unique and may even be symptoms of other issues, with their nature influenced by how discrepancies are explained.

Ethics training should prepare individuals to navigate the inherent complexity and uncertainty of wicked problems. Trainees must learn to accept that there may not be clear-cut answers and to develop comfort with ambiguity. Ethics training should foster critical thinking and encourage some flexibility in moral reasoning. Trainees should be equipped to evaluate solutions on a spectrum of better to worse and to adapt their strategies as new information emerges. Trainees should understand the weight of their decisions and the ethical implications of their actions. Ethics training should stress the importance of context and encourage participants to consider the broader implications and interconnectedness of the problems they face.

Wicked problems often require interdisciplinary solutions. Ethics training should promote collaboration and the integration of diverse perspectives to develop more comprehensive and effective responses. Since wicked problems have a multitude of mitigation strategies and possible solutions, ethics training should prepare individuals to operate without a single right answer. Trainees should learn to evaluate multiple potential solutions and their ethical ramifications critically. As the nature of a wicked problem's resolution depends on its explanation, ethics training should develop trainees' skills in justifying and explaining their ethical decisions. This includes articulating the reasoning behind their choices while acknowledging the validity of various viewpoints. Given the high stakes and significant responsibility involved, ethics training should instill ethical resilience. Trainees need to be prepared to face the moral and psychological challenges of dealing with complex, high-impact problems.

Duty-Oriented Ethics and Professional Codes

Referring to deontological ethics by its more accessible label, duty-oriented ethics, might be more appropriate in a training session for public sector employees. As popularized by Kant (1785/2012), this form of ethical analysis emphasizes adherence to rules and moral duties over outcomes. A training workshop might include a discussion of how obligation to duty as embodied by professional codes of ethics would be different than a more consequentialist approach focused on outcomes. Once again, the introduction of a new way to frame public decision-making gains more clarity for participants by contrasting with other perspectives. A review of relevant professional codes of ethics is well placed here. For example, the American Society for Public Administration (ASPA) offers a general code of ethics for public managers. ASPA has published a very helpful resource for working through its code of ethics (Svara et al., 2015) in training workshops.

One of the hallmarks of a fully developed profession are the standards embodied by and articulated in the code of ethics it advances. As Kipnis notes (1987), a code of ethics provides professionals with some protection when employers pressure them to engage in unethical behavior (p. 29). If a variety of professions are represented in a single training cohort, a comparison of the various approaches to codes of ethics by their more specialized associations might be quite useful. A crossover dynamic among the professions represented by the participants as they discuss their various codes among themselves would bring a welcome vitality to the training session. Often, a part of one code of ethics would have obvious applicability to another professional area. For example, the Hippocratic precept to "first do no harm" as first articulated for the medical profession has obvious value when contemplating intervention into the contemporary policy arena. In other words, make every attempt to ensure that a change in policy doesn't have unintended negative consequences.

Virtue Ethics

Virtue ethics is another very broad approach to the study and practice of ethics. In a training session, the instructor might facilitate a discussion among participants about the value of cultivating virtues such as caring, generosity, honesty, honor, loyalty, tenacity, and wisdom. Participants could be encouraged to reflect on their own character virtues with an eye toward improvement and self-development. The facilitator might ask how organizational culture can be best aligned to support virtuous behavior in the workplace.

Ethical administrators need a set of "moral qualities," as described by Bailey (1965). He identifies three key qualities: (1) optimism, which represents a belief in the possibility of achieving positive outcomes; (2) courage, defined by the ability to act "without fear or favor," resists illegitimate pressures from powerful interest groups and favor-seeking individuals; and (3) "fairness, tempered with charity," which Bailey considers the most essential moral quality for public servants. Fairness should be seen as "the principle above principle," reflecting the ability to provide equal, standardized treatment to all while remaining sensitive to individual differences (Cooper, 2006, p 191).

The Veil of Ignorance

The thought experiment proposed by Rawls (1971) that he called the "veil of ignorance" (pp. 136–142) is particularly relevant for public administrators. In a nutshell, Rawls states that when individuals craft a policy for their own society, they should imagine doing so without knowledge of their own socio-economic status, talents, or circumstances. This mental exercise is meant to control one's own biases in order to ensure equity and fairness. To incorporate the "veil of ignorance" into an ethics workshop, the trainer should start with an introduction to Rawls's theory and then use interactive lectures and real-world examples to illustrate the concept. The trainer should facilitate group discussions where participants apply the veil of ignorance to resolve ethical dilemmas to real or fictional case studies. An interesting tweak is to assign particular roles to individual participants as they design policies with the veil of ignorance in mind.

Social Capital

After nearly three decades of pioneering work on the contemporary study of the decline of social capital, Robert Putnam now advocates for promoting a sense of trust, that is, having "a stake in everybody's success—a very simple, moral principle" (Lindsay, 2024). The implications for ethics training are clear. Programs can emphasize building and strengthening social networks to promote ethical behavior and accountability. Since Putnam identifies trust and reciprocity as key components of social capital, ethics training should focus on encouraging individuals to engage in reciprocal behavior that develops trustworthiness. Likewise, ethics training can incorporate strategies for strengthening ties to the community.

Levels of Ethical Reflection

Henry David Aiken (1952) offers a framework for understanding how people engage in moral reasoning and discussion. He identifies four levels: the expressive level, where individuals simply express their feelings and preferences about a moral issue without justification; the level of moral rules, where people refer to societal or cultural norms and rules to justify their actions; the ethical principle level, where broader ethical principles like justice and equality are used to support or challenge moral rules; and the meta-ethical level, where individuals critically examine the foundations and justification of their ethical principles and the meaning of moral terms.

Models of Ethical Decision-Making

In a training module on ethical decision-making, a brief tour of various models from popular culture can provide unique insights that can enhance ethical analysis and foster a comprehensive understanding of complex moral dilemmas. In that spirit, here are some vivid examples that can be featured in the training setting.

Joseph Heller's concept of "Catch-22," introduced in his novel of the same name, describes a no-win situation where individuals are trapped by contradictory rules or conditions. In the story, a World War II bomber pilot, Yossarian, seeks to be declared insane to avoid flying dangerous missions. However, the military's rule, "Catch-22," states that if a pilot requests to be grounded due to insanity, the request demonstrates their sanity, thus making them ineligible to be grounded. This paradox illustrates the absurdity and futility of bureaucratic logic. In ethical decision-making, "Catch-22" situations highlight the complexity and often contradictory nature of moral dilemmas, where adhering to one ethical principle may inherently violate another. Such scenarios challenge individuals to navigate conflicting rules and find balanced, fair solutions despite the inherent contradictions (Heller, 1961).

"Hobson's Choice" refers to a situation where there appears to be a choice, but in reality, there is only one option available. The term originates from Thomas Hobson, a stable owner in 17th-century England, who offered customers the choice of either taking the horse nearest the door or none at all. In ethical decision-making, a Hobson's Choice represents scenarios where an individual must choose between an unappealing option or no option at all, creating an illusion of freedom of choice. This concept underscores the importance of recognizing genuine options and autonomy in ethical considerations. It challenges decision-makers to ensure that choices presented in ethical dilemmas are real and not manipulative, thus fostering true moral agency and fairness.

"Chesterton's Fence" is a principle derived from G.K. Chesterton's idea that one should not remove a fence until understanding why it was put up in the first place (1929, Chap. 3). This concept emphasizes the importance of understanding the purpose and context behind existing structures, rules, or practices before making changes to them. In ethical decision-making, Chesterton's Fence underscores the need for thorough analysis and consideration of the historical and functional reasons behind established norms and policies. It advises against hasty or uninformed alterations, advocating instead for a thoughtful approach that respects the underlying intentions and potential consequences of removing or changing established systems. This principle promotes careful evaluation and making informed decisions to ensure that changes lead to genuine improvements rather than unintended negative outcomes.

"Sophie's Choice," from William Styron's novel (1979), refers to an agonizing decision faced by the character Sophie, who is forced by a Nazi officer to choose which one of her two children will be sent to the gas chamber while the other is spared. This impossible and heart-wrenching decision highlights the extreme moral dilemma where any choice results in a profound loss and suffering. In ethical decision-making, "Sophie's Choice" represents situations where individuals must make decisions with devastating consequences, often involving a sacrifice of deeply held values or responsibilities. It underscores the complexity of moral dilemmas where no option leads to a fully ethical outcome, emphasizing the need for compassion, understanding, and the recognition of the profound impacts such decisions can have on individuals.

The "Kobayashi Maru Scenario" from the Star Trek universe is a training exercise designed to test Starfleet cadets' decision-making skills in a no-win situation (Meyer, 1982). In the simulation, cadets must choose between attempting a rescue mission of the civilian ship Kobayashi Maru, which is stranded in a dangerous zone facing almost certain destruction, or abandoning the ship and its crew to ensure their own survival. The scenario is designed to assess how individuals handle impossible choices and the inevitability of failure. In ethical decision-making, the Kobayashi Maru Scenario highlights the importance of leadership, creativity, and the willingness to face moral dilemmas where all possible outcomes involve significant compromise or loss. It underscores the value of maintaining integrity and courage even when no ideal solutions are available, and the need for innovative thinking to navigate complex ethical challenges.

Incorporating these and similar models into an ethics training course equips participants with a diverse set of tools and perspectives, fostering a deeper, more nuanced understanding of ethical decision-making. When available, brief clips of cinematic treatments of these types of decision-making models can help spark discussion. Participants learn to navigate complex and challenging situations with critical thinking, empathy, and informed judgment, ultimately enhancing their ability to make ethical decisions in their professional and personal lives.

Objective versus Subjective Responsibility

Objective responsibility refers to the duties and obligations that are formally assigned to individuals based on their roles and positions within an organization. It is grounded in clear, external standards and expectations, ensuring that public servants are aware of their specific responsibilities and the legal and institutional frameworks governing their actions. As evidenced by professional codes of conduct and formal oaths taken in a democracy, the ultimate objective responsibility is for a public administrator to look out for the public interest (or one of its usual stand-ins, a government's constitution). Cooper (2004) comments that "the public interest has a place in the construction of a normative administrative ethic as" the "moral compass, orienting us to a fundamental obligation" (p. 399).

On the other hand, *subjective responsibility* involves the personal, internal sense of duty and moral commitment that individuals bring to their roles. It encompasses the personal values, ethical principles, and conscience that guide their decision-making processes.

By exploring both concepts, a training workshop can help public servants recognize the importance of adhering to established rules and norms (objective responsibility) while also fostering a strong personal ethical compass (subjective responsibility). This dual focus encourages a balanced approach to ethical behavior, where adherence to external standards is complemented by a deep personal commitment to integrity and ethical excellence in public service.

Conflicts of Administrative Responsibility

Conflicts that might occur in areas of administrative responsibility can undermine the effectiveness and integrity of public administration. Three major types that should be covered in an ethics training setting include conflicts of authority, role conflicts, and conflicts of interest.

Conflicts of authority arise when there are overlapping or unclear lines of responsibility and decision-making within an organization. This can lead to confusion, inefficiency, and power struggles as different authorities assert control over the same issues. It is exemplified by the bit of biblical wisdom that one cannot serve two masters. In public administration, it is often articulated as the "unity of command" principle in which "a worker should receive orders from only one supervisor" (Sharp & Housel, 2004, p. 23). At a broader level for instance, a public agency might have conflicting directives from different levels of government or from various departments within the organization. In a training workshop, addressing conflicts of authority involves teaching participants about the importance of clear organizational structures, defined roles, and effective communication channels. Training should emphasize the need for establishing well-defined hierarchies and decision-making processes to prevent ambiguity and ensure smooth functioning.

Role conflicts occur when a public servant holds multiple roles that demand different and sometimes opposing actions. For example, a public official might struggle to balance their duty to enforce regulations with their role in advocating for community interests. In an ethics training workshop, it is essential to cover strategies for managing role conflicts, such as prioritizing responsibilities, seeking guidance from superiors or ethical committees, and maintaining transparency. Participants should learn to recognize the signs of role conflict and understand the importance of adhering to ethical guidelines while navigating these complex situations.

Conflicts of interest arise when personal interests or relationships interfere with the impartial performance of official duties. This can compromise the integrity of decisions and lead to corruption or favoritism. An example is when a public official is in a position to influence contracts that benefit their own business or that of a close relative. In a training workshop, covering conflicts of interest involves educating participants on identifying potential conflicts, understanding the legal and ethical implications, and implementing measures to avoid or manage such conflicts. Training should include practical exercises on disclosure, recusal, and maintaining transparency to ensure that personal interests do not compromise public trust.

These conflicts should be integrated into the training curriculum through a combination of theoretical discussions and practical applications. Case studies and real-life scenarios can be used to illustrate each type of conflict, allowing participants to analyze and resolve these issues in a controlled environment. Role-playing exercises can help participants practice navigating conflicts of authority and role conflicts. Interactive discussions can enhance their understanding of managing conflicts of interest. Additionally, the workshop should provide tools and frameworks for ethical decision-making, emphasizing the importance of accountability, transparency, and adherence to ethical standards in public service. By addressing these conflicts comprehensively, the training can equip public servants with the skills and knowledge needed to uphold ethical principles in their professional roles.

Group and Time Pressures

Public administrators often face significant pressures from both in-groups and time constraints that can profoundly impact their ability to act ethically. Understanding the influence of these pressures is critical to fostering ethical behavior in public administration.

Group pressure, or peer pressure, can strongly influence public administrators' ethical decision-making. The organizational culture and the behavior of colleagues can create an environment where certain ethical standards are either upheld or undermined. For instance, research has shown that ethical behavior is highly contagious within organizations; if peers and leaders exhibit ethical behavior, it sets a standard that others are likely to follow (Treviño et al., 2006). Conversely, if unethical behavior is normalized or goes unpunished, it can lead to a culture of ethical complacency or misconduct. Administrators may feel compelled to conform to group norms, even if those norms conflict with their personal ethical standards. This peer pressure can be especially intense in hierarchical organizations where dissenting from group norms may be perceived as insubordination or could jeopardize career advancement.

Groupthink, as theorized by Irving Janis in 1971, refers to the phenomenon where the desire for consensus within a group leads to poor decision-making outcomes. In such situations, critical thinking and dissent are suppressed as group members prioritize harmony and unanimity over rational analysis. This can result in ethical lapses, as the group fails to consider alternative viewpoints or the potential moral implications of their decisions. In a training course for public sector ethics, it is crucial to cover the concept of groupthink by illustrating its symptoms and consequences through historical case studies and examples from public administration. Participants should learn to recognize signs of groupthink, such as the illusion of invulnerability, collective rationalization, and self-censorship. The course should include strategies for mitigating groupthink, such as encouraging open dialogue, fostering a culture of dissent, and appointing a "devil's advocate" to challenge prevailing assumptions. Through interactive discussions and role-playing exercises, the training can equip public sector professionals with the skills to promote critical thinking and ethical decision-making in group settings.

Time pressure is another significant factor that can impact ethical decision-making. Public administrators often operate in fast-paced environments where decisions must be made quickly, sometimes without the luxury of thorough deliberation or ability to gather complete information. This urgency can lead to shortcuts and oversight, potentially compromising ethical standards. According to a study by Gunia et al. (2012), time pressure can impair moral judgment and decision-making by reducing cognitive resources available for ethical reflection. When under time constraints, administrators might prioritize efficiency and expediency over ethical considerations, increasing the risk of unethical behavior. Additionally, the pressure to meet deadlines and achieve quick results can lead to stress and burnout, further diminishing the capacity for ethical decision-making.

The combination of group and time pressures creates a complex environment for public administrators. Ethical lapses can occur when the pressure to conform to group norms coincides with the rush to meet tight deadlines. For instance, an administrator might overlook due process or the proper vetting of decisions due to the need to align with the expectations of colleagues and superiors while also adhering to strict timelines. This intersection of pressures can lead to ethical blind spots where the long-term implications of decisions are not fully considered.

Addressing these challenges requires a multifaceted approach. Organizations should cultivate an ethical culture that encourages open dialogue and supports ethical decision-making. Leadership plays a crucial role in setting the tone for ethical behavior. Leaders who model ethical conduct and prioritize ethical considerations in decision-making can positively influence the entire organization (Brown & Treviño, 2006). Additionally, providing training and resources to help administrators manage time pressures effectively can mitigate the negative impact of rushed decision-making. Techniques such as ethical decision-making frameworks and reflective practices can help administrators navigate complex situations even under time constraints.

The influence of group and time pressures on public administrators is significant and can impact their ability to act ethically. Understanding and addressing these pressures is essential for fostering an environment where ethical behavior is the norm rather than the exception. By promoting a strong ethical culture and providing tools to manage time pressures, public administration can support its officials in making decisions that uphold the highest ethical standards.

In an ethics training course, the influence of group and time pressures on public administrators should be addressed through a combination of interactive discussions and practical exercises. The module should begin with an overview of how group norms and organizational culture can shape ethical behavior, supported by research findings such as those by Treviño et al. (2006). Participants should engage in role-playing scenarios to experience the impact of peer pressure and discuss strategies for fostering an ethical culture. Time pressure's effect on ethical decision-making should be explored through case studies that illustrate the risks of rushed decisions, referencing Gunia et al.'s (2012) findings. The training should include techniques for managing time effectively and maintaining ethical standards under pressure, emphasizing the importance of reflective practices and ethical decision-making frameworks. By combining theory with practical application, the course can equip public administrators with the tools to navigate these pressures and uphold ethical principles in their work.

Rule-of-Thumb Ethics Tests

Simple, rule-of-thumb ethical tests are practical tools that help individuals evaluate the morality of their decisions by applying various principles and perspectives. Among these is the viral test (an update of the front-page test), which involves asking whether you would be comfortable if your decision were broadcast widely, such as on social media or in the news. It encourages transparency and accountability by considering the public's reaction and the potential reputational impact. The reciprocity test (also known as the reversibility test or the Golden Rule) asks you to consider if you would still find the decision acceptable if you were on the receiving end. The role model test involves considering whether a person you admire and respect would make the same decision. By using these types of ethical tests, individuals can critically assess their decisions from multiple perspectives, promoting ethical behavior and responsible decision-making. Incorporating these tests into an ethics training workshop can equip participants with practical tools to navigate complex moral dilemmas effectively.

Whistleblowing

Whistleblowing in the public sector involves the reporting of unethical, illegal, or otherwise questionable practices within government organizations by employees or insiders. This act is essential for maintaining transparency, accountability, and integrity in public administration. Whistleblowers play a crucial role in exposing corruption, fraud, and other misconduct, thereby safeguarding public interest and promoting ethical governance. Covering whistleblowing in an ethics training module should encompass several key components. Start by defining whistleblowing and its significance in the public sector. Explain how whistleblowers help uncover and prevent wrongdoing, thereby enhancing trust in public institutions and protecting public resources. Educate participants on the legal frameworks and protections available to whistleblowers. Discuss relevant laws, such as the Whistleblower Protection Act in the United States, which provides safeguards against retaliation and outlines the rights of whistleblowers. Emphasize the importance of understanding these protections to foster a safe environment for reporting misconduct. Explore the ethical dimensions of whistleblowing. Discuss the moral responsibility of public sector employees to report unethical behavior, balancing loyalty to the organization with the duty to act in the public interest. Highlight real-life examples of whistleblowing cases to illustrate the ethical dilemmas and challenges faced by whistleblowers.

Provide detailed information on the appropriate channels and procedures for reporting unethical behavior within the organization. Clarify the steps involved in filing a report, the role of internal and external oversight bodies, and the importance of maintaining confidentiality throughout the process. Discuss the support systems available for whistleblowers, such as counseling, legal advice, and peer support groups. Emphasize the organization's commitment to protecting and supporting individuals who come forward with concerns, reinforcing the message that whistleblowing is a courageous and valued act.

Incorporate case studies and role-playing exercises to give participants practical experience in handling whistleblowing scenarios. Analyze real or hypothetical cases to identify best practices and potential pitfalls. Role-playing can help participants understand the emotional and ethical complexities involved, preparing them to respond effectively in real-life situations. Highlight the importance of fostering an organizational culture that encourages ethical behavior and supports whistleblowers. Discuss strategies for creating an environment where employees feel safe and empowered to report misconduct without fear of retaliation. This includes leadership commitment, regular ethics training, and clear communication of whistleblowing policies.

Some Final Thoughts for Effective Ethics Training Design

In their facilitative role, trainers should not see their mission as providing complete and final answers to ethical dilemmas for their adult learners. Rather, the best that trainers can hope for is to help participants learn concepts and develop techniques so that they may continue to engage ethically in their future careers. Taking a long-range perspective is not only more realistic but also healthier.

Mixing different levels of an organization together in a training environment yields numerous benefits for all participants in terms of networking opportunities and interactions among those holding contrasting viewpoints. The training should be mindful to customize approaches for elected leaders, top administrators, and frontline workers. Table 3.1 summarizes how the lesson content and methods can be tailored according to organizational roles to address specific ethical challenges.

The shortcut method for designing an effective training program for public employees is to incorporate as many of the following features as practicable: (1) conduct in-person or synchronously remote; (2) locate off-site if possible; (3) provide for a full-day, at least six hours; (4) present a conceptual understanding and language for trainees to use in their own ethical analysis; (5) relegate smart phone usage to breaks; (6) break up training into easily digestible sections; (7) provide variety in modality delivery; and (8) ensure that the organization's top leaders attend themselves.

Table 3.1 Differentiated Ethics Training for Public Sector Roles

Role	Training Focus	Training Methods	Ethics Challenges Addressed
Elected Officials	Public accountability, transparency, and ethical policy-making	Workshops, seminars, retreats, and discussion panels	Balancing public interest with political pressures
Top Administrators	Ethical leadership, decision-making, and policy implementation	Case studies, leadership programs, and interactive workshops	Navigating complex policy issues and leading by example
Lower-Level Employees	Compliance, ethical awareness, and operational problem-solving	Online training, scenario-based learning, and practical simulations	Handling day-to-day ethical dilemmas and recognizing ethical implications

Conclusion

Ethics training is an essential component in cultivating a culture of integrity, accountability, and professionalism in public organizations. This chapter has explored the foundational frameworks and principles that guide ethical behavior in the public sector, as well as the importance of ethics training in fostering awareness, moral reasoning, and ethical decision-making among public employees. Examining different methods of delivering ethics training and tailoring approaches to specific roles within public organizations highlight the potential for ethics training to not only ensure compliance but also inspire true moral engagement.

The discussion emphasized that ethics training should move beyond minimal compliance with rules and regulations. Effective training must challenge public servants to analyze ethical dilemmas, recognize moral issues in their work, and make decisions that reflect a commitment to the public good. The use of innovative examples, case studies, and new technologies can further enhance the training experience, making it more impactful and applicable to real-life situations.

The importance of ethics training in public administration cannot be overstated, as public employees bear a unique responsibility to serve citizens with fairness and accountability. Encouraging ethical conduct in government strengthens public trust, enhances decision-making processes, and helps ensure that public resources are used equitably and effectively.

The theme of compliance and integrity runs throughout this chapter, emphasizing the idea that while compliance with rules and regulations is fundamental, it is only the starting point for ethical conduct in public administration. Ethics training must not only ensure that employees understand the laws and policies governing their actions but also foster a deeper commitment to integrity—acting not just because it is required, but because it is right. This chapter underscores that true integrity requires going beyond adherence to regulations; it involves cultivating a mindset that questions the ethical implications of decisions and prioritizes the public interest. By fostering both compliance and a culture of integrity, public organizations can better navigate ethical challenges and maintain the trust and confidence of the communities they serve.

Opportunities for future study include exploring the long-term effects of different ethics training methods on employee behavior, analyzing the effectiveness of blended learning approaches, and understanding how emerging technologies such as artificial intelligence can be integrated into ethics training. Research on tailored training approaches for diverse cultural and organizational contexts would also contribute significantly to the development of more effective public sector ethics programs.

References

Aiken, H. D. (1952). The levels of moral discourse. *Ethics, 62*(4), 235–248.

Argyris, C. (1960). *Understanding organizational behavior*. Dorsey Press.

Association for Talent Development. (2021, April 29). *The rise of online training in business*. Retrieved July 13, 2024, from www.td.org/professional-partner-content/the-rise-of-online-training-in-business

Bailey, S. K. (1965). The relationship between ethics and public service. In R. C. Martin (Ed.), *Public administration and democracy: Essays in honor of paul appleby*. Syracuse University Press.

Balfour, D. L., Adams, G. B., & Nickels, A. E. (2020). *Unmasking administrative evil* (5th ed.). Routledge.

Brown, M. E., & Treviño, L. K. (2006). Ethical leadership: A review and future directions. *The Leadership Quarterly, 17*(6), 595–616.

Chesterton, G. K. (1929). *The thing: Why i am a catholic*. Sheed & Ward.

Cooper, T. L. (2004). Big questions in administrative ethics: A need for focused, collaborative effort. *Public Administration Review, 64*(4), 395–407.

Cooper, T. L. (2006). *The responsible administrator: An approach to ethics for the administrative role* (5th ed.). John Wiley & Sons/Jossey-Bass.

Damasio, A. (1994). *Descartes' error: Emotion, reason, and the human brain*. Penguin Books.

Damasio, A. (1999). *The feeling of what happens: Body and emotion in the making of consciousness*. Harvest/Harcourt.

Damasio, A. (2003). *Looking for Spinoza: Joy, sorrow, and the feeling brain*. Harcourt.

Damasio, A. (2010). *Self comes to mind: Constructing the conscious brain*. Pantheon Books.

Damasio, A. (2018). *The strange order of things: Life, feeling, and the making of cultures*. Pantheon Books.

Ehrenberg, R. G., & Smith, R. S. (2012). *Modern labor economics theory and public policy*. Pearson Education.

Faragher v. City of Boca Raton, 524 U.S. 775 (1998).

Feeney, S., & Kipnis, K. (1985). Public policy report: Professional ethics in early childhood education. *Young Children, 40*(3), 54–58.

Flynn, J. R. (2013, March). Why our IQ levels are higher than our grandparents' [Video]. *TED Conferences.* Retrieved from www.ted.com/talks/james_flynn_why_our_iq_levels_are_higher_than_our_grandparents/transcript?subtitle=en

Gunia, B. C., Wang, L., Huang, L., Wang, J., & Murnighan, J. K. (2012). Contemplation and conversation: Subtle influences on moral decision making. *Academy of Management Journal, 55*(1), 13–33.

Heller, J. (1961). *Catch-22.* Simon & Schuster.

Herzog, R., & Claunch, R. (1997). Stories citizens tell and how administrators use types of knowledge. *Public Administration Review, 57*(5), 374–379.

Huizinga, K., & de Bree, M. (2021). Exploring the risk of goal displacement in regulatory enforcement agencies: A goal-ambiguity approach. *Public Performance & Management Review, 44*(4), 868–898.

Hummel, R. P. (2008). *The bureaucratic experience* (5th ed.). M.E. Sharpe.

Janis, I. L. (1971). Groupthink. *Psychology Today, 5*(6), 84–90.

Johnson, S. (2004). Antonio Damasio's theory of thinking faster and faster. *Discover, 25*(6), 44–49.

Kant, I. (2012). *Groundwork for the metaphysics of morals* (M. Gregor & J. Timmermann, Trans.). Cambridge University Press. (Original work published 1785).

Kappes, H. B., & Morewedge, C. K. (2016). Mental stimulation as substitute for experience. *Social & Personality Psychology Compass, 10*(7), 405–420.

Kipnis, K. (1987). How to discuss professional ethics. *Young Children, 42*(4), 26–30.

Lindsay, D. (2024). Why we're still bowling alone and how that could change. *Chronicle of Philanthropy, 36*(6).

Martin, J. B. (1948). The blast in Centralia no. 5: A mine disaster no one stopped. *Harper's Magazine, 196*, 1–38.

Marx, K. (1992). Economic and philosophical manuscripts. In (R. Livingstone & G. Benton (Trans.), *Early writings* (pp. 279–400). Penguin Classics. (Original work published 1844).

Meyer, N. (Director). (1982). *Star Trek: The Wrath of Khan.* Paramount Pictures.

Pfiffner, J. P. (2005). Torture and public policy. *Public Integrity, 7*(4), 313–329.

Rawls, J. (1971). *A theory of justice.* Belknapp/Harvard.

Rittel, H., & Webber, M. (1973, June). Dilemmas in a general theory of planning. *Policy Sciences, 4*(2), 155–169.

Roland, J. (2019). The pros and cons of Obamacare. *Healthline.* Retrieved July 14, 2024, from www.healthline.com/health/consumer-healthcare-guide/pros-and-cons-obamacare

Sharp, B. S., & Housel, S. W. (2004). Ghosts in the bureaucratic machine: Resurrecting the principles of administration in the Oklahoma Health Department. *American Review of Public Administration, 34*(1), 20–35.

Stewart, D. W. (1985). Professionalism vs. democracy: Friedrich vs. Finer revisited. *Public Administration Quarterly, 9*(1), 13–25.

Strother, S. (2018). When making money is more important than saving lives: Revisiting the Ford Pinto case, *Journal of International & Interdisciplinary Business Research, 5*, Article 11. https://doi.org/10.58809/SAJH3330

Styron, W. (1979). *Sophie's choice: A novel.* Random House.

Sullivan, J., Orris, A., & Luken, G. (2024, March 25). *Entering their second decade, Affordable Care Act coverage expansions have helped millions, provide the basis for further progress.* Center on Budget and Policy Priorities. Retrieved July 14, 2024, from www.cbpp.org/sites/default/files/3-18-24health.pdf.

Svara, J., Braga, A., de Lancer Julnes, P., Massiah, M., Gilman, S., Ward, J., & Shields, W. (2015, November 22). *Implementing the ASPA code of ethics: Workbook and assessment guide.* American Society for Public Administration. Retrieved from www.aspanet.org/Common/Uploaded%20files/ASPADocs/Membership/Ethics_Assessment_Guide.pdf

Treviño, L. K., Weaver, G. R., & Reynolds, S. J. (2006). Behavioral ethics in organizations: A review. *Journal of Management*, *32*(1), 951–990.

Weber, M. (2004). *The vocation lectures* (R. Livingstone & D. Owen, Trans.; Original work published 1919). Hackett Publishing Company.

Witesman, E. M., & Wise, C. R. (2008). The centralization/decentralization paradox in civil service reform: How government structure affects democratic training of civil servants. *Public Administration Review*, *69*(1), 116–127.

4 Sanctions and Incentives in Public Ethics Management

Nevbahar Ertas

Sanctions, Incentives, and Their Relation to Public Ethics Management

Sanctions and incentives are key tools in public ethics management systems. While sanctions are penalties to deter or punish unethical actions, incentives are rewards or benefits to encourage ethical behavior. In fact, the various approaches to ethics management can be understood in terms of the relative priority they assign to the development and application of sanctions or incentives. This chapter starts by a brief discussion of the role sanctions and incentives play in relationship to traditional and integrity-based approaches to ethics management. The next section delves into examples of sanctions and incentives at the institutional and organizational levels. The subsequent section summarizes research regarding the impact of sanctions and incentives on shaping ethical and unethical behavior. The conclusion identifies some gaps in the literature that could suggest avenues for additional research. Overall, this chapter highlights how the strategic use of rewards and punishments may operate as part of a larger ethics management strategy that considers individual motivations, organizational culture, and long-term goals.

The pursuit of integrity within organizations has a rich history. Most historical accounts of administrative ethics in the public sector refer to the classic Friedrich–Finer debate on the role of discretion in guiding public administrative decision-making (Cooper, 2012; Dobel, 2006; Reddick et al., 2020). In a series of exchanges, Friedrich (1940) emphasized internal controls, such as professional standards and technical knowledge, as primary mechanisms to hold public officials accountable. In response, Finer (1941) emphasized the priority of external political and institutional controls to limit administrative discretion and to manage and impose accountability on public servants. These perspectives represent the origins of the traditional dichotomy between compliance-based and integrity-based approaches to ethics management.

The compliance-based approach to ethics management emphasizes adherence to rules and prevention of unethical or illegal conduct by appealing to employees'

DOI: 10.4324/9781003416258-5

extrinsic motivations. This is sometimes referred to as the "low road" approach to ethics, as it aims to spur obedience to minimum standards and legal prohibitions (Lewis & Gilman, 2005). The integrity-based approach to ethics management, by contrast, highlights adherence to professional values and standards and to organizational norms to elicit ethical behavior. This is often deemed the "high road" approach because the path to ethical practice is seen as normative and persuasive, and includes positive inducements to internalize values, not external penalties (Lewis & Gilman, 2005). Proponents of the integrity-based approach underscore the importance of engaging employees' intrinsic motivations through professional and organizational socialization. From this perspective, the difference between Friedrich and Finer might be understood as a tension between accountability and responsibility (Gregory, 2017; Reddick et al., 2020).

The Interconnectedness of Sanctions, Incentives, Accountability, and Responsibility

Accountability involves answerability to authorities in a relationship designed to ensure compliance and control (Gregory, 2017). In a public organization, this corresponds not only to employee-to-employer accountability but also to accountability to elected representatives and the public, as they are stewards of public power, resources, and trust. Enforcement requires sanctions—penalties or consequences imposed upon employees who violate laws, regulations, codes of conduct, or ethical standards. Sanctions and accountability are interconnected in the sense that sanctions are often used to reinforce accountability by imposing consequences for misconduct or non-compliance. Responsibility, on the other hand, pertains to the related but distinct realm of individual moral choice (Gregory, 2017), and for employees of public organizations this often means acting on the principle of public interest while performing on-the-job duties and obligations. Public managers may employ incentives—tangible or intangible rewards or privileges intended to motivate, recognize, or reward exemplary performance, dedication, and ethical conduct within the workplace—and such inducements can play a significant role in shaping behavior and promoting responsibility by aligning actions with goals and reinforcing intrinsic prosocial motivation.

This critical point of contention—the relative importance placed on "enforcing" versus "eliciting" responsible conduct—has persisted as component of the practical and scholarly debate on ethics management. Lewis and Gilman (2005, p. 16) observed that the US system has been "preoccupied with accountability from its inception." As a case in point, they highlighted what is arguably the single most important travel reimbursement in US history, the bill that Paul Revere, the folk hero of the American Revolution, presented to the Massachusetts legislature for "printing and riding for the Committee of Safety" in 1775. The record of approved payment, "in full discharge of the written account," although for less than the amount requested, demonstrates that controls were enforced to implement accountability, even during the revolutionary period (Lewis & Gilman, 2005, p. 16). With the post-war era in many Western democracies being defined by the growth of the government sector, Friedrich's emphasis on professional public service gained prominence; however, from the early 1960s onwards, there has been a surge in both governmental and nongovernmental ethics programs centered around compliance (Roberts, 2009).

While there is broad consensus that ethics is essential for good governance and that managerial actions involving sanctions and rewards can influence conduct, there is a lack of robust theory regarding the optimal combination of value-based and compliance-based policies (Six & Lawton, 2013). Additionally, compared to business ethics, there has been insufficient empirical testing of theoretical frameworks in this area (Downe et al., 2016). A 2005 review of the state of public administration ethics research published in two premier journals concluded that the "developments in the areas of performance and ethics management were still at an embryonic stage," and an updated 2015 review indicated that ethics management remains an understudied topic, although it had received more attention over time (Menzel, 2015, p. 343). The existing body of research on ethics management predominantly revolves around integrity-based approaches such as leadership, training, and public values, while sanctions and incentives are often regarded as peripheral, if they are considered at all.

Sanctions and Incentives at the Institutional and Organizational Level

The ethical standards that public servants devise, communicate, and enforce are significantly influenced by the system within which they operate. In other words, sanctions and incentives can be devised and implemented at the institutional, organizational, and individual levels. The primary emphasis of this section will be directed toward strategies employed at the organizational level, that is, within specific government departments or public organizations. Public managers interested in building organizations of integrity have some tools at their disposal in the form of sanctions and incentives to communicate and reinforce ethical norms and standards; however, they are also bound by the larger institutional system in which they operate. Institutional-level ethics infrastructure is a typical consideration of research and practice focused on cross-country analysis of fraud and corruption (Rose-Ackerman, 2008). Institutional-level ethics infrastructure pertains not only to existence of clear legal guidelines regarding corruption, procurement, and administrative procedures at the national level, but also to the strength of democratic foundations such as open, free, and fair elections; separation of powers; free press; and a robust civil society.

Institutional Level

The concept of an institution refers to a social structure or system established and enforced by both state and nonstate actors to guide behavior and interactions within a particular domain in a society. As such, institutions are larger than specific organizations and constrain and prescribe their actions. The focus of ethics initiatives at the institutional level is to establish a well-functioning system where the government makes a commitment to responsible and accountable conduct, respects checks and balances to prevent concentrations of power, and maintains pathways for inclusive citizen engagement and participation. Many international organizations, such as the Organization for Economic Cooperation and Development (OECD), World Bank, the United Nations, the International Monetary Fund (IMF), and Transparency International, establish benchmarks for governmental integrity and offer incentives to encourage adherence to these standards: for example, countries that borrow from the IMF might be subject to "conditionalities" that require measures to strengthen governance such as adopting anti-corruption programs, audits, and financial controls (Grant, 2011). Furthermore, the standards and benchmarks often offer incentives and sanctions as strategies that governments may use within public service or in their relationships with the private sector to deter corruption or to promote ethical conduct. For instance, the OECD Public Integrity Handbook (2020) advises governments on implementing OECD recommendations by advocating for national public integrity systems to incorporate standards and processes for public officials into criminal, civil, and administrative law, complete with appropriate investigative procedures and sanctions. The guidelines emphasize the importance of "clear and proportionate" administrative or disciplinary sanctions in the form of:

- Warnings and reprimands (either written or oral)
- monetary disadvantages (e.g. fines, salary penalties)
- impact on current or future career (e.g. demotions, transfers)
- ban from public office, i.e., preventing offending former officials from occupying public office for specific periods
- dismissal from office.

(OECD, 2020)

These types of benchmarks from intergovernmental organizations also refer to incentives-driven approaches, often in the context of providing appropriate incentives to private sector entities to comply with the regulatory framework of the national governments or the international organization. For example, the OECD Working Group on Bribery in International Business Transactions issued the first international guidance on anti-corruption compliance programs in 2010, and then in 2021 parties to the Convention agreed to new measures to reinforce their efforts to prevent, detect, and investigate wrongdoing. One of the key elements of the recommendation was to "encourage countries to incentivize enterprises to develop internal controls, ethics and compliance programmes or measures to prevent and detect foreign bribery" (OECD, 2020). The aforementioned OECD Public Integrity Handbook (2020) also mentions that performance assessments may be used to promote and reward integrity leadership, which "needs to be reinforced by rewards and sanctions," but they do not specify any examples of rewards other than "career development opportunities."

The development of the ethical framework for government in the United States has mirrored global trends and concerns about conduct and declining public trust. According to Roberts (2009), the surge in both governmental and nongovernmental compliance-based ethics programs was driven by rising concerns over the objectivity and impartiality of public officials, criticism of big government, impact of the Watergate Scandal, and the increased outsourcing of government services instigated by the "reinventing government" movement. In the federal government as well as states and local governments, there is a prevailing tendency to view ethical behavior primarily through a compliance lens. Training materials provided by federal authorities for ethics officials and employees tend to approach conduct solely within the framework of legally enforceable standards, treating ethical dilemmas predominantly as legal issues to be addressed by recourse to statutes like the US Code.

The US government established the Office of Government Ethics (OGE) with the passage of the Ethics in Government Act of 1978. The 1988 reauthorization act transformed the OGE into a separate agency from the federal Office of Personnel Management, and over time its role has expanded into education, guidance, interpretation, and enforcement alongside regulation (Lewis & Gilman, 2005). Under the Ethics in Government Act, each agency has appointed designated agency ethics officials (DAEOs). Executive Order 12674 in 1989, later modified by Executive Order 12731 in 1990, directed the OGE to "write a single comprehensive, and clear set of executive branch standards of conduct that shall be objective, reasonable and enforceable" (Roberts, 2009, p. 268) and established the framework for the ethical behavior required of all federal employees in the United States. The United States Code (USC) is made up of the official federal statutes of the United States, and the Code of Federal Regulations (CFR) contains all of the regulations promulgated by executive agencies. Criminal Conflict of Interest Laws (18 U.S.C. §§ 201–209) regulate issues related to bribery, improper gifts and compensation, representation, financial conflicts of interest, and impartiality, and carry criminal penalties for non-compliance.

Overall, by the mid-1990s many countries worldwide had institutionalized ethics systems in the public sector and several major efforts have since been undertaken at the global level. These initiatives form the basis of the institutional ethics infrastructure: for instance, executive branch public employees in the United States are subject to these detailed criminal conflict of interest laws. They also serve as a basis for the ethics regulations known as the Standards of Ethical

Conduct for Employees of the Executive Branch (5 C.F.R. part 2635) (US Office of Government Ethics [OGE], 2023). As an indicator of the extent to which the law plays a role in the sanctions function, it might be of interest to review a number of statistics. According to the National Conference of State Legislatures, in 2023 a total of 392 ethics bills were introduced, and 72 measures were enacted in 31 states. According to the US Office of Government Ethics (OGE, 2020), there were 13 successful prosecutions of violations of ethics laws (18 U.S.C. §§ 202–209 and other related statutes) in 2019. In addition, 1,036 administrative penalty actions were taken in the executive branch agencies for less severe violations of ethics rules and regulations. These actions involved corrective training, reprimands, monetary penalties, and termination. Sanctions via criminal, civil, and administrative law are a standard aspect of public sector work. As a case in point, relying on data from 1,189 participants in the 2015 survey of National Administrative Studies Project, Jung et al. (2020) examined differences in fear of punishment according to sector and found that public sector employees were more likely than their private sector counterparts to express a fear of punishment for bending rules.

Organizational Level

Having a strong institutional ethics infrastructure in place creates a foundation for strategies and mechanisms that are capable of fostering and maintaining ethical behavior at the organizational level. While ethics researchers in the field of public administration have elevated the status of integrity-based ethics management within academic literature, much of the practitioner effort in this arena is confined to the compliance rather than the integrity aspect of administrative ethics. One of the predominant textbooks in public personnel management refers to sanctions as the fourth core function of personnel management, alongside planning, acquisition, and development, and defines the sanction function as establishing, maintaining, and enforcing the "terms of the relationship between the employee and the employer" (Klingner et al., 2015, p. 306). Given that controls are deeply embedded in traditional managerial activities like personnel management and budgeting, compliance primarily translates into supervision and regulation from a managerial perspective.

As noted earlier, sanctions and especially incentives are often regarded as peripheral in public administration ethics research, as the majority of the empirical scholarship focuses on attitudes and perceptions regarding ethics using small samples or specific cases (Menzel, 2015). However, new scholarship on local governments in the United States (Demir et al., 2023a, 2023b) and the UK (Downe et al., 2016) offers promising new avenues to systematically examine sanctions and incentives in government. For instance, based on a comprehensive literature review, scholars have identified awareness and knowledge, enforcement, incentives, and policy support as the four building blocks for a public organization's ethics infrastructure, and analyzing comprehensive data from local governments in the United States confirmed that only few local governments employed all of these building blocks in their ethics management efforts (Demir et al., 2023b). The most popular actions were having an ethics code, training, and enforcement of rules. This analysis provides much-needed descriptive information from local governments and a way to classify the critical components of an ethics infrastructure at the organizational level. It also reveals two major gaps in the research literature. First, there is a need for more information from other public organizations with regard to the sanctions and reward systems they use to promote ethical behavior. Most empirical evidence related to ethics management comes from business ethics research conducted in the private sector. This is especially critical, because the sanctions' function in public employment differs from that in private sector employment due to the existence of certain rights regarding speech, association, privacy, and equal treatment conferred upon government employees (Klingner et al., 2015). Second, there is a need for empirical research to bridge theory and practice and so to investigate the relationship between these critical components and ethical outcomes and behaviors at the organizational and individual levels.

Codes, Rules, Sanctions, and Leaders

At the organizational level, the personnel manual consisting of the relevant policies, rules, regulations, procedures, and practices is one of the formal mechanisms through which obligations and expectations are recognized. Many public organizations develop a formal code of conduct and/or a code of ethics to outline the ethical standards, principles, and expectations for behavior within the organization. While a code of conduct delineates the restrictions and sanctions in detail, a code of ethics is more intended to reflect the values and aspirations of an organization or profession. Critical elements of an effective code of conduct include a "set of enforceable, meaningful sanctions," alongside clear objectives and standards, affirmative values, and procedural safeguards (Lewis & Gilman, 2005, p. 194). Sanctions and penalties might include reference to criminal sanctions, as well as recusal and administrative interventions. Most studies of codes in public administration ethics research are descriptive and comparative in nature, investigating similarities and differences across organizations, public service professions, or countries (Menzel, 2015); the scant empirical knowledge about whether and to what extent codes prevent unethical behavior in the workplace comes rather from business ethics research. For instance, using a sample of working adults, Kaptein concluded that the mere existence of codes does not influence observed unethical behavior at work (Kaptein, 2011). The codes reduced unethical behavior only when workers perceived that the values contained within the code had become embedded in management and were communicated in an accessible, clear, and usable manner (Kaptein, 2011).

This suggests that even when the organization has a detailed code of conduct or an aspirational code of ethics, managers play a key role in translating the principles outlined in the code into practical, actionable rules and standards, and in offering guidance for specific situations. Although there is consensus on ethical leadership being a key component of good governance (Hassan et al., 2014), there is still limited research on how leadership influences ethical conduct (Menzel, 2015) or how different aspects of leadership interact with sanctions and incentives. One recent exception is a qualitative study of local governments in England, where Downe and colleagues (2016) conducted over 100 semi-structured interviews with key informants from nine local councils to investigate the role that leaders play in promoting and reinforcing ethical conduct. Conversations about the informants' perceptions regarding how norms of conduct were shaped and transmitted, and how misconduct was identified and addressed, revealed that sanctions did not lead to a significant change of behavior. Furthermore, where leaders exemplified ethical conduct and acted as role models there was less need for disciplinary measures. However, they also noted that the leaders in their case studies mostly had few rewards to offer for good behavior and perceived the formal sanctions as inadequate. This is a critical observation, because previous research has shown that the use of sanctioning systems to promote ethics in organizations might backfire if the sanctions are weak. Tenbrunsel and Messick (1999) showed that weak sanctions increase unethical behavior more than no sanctions at all. Therefore, when rewards are absent, and sanctions are weak, ethical leadership matters even more.

While a code is not a panacea, the public sector manager can use a code as the core of an effective ethics program by critically incorporating missing elements, strengthening sanctions and incentives, and connecting them more tightly to general enforcement, implementation, and protection processes. For an effective code, meaningful sanctions should be complemented by clear information concerning general processes of enforcement, implementation, and protections (Gilman, 2005). Enforcement mechanisms typically include procedures for financial disclosure, investigation, and audit, and specify the commission or agency that is vested with investigatory authority. Implementation processes include organizational strategies and activities related to the orientation of new employees, the training of all employees, and the evaluation of compliance and ethics programs. Protection refers to the procedural protections afforded to employees and others regarding grievance and appeal procedures, as well as whistleblowers' rights and protections. Looking from the opposite perspective, even if the legal and institutional support systems are in place, codes fail when components are missing, vague, or overly complicated, when a code clashes with the values and norms in the organization, and when a code gets dated.

Research suggests that providing employees with the opportunity to contribute to the organization's ethics policy increases the likelihood that they will internalize its values and actively participate in ethical decision-making in the future (Beeri et al., 2013). Therefore, public managers may consider the ways in which employees at different levels and units may be engaged as collaborators in developing, implementing, or monitoring the organization's ethics code. The Ethics Research Center, a nonprofit organization dedicated to building integrity in organizations, recommends using a taskforce or committee which represents the diversity of the organization and engaging in extensive data collection efforts during code development, so that the code is meaningful and reflects employees' needs and values. After the code is in place, it is best practice to conduct periodic ethics audits, which may be undertaken in the form of a task force with rotating membership, and periodic data collection exercises via interviews, surveys, needs assessments, or document reviews (Lewis & Gilman, 2005). This approach ensures that the code aligns with the organization's administrative realities and fosters a sustained commitment to an ethical environment. Furthermore, the process then can serve as a way to track commitment and contribution, so as to be of use in the incentives system.

Incentives and Reinforcement

The literature also suggests several ways in which managers may build ethical concerns directly into the work environment and agency operations. Many of these techniques may be included in the organization's incentives system. Organizations may, for example, engage in both compliance and integrity training on a recurring basis (Bowman & West, 2021; Cooper, 2012). It is also best practice to provide precise instructions and essential information for new hires and upon termination of employment (Lewis & Gilman, 2012): this might include information about the standards and the code, designated ethics officers and offices, sanctions and incentives in place, general enforcement, implementation and protection processes, common ethical problems on the job, and potential ethics issues that might arise in postemployment. An independent grievance process or a designated high-level manager to oversee integrity issues, in addition to the units responsible for compliance or investigation, is also a best practice recommended by leading government agencies and professional organizations such as the Office of the Inspector General and the Organization for Economic Co-operation and Development (Klingner et al., 2015).

To the extent possible, a proactive manager would link ethical behavior to incentives. Implementing visible, substantial rewards, whether monetary or nonmonetary, for ethical behavior can be challenging, because of inherent difficulty of measuring ethical conduct (Cooper, 2012). One approach to address this is to collaborate with HR and keep the focus on evaluating what individuals or managers do on the job routinely (e.g., whether trainings are completed or completed on time, whether supervisors are perceived to use the code of conduct as a guide and to enable employees to voice concerns) (Murphy, 2011). Another strategy is to reserve recognition for outstanding performance or dramatic "instance of ethical courage within the organization—for example when employees take action to rectify corrupt organizational activities at some risk to their own careers" (Cooper, 2012, p. 210). While organizations with an ethics program typically have established processes that govern how allegations of misconduct are investigated and sanctioned, not many have a strategy to reward or positively incentivize ethical behavior. Strategies to incentivize ethical behavior are often discussed within the context of corporate compliance or for organizations contracting with government agencies, rather than as a way to reward employees within public organizations (Ethics & Compliance Initiative, 2018; Murphy, 2011). For example, the revised US Federal Sentencing Guidelines states that organizations should both "exercise due diligence to prevent and detect criminal conduct" and "otherwise promote an organizational culture that encourages ethical conduct and a commitment to compliance with the law" (US Sentencing Commission, 2023).

Incentives may become part of the compliance and ethics program in several ways. First, they can be included in the performance evaluation system, so that the organization tracks compliance and ethics performance in employees' assessments and evaluations; Murphy (2011) provides a sample evaluation form that lists expectations that may form the basis of an evaluation of integrity leadership, such as using and promoting the code and implementing trainings. Second, information on compliance and ethics may be used as an input in promotions and other reward systems. This information can be utilized as a minimum standard to be considered for promotion, or the compliance and ethics office may be officially brought into the organization's promotions process. Third, employees and managers who demonstrate outstanding commitment to ethics may be recognized and rewarded; similar recognition and rewards for the compliance and ethics staff of the organization may also serve as a signpost to signal that the organization values high ethical standards, and that leaders are committed to maintaining an ethical environment. Finally, a relatively new and somewhat contentious strategy is to also recognize and reward whistleblowers. In the United States, the False Claims Act, the Dodd–Frank Act, and the IRS whistleblower law require financial incentives for whistleblowers to report evidence of wrongdoing. According to the National Whistleblower Center (2024), since 2011 law enforcement agencies have paid nearly $6.7 billion in rewards to whistleblowers and have recovered $43.4 billion for the benefit of taxpayers. Since 2013, July 30 has been designated as National Whistleblower Appreciation Day by passage of resolutions in the US Congress. The US Office of Personnel Management (OPM) and the OPM Office of the Inspector General (OIG) typically use the occasion to express appreciation for the role that whistleblowers play in government oversight and to raise awareness about reporting procedures and whistleblower protections available to federal employees.

A common objection raised is that rewarding employees for ethical behavior should not be necessary as it is an inherent expectation of their conduct. Yet this is a myopic attitude toward rewards, because the notion is not about "paying people to be good," but rather both a reflection and a shaper of the organizational culture (Cooper, 2012). The rewarding process serves a "dual role modelling" strategy, in that both those who do the giving and those receiving the rewards exemplify ethical strength and thus signal organizational values to employees and the public (Cooper, 2012). According to Murphy (2011), these objections underscore that incentives, assessments, and rewards have a significant influence on behavior and wield considerable power, because integrating ethical values into compensation and acknowledgment systems shows that the leadership is putting words into action and signals genuine commitment to ethical values and principles. This, however, is not the only objection to the use of incentives in shaping behavior. A growing body of behavioral ethics literature identifies various shortcomings and limitations of individual decision-making processes and offers critical insights into the relationship between (dis)incentives and (un)ethical decisions.

How and Why Incentives Elicit (Un)ethical Behavior

Different perspectives to maintaining responsible conduct within public organizations align with different theoretical orientations to human behavior. Traditional philosophical approaches to ethics focus on the understanding of how people form moral judgments and on the process of moral development, whereas behavioral ethics, drawing heavily from psychology and behavioral decision research, examines how situational and social forces interact with individual psychological frames and individual biases (Bowman & West, 2021). A behavioral approach to ethics argues that rational decision-making models overlook individuals' unconscious psychological responses to problems, including ethical dilemmas. Psychological research reveals that even well-meaning individuals can display unethical behavior when their self-control becomes depleted (Gino et al., 2011): in other words, unethical behavior is not necessarily a result of ill-intention or underdeveloped moral reasoning. In fact, according to Bazerman and Gino (2012), "most of the unethical behavior we observe in organizations is the result of the actions of several individuals who, although they value morality and want to be seen as ethical people, regularly fail to resist the temptation to act dishonestly or even fail to recognize that there is a moral issue at stake in the decision they are making" (p. 13).

The field of behavioral research has grown rapidly in the last few decades, and a prolific research literature has examined how incentives and nudges influence individual decision-making. It is prudent to note that nudges are not the same as incentives. The concept of a "nudge" focuses on the design of the decision environment. A nudge is a targeted change in the "choice architecture"—the decision-making context—intended to increase the likelihood of a desired action (Sunstein, 2018), whereas incentives involve explicit rewards or penalties. In fact, Sunstein (2018) explicitly notes that "to qualify as a nudge, an initiative must not impose significant material incentives (including disincentives)" (p. 61). Regardless, both incentives and nudges aim to shape behavior by leveraging reactive responses and counteracting behavioral biases, and this line of research offers implications for ethics training and policymaking process by clarifying relationships between sanctions, incentives, and ethical decision-making. The use of such behavioral insights and nudges has proliferated to many countries around the world. For example, in 2010 the British Behavioural Insights Team, popularly known as the "Nudge Unit," was established at the British Cabinet Office to apply behavioral science to public policy. In 2015 a presidential Social and Behavioral Sciences Team (SBST) was established in the United States to develop and use behavioral science research to create policy solutions (Executive Order No. 13707, 2015).[1]

How and why incentives elicit (un)ethical behavior is a critical topic of discussion for managers interested in cultivating organizations of integrity in the public sector, because sanctions and incentives interact with both internal psychological frames and external contextual factors. Subjective perceptions of the meanings of incentives may determine whether incentives have their intended effects. There are several objections raised against using incentives to elicit ethical behavior, both on grounds of morality and on potential unintended consequences. Park et al. (2022) define incentives as "any form of return offered to a person for actions and behaviors that they would not have otherwise chosen" (p. 300), whether they take the form of tangible (e.g., annual merit increases) or intangible (e.g., praise), or positive (e.g., reward) or negative (e.g., penalty) inducements. After reviewing 361 research studies across multiple academic disciplines, Park et al. (2022) identified three main explanations for why incentives might catalyze unethical behavior: Cost–benefit comparison, motivated reasoning, and decreases in prosocial motivation.

Cost–Benefit Comparison and Motivated Reasoning

The simple cost–benefit model of unethical behavior posits that incentives influence unethical actions by altering the perceived benefits and costs associated with those actions. Individuals may make such comparisons without even realizing the ethical implications of their decisions. There is mixed evidence regarding this relationship. For example, while some studies have shown that increased monitoring decreases unethical behavior in the workplace (Bellé & Cantarelli, 2017), others have shown that they may—unexpectedly—contribute to unethical behavior, especially if the employees' perceptions of organizational justice are low (Thiel et al., 2023). In fact, there is an interdependent relationship between employee perceptions of overall justice in the organization and an organization's incentives system. Perceptions of fairness represent a key heuristic in interpreting incentives (Thiel et al., 2023), and incentives serve as a lens through which employees evaluate justice within their organization (Klingner et al., 2015).

Motivated reasoning refers to situations where an individual actively searches for ways to justify a potentially unethical decision. Incentives may and do affect this reasoning process by commodifying subjective values. In a classic example, Gneezy and Rustichini (2000) showed how daycare centers which instituted a marginal fine to incentivize timely pickups experienced double the rate of late arrivals, and that the increased rate of tardiness persisted even after fines were removed. They explained that parents perceived the fine as a price for lateness, and so considered the decision with a market mindset rather than as an ethical obligation to avoid inconveniencing the teachers. Another mechanism that may increase unethicality is overreliance on outcomes in designing or implementing an incentives system. For example, the Occupational Safety and Health Administration (OSHA) has challenged the efficacy of outcome-based safety incentive programs, which reward workers when no or low incidences of accidents or injuries are reported over a specific period of time. Rewarding the absence of violations or injuries may pressure individuals to underreport them, and discouraging reporting goes against the very essence of creating a safer workplace (Laws, 2017).

Decreases in Prosocial Motivation

Another theory concerning the link between incentives and unethicality is the idea of moral crowding-out. When individuals are promised an extrinsic reward for an activity, they lose an intrinsic desire to perform that task (Frey & Oberholzer-Gee, 1997). In their seminal study, economists Bruno Frey and Felix Oberholzer-Gee provided a striking example to demonstrate how introducing financial incentives can change people's attitudes and crowd out moral and civic commitments. For this study, they surveyed the residents of the Swiss village of Wolfenschiessen, which was designated by the Swiss parliament as a potential site for a nuclear waste repository. Even though the prospect was undesirable, 51 percent of residents reported they would vote to accept the facility in their community in the upcoming referendum because of their sense of civic duty. However, when the researchers asked how they would vote if the parliament offered to financially compensate each resident, not only did the approval rate drop to 25 percent, but increasing the monetary offer did not increase the approval rate. In other words, contrary to traditional economic wisdom, financial incentives did not increase compliance. The moral crowding-out literature explains that rewards alter the character of the propositions and the nature of the decisions, and such studies go on to caution that relying solely on external rewards to induce behavior can be corrupting, should these incentives replace consent derived from thoughtful deliberation and reflection. Moral crowding-out refers to this larger idea of the gradual erosion of intrinsic motivations toward ethical or civic behaviors (Sandel, 2012; Bowles, 2016).

Key Takeaways From Behavioral Research

There are key lessons to be learned from this behavioral research literature. First, (dis)incentives are not universal remedies, and their indiscriminate application may result in adverse consequences. Ethical competence requires reflection, and overreliance on reactive behavioral interventions can impede its long-term development. Therefore, an informed manager should deploy incentives strategically to complement other strategies that aim to develop ethical competence and the capacity for reflection. Bowman and West (2021, p. 153) suggest organizational training activities that involve "showing how vulnerable employees are to mental shortcuts," "engaging in critical reflection to legitimize and incentivize doubt," and "being wary of rationalizations" (i.e., "it's legal," "I had no choice," "everyone does it") as behaviorally informed techniques to improve ethical decision-making.

Second, to be effective and functional, (dis)incentives should be designed to counteract common biases regarding cost–benefit comparison and motivated reasoning. Based on their extensive review of the empirical literature, Park et al. (2022) concluded that negative incentives are effective to reduce unethicality, but only when the sanctioning system is strong; and even then, their very existence alters the foundation for compliance and cooperation from ethical reflection to economic calculation (Tenbrunsel & Messick, 1999). Although the research on the influence of different sanctioning systems on behavior is limited and widely dispersed across disciplines, existing evidence demonstrates that "increasing the probability of unethicality detection" is more effective than "increasing the severity of negative outcomes (i.e., penalty or punishment)" (Park et al., 2022). Organizational leaders, as designers and implementers of incentive structures, are in a good position to improve detection mechanisms in the sanctioning systems. A strong detection system is a strong disincentive for unethical conduct. Furthermore, employee perceptions regarding the justice of an organization's policies and procedures mediate their reaction to the incentives, and organizational justice perceptions relate to ethical and unethical forms of work behavior in both the private (Jacobs et al., 2014) and the public sector (Moon, 2017). This suggests that the primary task for managers is to improve their organization's justice climate, so as to increase the likelihood of success for any (dis)incentive. The key factors in shaping perceptions of organizational justice are fair and transparent procedures, the extent to which employees feel that they are involved in organizational decision-making, the quality of organizational and managerial communication, and the perceptions of co-workers and team members (Jacobs et al., 2014; Moon, 2017).

Finally, the research evidence also emphasizes that the form of the incentives (e.g., whether monetary or nonmonetary, or process or goal-based) affects how employees perceive and react to their organization's incentive systems. Extrinsic rewards and penalties activate a market mindset and a cost–benefit calculus and may even lead to a gradual erosion of prosocial intrinsic motivations toward ethical behaviors. Therefore, the use of monetary incentives needs to be carefully considered in all areas where intrinsic motivation is important. This is especially relevant for public sector work, because public administration and management scholars have long argued that the differences in values and motivations among public sector and private sector workers carry important implications for improving management practices in public organizations. Research comparing employees in the private and public sectors has shown that public sector workers prioritize prosocial intrinsic rewards—for example, having meaningful work, contributing to the public interest, helping others—over extrinsic rewards—for example, higher pay, fewer hours, bonuses—which are more valued by their private sector counterparts (Brewer, 2003). An extensive empirical literature has developed around the concept of public service motivation (PSM), which suggests that "the alignment of values may explain sorting into public service work" (Holt, 2018). Much of this research focuses on employment decisions and employee performance, and empirical evidence addressing the relation between PSM and (un)ethical behavior remains scarce; however, experimental studies conducted in Chili (Meyer-Sahling et al., 2019), South Korea (Lee & Park, 2023), and the United States (Wright et al., 2016) have suggested that PSM activation enhances willingness to report unethical behavior in the public sector organizations. Managers of public organizations may tailor rewards to align with the public interest values that their employees prioritize. Incentives, evaluations, and employee recognition programs can be used to communicate the underlying mission and values of the organization.

Conclusion

The discussion began by juxtaposing the so-called "low road" of compliance and the "high road" of integrity as the two approaches to ethics management. Public administration and management theory and practice have repeatedly demonstrated that a dual approach is necessary to build and sustain organizations of integrity (Frederickson & Ghere, 2014; Lewis & Gilman, 2005; Menzel, 2014, 2019; Svara, 2021). Furthermore, behavioral ethics researchers call for integration of a design approach, which combine specific (dis)incentives with specific decision scenarios, to counter human bias and to reduce contextual temptations for dishonest behavior (Zhang et al., 2014). The main takeaway from this chapter is that public managers should recognize that ethics management is not about choosing between strict control-based compliance, a system based completely on integrity, and a purely incentives-based approach. Instead, it involves a nuanced blend of each, tailored to the specific needs and contexts of the organization.

This conclusion is closely connected to the fundamental ideas of integrity and compliance approaches in public ethics management, particularly public accountability and administrative responsibility. Public management demands the stewardship of public trust, so administrative controls and legal sanctions are essential to the conduct of public employees and public affairs. Public accounta-bility is not only the underlying principle in sanctioning systems in public organ-izations but also one of the defining characteristics of democratic governance. As such, public administration research continues to track the evolution of our understanding and measurement of public accountability, the implementation and consequences of accountability reforms, including their impact on agency performance, employee behavior, and citizens' trust (Pérez-Durán, 2023). Nev-ertheless, leadership in the public sector requires aiming higher than simply meeting minimum standards of conduct. Administrative responsibility, which has been a core value guiding the growth and formalization of public admin-istration profession and scholarship, is a crucial component of administrative ethics. Through this literature, we observe that the managerial theories of moti-vation have evolved over time to emphasize internal factors that contribute to a more engaged and fulfilled workforce (Meyer-Sahling et al., 2019; Wright et al., 2016). This suggests that the strategic use of rewards and punishments should be part of a larger ethics management strategy that considers research evidence on individual motivations, organizational culture, and long-term goals.

Nevertheless, the discussion has also revealed several gaps in the research literature regarding sanctions and incentives. First, an inventory of sanctions and incentives at the disposal of public managers at different levels of public organizations would provide much-needed descriptive baseline information. What sanction and reward systems are being used to promote ethical behav-ior in public organizations? How do they vary among different levels and types of public sector organizations? How similar or different they are from those in private sector organizations? Second, public administration and public manage-ment scholarship may contribute to the scattered and limited, but growing lit-erature on the influence of different sanctioning systems on behavior. How do different aspects of the system such as the severity of punishment, the strength of the detection system, or the transparency of the procedures affect behavior? How do these systemic aspects interact with individual dispositions such as PSM or organizational factors such as ethical climate to shape behavior? Third, we need research to clarify the roles managers play in translating and communicat-ing principles and rules into actionable penalties and rewards, and how different aspects of leadership interact with perceptions and implementation of sanctions and incentives. How much discretion public managers have when it comes to devising and implementing sanctions or incentives? How do different types of ethical leadership—for example, proactive management, where steps are taken in advance to build an ethical infrastructure versus passive management focusing on responding to problems as they happen—influence ethical perceptions and behavior? Finally, behavioral interventions require attention from scholars inter-ested in both normative and empirical aspects of public sector ethics. What is the right balance between ethical reflection and behavioral reaction by means of external sanctions and incentives? How common are behavioral versus reflective ethical interventions in the public sector? How does the purported trade-off between incentivizing and ethical prosocial motivation operate for public sector employees? How can public managers tailor reward systems so that they align with the underlying public service mission of their organization, activate the public interest values of their employees, and counteract common human biases such as cost–benefit comparison and motivated reasoning?

This line of research would move sanctions and incentives from the periphery to the center of public administration ethics research and help clarify the specific challenges and constraints public organizations face when devising and implementing sanctions and rewards to promote ethical behavior. Robust theory building and empirical testing regarding the optimal combination of value-based and compliance-based policies can bridge theory and practice and guide public leaders in their efforts to build organizations of integrity. Public managers possess significant discretion in their roles, which may extend to writing and implementing rules, overseeing contracts, making budget decisions, and balancing multiple purposes and priorities. They must also navigate conflicts within laws and engage in negotiation and discretion as they interact with citizens. Such discretion highlights the moral responsibility and the initiative of public managers as leaders. Aligning management discretion with ethics is to view law as a facilitator, rather than as an obstacle, in ensuring that sanctions and incentives match promulgated values and promote desirable actions. A comprehensive public management approach to ethics must involve both compliance-based and value-based strategies, reinforced by sanctions and incentives.

Note

1 The SBST was discontinued in 2017, but the Biden White House re-chartered the Subcommittee on Social and Behavioral Sciences until 2025. See the Federation of Associations in Behavioral and Brain Sciences (FABBS) (April 4, 2014). SBS Subcommittee of the NSTC Updates NIH Community. https://fabbs.org/news/2024/04/sbs-subcommittee-of-the-nstc-updates-nih-community/.

References

Bazerman, M. H., & Gino, F. (2012). Behavioral ethics: Toward a deeper understanding of moral judgment and dishonesty. *Annual Review of Law and Social Science, 8*, 85–104.

Beeri, I., Dayan, R., Vigoda-Gadot, E., & Werner, S. B. (2013). Advancing ethics in public organizations: The impact of an ethics program on employees' perceptions and behaviors in a regional council. *Journal of Business Ethics, 112*, 59–78.

Bellé, N., & Cantarelli, P. (2017). What causes unethical behavior? A meta-analysis to set an agenda for public administration research. *Public Administration Review, 77*(3), 327–339.

Bowles, S. (2016). *The moral economy: Why good incentives are no substitute for good citizens*. Yale University Press.

Bowman, J. S., & West, J. P. (2021). *Public service ethics: Individual and institutional responsibilities*. Routledge.

Brewer, G. A. (2003). Building social capital: Civic attitudes and behavior of public servants. *Journal of Public Administration Research and Theory, 13*(1), 5–25.

Cooper, T. L. (2012). *The responsible administrator: An approach to ethics for the administrative role.* John Wiley & Sons.

Demir, T., Reddick, C. G., & Perlman, B. J. (2023a). Ethical performance in local governments: An empirical study of organizational leadership and ethics culture. *The American Review of Public Administration.* https://doi.org/02750740231175653

Demir, T., Reddick, C. G., & Perlman, B. J. (2023b). In search of ethics infrastructure in US local governments: Building blocks or dead end? *Administration & Society, 55*(10), 1866–1892.

Dobel, J. P. (2006). Public management as ethics. In *Public Management as Ethics." The Oxford handbook of public management* (pp. 161–181). Oxford University Press.

Downe, J., Cowell, R., & Morgan, K. (2016). What determines ethical behavior in public organizations: Is it rules or leadership? *Public Administration Review, 76*(6), 898–909.

Ethics & Compliance Initiative (ECI). (2018). *Using your organization's performance evaluation system to drive ethical conduct. Best practices paper.* Retrieved from www. ethics.org/wp-content/uploads/2018-ECI-WP-Using-Performance-Evaluation-to-Drive-Ethical-Conduct.pdf

Finer, H. (1941). Administrative responsibility in democratic government. *Public Administration Review, 1*(4), 335–350.

Frederickson, H. G., & Ghere, R. K. (2014). *Ethics in public management.* Routledge.

Frey, B. S., & Oberholzer-Gee, F. (1997). The cost of price incentives: An empirical analysis of motivation crowding-out. *The American Economic Review, 87*(4), 746–755.

Friedrich, C. J. (1940). The nature of administrative responsibility. *Public Policy, 1,* 3–24. Reprinted in P. Woll (Ed.). *Public administration and public policy.* Harper Torch Books.

Gilman, S. C. (2005). Ethics codes and codes of conduct as tools for promoting an ethical and professional public service: Comparative successes and lessons. *Prepared for the PREM, the World Bank.* Retrieved from https://knowledgehub.transparency.org/assets/uploads/kproducts/Topic_Guide_Codes_of_Conduct.pdf

Gino, F., Schweitzer, M. E., Mead, N. L., & Ariely, D. (2011). Unable to resist temptation: How self-control depletion promotes unethical behavior. *Organizational Behavior and Human Decision Processes, 115,* 191–203.

Gneezy, U., & Rustichini, A. (2000). A fine is a price. *The Journal of Legal Studies, 29*(1), 1–17. https://doi.org/10.1086/468061

Grant, R. W. (2011). *Strings attached: Untangling the ethics of incentives.* Princeton University Press.

Gregory, R. (2017). Accountability and responsibility. *Oxford Research Encyclopaedia.* https://doi.org/10.1093/acrefore/9780190228637.013.525

Hassan, S., Wright, B. E., & Yukl, G. (2014). Does ethical leadership matter in government? Effects on organizational commitment, absenteeism, an willingness to report ethical problems. *Public Administration Review, 74*(3), 333–343.

Holt, S. B. (2018). For those who care: The effect of public service motivation on sector selection. *Public Administration Review, 78*(3), 457–471.

Jacobs, G., Belschak, F. D., & Den Hartog, D. N. (2014). (Un)ethical behavior and performance appraisal: The role of affect, support, and organizational justice. *Journal of Business Ethics, 121,* 63–76.

Jung, J., Bozeman, B., & Gaughan, M. (2020). Fear in bureaucracy: Comparing public and private sector workers' expectations of punishment. *Administration & Society, 52*(2), 233–264.

Kaptein, M. (2011). Toward effective codes: Testing the relationship with unethical behavior. *Journal of Business Ethics, 99,* 233–251.

Klingner, D. E., Nalbandian, J., & Llorens, J. J. (2015). *Public personnel management: Contexts and strategies*. Routledge.

Laws, J. (2017, September 1). Safety incentives: It's a small world, after all. [Conversation with Certified Professional of Incentive Management (CPIM) Sean Roark]. *Occupational Health & Safety*. Retrieved from https://ohsonline.com/articles/2017/09/01/small-world-after-all.aspx

Lee, D. S., & Park, S. (2023). Do motivated public servants behave more ethically? *Review of Public Personnel Administration*. https://doi.org/0734371X231216944

Lewis, C. W., & Gilman, S. C. (2005). *The ethics challenge in public service: A problem-solving guide*. John Wiley & Sons.

Lewis, C. W., & Gilman, S. C. (2012). *The ethics challenge in public service: A problem-solving guide* (3rd ed.). John Wiley & Sons.

Menzel, D. C. (2014). *Ethics management for public administrators: Building organizations of integrity*. Routledge.

Menzel, D. C. (2015). Research on ethics and integrity in public administration: Moving forward, looking back. *Public Integrity, 17*(4), 343–370.

Menzel, D. C. (2019). Ethics management in public organizations: What, why, and how? In *Handbook of administrative ethics* (pp. 355–366). Routledge.

Meyer-Sahling, J. H., Mikkelsen, K. S., & Schuster, C. (2019). The causal effect of public service motivation on ethical behavior in the public sector: Evidence from a large-scale survey experiment. *Journal of Public Administration Research and Theory, 29*(3), 445–459.

Moon, K. K. (2017). Fairness at the organizational level: Examining the effect of organizational justice climate on collective turnover rates and organizational performance. *Public Personnel Management, 46*(2), 118–143.

Murphy, J. E. (2011). Using incentives in your compliance and ethics program. *Society of Corporate Compliance and Ethics*. Retrieved from https://assets.hcca-info.org/Portals/0/PDFs/Resources/library/814_0_IncentivesCEProgram-Murphy.pdf

National Whistleblower Center [NWC] (2024). *Whistleblower protections and rewards*. Retrieved from www.whistleblowers.org/whistleblower-protections-and-rewards/

The Organisation for Economic Co-operation and Development [OECD]. (2020). *The OECD public integrity handbook*. OECD Publishing. https://doi.org/10.1787/ac8ed8e8-en

The Organisation for Economic Co-operation and Development [OECD]. (2021). *2021 OECD anti-bribery recommendation*. Retrieved from www.oecd.org/corruption/2021-oecd-anti-bribery-recommendation.htm

Park, T. Y., Park, S., & Barry, B. (2022). Incentive effects on ethics. *Academy of Management Annals, 16*(1), 297–333.

Pérez-Durán, I. (2023). Twenty-five years of accountability research in public administration: Authorship, themes, methods, and future trends. *International Review of Administrative Sciences, 90*(3), 546–562.

Reddick, C. G., Demir, T., & Perlman, B. (2020). Horizontal, vertical, and hybrid: An empirical look at the forms of accountability. *Administration & Society, 52*(9), 1410–1438.

Roberts, R. (2009). The rise of compliance-based ethics management: Implications for organizational ethics. *Public Integrity, 11*(3), 261–278.

Rose-Ackerman, S. (2008). Corruption and government. *International Peacekeeping, 15*(3), 328–343.

Sandel, M. J. (2012). *What money can't buy: The moral limits of markets*. Farrar, Straus and Giroux.

Six, F., & Lawton, A. (2013). Towards a theory of integrity systems: A configurational approach. *International Review of Administrative Sciences, 79*(4), 639–658.

Sunstein, C. R. (2018). Misconceptions about nudges. *Journal of Behavioral Economics for Policy, 2*(1), 1–67.

Svara, J. H. (2021). *The ethics primer for public administrators in government and non-profit organizations*. Jones & Bartlett Learning.

Tenbrunsel, A. E., & Messick, D. M. (1999). Sanctioning systems, decision frames, and cooperation. *Administrative Science Quarterly, 44*(4), 684–707.

Thiel, C. E., Bonner, J., Bush, J. T., Welsh, D. T., & Garud, N. (2023). Stripped of agency: The paradoxical effect of employee monitoring on deviance. *Journal of Management, 49*(2), 709–740.

US Office of Government Ethics [OGE]. (2020). *Annual performance report 2020*. Retrieved from https://www.oge.gov/Web/OGE.nsf/Resources/Annual+Performance+Report+(FY+2020)

US Office of Government Ethics [OGE]. (2023). *Compilation of federal ethics laws*. Retrieved from www.oge.gov/Web/oge.nsf/Resources/Compilation+of+Federal+Ethics+Laws

US Sentencing Commission. (2023). *The U.S. federal sentencing guidelines (§8B2.1. Effective Compliance and Ethics Program)*. Retrieved from https://guidelines.ussc.gov/apex/r/ussc_apex/guidelinesapp/guidelines?app_gl_id=%C2%A78B2.1

Wright, B. E., Hassan, S., & Park, J. (2016). Does a public service ethic encourage ethical behaviour? Public service motivation, ethical leadership and the willingness to report ethical problems. *Public Administration, 94*(3), 647–663.

Zhang, T., Gino, F., & Bazerman, M. H. (2014). Morality rebooted: Exploring simple fixes to our moral bugs. *Research in Organizational Behavior, 34*, 63–79.

5 Comparing and Bridging Ethics Management Approaches

Edgar Karssing and Alain Hoekstra

Introduction

In the public sector, the purpose of ethics management is to ensure the accountability of public officials. They should act with integrity and adhere to ethical standards in all their actions. Currently, and perhaps more so than in the past, ethics and integrity are highly regarded as valuable qualities for public organizations and as critical aspects of good governance (Huberts, 2014). This is due to the unique powers vested in public organizations (such as the ability to use violence; to issue passports, permits, and licenses; and to grant subsidies and social benefits) and the strong dependency of citizens on public service delivery (Hoekstra & Heres, 2016). Public integrity is a condition for achieving and maintaining public support and thus for the legitimacy of the government and its administration. Moreover, for public organizations and their officials upholding integrity and ethical leadership is important if they want their citizens to respect the law and to act according to the public norms. As public organizations are funded by taxes, taxpayers have the right to expect their money to be spent correctly and in accordance with the values of transparency, accountability, and integrity.

Although government organizations pay increasing attention to ethics, this is not a new trend or norm. As the 14th-century frescoes of "Good and Bad Government" (Meoni, 2005) demonstrate, the concern for good governance has a much longer tradition. These frescoes in Siena's Palazzo Pubblico (formerly the city hall) were intended to remind public office holders to act ethically. The wall paintings served as an early code of conduct, based on Aristotelian virtues such as courage, justice, prudence, and temperance, and provided ethical guidance to the city's governors and administrators. The tantalizing images illustrate that good (i.e., ethical) governance leads to a well-maintained, safe, and prosperous city, whereas bad (i.e., unethical) governance results in poverty, injustice, and ultimately total chaos. This example illustrates that concerns for (and thus the importance of) public integrity are as old as government itself.

Nowadays, most government organizations have implemented ethics policies. Although the precise set of prescribed measures differs by country, widely

DOI: 10.4324/9781003416258-6

adopted measures include the oath of office, a code of conduct, whistleblowing procedures, integrity training, screening of new personnel, and specific rules for gift acceptance, side-activities, public procurement, and other vulnerable topics. In recent times, numerous scholars and practitioners have advocated an integrity approach to ethics management (e.g., Perlman et al., 2023, Tremblay et al., 2016), also referred to as the high-road or a values-based approach. This approach is often contrasted with a compliance approach, also referred to as the low-road or a rules-based approach. Although they may have the same purpose—ensuring the accountability of public officials—the two approaches have different goals. The compliance approach aims to impede unethical behavior, whereas the integrity approach is designed to promote ethical behavior. This chapter provides a critical overview of the history, purpose, objectives, and characteristics of the integrity approach by contrasting it with the compliance approach. We examine several dimensions where the approaches differ and the arguments advanced by some critics who believe that a two-dimensional framework "trivializes the actual complexity of ethical behavior and the intricate nature of organizational ethics" (Tremblay et al., 2016, p. 2). Ultimately, most scholars and practitioners concur that a combination of both approaches is the most effective way to manage ethics. This prompts the question of how to bridge the low-road and the high-road. We discuss how an integrated systems approach could help, and how this can take shape. We conclude the chapter with some remarks and questions for further research.

The Integrity Approach

The distinction between an integrity approach and a compliance approach was identified by Paine (1994; see also 1997a) in an article primarily concerned with corporate ethics. In this article, she responds to the damaging effects of corporate misconduct. Thirty years later, in a reflection on her seminal paper, Paine (2024, p. 8) reiterates the main premise: that corporate failures cannot be attributed solely to "bad apples"—to the actions of unethical individuals. She notes that many ethical lapses "involved ordinarily decent people either not recognising the ethical aspects of issues they were dealing with or simply acting in response to organisational pressures and directives". Given that "corporate misconduct and irresponsibility are often rooted in organisational and management choices", it is necessary to consider "organisational features and management behaviours" when attempting to manage ethics (ibid.). She concludes: "How managers make decisions and what they decide—what opportunities to pursue, what goals to set, how to measure performance, how to pay people, how much to invest in risk management, technology, training and so on—together have a profound influence on how individuals do their jobs and whether the company as a whole acts responsibly. While we believe this connection is more widely understood today than it was in 1994, the steady stream of cases involving large-scale corporate malfeasance over the last three decades suggests that it is worth repeating" (Paine, 2024, p. 12). By distinguishing between the two approaches, she provides management with a tool to reflect on measures and instruments for ethics management.

Similar Distinctions in Public Management

In the field of public management, Paine's distinction resembles the Friedrich-Finer debate in the late 1930s and early 1940s and the often-discussed difference between the low-road and the high-road by Rohr (e.g., Maesschalck, 2005; Perlman et al., 2023; Tremblay et al., 2016). The crux of the Friedrich-Finer debate concerns the optimal means of ensuring the accountability of public officials. Both Friedrich and Finer initially addressed the role of the public servant in their relationship with ministers (Jackson, 2009; cf. Cooper, 2006). Finer posited that the public servant must obey the minister precisely: politicians should be making the decisions and issuing orders to the administrator. Friedrich believed that it was impossible for ministers to supervise public servants in detail and that administrative discretion was therefore necessary. He concluded "that enforcement can be effective for preventing undesirable actions like corruption, but not for securing good effects. To secure good results performance must be elicited not compelled" (Jackson, 2009, p. 72). An important topic in the discussion was how public servants should be managed. Finer emphasized the necessity of "external controls", namely formal and detailed rules and regulations designed to direct public servants. Friedrich, by contrast, advocated "internal controls", whereby public officials exercise control over themselves. Friedrich thus proposed that officials should be educated and motivated "to act responsibly by increasing their professionalism through education" (Jackson, 2009, p. 71). Many years later, but prior to Paine's arguments, in 1978, Rohr (1989/1978) made his now-famous distinction between the low-road and the high-road to ethics management, discussing professional education for bureaucrats. The low-road stresses compliance with formal rules—to stay out of trouble—whereas the high-road refers to moral character. The high-road "blends accepting responsibility for one's behavior with honorable intentions and personal integrity, that is, adherence to morals and principles" (Menzel, 2007, p. 36). As such, in the field of public management, similar distinctions can be observed as those made by Paine (e.g., Demmke, 2004; Maesschalck & Bertok, 2009; Perlman et al., 2023; Timmermans, 2022). As most scholars contributing to the debate on the integrity approach to ethics management begin with Paine, this will be the starting point for our overview.

Purpose, Objectives, and Characteristics

The purpose of ethics management, as outlined by Paine (1994, 1997a, 2024), is to assist organizations in acting in a more responsible manner. However, while the two approaches to managing conduct in organizations share this same purpose, they have different objectives (cf. Timmermans, 2022). The objective of the compliance approach is to impede individual misconduct, whereas the objective of the integrity approach is to enable responsible conduct (cf. Hartman, 2000, p. 158). Both approaches view employees as the main actors (Lartey, 2021, p. 52). The compliance approach does so by "disciplining individuals for narrow low-road violations" (Roberts, 2009, p. 265), while the integrity approach does so by supporting and nurturing high-road moral values. The essence of the compliance approach is conformity with externally imposed standards: "In compliance-based programs, employees are motivated to act out of fear of consequence as opposed to being motivated because of some moral or ethical compass" (Geddes, 2017, p. 424).

The essence of the integrity approach is self-governance based on standards chosen by the organization. Organizations could cultivate these internal controls by building moral character and improving decision-making from an ethical standpoint. As previously noted, scholars and practitioners employ different terminologies to describe the two approaches. This is partly due to historical influences—low-road versus high-road—and partly due to accentuating the essential difference between the two approaches: rules-based versus values-based. Verhezen (2010, p. 190), for example, calls the two approaches "command-and-control" and "values-and-integrity". Furthermore, confusion can arise because the term "integrity" is used to refer to both the genus (integrity policy) and the species (a specific management approach to give substance to the integrity policy) (cf. Jeurissen, 2002, p. 185), or because the term "integrity" is already used to describe one of the objectives of ethics management—to promote integrity—or "integrity" is one of the high-road values that ethics management seeks to cultivate.

It is often unclear from the outside whether an organization emphasizes a compliance approach or an integrity approach (Paine, 1994, p. 111). In both, several similar tools and measures are in place within the organization, such as codes of conduct, audits, reporting procedure, and training. In a compliance approach, these tools and measures are used to increase the supervision and control of employees with an emphasis on enforcing norm-compliant behavior: "The goal of these programs is to prevent, detect, and punish legal violations" (Paine, 1994, p. 106). By contrast, an integrity approach employs these measures and tools to encourage employees to take responsibility and to support them in identifying and addressing moral issues. "From the perspective of integrity, the task of ethics management is to define and give life to an organization's guiding values, to create an environment that supports ethically sound behavior, and to instill a sense of shared accountability among employees. The need to obey the law is viewed as a positive aspect of organizational life, rather than an unwelcome constraint imposed by external authorities" (Paine, 1994, p. 111).

Box 5.1   Paine's Understanding of Integrity

Integrity has many faces and, therefore, it is crucial for those involved in integrity-related activities to first clarify the definition of integrity being used (Audi & Murphy, 2006). Otherwise, integrity is mainly a source of confusion that provides little guidance in everyday practice. Interestingly, Paine provides minimal elaboration on her understanding of the concept of integrity that she employs in her initial article and book, in which she introduces the two approaches. In the article she states that "organizational integrity is based on the concept of self-governance in accordance with a set of guiding principles" (Paine, 1994, p. 111). In the book, she provides a more detailed explanation. In the introduction, she writes that "the term integrity is not being used in its narrow sense as a synonym for honesty, but in its broad sense to refer to the qualities of self-governance, responsibility, moral soundness, adherence to principle, and constancy of purpose" (Paine, 1997a, p. vii). She later elaborates on this, stating that the term "integrity" is rich in meaning and history: "Derived from the Latin word *integritas* meaning wholeness or purity, integrity is often identified with the qualities of honesty, reliability, and fair dealing. But is also implies a general sense of responsibility, a set of commitments, and a capacity for self-governance. In its broad sense, integrity suggests a coherent integration of identity and responsibility. As with many qualities, integrity comes in degrees. The highest levels are associated with principled behavior in the face of adversity or temptation" (Paine, 1997a, p. 98). In an article on ethics education, Paine (1991, p. 75) emphasized the importance of "self-awareness" and "self-assessment" and again links integrity to morality when she indicates that people of integrity at least "appreciate fundamental ethical principles, recognize situations in which they apply, and be able to resist the normal, routine pressures and temptations to compromise them". In a contribution to an encyclopedia, Paine (1997b, p. 336) defines integrity as "the quality of moral self-governance".

This can be compared to the distinction that Adler and Borys (1996) made between two types of bureaucracy: enabling and coercive. The integrity approach enables employees to master their tasks or functions, whereas the compliance approach attempts to coerce rule-abiding behavior. Paine (1994, p. 111) views the integrity approach as broader, deeper, and more demanding than the compliance approach:

> Broader in that it seeks to enable responsible conduct. Deeper in that it cuts to the ethos and operating systems of the organization and its members, their guiding values and patterns of thought and action. And more demanding in that it requires an active effort to define the responsibilities and aspirations

that constitute an organization's ethical compass. Above all, organizational ethics is seen as the work of management.

While both approaches can utilize the same tools, the specifics will vary from one approach to the other. In *Towards a Sound Integrity Framework: Instruments, Processes, Structures and Conditions for Implementation*, Maesschalck and Bertok (2009) provide several examples. In the compliance approach, a code "will describe, as specifically and unambiguously as possible, which behaviour is expected" (ibid, p. 32). By contrast, in the integrity approach, a code "focuses on general values, rather than on specific guidelines for behaviour, thus putting more trust in the organisational members' capacities for independent moral reasoning. Rather than telling what to do, the organisation provides its members with a general framework that identifies the general values and provides support, training and coaching for the application of these values in daily real-life situations" (ibid., p. 32).

A typical format for training in the compliance approach "would be a classroom setting where the trainer would be talking most of the time, explaining what is expected from the organisational members according to the laws, rules and codes and what the consequences are if one does not follow these directions" (ibid., p. 45). By contrast, training sessions in the integrity approach are "better described as discussion sessions. The trainees will do most of the thinking and talking and the trainer is only there as a facilitator, stimulating discussion, provoking thinking, playing the devil's advocate. A well-known example of this type of training is the Socratic Method" (ibid., p. 45; cf. OECD, 2020, pp. 125–126).

In her 1994 article, Paine summarizes the most significant characteristics of both approaches to ethics management (Table 5.1).

Table 5.1 The Main Characteristics of the Compliance Approach and the Integrity Approach

Compliance approach		*Integrity approach*	
Ethos	Conformity with externally imposed standards	*Ethos*	Self-governance according to chosen standards
Objective	Prevent criminal misconduct	*Objective*	Enable responsible conduct
Leadership	Lawyer-driven	*Leadership*	Management-driven with the aid of lawyers, HR, and others
Methods	Education, reduced discretion, auditing and controls, penalties	*Methods*	Education, leadership, accountability, organizational systems and decision processes, auditing and controls, penalties
Behavioral assumptions	Autonomous beings guided by material self-interest	*Behavioral assumptions*	Social being guided by material self-interest, values, ideals, and peers

Source: Paine (1994, p. 113).

While we have discussed ethos, objectives, and methods, leadership is of great importance in adopting an integrity approach to promote ethics in the organization (Heres, 2014; Perlman et al., 2023, p. 827). Paine (1994, p. 112) asserts that the concrete implementation of an integrity approach is tailored to specific circumstances, influenced by factors such as management personality, company history, culture, lines of business, and industry regulations. She notes that there is no one right integrity strategy but identifies the hallmarks of an effective integrity approach (Paine, 1994, p. 112):

- The guiding values and commitments make sense and are clearly communicated.
- Company leaders are personally committed, credible, and willing to take action on the values they espouse.
- The espoused values are integrated into the normal channels of management decision-making and are reflected in the organization's critical activities.
- The company's systems and structures support and reinforce its values.
- Managers throughout the company have the decision-making skills, knowledge, and competencies needed to make ethically sound decisions on a day-to-day basis.

The two approaches exhibit a clear distinction in their underlying behavioral assumptions. This was also evident in the Friedrich-Finer debate: can we trust internal controls or do we have to rely on external controls? Paine (1994, p. 110) posited that the underlying model for the compliance approach is "deterrence theory, which envisions people as rational maximizers of self-interest, responsive to the personal costs and benefits of their choices, yet indifferent to the moral legitimacy of those choices". In this approach, employees are regarded as "homo economicus", motivated solely by (material) self-interest (Timmermans, 2022, p. 103). This results in the implementation of oversight systems to detect, investigate, and sanction inappropriate behavior by employees. Anechiarico and Jacobs (1996) termed this the panoptic approach. Perlman et al. (2023, p. 824) observe that the compliance approach is based on contractual exchange theory, whereas the integrity approach is founded on social exchange theory. The integrity approach assumes that civil servants are intrinsically motivated to self-commitment and self-control, and the self-responsibility of the individual is emphasized (Herold & Schlegel, 2023). Consequently, employees are perceived as social-dependent beings guided by material self-interest and also by ideals and values.

Either . . . or . . .

There are no strong views among scholars as to one approach being superior to the other; rather a need is seen for both approaches: compliance and integrity reinforce each other (e.g., Calderón et al., 2018; Geddes, 2017; Maesschalck,

2005; Maesschalck & Bertok, 2009; OECD, 2020; Perlman et al., 2023). Or, as Maesschalck (2005, p. 22) summarizes the prevailing view: "these two approaches do not constitute a simple dichotomy but should be seen as the opposite ends of a continuum, and in practice they should always be combined and considered complementary". The compliance approach provides the necessary enforcement mechanisms as the "teeth" that are essential to ensure a minimum ethical behavior (Maesschalck & Bertok, 2009, p. 12). Nevertheless, as Paine (1994, p. 111) notes, "managers who define ethics as legal compliance are implicitly endorsing a code of moral mediocrity for their organizations". This approach leaves little room for individual conscience (Roberts, 2009, p. 263). Although this approach may help avoid wrongdoing, "organizations that work to achieve compliance are unlikely to exceed it" (Sekerka, 2012, p. 286). The integrity approach could strengthen the compliance approach by clarifying the importance of rules through adding values: "it introduces guiding principles and values that are crucial for motivating human action" (Herold & Schlegel, 2023, p. 123). However, these principles and values might be too vague to provide clear guidance. Indeed, Finer criticized Friedrich for referring to "abstract and ethereal" concepts that would not help to ensure the accountability of public officials (Jackson, 2009, p. 70). Although relying solely on a compliance approach can have detrimental effects, the opposite is also true. Implementing only integrity measures "would result in an organization without proper guiding rules to structure ethical decision-making, activities, and the system itself. It would equally mean that the organization relies entirely on the goodwill of its members and the idea that everyone is fundamentally ethical" (Tremblay et al., 2016, p. 4). Therefore, in practice, organizations should seek an appropriate balance between the two approaches. As Maesschalck and Bertok (2009, p. 13) noted, "Because most governments traditionally emphasised the rules-based approach, this often implies a move towards a values-based approach. Yet, the balance should be maintained and one should also beware of a too enthusiastic and radical switch towards the values-based approach, particularly in a culture that is traditionally rules-based". In certain instances, it may be beneficial to intentionally create a temporary imbalance within the organization to facilitate a significant transition. "For example, in an organization where one wants to eradicate pervasive and serious corruption, one might decide for a temporary emphasis on the rules-based approach: making strict rules and strictly controlling and enforcing them" (Maesschalck & Bertok, 2009, p. 78). After the transition has been achieved, it is then possible to re-establish a balance between the two approaches. Furthermore, this balance should not be assessed at the level of each measure or tool, but in the overall approach to ethics management, including complementary structural measures "such as measures within personnel management, procurement and contract management or financial management" (Maesschalck & Bertok, 2009, p. 28). To help in the search for balance, Lartey (2021) examined the key differences between the two approaches with reference to the four phases of program management: initiation, planning, implementation, and control. Timmermans (2022) differentiates between process (or act) and content (or object) in order to capture the range of similarities and differences between integrity and compliance: "The different activities and methods of compliance and integrity, for example, are covered by process, while the implied (moral, social or legal) standards fall under content" (ibid., p. 105). He believes that this approach better reflects the intricacies and multilayered character of the relationship.

Box 5.2   Rohr (1989/1978, p. 85), on "Follow Your Conscience"

In upholding the duty of bureaucrats to 'follow their consciences', we are not suggesting that they simply 'do their own thing'. It is unfortunate that these two phrases have become confused in popular speech. We can hope that our method might help to provide bureaucrats with informed consciences that would lead them into dialogue with the political society they serve and that they would ponder its values seriously. After submitting themselves to this discipline, they would be free to follow their consciences.

Some scholars have criticized the compliance-integrity continuum. Timmermans (2022) asserts that the two approaches could conflict with each other. Maesschalck (2005) proposed extending the compliance-integrity continuum in the form of a fourfold typology inspired by grid-group theory. Tremblay et al. (2016) and Martineau et al. (2017) suggested adopting a new pluralistic contingency approach to integrate the individual, collective, and strategic levels of the compliance and integrity approaches: "If one of the levels is neglected, the organization might be confronted with ethical problems relating to this level. For example, a public organization that does not consider environmental issues in its decision-making might find civil society turning against it" (Tremblay et al., 2016, p. 6). This theory is empirically derived from a "statistical analysis of responses to an ad hoc questionnaire on organizational ethics practices" (Martineau et al., 2017, p. 791). The analysis identified six different orientations to ethics programs, corresponding to distinct types of organizational ethics practices. However, these criticisms can be seen as elaborations of the basic ideas of Rohr and Paine rather than a denial of the primary distinction between the low-road and the high-road—between compliance and integrity approaches.

Thirty years have passed since the distinction between compliance and integrity was made. Compliance approaches have undergone considerable development in that time. As Paine (2024, p. 14) points out in her retrospective: "compliance programmes have gotten much more sophisticated over the last three decades". Many organizations have improved their performance, and the integrity approach has been embraced by these organizations. Compliance has "expanded from the original pure adherence to legal provisions to include adherence to internal guidelines" (Herold & Schlegel, 2023, p. 112). Nowadays, if you look around in organizations, and watch what managers, compliance officers, and the compliance department are doing, you can distinguish between legal compliance and value-based compliance (Herold & Schlegel, 2023).

One might ask whether the compliance approach and the integrity approach genuinely exist in practice, as the literature suggests, and are they really distinct? To which we would answer: yes, and yes. For instance, Perlman et al. (2023) conducted an empirical analysis of local government practice. The results indicated "that integrity and compliance are not just separate and distinct ideas but are related sets of practices that have an empirical basis. Both of these need to be used to understand ethics management in local government" (ibid., p. 823). A few years after the publication of Paine's seminal article, Treviño, Weaver and colleagues conducted empirical research into the two approaches (e.g., Treviño et al., 1999; Treviño & Weaver, 2003; Weaver & Treviño, 1999). This demonstrated that the distinction between the two approaches was evident in practice, that the two approaches often coexist simultaneously, and that there are significant differences in the effectiveness of the approaches in achieving the objectives of ethics management. According to their research, the two approaches are not fully interchangeable, and which approach is chosen certainly determines the effectiveness of ethics management. The compliance approach primarily encourages employees to adopt an attitude of "make sure you don't get caught!". Such an attitude clearly has a positive influence on employee behavior and contributes to achieving the objectives of ethics management. However, the effect is much greater with an integrity approach, and more objectives are achieved. On a note of caution, Stimmler-Caesmann (2022, p. 27) concluded, after reviewing the measurement tools: "this first attempt at measuring the mode of ethics programs still lacks validation to date, and not one standardized measurement model has been developed". Furthermore, she is skeptical about the pluralistic theory of ethics program orientations by Martineau et al. (2017), the only other method she is aware of for measuring ethics management approaches. Consequently, she developed and validated her own measurement instruments. To the best of our knowledge, we are unaware of any research that has yet utilized her instruments.

Integrity Management Systems: Bridging the High and the Low Roads

The management of public sector ethics is complex (Huberts et al., 2025). There are many different types of integrity violations (Lasthuizen et al., 2011), which are often the result of a combination of different causes (Kish-Gephart et al., 2010). Consequently, there are no simple "silver bullet" interventions to ensure public integrity. On the contrary, managing ethics requires a diverse set of measures and instruments that need to be carefully orchestrated (Kaptein, 2015; Maclean et al., 2015). Moreover, as different organizational departments (e.g., HR, finance, legal, compliance) are responsible for the implementation of these measures and instruments, it is essential to ensure sufficient coherence between these actors (Hoekstra, 2016). In the preceding section, we discussed two approaches to ethics management and the need for a balance between them and, indeed, a combination of both approaches is generally considered to be the most effective way to manage ethics. This prompts the question: how to bridge the low-road and the high-road?

This section will explore how a new and growing trend in ethics management research and the associated literature may help to bridge the high and low roads. This trend involves the development of integrity management systems (IMSs). An IMS comprises the whole set of measures necessary to create an ethical culture, to impede unethical conduct, and to promote ethical behavior within an organization. Thus, just as with the original meaning of the word integrity itself (derived from the Latin word *integritas*), an IMS refers to (and pursues) wholeness: it brings together all the relevant aspects of managing integrity. We will begin by summarizing some common characteristics of IMSs based on a recent study (Maesschalck et al., 2024). Subsequently, we will reflect on the manner in which these systems facilitate the integration of the high- and low-road approaches.

Characteristics of Integrity Management Systems

Based on a study of the ethics management literature, Maesschalck et al. (2024) identified four characteristics of IMSs: interconnectedness, the requisite variety, a processual perspective, and grassroots participation. These characteristics are summarized in the following sections.

Interconnectedness

The notion of interconnectedness reflects that an IMS looks beyond individual ethics management measures and focuses on their connections, and how they jointly contribute to organizational integrity. Measures that are aligned and support each other are more effective, both individually and collectively (Hoekstra & Kaptein, 2020; Kaptein, 2015). As an illustration, a new code of ethics that is reinforced by training sessions, frequently referred to by senior management, and discussed in team meetings will have a more profound impact than a code that is introduced as a stand-alone measure. Interconnectedness also plays a role with other organizational interventions that need not be directly focused on ensuring responsible conduct but may still have an impact on organizational integrity. For instance, if management pushes employees to achieve certain targets in ways that contradict the code of ethics, this will undermine the code's credibility and, consequently, its effectiveness. Interconnectedness also relates to external actors. For example, the implementation of a code will be much easier when contractors are also aware of the code and recognize the consequences of violating it. Consequently, it is often recommended that external actors are involved in both the design and the implementation of ethics management measures.

Requisite Variety

An often-repeated mantra in the ethics management literature is the need for variation as well as comprehensiveness. Kaptein (2015), for example, advocates having a large number of measures, arguing that they can fulfill a greater number of functions and also reinforce the message that the organization takes ethics seriously. Van Montfort et al. (2018) promote the value of comprehensiveness, suggesting that all appropriate measures of an integrity system should be present. That is, the range of (different types of) integrity measures that constitute an IMS should be broad. Maesschalck and Bertok (2009) distinguish four groups of functions in categorizing these measures, and argue the need to fulfil each of those functions. Alongside the various classifications of ethics management instruments, there are also classifications of broader approaches to ethics management. Paine's (1994) discussed distinction between compliance and integrity approaches to ethics management is certainly the most groundbreaking, but nowadays most authors recommend that both approaches should be combined in a well-balanced mix.

Processual Perspective

Researchers increasingly emphasize the importance of a processual approach to ethics management design and refer, for instance, to the "Deming cycle" to conceptualize this process (Constantinescu & Kaptein, 2020; Hoekstra & Kaptein, 2020; Maesschalck & Bertok, 2009). This cycle conceptualizes the development, implementation, and evaluation of interventions in four steps: plan, do, check, and adapt (the PDCA cycle). The application of such a cycle with an IMS ensures that it is based on a clear and well-developed plan. In the absence of a clear plan, measures and instruments are likely to remain somewhat incident-driven, prompted by scandals, or driven by erratic political or financial decisions (Hoekstra & Kaptein, 2021). A processual approach also enables the IMS to learn from its implementation and adapt when interventions do not appear to be effective or need to be adjusted due to changing circumstances. This may also help to avoid the common "implementation deficit" of ethics management, wherein lofty ambitions are not implemented or are quickly forgotten when other organizational concerns and priorities take center stage (Maesschalck & Bertok, 2009). The expectation is that such a deficit will be less likely in organizations that commit themselves to systematically monitoring, evaluating, and adapting their ethics management instruments.

Grassroots Participation

The fourth characteristic of IMSs is the involvement of both internal employees and other, external, stakeholders. Employee participation can help avoid the risk of excessive emphasis on compliance and control, which can easily lead to resistance among employees to accepting ethics management and thus undermine its goals. Through an emphasis on compliance and control, ethics management can also reduce individual employees' ability to manage ethical ambiguity, thus leading to atrophy of competency. Stansbury and Barry (2007) hypothesize that the potentially perverse effects of ethics management can be avoided by allowing greater participation, for example, by allowing employees sufficient discretion or by organizing regular opportunities for criticism of the ethics program itself. Another argument for employee participation is that their input may improve not only the quality but also the acceptance and implementation of the ethics management (Andersson & Ekelund, 2022; Tremblay et al., 2016). Similar arguments can be made for the participation of external parties (e.g., Tremblay et al., 2016). Indeed, this can help to improve the quality of the IMS itself. For example, taking activists from outside the organization seriously and giving them a voice, including in the development and implementation of an IMS, can help to prevent resistance.

Bridging Qualities of Integrity Management Systems

How do IMSs contribute to bridging the high-road and low-road approaches to ethics management? To answer this question, and to build our argument, we use the first three characteristics (or features) of IMSs, starting with requisite variety.

Requisite variety is a key feature of an IMS. It implies that ethics management requires a diverse set of measures and activities. From this perspective, it is also strongly recommended that the combined set of measures and activities gives substance to a well-balanced (both compliance-based and integrity-based) ethics management approach.

This brings us to interconnectedness, another key IMS feature. Due to its integrative character, an IMS also promotes the fitting together of these measures and activities such that they reinforce each other. This leads to synergies that enhance the effectiveness of both the individual measures and the IMS as a whole (Brenner, 1992; De Graaf & Macaulay, 2014; Foote & Ruona, 2008; Hoekstra, 2022; Six et al., 2012). Consequently, organizations should avoid implementing "standalone" measures. Rather, they should ensure that the measures are mutually aligned. Similarly, instead of viewing the two (compliance- and integrity-based) approaches as independent and isolated ethics management approaches, seeking alignment and coherency aligns with IMS theory.

To design a well-balanced and coherent IMS, a well thought-out strategy or plan is required. Foote and Ruona (2008, p. 298) posit that a superficial and reactive approach to promoting ethics in the workplace will not remedy unethical organizational behavior. Rather, this requires a well-developed strategy to build the foundations for an organizational culture that promotes and supports ethical behavior. This brings us to the planning and process phase of ethics management (the third IMS feature). This phase is where the organization's overall ethics management strategy is developed. It could easily also be called the "design" or "bridging" phase since it transcends individual measures and approaches. From a strategic and integrating perspective, not only is the right combination of integrity measures determined, but also how these are to be aligned to constitute a coherent and well-balanced IMS (both high-road and low-road). Moreover, as organizations and societies are in constant transformation, the IMS should be dynamic and adaptable to new situations and developments. This requires the implementation of a continuous learning cycle, involving the monitoring, evaluation, and adaptation of the entire IMS. This implies that the IMS strategy, measures, balance, and coherence should be reassessed on a regular basis. As an immediate reaction to a high-impact integrity violation, it is understandable that one might put more emphasis on a compliance-based approach. This may lead to an imbalance, which is acceptable as long as the emphasis on compliance is not excessive and the balance is eventually restored.

This leads to the conclusion that the "interconnectedness" and "processual perspective" features of an IMS contribute to bridging the high- and the low-roads. Further, this bridge should be assessed in the overall approach to ethics management, rather than at the level of each individual measure or tool.

Integrity Management Systems: Current Circumstances and Challenges

Given that IMSs are a relatively new development, there are only a few organizations that have already implemented a full-fledged IMS. To the best of our knowledge, IMSs are currently mainly applied in a prescriptive manner and used to evaluate existing integrity polices in order to determine which measures are missing in organizations. The evaluation by Hoekstra et al. (2022) of the comprehensiveness of integrity policies and measures being applied in three major cities (Antwerp, Munich, and Amsterdam) based on a developed IMS framework is a good example in this regard.

The introduction of comprehensive IMSs in public organizations is not without challenges. There are several reasons that may discourage organizations from implementing IMSs, at least in the short term. First, it seems that paying attention to integrity is not a top priority within most public organizations. Here, adopting a less comprehensive approach provides more opportunities to prioritize other organizational goals, whereas a thorough IMS approach may have, possibly unwanted, consequences for the everyday organizational goals and operations. Second, setting up an IMS could be rejected as undesirable bureaucracy for which the organization lacks capacity and resources. Third, the introduction of a comprehensive IMS may suggest that the organization has serious integrity problems. This negative (and quite possibly incorrect) image discourages organizational leaders from introducing such systems. Fourth, organizations often tend to only implement formal requirements. As IMSs are still a relatively new, and somewhat academic, concept, it will take some time before one becomes a formal requirement and therefore implemented in public organizations. Despite the current situation and challenges, we expect, and given the advantages of IMS, hope that public organizations will introduce IMSs in the near future.

Concluding Remarks

This chapter started out by referring to the 14th-century frescoes of "Good and Bad Government" painted on the walls of Siena's Palazzo Pubblico. These frescoes provided ethical guidance to the city's public office holders, instructing them to act in accordance with the moral code and warning them of the societal harm caused by political and administrative vices such as greed and pride. As such, the frescoes symbolize the high road to ethics management: cultivating internal controls by building moral character and improving decision-making from an ethical standpoint. However, it is also necessary to implement a compliance approach that provides the teeth that are essential to ensure minimal ethical behavior.

For control systems, one can again look back to Italian cities for an example. Precursors of today's whistleblowing systems can be found in Venice. The famous lions' heads with open mouths (*bocche di leone*), often plastered on the outer walls of official buildings, served as letterboxes where citizens could anonymously post or report suspicions of wrongdoings of public officials. Each state department had its own box, so different boxes addressed different issues—such as taxes, pollution, market fraud, or trade disputes (Dietz, 2020). The lions' head that is attached to the Doge's Palace in Venice is accompanied by the following engraved text: "*Denontie secrete contro chi occultera gratie et officii o colludera per nascon der la vera rendita d essi*" (which can be translated as: "Secret denunciations against anyone who will conceal favors and services or will collude to hide the true revenue from them"). Each letter was read and addressed by the relevant state department, or by the "Council of Ten" (Venice's main governing body). When the accusation proofed to be right the consequences could be dire and lead to imprisonment, or even death. According to Cowan (2009), many European cities and countries had similar systems for anonymous denunciation, during the medieval and Renaissance periods. Next to these *bocche di leone* there also exists the famous *bocca della verità* (the mouth of truth), an ancient marble mask in Rome. According to a medieval legend, it will bite off the hand of any liar who places their hand in its mouth, or, alternatively, any who utters a lie while their hand is in the mouth (Wikipedia, 2024). This resembles the lie detector we use nowadays, which also fits in the compliance-based approach. Obviously both systems had flaws, as sometimes innocent people were condemned, or guilty people were unjustly acquitted.

Two distinct approaches to managing ethics can be employed to ensure the accountability of public officials: the low road and the high road (or the compliance approach and the integrity approach). Both approaches are necessary since "it takes two to Tango". The challenge is to balance the two approaches: to bridge the low- and the high-roads. An important question is: "how much regulation and control are necessary to allow sufficient ethical room for maneuver for self-responsibility" (Herold & Schlegel, 2023). More empirical research is needed to assess the effectiveness of the wide range of ethics management systems, and the frameworks and models that have been developed and propagated (cf. Kaptein, 2015). Further research could provide insight into the relationship between integrity and compliance, both in theory and in organizational practice. The insights gained from this research would help corroborate, and refine, the conceptual framework (Timmermans, 2022). We support the conclusion of Treviño et al. (2024) that there is a need for more research into positive behavioral ethics. While significant research has been conducted to understand "the causes and prevention of *unethical* behaviour in the workplace" (ibid., p. 129), to further develop the integrity approach requires a deeper insight into the causes of *good* behavior, as well as the ways in which character and conscience can be cultivated. This would enable, as Rohr observed, public officials to follow their conscience.

Research has shown that it can be challenging for smaller organizations to develop, implement, and maintain adequate integrity policies (Hoekstra, 2022). This is likely because most guidelines for ethics management are designed for larger organizations. This raises the question as to whether it is possible to adapt the existing ethics management guidelines to smaller organizations. Further research is needed in this regard.

A final aspect to consider refers to the so-called Western bias (cf. Tremblay et al., 2016). Most of the literature and research that we have drawn on, as well as our own insights and experiences, originate in Western countries and their governmental organizations. These countries and organizations share a similar cultural background. It is unclear to what extent the distinction made between the two ethics management approaches is relevant for non-Western public administrations with different cultural backgrounds who are likely to face different ethics and integrity problems. Do they require a high-road or a low-road ethics management approach, or a combination thereof? Are the components of IMSs the same, or do they require different models for managing public sector ethics and integrity? Comparative, cross-cultural research would help answer these questions.

References

Adler, P. S., & Borys, B. (1996). Two types of bureaucracy: Enabling and coercive. *Administrative Science Quarterly*, 61–89.

Andersson, S., & Ekelund, H. (2022). Promoting ethics management strategies in the public sector: Rules, values, and inclusion in Sweden. *Administration & Society, 54*(6), 1089–1116.

Anechiarico, F., & Jacobs, J. B. (1996). *The pursuit of absolute integrity: How corruption control makes government ineffective*. The University of Chicago Press.

Audi, R., & Murphy, P. (2006). The many faces of integrity. *Business Ethics Quarterly, 16*, 3–21.

Brenner, S. N. (1992). Ethics programs and their dimensions. *Journal of Business Ethics, 11*, 391–399.

Calderón, R., Piñero, R., & Redín, D. M. (2018). Can compliance restart integrity? Toward a harmonized approach. The example of the audit committee. *Business Ethics: A European Review, 27*(2), 195–206.

Constantinescu, M., & Kaptein, M. (2020). Ethics management and ethical management: Mapping criteria and interventions to support responsible management practice. In O. Laasch, R. Suddaby, R. Freeman & D. Jamali (Eds.), *Research handbook of responsible management* (pp. 155–174). Edward Elgar.

Cooper, T. L. (2006). *The responsible administrator: An approach to ethics for the administrative role* (5th ed.). Jossey-Bass.

Cowan, A. (2009). Information and communication in Venice: Rethinking early modern politics. By Filippo de Vivo. *Cultural and Social History, 6*(4), 518–519. https://doi.org/10.2752/147800409X467659

De Graaf, G., & Macaulay, M. (2014). Introduction to a symposium on integrity and integrity systems. *International Journal of Public Administration, 37*, 65–66.

Demmke, C. (2004). Working towards common elements in the field of ethics and integrity. In *Study for the 43rd Meeting of the Directors-General of the Public Services of the Member States of the European Union*, EIPA.

Dietz, K. (2020). Need to complain? Here's how Renaissance-era Venetians did it Trade disputes. *Tax gripes. All manner of ancient accusations were dropped into the 'bocche di leone,' or lions' mouths*. Retrieved from www.nationalgeographic.com/travel/article/need-to-complain-heres-how-renaissance-era-venetians-did-it.

Foote, M. F., & Ruona, W. E. A. (2008). Institutionalizing ethics: A synthesis of frameworks and the implications for HRD. *Human Resource Development Review, 7*(3), 292–308.

Geddes, B. H. (2017). Integrity or compliance based ethics: Which is better for today's business? *Open Journal of Business and Management, 5*(3), 420–429.

Hartman, L. (2000). Compliance versus integrity: The process of ethics integration. *Journal of Employment Discrimination Law, 2*(2), 157–159.

Heres, L. (2014). *One style fits all? The content, origins, and effect of follower expectations of ethical leadership* [PhD-thesis—Research and graduation internal, Vrije Universiteit Amsterdam]. Ipskamp Drukkers.

Herold, T., & Schlegel, F. (2023). Value-based compliance: Integrating integrity and compliance management. In J. lange (Ed.), *Value-oriented leadership in theory and practice: Concepts-study results-practical insights* (pp. 111–126). Springer International Publishing.

Hoekstra, A. (2016). Institutionalizing integrity management: Challenges and solutions in times of financial crises and austerity measures. In A. Lawton, Z. van der Wal & L. W. J. C. Huberts (Eds.), *Ethics in public policy and management: A global research companion* (pp. 147–164). Routledge.

Hoekstra, A. (2022). *Integrity management in public organizations. Content & Design.* Erasmus University.

Hoekstra, A., & Heres, L. (2016). Ethical probity in public service. In *Global encyclopedia of public administration, Public Policy, and Governance.* Springer International Publishing.

Hoekstra, A., & Kaptein, M. (2020). Ethics management: A pluralistic and dynamic perspective. In C. L. Jurkiewicz (Ed.), *Global corruption and ethics management: Translating theory into action* (pp. 109–118). Roman & Littlefield Publishers.

Hoekstra, A., & Kaptein, M. (2021). The integrity of integrity programs: Toward a normative framework. *Public Integrity, 23*(2), 129–141.

Hoekstra, A., Huberts, L., & van Montfort, A. (2022). Content and design of integrity systems: Evaluating integrity systems in local government. *Public Integrity, 25*(2), 137–149.

Huberts, L. (2014). *The integrity of governance. What it is, what we know, what is done, and where we go to.* Palgrave Macmillan.

Huberts, L., Hoekstra, A., & Van Montfort, A. (2025). Integrity management systems: What integrity is about, how it relates to corruption and what helps to protect integrity and curb corruption. In J. Pozsgai-Alvarez & R. Bratu (Eds.), *Routledge handbook of anti-corruption research and practice.* Routledge.

Jackson, M. (2009). Responsibility versus accountability in the Friedrich-Finer debate. *Journal of Management History, 15*(1), 66–77.

Jeurissen, R. (2002). Benaderingen van integriteitsmanagement [Approaches of integrity-management]. In *Integriteit in bedrijf, organisatie en openbaar bestuur.* Van Gorcum.

Kaptein, M. (2015). The effectiveness of ethics programs: The role of scope, composition and sequence. *Journal of Business Ethics, 132,* 415–431.

Kish-Gephart, J. J., Harrison, D. A., & Treviño, L. K. (2010). Bad apples, bad cases and bad barrels: Meta-analytic evidence about sources of unethical; Decision at work. *Journal of Applied Psychology, 95*(1), 1–31.

Lartey, F. M. (2021). Integrity-based and compliance-based ethics programs: A critical analysis of key differences. *International Journal of Economics, Business and Management Research, 5*(5), 43–53.

Lasthuizen, K., Huberts, L. W. J. C., & Heres, L. (2011). How to measure integrity violations. Towards a validated typology of unethical behavior. *Public Management Review, 13*(3), 383–408.

MacLean, T., Litzky, B. E., & Holderness, D. K. (2015). When organizations don't walk their talk: A cross-level examination of how decoupling formal ethics programs affects organizational members. *Journal of Business Ethics, 128,* 351–368.

Maesschalck, J. (2005). Approaches to ethics management in the public sector: A proposed extension of the compliance-integrity continuum. *Public Integrity, 7*(1), 20–41.

Maesschalck, J., & Bertok, J. (2009). *Towards a sound integrity framework: Instruments, processes, structures and Conditions for implementation.* OECD Publications.

Maesschalck, J., Hoekstra, A., & Van Montfort, A. (2024). Integrity management systems. In M. Kaptein (Ed.), *Research handbook on organisational integrity* (pp. 542–557). Edward Elgar Publishing.

Martineau, J. T., Johnson, K. J., & Pauchant, T. C. (2017). The pluralist theory of ethics programs orientations and ideologies: An empirical study anchored in requisite variety. *Journal of Business Ethics, 142,* 791–815.

Menzel, D. C. (2007). *Ethics management for public administrators. Building organizations of integrity.* M.E. Sharpe.

Meoni, M. L. (2005). *Utopia and reality in Ambroggio Lorenzetti's Good Government. Formal example in the representation of human activity. An anthropological analysis.* Edizioni IFI.

OECD. (2020). *OECD public integrity handbook*. OECD Publishing.

Paine, L. S. (1991). Ethics as character development: Reflections on the objective of ethics education. *The Ruffin Series in Business Ethics*, 67–86.

Paine, L. S. (1994). Managing for organizational integrity. *Harvard Business Review, March-April*, 106–117.

Paine, L. S. (1997a). *Cases in leadership, ethics, and organizational integrity: A strategic perspective*. McGraw-Hill.

Paine, L. S. (1997b). Integrity. In P. Werhane & R. Freeman (Eds.). *The Blackwell Encyclopedia of Management: Business Ethics* (pp. 335–337). Blackwell Publishing.

Paine, L. S. (2024). Managing for organisational integrity. In M. Kaptein (Ed.), *Research Handbook on Organisational Integrity* (pp. 8–23). Edward Elgar Publishing.

Perlman, B. J., Reddick, C., & Demir, T. (2023). A compliance—integrity framework for ethics management: An empirical analysis of local government practice. *Public Administration Review, 83*(4), 823–837.

Roberts, R. (2009). The rise of compliance-based ethics management: Implications for organizational ethics. *Public Integrity, 11*(3), 261–278.

Rohr, J. A. (1989/1978). *Ethics for bureaucrats: An essay on law and values* (2nd ed.). Marcel Dekker.

Sekerka, L. E. (2012). Compliance as a subtle precursor to ethical corrosion: A strength-based approach as a way forward. *Wyoming Law Review, 12*, 277–302.

Six, F., Van der Veen, M., & Kruithof, N. (2012). Conceptualizing integrity systems in governments and banking. *Public Integrity, 14*(4), 361–382.

Stansbury, J., & Barry, B. (2007). Ethics programs and the paradox of control. *Business Ethics Quarterly, 17*(2), 239–261.

Stimmler-Caesmann, D. (2022). *An ethical culture approach to compliance and integrity management: What works and what hurts to prevent misconduct and promote ethical behavior in organizations*. Zeppelin Universität.

Timmermans, J. (2022). Exploring the multifaceted relationship of compliance and integrity—the case of the defence industry. *NL ARMS Netherlands Annual Review of Military Studies 2021: Compliance and Integrity in International Military Trade*, 95–113.

Tremblay, M., Martineau, J. T., & Pauchant, T. C. (2016). Managing organizational ethics in the public sector: A pluralist contingency approach as an alternative to the integrity management framework. *Public Integrity, 19*(3), 219–233.

Treviño, L. K., den Nieuwenboer, N. A., & Kish-Gephart, J. (2024). A positive behavioural ethics perspective on organisational integrity. In M. Kaptein (Ed.), *Research handbook on organisational integrity* (pp. 129–161). Edward Elgar Publishing.

Treviño, L. K., & Weaver, G. R. (2003). *Managing ethics in business organizations: Social scientific perspectives*. Stanford University Press.

Treviño, L. K., Weaver, G. R., Gibson, D. G., & Toffler, B. L. (1999). Managing ethics and legal compliance: What works and what hurts. *California Management Review, 41*(2), 131–151.

Van Montfort, A., Ogric, B., & Huberts, L. (2018). The (in)completeness of local integrity systems, a cross-sectional study on municipal integrity systems for civil servants in the Netherlands. *Archives of Business Research, 6*(9), 70–90.

Verhezen, P. (2010). Giving voice in a culture of silence. From a culture of compliance to a culture of integrity. *Journal of Business Ethics, 96*, 187–206.

Weaver, G. R., & Treviño, L. K. (1999). Compliance and values oriented ethics programs: Influences on employees' attitudes and behavior. *Business Ethics Quarterly, 9*(2), 315–335.

Wikipedia. (2024). Retrieved September 24, 2024 from https://en.wikipedia.org/wiki/Bocca_della_Verità

6 Does Leadership Matter? Why and How?

Rusi Sun and Yahong Zhang

Introduction

Ethics and integrity are the core democratic values of public and nonprofit organizations and affect the legitimacy of the organization. Nowadays, citizens' trust in governments has reached an all-time low in the United States (Pew, 2023). The lack of trust stems not only from dissatisfaction with public services and policies but also from public administrators' involvement in unethical activities and high-profile scandals. To restore confidence in the government, implementing measures that combat unethical conduct and enhance integrity has become one of the top priorities for governments at all levels.

Ethics codes and formal policies outlining ethical principles and setting the standards for public officials and employees' accountability have been extensively developed and enacted in public organizations. However, those codified principles are generally broad and cannot anticipate every situation where ethical issues may arise. They cannot provide specific instructions on how to make decisions in complex and diverse circumstances. Therefore, simply implementing a code of ethics and other formal policies to promote ethical behavior across an organization is not adequate (Downe et al., 2016).

Furthermore, the traditional approach to addressing unethical behaviors focuses on identifying "rotten apples" (Tasdoven & Kaya, 2014, p. 530). Deviant behavior was often attributed to the moral deficiency of individual members within the organization (Tasdoven & Kaya, 2014). However, in some cases, the problem lies not only with the individual engaging in unethical behavior but also with the entire group or organization failing to detect integrity-related violations and lack of proper culture to promote ethical conduct (Tasdoven & Kaya, 2014). Therefore, the traditional approach does not address the organizational arrangements and dynamics from which unethical conducts emerge (Frost & Tischer, 2014).

These limitations make it imperative to find a way to enhance an organization's ethics management through the moral leadership of public managers who set an example of how to do the right things and shape the organizational environment to support the ethical conduct of public employees. Empirical studies

DOI: 10.4324/9781003416258-7

indicate that the presence of ethical leadership can further enhance the effectiveness of other ethics management infrastructures, such as the code of ethics and ethics training for improving ethical practices in public sector organizations (Asencio, 2022; Hassan et al., 2014).

In this chapter, we focus on the significant role of leadership in shaping an organization's ethics. Our discussion is organized into several sections. We begin by identifying and examining various models of moral aspects of leadership, with a particular focus on their implications for leadership in the public sector. Following this, we delve into the mechanisms through which leaders influence the ethical conduct of their employees and offer actionable recommendations for leaders committed to ethical excellence. We then discuss the role of leadership in ethics management within the context of inter- and intra-organizational collaboration. Finally, we will outline key strategies for cultivating ethical leadership. See Figure 6.1 for the roadmap of the chapter.

What Is Ethical Leadership in the Public Sector?

Ethics, morality, and integrity are essential components of effective leadership. In particular, several leadership constructs in the literature are directly linked to ethics. Those leadership styles have some theoretical and empirical similarities. The leadership style with an ethical perspective introduced to the literature earliest is transformational leadership (Peus et al., 2010). In its initial definition coined by Burns, transformational leadership occurs only when "leaders and followers raise one another to higher levels of morality and motivation beyond self-interest to serve the collective interests" (1978, p 20). Bass (1985) further expanded and developed this leadership construct, focusing on transforming leaders' ability to influence positive follower outcomes beyond ordinary limits. Bass's framework is seen to take on a more value-neutral perspective (Denhardt & Campbell, 2006). Even though the literature indicates that transformational leaders are adept at moral reasoning (Turner et al., 2002), the morality of transformational leadership is only implicitly embedded in his four I's conceptualization: idealized influence, inspirational motivation, intellectual stimulation, and individualized consideration.

Bass's model of transformational leadership is most widely employed; however, a strong, explicit moral dimension is absent from his conceptualization. On the one hand, scholars such as Denhardt and Campbell (2006) argue for bringing the moral and normative elements back to the transformational leadership construct. Particularly in the context of public service, public transformational leadership should integrate democratic values such as integrity, justice, social equity, accountability, citizenship, and public interests.

On the other hand, extensive research and theory development on leadership styles with a clear ethical focus has been conducted. Moral leadership styles, including ethical, authentic, and servant leadership, have been developed and

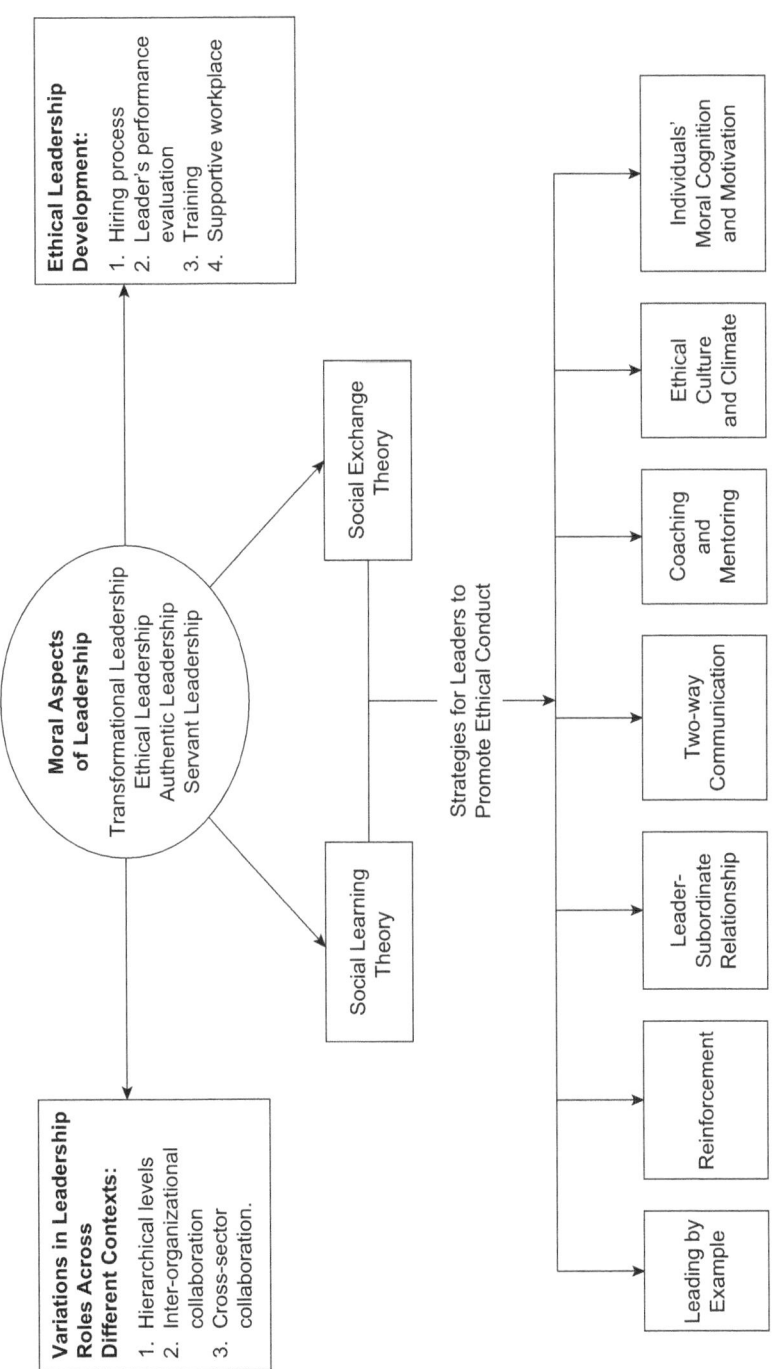

Figure 6.1 The Chapter Structure and the Main Findings.

have gained increasing attention in public management and administration literature over recent decades.

Recognized as one of the positive leadership styles, ethical leadership particularly focuses on the ethical aspects of leading (Mostafa & Abed El-Motalib, 2020). The most comprehensive and widely cited definition of ethical leadership is offered by Brown et al. (2005): "the demonstration of normatively appropriate conduct through personal actions and interpersonal relationships, and the promotion of such conduct to followers through two-way communication, reinforcement, and decision making" (Brown et al., 2005, p. 120). A synthesis of existing studies reveals three major components within the concept of ethical leadership: (1) the leader is an ethical role model, (2) the leader treats people with fairness and respect, and (3) the leader actively manages ethics in the organization (Hassan, 2015; Hassan et al., 2014). The first two components address the moral person facet of ethical leadership, while the last one highlights the idea of being a moral manager (Hassan et al., 2014).

Scholars have suggested that being a moral or virtuous person constitutes the basic expectation for ethical leadership (Shakeel et al., 2019). The fundamental attributes linked to this minimal virtue encompass honesty, altruism, integrity, compassion, and maintaining ethical conduct even when faced with adversity or pressure (Bashir & Hassan, 2020; Brown et al., 2005; Hassan et al., 2014; Shakeel et al., 2019). Furthermore, this type of leader steers an organization not just through their personal virtues and disciplined behavior but also through proficient interpersonal communication and cooperation. To ensure effective communication and cooperation, ethical leaders actively listen to their team members; show them respect; and treat them with fairness, consideration, and dignity (Brown et al., 2005; Brown & Treviño, 2006; Moon & Christensen, 2022). Finally, ethical leaders actively manage ethics within an organization by providing direct guidance and discipline to their subordinates. They encourage ethical behavior among their followers through explicit discussions about ethics, establishing ethical standards, clarifying ethical expectations, rewarding ethical behavior, and sanctioning unethical conduct (Bashir & Hassan, 2020; Brown et al., 2005; Mostafa & Abed El-Motalib, 2020; Shakeel et al., 2019; Wright et al., 2016).

Authentic leaders are known for their strong internal moral standards. Such leaders see themselves as their organizations' "moral standard bearer" (May et al., 2003, p. 253). They possess self-awareness and self-regulation (Luthans & Avolio, 2003). They tend to act ethically and develop ethical leadership not because of external pressure or social forces but because it aligns with their internalized positive virtues and high moral character. When faced with tough ethical challenges, authentic leaders demonstrate a higher moral capacity to deeply and comprehensively assess ethical issues. They consider the perspectives and opinions of various stakeholders before making decisions, even if such insights challenge their own strong beliefs. Moreover, authentic leaders engage with followers in a transparent and balanced manner (May et al., 2003; Vogel et al.,

2023). Authentic leadership has substantial implications for the public sector (Vogel et al., 2023), as it aligns with the relational approaches of leadership style championed by the scholars in public management and administration and is instrumental to "[tackle] public policy issues and [address] organizational and societal problems" (Avolio et al., 2004, p. 802).

Servant leadership is characterized by two critical aspects: "the prioritization of subordinates' concern" and "ethical behavior" (Ehrhart, 2004, p. 70). By examining servant leadership in the context of local government, public administration scholars summarized the key dimensions of public sector servant leadership (Awasthi & Walumbwa, 2022, p. 1089):

> [S]ervant leaders are ethically centered and genuinely people-oriented leaders who strive to maximize the value for followers and various community stakeholders. In addition, they are adept at understanding organizational needs and ensuring organizational goals are met to eventually benefit all the stakeholders, both internal and external to the organization, including the community.

How Can Leaders Influence Followers' Ethical Behaviors?

Existing empirical studies in the public management and administration literature have found a direct positive relationship between ethical leadership and various ethics-related outcomes. These include the integrity of public employees (Tasdoven & Kaya, 2014), their commitment to behaving ethically (Asencio, 2022), and their willingness to report wrongdoing within the organization (Hassan et al., 2014; Wright et al., 2016). Moreover, leaders are found to play an important role in preventing employees from engaging in deviant behaviors such as disobedience of supervisors (De Wolde et al., 2014), bribing and favoritism (Asencio, 2019), workplace incivility (Young et al., 2021), and race-based employment discrimination (Moon & Christensen, 2022).

Two theories, social learning theory and social exchange theory, are useful for explaining how leaders could play an important role in influencing their followers' ethical conduct. Social learning theory suggests that leaders influence ethical and unethical conduct through modeling processes (Brown & Treviño, 2006). According to the theory, people in an organization learn not only from their direct experience but also by observing others' behaviors, including the behaviors of leaders and their consequences. If the consequences of certain behaviors are seen as positive, those behaviors become examples of ethical behavior and are then translated into their own actions under the right circumstances (Asencio, 2019). Given their power, role, and status in the organization, the behavior of leaders serves as a powerful communication mechanism that conveys the ethical values and expectations of appropriate behaviors to the rest of the organization. Leaders who engage in unethical behaviors send a message that deviant behaviors are acceptable, and thus, employees observe and are likely to imitate the unethical conduct; however, if the leaders demonstrate just behaviors and make ethical decisions, their subordinates follow their leaders to be ethical (Moon & Christensen, 2022).

Bandura (1977) emphasized that effective role modeling requires the role model to be a trustworthy source of information on proper and acceptable behaviors. Essentially, managers need to be "moral persons" first (Asencio, 2019). When leaders are seen as legitimate and admirable, employees are inclined to imitate their values and behaviors (Mayer et al., 2009). Jordan et al. (2013) noted that leaders with stronger ethical reasoning compared to their followers are likely to be prominent ethical role models who capture their followers' attention. Additionally, leading by example is not just about grand gestures or effectively handling ethical dilemmas; leaders' everyday behaviors in their personal and professional lives are most influential when it comes to setting an example for followers (Treviño & Brown, 2005).

Leaders can further enhance the ethical conduct of followers through the imposition of consequences on employees. Social learning and modeling involve more than just imitating leaders' behavior. It includes learning from the potential rewards and discipline that result from following or breaking the rules (Bandura, 1986). People tend to repeat behaviors that are rewarded and avoid those that are punished. Employees vicariously and anticipatorily learn what to do, as well as what not to do, through observing the reinforcement actions of the leaders (Brown et al., 2005; Mayer et al., 2009). Therefore, leaders not only act as role models themselves but also turn other employees into models by rewarding their appropriate conduct and disciplining inappropriate conduct (Treviño & Brown, 2005). Integrating moral and integrity values and norms into rewards, recognition, advancement, and punishment processes is a crucial approach a leader can utilize to influence employees' ethical conduct (Grojean et al., 2004; Moon & Christensen, 2022). Leaders should also measure success not solely by the outcomes achieved but also by the processes used to achieve them. This approach rejects unethical methods for increasing performance, stressing that the means are equally important as the ends.

When comparing two influencing approaches from a social learning perspective, it is observed that leaders inspiring employees to mimic their ethical conduct is more effective in influencing employees' ethical behavior compared to reinforcement through reward and punishment. Nostrom (2006, p. 271) asserted that

> employees do not passively fall into line and intimidation and threat do not work . . . the fact that the workforce is no longer subservient doesn't mean that leadership is redundant; however, on the contrary, the new world of work requires even more thoughtful and meaningful leadership.
>
> (Nostrom, 2006, p. 271)

The social exchange process is a second theory that can be used to explain how leaders influence employees' ethical conduct. Social exchange is premised on reciprocity (Gouldner, 1960), where one party in a relationship does something positive for the other, creating an obligation for the other party to pay back with something beneficial (Cropanzano & Mitchell, 2005). High-quality relationships between employees and their leaders that are able to initiate the social exchange processes are characterized by fair treatment of employees, trust in leaders, and employee liking and admiration of their leader (Treviño & Brown, 2005).

Leaders should treat their followers with fairness, respect, consideration, and dignity (Hassan et al., 2014). They should be fair and just when assigning tasks, evaluating performance, and rewarding team members. It is also important for leaders to be skilled in resolving conflicts impartially and to consider their team members' perspectives, ensuring their decisions and actions are fair and just. Leaders should also consider the moral implications of their choices when making significant decisions that could impact others' well-being (Brown et al., 2005; Hassan et al., 2014). Because of the fair and caring treatment and trust they feel, employees tend to identify with the leaders. Therefore, they are more likely to repay favorable treatment from their leaders by behaving in ways that benefit the entire work group and by refraining from unethical behaviors.

As implied by the social exchange theory, leaders can promote ethical conduct among employees through clear and frequent two-way communication about ethics (Asencio, 2019). On the one side, this involves openly emphasizing the importance of ethical conduct, discussing the implications of moral decision-making, clearly defining ethical issues, and communicating clear norms and expectations for ethical behavior.

On the other side, leaders must ensure that the environment is conducive to open and honest dialogue where employees feel comfortable discussing ethical issues and voicing concerns about unethical behavior without fear of retaliation. They should be approachable listeners who welcome open communication and are receptive to employees' mistakes (Asencio, 2019). They can encourage members to share their perspectives and experiences related to ethical issues. The importance of creating a safe environment is supported by a study that examined the shared efficacy beliefs among group members regarding their ability to speak up on ethical issues. Huang and Paterson (2017) found that evaluating the risks in a given environment is essential for employees to make the decision to raise ethical concerns. Group ethical voice efficacy plays an important role in translating the positive influence of leadership to the group's ethical performance (Huang & Paterson, 2017). This implies that leaders should actively work on creating an environment in which employees have the confidence to express their views on ethical matters (Huang & Paterson, 2017).

Additionally, leaders can support their employees' ethical behaviors through coaching and mentoring. By identifying specific ethical challenges faced by employees and providing individualized guidance on the appropriate course of action, leaders can help reduce ambiguity surrounding ethical events, increase ethical awareness, and strengthen employees' ability to address ethical issues and make ethical decisions (Grojean et al., 2004).

Following social learning and social exchange theories, empirical studies have identified additional organizational and individual factors that translate leaders' influence on ethics-related outcomes. The first mechanism is an ethical culture and climate. A favorable ethical culture works as a shared understanding among members that effectively convey ethical norms in the workplace environment. Leadership should play a pivotal role in creating the right conditions and organizational culture for ethics (Kuenzi et al., 2020; Liu et al., 2018; Mayer et al., 2010). Some examined the organization's politics, which is part of the organization's climate. Ethical behavior may be discouraged in an organization with a high level of perceived organizational politics. This is because employees may feel that they would face complicated entanglement of interests and do not have enough support to speak up against unethical behaviors. Therefore, Cheng et al. (2019) suggested that ethical leaders can reduce employees' perceptions of organizational politics and encourage a positive climate to facilitate ethical behaviors.

While organizational factors and processes shape the choices that individuals make regarding ethical issues, individuals' core moral cognition and motivation also influence their behavior independently of external forces. Moral disengagement refers to the cognitive structures individuals use to justify their unethical behaviors without experiencing distress (Bandura, 1999). This is a significant factor in predicting the likelihood of individuals engaging in actual deviant behaviors (Bandura et al., 1996). Research indicates that leaders play a crucial role in preventing their followers from relying on morally disengaged thinking in the workplace by activating their internal self-regulatory systems. This can be done by reminding employees of their own internal sanctions against immoral behavior (Moore et al., 2019).

Another important cognitive mechanism is role ethicality, which refers to the degree to which acting ethically is seen as part of the job requirements among organizational members (Paterson & Huang, 2019). Even when not driven by their own moral conscience, employees who view ethical behavior as part of their role expectations are less likely to engage in unethical behaviors. The role of the leader is especially important in shaping the followers' role expectations. In their empirical study, Paterson and Huang (2019) found that ethical leadership had a negative indirect effect on employees' unethical behavior by constructing their role ethicality.

Leaders have the ability to influence the ethical behavior of public employees by nurturing their desire to serve the public, also known as public service motivation (PSM). Public employees with a high level of PSM typically hold internalized public values and interests, making them more likely to see unethical conduct within their organizations as conflicting with their personal values. Therefore, public leaders can work on enhancing their followers' PSM to improve their ethical awareness and their willingness to engage in ethical conduct (Wright et al., 2016).

Implications of how leaders influence organizational ethics can also come from studies examining what may be driving costly misconduct in organizations. According to Buckingham and Coffman (1999), it is important for managers to understand the limitations of their employees and to be mindful of the goals they set for them. Setting unrealistic goals that cannot be achieved legally may imply that employees "should achieve this target through whatever means" (Yeboah-Assiamah et al., 2016, p. 327). Unrealistic goals can drive public employees to engage in deviant behaviors.

Roles of Multiple Leaders

When discussing the role of leadership, we should also place it in a broader and complex organizational and inter-organizational context. First, leaders can come from different hierarchical levels of the organization. Each has different levels of authority and functions, interacts with employees in different ways, and thus applies different mechanisms to transmit values and expectations (Mayer et al., 2009). Some literature pays attention to the different roles of executive-level and supervisory-level leaders in shaping ethics-related outcomes. Top leaders have a wide-ranging impact as they convey the organization's overall vision and objectives; make decisions on broad strategies and policies; and establish formal structures, work processes, and control systems. Executive-level leaders mostly shape the ethical conduct of the organization through their broader influence on the organization's overall culture and ethical value system, as well as through communicating a strong message about ethics and values. They also establish structures and policies that provide clear expectations regarding ethics to the members (Grojean et al., 2004). Even though often perceived from a distance, executive leaders as a "reputational phenomenon" should be playing visible and salient ethical role models to their subordinates (Brown & Trevinño, 2006, p. 597). Finally, top leaders develop and mentor immediate supervisors to instill ethical values and make sure that "what 'trickles down' [throughout the organization] is truly representative of their presumably good ethical intentions" (Weaver et al., 2005, p. 324).

Direct supervisory leaders act as a bridge between top management and employees. They interpret the strategies and policies (e.g., ethical guidelines) set by executives and exercise their discretion to carry them out. Therefore, they play a crucial role in reducing employees' uncertainty regarding ethical policies and ensuring their consistent implementation throughout the organization (Grojean et al., 2004). Additionally, employees interact with their supervisors more often and more intimately than with top management. The role modeling effects from direct managers and supervisors might have the strongest effect and thus often serve as the main influence on individual ethical behavior. When faced with ethical dilemmas, employees are more likely to observe their immediate supervisors' behaviors and attitudes for guidance on appropriate responses to ethical situations (Posner & Schmidt, 1984). Lastly, direct leaders are better positioned to monitor and assess employee behavior, allowing them to provide coaching and mentoring to promote ethical behavior through social interactions (Mayer et al., 2009).

In a collaborative networking setting, such as local government, there are leaders from various hierarchical positions, as well as leaders with managerial authority and those with electoral power. In this context, leadership is distributed, collaborative, and interconnected, and involves overlapping responsibilities (Gronn, 2002). Therefore, the traditional model of ethical, values-based leadership at the level of specific stakeholder groups is of limited use in such a collaborative networking setting (Iles & Macaulay, 2007). This requires that political leaders and managerial leaders take different roles to promote good conduct and foster an ethical culture, where the former "set an example by endorsing exemplary behavior, denouncing improper conduct, using rhetoric such as making speeches, and influencing their political group," while the latter "provide resources to show that they take the issue seriously by appointing officers to support training and process complaints" (Downe et al., 2016, p. 907).

When managing ethics with various leaders, whether across different hierarchical levels or between political and managerial leaders, it is crucial for these leaders to work together to promote ethical conduct. They need to have a shared vision for the organization's ethics, consistently communicate, and apply ethical standards. By working together in this dedicated manner, we can guarantee the preservation of a sustainable and stable ethical environment (Grojean et al., 2004).

Sector Differences in Leaders' Role in Ethics Management

This chapter has reviewed studies on the importance of leaders and how they influence their followers' ethical and unethical behavior, drawing from both generic and public management literature. Those mechanisms and managerial practices for leaders to promote ethical conduct can be applied to both public and private sector contexts. Moral aspects of leadership are crucial in all types of organizations. However, any single style of leadership that is ethically oriented may not be suitable for all types of organizations. Some scholars assert that it is important to understand how ethical leadership differs across public, private, and nonprofit sectors (Heres & Lasthuizen, 2012). Given the long-standing discussion of public-private distinction, it is reasonable to expect that what constitutes ethical leadership behavior may vary across these sectors. On the one hand, public and nonprofit organizations are subject to political control and external scrutiny and are expected to uphold public values and the common good. As a result, managers in these organizations may feel compelled to exhibit more explicit ethical leadership and implement formal ethics programs (Heres & Lasthuizen, 2012).

On the other hand, public and nonprofit organizations face multiple and even competing stakeholders' needs and interests. Ethical dilemmas are more intricate and prominent in these organizations, putting managers in ethically challenging situations more frequently. As a result, public and nonprofit managers need to possess stronger ethical competencies to address these moral dilemmas effectively than their private counterparts (Heres & Lasthuizen, 2012). Additionally, employees in public organizations are believed to be intrinsically motivated by prosocial attitudes, such as PSM. Therefore, the way leaders in the public sector communicate the significance of ethical values may be different from those in the private sector (Heres & Lasthuizen, 2012). Heres and Lasthuizen (2012) interviewed a non-random sample of public, hybrid, and private sector managers in the Netherlands and found that even though managers' views on ethical leadership are similar across public, private, and nonprofit organizations, there are subtle differences across sectors in how these managers conceive ethical leadership. Managers in the public sector place more emphasis on values and traits with a specific societal focus, while their counterparts in the private sector tend to prioritize traits such as honesty when defining ethical leadership. Additionally, public and private managers differ in the frequency and style of communication about ethics. Public managers tend to communicate ethics more frequently and regularly, preferring a more explicit way to communicate ethical values compared to private managers. It is essential to be aware of these differences in ethics management in public-private sector collaborations.

How to Cultivate Ethical Leadership?

Given the positive impact of ethics-related leadership on fostering employee ethical attitudes and behavior, it is worthwhile for public organizations to utilize general human resource practices to increase ethical leadership. One way to achieve this is through the hiring process. Dan Burnham, Raytheon Company's chairman and CEO, pointed out: "What do we look for in a leadership candidate with respect to integrity? What we're really looking for when we recruit leaders are people who have developed an inner gyroscope of ethical principles. We look for people for whom ethical thinking is part of what they do" (Fulmer, 2004, p. 311). Organizations can outline specific ethical traits such as fairness, integrity, honesty, trustworthiness, caring, and the ability to listen to employees' concerns for the particular leadership role (Hoch et al., 2018; Moon & Christensen, 2022). They can also utilize selection tools to identify candidates who are both moral people and moral managers. Integrity assessment tests that evaluate the managerial style and ethical dispositions of candidates can be effective tools. Discussing moral issues and ethical dilemmas during job interviews can also increase the likelihood of selecting leaders with high ethical standards for an organization (Mayer et al., 2009; Mayer et al., 2010).

Aside from the hiring process, it is also crucial to incorporate an integrity and morality dimension into the leaders' performance evaluation structure (Hoch et al., 2018; May et al., 2003). For example, the performance metric can assess leaders' commitment to ethical role modeling, their orientation to prioritize long-term ethical actions over short-term pressures, and their use of transactional rewards to promote ethical behavior among their team members (May et al., 2003).

Organizations should consider investing in ethical training programs to enhance the ethical capabilities of their leaders. Training is widely considered essential for shaping the ethical conduct of individuals within an organization. According to Perlman et al. (2021), ethics-related training programs can differ in their approach, emphasizing either compliance or integrity. Compliance-focused programs concentrate on ensuring individuals follow the rules and regulations, making sure they understand what is expected of them and the repercussions of non-compliance. Conversely, integrity-focused programs seek to embed ethical values and emphasize the significance of ethical behavior, helping individuals internalize these principles as a guide for their actions in the workplace. "While the compliance-based approach can be effected through a short-term program . . . the integrity-based . . . requires the more difficult and longer-term task of transmitting values in training content to build an ethical culture" (Perlman et al., 2021, p. 496).

Many organizations prioritize ethics training for employees, often overlooking the crucial need for training managers (Mayer et al., 2009). It is essential to offer specialized training aimed at enhancing public managers' skills in promoting ethical decision-making, encouraging ethical behavior among their teams, and upholding the integrity of public organizations. The training programs should be designed as integrity-based training, seeking to help public managers comprehend the fundamental principles and characteristics of ethical leadership (Asencio, 2019; Hoch et al., 2018). The programs should also assist public managers in developing the skills and competence needed to cope with the challenges facing the exercise of ethical leadership behaviors and effectively manage an organizational culture that discourages misconduct and promotes ethical behaviors among employees. These trainings can cover topics such as increasing leaders' awareness of the moral aspects of a given situation, strengthening leaders' moral efficacy and moral courage, enhancing their moral reasoning, and the significance of trusting relationships in influencing employee attitudes and behavior (Mayer et al., 2010).

A workplace dedicated to upholding morality is also essential in sustaining and nurturing moral leadership. It enables leaders with high ethical standards to consistently exhibit behaviors that reflect their moral values (Mayer et al., 2012). Mentoring relations with role models they respect, including other leaders or individuals above them in the organizational hierarchy, should be established (May et al., 2003).

It is essential to acknowledge that the methods and strategies described earlier should target all levels of leadership within an organization. Training programs created for supervisors and middle managers are likely to produce the quickest effects on employees, while those intended for top executives will mainly influence supervisors, ultimately reaching all members of the organization. Applying ethical interventions across various levels will yield superior outcomes, enabling organizations to maximize the return on their investment in leadership training and performance management (Mayer et al., 2009).

Conclusion

Public leaders play a crucial role in shaping followers' ethical behavior, especially with the growing public concern about ethics and integrity in the public sector. In this chapter, we reviewed the literature to understand the characteristics of moral aspects of leadership and their impact on ethical outcomes. Social learning theory and social exchange theory have offered theoretical frameworks for comprehending how leaders can shape the ethical behavior and integrity of their employees.

We also provide an overview of strategies that leaders can employ for ethical purposes, including role modeling, reinforcement, high-quality leader-subordinate relationships, two-way communication about ethics, coaching and mentoring, cultivating an ethical work environment, and shaping employees' cognitive structure for ethical decision-making.

In the midst of collaborations and cooperation across various government agencies, as well as between government agencies, nonprofit organizations, and private entities, we also highlight the diverse effects leadership can have on ethics management in more intricate settings. It is essential to recognize the differences in roles, expectations, and strategies among leaders from different organizational contexts, including different hierarchical levels, varying sources of power, and different sectors. Given these differences, when leaders collaborate, they should strive to cultivate mutual understanding to improve the ethical execution of public policies and service provision.

Finally, this chapter concludes with strategies for fostering ethical leadership. The literature suggests two primary methods: incorporating ethics as a key factor in hiring and promotion decisions and offering ethics training to leaders. Furthermore, it is essential to have a supportive environment and system dedicated to encouraging moral leadership. Future research can explore under what circumstances public ethical leadership is more or less effective. Apart from the study by Bashir and Hassan (2020), which discovered that implementing a fair performance evaluation system can boost the impact of ethical leaders in fighting corruption in government and nonprofit organizations, there is limited research on the factors (e.g., job characteristics, follower characteristics) that can moderate the effects of moral leadership behaviors. This area of research could further enhance our understanding of the influences of ethical leadership in shaping the integrity of public organizations.

References

Asencio, H. D. (2019). The effect of ethical leadership on bribing and favoritism: A field research study. *Public Integrity*, *21*(3), 263–285.

Asencio, H. D. (2022). Ethical leadership and commitment to behave ethically in government agencies. *International Journal of Public Administration*, *45*(12), 907–916.

Avolio, B. J., Gardner, W. L., Walumbwa, F. O., Luthans, F., & May, D. R. (2004). Unlocking the mask: A look at the process by which authentic leaders impact follower attitudes and behaviors. *The Leadership Quarterly*, *15*(6), 801–823.

Awasthi, P., & Walumbwa, F. O. (2022). Antecedents and consequences of servant leadership in local governance: Evidence from three case studies. *Public Administration Review*, *82*(6), 1077–1094.

Bandura, A. (1977). *Social learning theory*. Prentice Hall.

Bandura, A. (1986). *Social foundations of thought and action: A social cognitive theory*. Prentice-Hall.

Bandura, A. (1999). Moral disengagement in the perpetration of inhumanities. *Personality and Social Psychology Review*, *3*, 193–209.

Bandura, A., Barbaranelli, C., Caprara, G. V., & Pastorelli, C. (1996). Mechanisms of moral disengagement in the exercise of moral agency. *Journal of Personality and Social Psychology*, *71*, 364–374.

Bashir, M., & Hassan, S. (2020). The need for ethical leadership in combating corruption. *International Review of Administrative Sciences*, *86*(4), 673–690.

Bass, B. M. (1985). *Leadership and performance beyond expectations*. Free Press, Collier Macmillan.

Brown, M. E., & Treviño, L. K. (2006). Ethical leadership: A review and future directions. *The Leadership Quarterly*, *17*(6), 595–616.

Brown, M. E., Treviño, L. K., & Harrison, D. A. (2005). Ethical leadership: A social learning perspective for construct development and testing. *Organizational Behavior and Human Decision Processes*, *97*(2), 117–134.

Buckingham, M., & Coffman, C. (1999). First break all the rules; What the world's greatest managers do differently. Simon and Schuster.

Burns, J. M. (1978). *Leadership*. Harper and Row Publishers.

Cheng, J., Bai, H., & Yang, X. (2019). Ethical leadership and internal whistleblowing: A mediated moderation model. *Journal of Business Ethics*, *155*, 115–130.

Cropanzano, R., & Mitchell, M. S. (2005). Social exchange theory: An interdisciplinary review. *Journal of Management*, *31*(6), 874–900.

De Wolde, A., Groenendaal, J., Helsloot, I., & Schmidt, A. (2014). An explorative study on the connection between ethical leadership, prototypicality and organizational misbehavior in a Dutch fire service. *International Journal of Leadership Studies*, *8*(2), 18–43.

Denhardt, J. V., & Campbell, K. B. (2006). The role of democratic values in transformational leadership. *Administration & Society*, *38*(5), 556–572.

Downe, J., Cowell, R., & Morgan, K. (2016). What determines ethical behavior in public organizations: Is it rules or leadership? *Public Administration Review*, *76*(6), 898–909.

Ehrhart, M. G. (2004). Leadership and procedural justice climate as antecedents of unit-level organizational citizenship behavior. *Personnel Psychology*, *57*(1), 61–94.

Frost, J., & Tischer, S. (2014). Unmasking collective corruption: The dynamics of corrupt routines. *European Management Review*, *11*(3–4), 191–207.

Fulmer, R. M. (2004). The challenge of ethical leadership. *Organizational Dynamics*, *33*(3), 307–317.

Gouldner, A. W. (1960). The norm of reciprocity. *American Sociological Review*, *25*, 165–167.

Grojean, M. W., Resick, C. J., Dickson, M. W., & Smith, D. B. (2004). Leaders, values, and organizational climate: Examining leadership strategies for establishing an organizational climate regarding ethics. *Journal of Business Ethics*, *55*, 223–241.

Gronn, P. (2002). Distributed leadership. In K. Leithwood & P. Hallinger (Eds.), *Second International handbook of educational leadership & administration*. Springer International Publishing.

Hassan, S. (2015). The importance of ethical leadership and personal control in promoting improvement-centered voice among government employees. *Journal of Public Administration Research and Theory, 25*(3), 697–719.

Hassan, S., Wright, B. E., & Yukl, G. (2014). Does ethical leadership matter in government? Effects on organizational commitment, absenteeism, and willingness to report ethical problems. *Public Administration Review, 74*(3), 333–343.

Heres, L., & Lasthuizen, K. (2012). What's the difference? Ethical leadership in public, hybrid and private sector organizations. *Journal of Change Management, 12*(4), 441–466.

Hoch, J. E., Bommer, W. H., Dulebohn, J. H., & Wu, D. (2018). Do ethical, authentic, and servant leadership explain variance above and beyond transformational leadership? A meta-analysis. *Journal of Management, 44*(2), 501–529.

Huang, L., & Paterson, T. A. (2017). Group ethical voice: Influence of ethical leadership and impact on ethical performance. *Journal of Management, 43*(4), 1157–1184.

Iles, P., & Macaulay, M. (2007). Putting principles into practice: Developing ethical leadership in local government. *International Journal of Leadership in Public Services, 3*(3), 15–28.

Jordan, J., Brown, M. E., Treviño, L. K., & Finkelstein, S. (2013). Someone to look up to: Executive–follower ethical reasoning and perceptions of ethical leadership. *Journal of Management, 39*(3), 660–683.

Kuenzi, M., Mayer, D. M., & Greenbaum, R. L. (2020). Creating an ethical organizational environment: The relationship between ethical leadership, ethical organizational climate, and unethical behavior. *Personnel Psychology, 73*(1), 43–71.

Liu, Y., Fuller, B., Hester, K., Bennett, R. J., & Dickerson, M. S. (2018). Linking authentic leadership to subordinate behaviors. *Leadership & Organization Development Journal, 39*(2), 218–233.

Luthans, F., & Avolio, B. J. (2003). Authentic leadership development. *Positive Organizational Scholarship, 241*(258), 1–26.

May, D. R., Chan, A. Y., Hodges, T. D., & Avolio, B. J. (2003). Developing the moral component of authentic leadership. *Organizational Dynamics, 32*(3), 247–260.

Mayer, D. M., Aquino, K., Greenbaum, R. L., & Kuenzi, M. (2012). Who displays ethical leadership, and why does it matter? An examination of antecedents and consequences of ethical leadership. *Academy of Management Journal, 55*(1), 151–171.

Mayer, D. M., Kuenzi, M., & Greenbaum, R. L. (2010). Examining the link between ethical leadership and employee misconduct: The mediating role of ethical climate. *Journal of Business Ethics, 95*, 7–16.

Mayer, D. M., Kuenzi, M., Greenbaum, R., Bardes, M., & Salvador, R. B. (2009). How low does ethical leadership flow? Test of a trickle-down model. *Organizational Behavior and Human Decision Processes, 108*(1), 1–13.

Moon, K. K., & Christensen, R. K. (2022). Moderating diversity, collective commitment, and discrimination: The role of ethical leaders in the public sector. *Journal of Public Administration Research and Theory, 32*(2), 380–397.

Moore, C., Mayer, D. M., Chiang, F. F., Crossley, C., Karlesky, M. J., & Birtch, T. A. (2019). Leaders matter morally: The role of ethical leadership in shaping employee moral cognition and misconduct. *American Psychological Association, 104*(1), 123.

Mostafa, A. M. S., & Abed El-Motalib, E. A. (2020). Ethical leadership, work meaningfulness, and work engagement in the public sector. *Review of Public Personnel Administration, 40*(1), 112–131.

Nostrom, K. (2006). Leading in interesting times. In *Business, the ultimate resources* (2nd ed.) Basic Books.

Paterson, T. A., & Huang, L. (2019). Am I expected to be ethical? A role-definition perspective of ethical leadership and unethical behavior. *Journal of Management, 45*(7), 2837–2860.

Perlman, B. J., Reddick, C. G., Demir, T., & Ogilby, S. M. (2021). What do local governments teach about in ethics training? Compliance versus integrity. *Journal of Public Affairs Education, 27*(4), 490–507.

Peus, C., Kerschreiter, R., Frey, D., & Traut-Mattausch, E. (2010). What is the value? Economic effects of ethically oriented leadership. *Zeitschrift für Psychologie/Journal of Psychology, 218,* 198–212.

Pew. (2023, September 19). *Public trust in government: 1958–2023.* Retrieved from www.pewresearch.org/politics/2023/09/19/public-trust-in-government-1958-2023/#:~:text=Public%20trust%20in%20the%20federal,the%20time%E2%80%9D%20(15%25).

Posner, B., & Schmidt, W. (1984). Values and the American manager: An update. *California Management Review, XXVI,* 202–216.

Shakeel, F., Kruyen, P. M., & Van Thiel, S. (2019). Ethical leadership as process: A conceptual proposition. *Public Integrity, 21*(6), 613–624.

Tasdoven, H., & Kaya, M. (2014). The impact of ethical leadership on police officers' code of silence and integrity: Results from the Turkish national police. *International Journal of Public Administration, 37*(9), 529–541.

Treviño, L. K., & Brown, M. E. (2005). The role of leaders in influencing unethical behavior in the workplace. *Managing Organizational Deviance, 5,* 69–87.

Turner, N., Barling, J., Epitropaki, O., Butcher, V., & Milner, C. (2002). Transformational leadership and moral reasoning. *Journal of Applied Psychology, 87*(2), 304.

Vogel, R., Vogel, D., & Reuber, A. (2023). Finding a mission in bureaucracies: How authentic leadership and red tape interact. *Public Administration, 101*(4), 1503–1525.

Weaver, G. R., Treviño, L. K., & Agle, B. (2005). "Somebody I look up to": Ethical role models in organizations. *Organizational Dynamics, 34*(4), 313–330.

Wright, B. E., Hassan, S., & Park, J. (2016). Does a public service ethic encourage ethical behaviour? Public service motivation, ethical leadership and the willingness to report ethical problems. *Public Administration, 94*(3), 647–663.

Yeboah-Assiamah, E., Asamoah, K., Bawole, J. N., & Buabeng, T. (2016). Public sector leadership-subordinate ethical diffusion conundrum: Perspectives from developing African countries. *Journal of Public Affairs, 16*(4), 320–330.

Young, K. A., Hassan, S., & Hatmaker, D. M. (2021). Towards understanding workplace incivility: Gender, ethical leadership and personal control. *Public Management Review, 23*(1), 31–52.

7 The Power of Organizational Values

Communication, Conflict, and Alignment in Shaping Employee Behavior and Decision-Making

Chevanese Samms Brown and Karen D. Sweeting

Introduction

Values exist as core beliefs embedded within organizational systems and culture to provide direction and purpose (Weston, 2021), ultimately impacting what is practiced, prioritized, and operationalized in organizations (Daft, 2008; Denhardt & Denhardt, 2015; Kaufman, 1956). Public sector values of transparency, ethics, trust, accountability, integrity, and fairness are expected components of organizational value systems. Values serve as the bedrock of ethical frameworks within organizations (Molina, 2015; Schermerhorn, 2013; Van Wart, 1998; Waldo, 1984).

Leadership and management are crucial in shaping, sustaining, and facilitating organizational values. Leaders set the tone and direction of the organization (Maidment & Eldridge, 2000), serve as role models, and establish top-level influence (Sweeting, 2022). Through a commitment to ethical standards and organizational values, leaders demonstrate value hierarchies that employees interpret and internalize, shaping their behavior in the workplace.

In May 2024, for the first time in America's history, a former president was convicted of felony crimes (e.g., falsifying records to conceal hush money) (Sisak et al., 2024). Another historical moment was cemented in September of the same year when New York City's (NYC's) first *modern-era* mayor (Barry, 2024) was charged with accepting bribes and was the first to be indicted while in office (McHugh, 2024). The implications of these two examples demonstrate how individual behaviors and actions through the promotion of self-interest, a lack of integrity and accountability, and disrespect for public office and core public service values can generate negative externalities in public service. The first example demonstrates a violation of public trust with implications that erode confidence in government and credibility of public service. Similarly, the indictment of NYC's mayor exposes the violation of public service values of integrity, trust, and transparency. These examples indelibly taint behaviors and the reputation of public service employees and organizations they represent. Considering

DOI: 10.4324/9781003416258-8

that leadership behaviors influence employee behaviors (Detert & Burris, 2007) and values act as a criterion for action (Waldo, 1984), the failure of these two public figures to exemplify core public service values may create a ripple effect, extending, expanding, and normalizing a detachment from public service value positions.

This means that the behaviors leading to conviction of the former president and charges against the NYC mayor translate into an assault on the values of the public organizations they serve(d) resulting in a misalignment of organizational priorities, negatively altering employee and leadership attitudes and behaviors. Denhardt and Denhardt (2002) argue that values shape attitudes toward goals, legitimacy, and standards of conduct, highlighting the need to bridge existing gaps.

Kaufman (1956) asserts that institutions are organized and operate in alignment with shifting values over time. He argues that while one set of values may dominate, other values are never totally disregarded but are often subordinated. Dose (1997) further defines values as "evaluative standards relating to work or the work environment by which individuals discern what is 'right' or assess the importance of preferences" (pp. 227–228). These definitions highlight the political, economic, technological, legal, and sociological factors that continue to shape the prioritization of values over time, emphasizing the importance of context, leadership, and external influences as key variables. In today's volatile political landscape, values are critical to democratic governance. Van Wart (1998) cautions that values are often confused with ethics, which is just one part of the broader values discussion.

This chapter explores the significance of organizational values in shaping employee behavior, focusing on how values are communicated, shared, and sometimes in conflict. It introduces nine primary value types that influence decision-making, leadership, and employee behavior, leading into a discussion on value alignment with employee actions and the paradigms of Traditional Public Administration, New Public Management (NPM), and New Public Service (NPS). By offering a comprehensive analysis, the chapter fosters dialogue on the transformative nature of values and their dynamic role in organizational systems. It emphasizes value-based management as a key driver in creating effective and adaptable value systems. The chapter concludes by advocating for an integrated approach that weaves integrity and value-congruence into evolving organizational values, ethical standards, and culture, forming a cohesive and effective framework for public management.

Values at the Core: Communicating Organizational Values in the Workplace

Organizational values reflect the core drivers of an organization's behaviors and actions (Barnard, 1938; Box, 2015; Denhardt & Denhardt, 2002; Weston, 2021). The literature portrays these values as multi-dimensional and shaped by different temporal orientations (Finegan, 2000). They are influenced by factors such as culture (Bowman, 1990; Schein & Schein, 2017), identity, socialization (Barnard, 1938; Dose, 1997), social control (Argandoña, 2003), and person-organization fit (Amos & Weathington, 2008; Kroeger, 1995). Additionally, research highlights that an organization's ethos and culture are critical in shaping employee behavior and decision-making, particularly when values conflict (Spicer, 2009).

In the context of administration and management, organizational values play a crucial role in defining the ethical framework and operational ethos that guide employees as they navigate competing moral perspectives and make decisions that impact those they serve (Spicer, 2009). In highly competitive industries, organizations rely upon their core, functional, and pragmatic values, along with discretionary authority, to distinguish between right and wrong in how they improve their products or services. The outcomes of these decisions may be both positive and negative.

Employees often express support for "the values of the organization," but what does this truly mean? How do individuals identify with, support, and embody organizational values in their behavior? Employees are typically bound by organizational policies and practices, with values communicated through formal mechanisms like mission statements, codes of conduct, and policy documents, as well as informal channels such as organizational norms, practices, stories, and leadership behaviors (Bourne & Jenkins, 2013; Schein & Schein, 2017; Stevens, 1999; Weston, 2021). The effective communication and integration of these values into daily activities of employees are pivotal for organizational coherence. To this end, several authors (Herold & Schlegel, 2023; Jannat et al., 2022; Paine, 1994) have clarified distinct differences between integrity-based (based on values) and compliance-based (Roberts, 2009) (based on adherence to standards) approaches to public management, while Perlman et al. (2023) advocate for an integrated approach that combines integrity-based with compliance-based elements.

However, the translation of these values into tangible actions is often a complex process. Figure 7.1 illustrates how an employee may be introduced or socialized into value orientations, shaping their perception of value alignment or misalignment with the organization.

The communication of organizational values can be both symbolic and substantive, embedded in "the most mundane everyday choices" (Spicer, 2009, p. 541). Employees' awareness of these values within an organization is shaped by employee orientation programs (shared); mission and values statements (espoused); and materials such as the code of conduct, organizational policies, and collective bargaining agreements (written). Employees also learn values through socialization (shared and practiced), direct application (practiced), verbal communication (stated), and aims (aspirational).

Bourne and Jenkins (2013) discuss the temporal nature of how organizational values are communicated, highlighting gaps between espoused, written, and shared values versus those actually practiced. The way values are shared has a

Figure 7.1 How Organizational Values May Be Communicated.

profound impact on organizational culture and influences employee perception of their roles and responsibilities. These perceptions are tied to how employees understand problems and what they have been socialized to see as normative behavior (Bourne & Jenkins, 2013; Schein & Schein, 2017; Weston, 2021).

Individuals encounter, internalize, and practice values in diverse ways, and their responses vary depending on context, awareness, and their analysis of a situation. Recognizing that value tradeoffs may conflict with individual or organizational priorities and expectations is crucial in managing these dynamics effectively. In the same way that employers develop a code of ethics, they should develop a *code of values* embedding organizational values into policies, behaviors, and procedures. Further empiricism is warranted to explore and develop this mechanism that aligns employees' actions with organizational values. To incentivize employees to uphold these values, organizations should consider incorporating them into performance management systems, so that employees are evaluated and rewarded for demonstrating value-aligned behaviors. Merely requiring employees to acknowledge a code of values in the same way they do a code of ethics or organizational manual during onboarding is not enough—organizations need to actively promote a culture where employees internalize and practice the organization's values. By actively championing a culture of organizational commitment and employee ownership of values, public organizations can foster ethical conduct and build trust with stakeholders.

It is not enough to state values in a code of conduct; while this introduces values through orientation and socialization, it is primarily regulatory and compliance-based. It does not guide employees on how to reflect on and reason through specific situations. When employees want to do the right thing and the "right" thing is not clear, how do employees make the "right" value-based decision? In their daily responsibilities, employees are often forced to make tough choices and decisions and often rely on colleagues they trust or who may have experienced similar situations. However, an organization's culture that clearly communicates core values builds a support system that helps employees make better decisions. This clarity reduces the risk of compromised decision-making and ensures actions align with the organization's values, ultimately serving the best interest of the public.

A lack of clarity around values creates ethical dilemmas and fosters an environment where ethical lapses can easily occur (Weston, 2021), as demonstrated in earlier examples. Significant gaps often exist between what is written, stated, and practiced within organizations, leading to pressure for employees to conform to these inconsistent standards. These gaps are also evident in the disconnect between how values are communicated and the expectation that employees live out those values versus the reality they face (Durand et al., 2019). While employees are expected to embody organizational values, shifting priorities, leadership tensions, and varying conditions of stability or uncertainty can cause values to fluctuate (Bourne & Jenkins, 2013). As discussed earlier, employees often rely on informal networks and peers for guidance when values are unclear, underscoring the need for a supportive culture that reinforces core values. Clear communication of values is essential not only in formal documents like codes of conduct but also in everyday actions and decisions. This ensures employees understand how to adopt and apply these values in their behavior, aligning their actions with organizational goals and reducing ambiguity to promote value-congruence. Ultimately, clarity around values strengthens ethical decision-making and promotes organizational integrity.

Building on the discussion of value communication and gaps between what is espoused and practiced, employees are frequently required to navigate the multifaceted, abstract, and often conflicting values that they encounter daily. They face the challenge of determining which values should guide their behavior and how to reconcile value pluralism and incongruence. As Spicer notes, value conflict "represents not simply an ethical problem in terms of what we should do, but also a political problem in terms of how we are to coexist with others" (p. 539). This highlights the complexity of aligning personal, organizational, and societal values within decision-making processes.

To provide a clearer framework for understanding the impact of values on behavior, we introduce in Table 7.1 nine key types of organizational values, each

Table 7.1 Key Organizational Value Types and Their Associated Behavioral Drivers

Value Types	Description	Associated Values	Sources
Organizational Values	Espoused or stated guiding principles that shape the behaviors, decisions, and actions within an organization. These values reflect the organization's ethos and culture, influencing how it interacts with internal and external stakeholders.	Collective responsibility Accountability Trust Humanness Participative	Box, 2015; Bowman, 1990; Bozeman, 2007; Finegan, 2000; Van Wart, 1998; Weston, 2021
Public Service Values	Principles and standards that guide the conduct, decisions, and actions of individuals and organizations. These values are rooted in the ethos of serving the public interest and ensuring the welfare of the community served.	Respect for democratic principles Integrity Accountability Efficiency Transparency Equity	Box, 2015; Denhardt & Denhardt, 2002; Waldo, 1984
Professional Values	Core principles and ethical standards guide the behavior, decisions, and practices of individuals within a specific profession. These values reflect the ideals and responsibilities inherent in the professional role, providing a framework for responding to cues, pressures, and demands from the organization.	Integrity Competence Accountability Fairness Professionalism Professional Competence	Molina & McKeown, 2012; Spicer, 2009; Weston, 2021
Personal/Individual Values	Individual interpretation of values based on fundamental beliefs and guiding principles shape an individual's attitudes, behaviors, and decisions in life. These values represent what is important to a person, influencing how they perceive the world, interact with others, and prioritize their goals. They are often developed through life experiences, cultural background, and personal reflections, and they form the foundation of one's moral compass and ethical framework.	Honesty Responsibility Empathy Freedom Culture Personal Credibility	Molina & McKeown, 2012; Weston, 2021
Social Values	These values reflect the collective attitudes and beliefs about what is considered desirable, appropriate, and beneficial for the common good according to social value priorities and shared principles and norms that a community or society collectively recognizes as important.	Equity Responsibility Empathy Justice Community	Schein & Schein, 2017; Weston, 2021

(Continued)

Table 7.1 (Continued)

Value Types	Description	Associated Values	Sources
Leadership/ Managerial Values	Core principles and beliefs that guide the behavior, decision-making, and leadership style of individuals in management or leadership positions. Values sanctioned and practiced by leaders/managers influence how they interact with their teams, make strategic decisions, and influence the organizational culture.	Integrity Fairness Transparency Collaboration Innovation	Bansal, 2003; Bourne & Jenkins, 2013
Ethical Values	Ethical values are part and parcel of organizational values. They are the fundamental principles and standards that guide individuals and organizations in distinguishing right from wrong and making decisions that are morally sound and socially responsible. These values reflect the ethical beliefs and commitments that shape behavior and interactions, promoting integrity, fairness, and respect for others.	Integrity Respect Courage Benevolence Honesty	Loyens & Maesschalck, 2010; Weston, 2021
Public Interest Values	Prioritize the well-being and welfare of the general public over individual or special interests. These values guide the actions and decisions of public practitioners, organizations, and government entities to ensure that the common good is served and that public resources are used ethically and effectively to benefit public life.	Fairness Equity Transparency Social Responsibility Responsiveness Inclusivity Accountability Justice	Box, 2015; Denhardt & Denhardt, 2015; Weston, 2021
Legal Values	These values reflect society's moral and ethical commitments and ensure that laws are just, fair, and equitable. Legal values may conflict with ethical values and personal/individual values as they focus on compliance.	Justice Lawfulness Rule of Law Human Dignity Transparency Due Process	Bozeman, 2007; Spicer, 2009; Weston, 2021

accompanied by working definitions that employees navigate. Drawing from Molina and McKeown's (2012) comprehensive value-based research, which identified 40 distinct values, we paired each value type with its associated values. Van Wart (1998) emphasizes that clarity around values is of paramount importance for fostering employee behavior and enhancing administrative competence. By offering this structured approach to understanding value types, we aim to equip employees and leaders with the tools necessary to navigate the complex landscape of organizational values, bridging the gap between value alignment and action.

It is important to acknowledge that there is no singular objective guide to navigating values and behavior in organizations. Values may be either compatible or fundamentally incommensurable, which raises the critical question: when values conflict, what is truly at stake? Conflicting values challenge an individual's core beliefs, potentially putting the organization at risk and fostering misunderstanding or conflicts among employees which can harm social cohesion in the workplace (Spicer, 2009). These conflicts can lead to ethical dilemmas and value dissonance, forcing individuals to choose between competing values and potentially may feel as though they are compromising their principles—for example, in the high-profile case of former Kentucky Clerk Kim Davis, who refused to issue same-sex marriage licenses in 2015.

Barnard's (1938) seminal work discusses the pressures for conformity and the problems that arise when values converge or clash. Similarly, Spicer (2009) argues for a more "self-conscious cultivation of the process of practical reasoning" to resolve moral conflicts (p. 537). When individuals or organizations prioritize different values, the potential for conflict increases, impacting decisions and actions (Bourne & Jenkins, 2013). Goodsell's (1989) five-part characterization of values (means, morality, multitude, market, and mission) provides a framework for balancing competing value orientations. Additionally, Van Wart (1998) highlights how centralized and institutionalized values, such as individual, professional, organizational, legal, and public interest value, shape individuals' capacity to choose effective solutions.

Clear communication of prioritized values helps guide employees in making ethical decisions and fosters positive behavior by providing a strong sense of purpose. When employees understand and embrace the organization's values, they are more likely to act in ways that align with those principles. For instance, an organization that emphasizes humanism, equity, transparency, and accountability can create a culture where employees feel responsible for their actions and are motivated to act with integrity and respect for those they serve.

Political and economic conditions further influence value prioritization, as cultural, legal and institutional values can both constrain and shape behavior and outcomes (Molina & McKeown, 2012; Van der Wal & Huberts, 2008; Weston, 2021). Identifying, discussing, and negotiating which values to act upon can be mentally and emotionally taxing. Organizations can help alleviate this burden by cultivating a culture where employees can rely on peer support to engage in thoughtful dialogue, deliberate on clashing values, and broaden their scope of reasoning. Molina and McKeown (2012) discuss how job responsibilities, accountability, legal implications, and organizational expectations all shape value-based decisions (see also Molina, 2015; Van der Wal & Huberts, 2008). By fostering such a culture, organizations can better equip their employees to navigate the complexities of value conflicts, ensuring more thoughtful and ethical decision-making.

Based on the discussion, the fluid nature of organizational values becomes clear. Individuals often draw on different value types depending on their roles and the specific situations they face. The complexity and contradictions inherent in organizational cultures frequently place employees in circumstances that may conflict with their personal values (Finegan, 2000). This raises critical questions about value tradeoffs and the factors that drive choices, shaping how individuals respond to ethical dilemmas and make decisions (Amos & Weathington, 2008; Box, 2015).

While organizations may clearly espouse certain values, their application in practice is often subjective and varies based on context. This subjectivity underscores the challenge of aligning personal values and organizational expectations and highlights the importance of understanding the factors that influence behaviors. As discussed earlier, political, economic, and social conditions play a significant role in how values are prioritized and acted upon. Additionally, the way values are communicated—whether formally or informally—can greatly impact how employees navigate these tradeoffs. Recognizing the dynamic nature of values and the potential for conflict is essential for fostering a work environment where employees can reconcile these differences and make informed, ethical decisions.

Aligning Values: How Organizational Values Drive Employee Behavior?

Public service organizations often encounter significant tensions due to the diverse and sometimes competing demands of stakeholders. For instance, the need for efficiency and cost-effectiveness (public service values) may directly conflict with the goal of providing equitable service to all people (public service values, fairness). Similarly, an emphasis on performance measurement might prioritize short-term results over long-term public interest. These conflicts create ethical dilemmas for employees who must navigate competing values in their day-to-day decision-making.

To address these challenges, employees need to be introduced to the foundational elements of values—different types of values and how they manifest within organizations. As discussed earlier, values can be established, accepted, practiced in various ways, or at times, not enacted at all (Box, 2015; Molina & McKeown, 2012; Van der Wal & Huberts, 2008). Ethical training, clear guidelines, and open communication channels are good practices and critical strategies to help employees mitigate the impact of value conflicts and moral choices. It is essential for organizations to implement mechanisms that support employees in reasoning through complex value-based dilemmas.

When values are in conflict, employees must make tradeoffs, but which values should take precedence? It is vital for values to be clearly articulated, communicated, and deeply embedded within the organizational culture. How values are normalized and communicated in day-to-day operations sets the stage for individual behavioral responses and how tradeoffs are managed. Public value failure and conflict are inevitable given the plurality of values and ethical dilemmas that arise, and they can have serious consequences, including conflicts of interest (Bozeman, 2007; Moynihan, 2009; Spicer, 2009).

According to Dickson et al. (2001), ethical responses from an organization positively correlate with individual motives, personal ideals, and adherence to a code of conduct. Whether the organization prioritizes collaboration, creativity, quality, fairness, equity, or humane treatment (Meyer et al., 2022), its identity is shaped by both espoused and practiced values. Ultimately, organizational values influence how policies are interpreted; how decisions are made; and the choices, changes, and behaviors that prevail in the ethical stance of an organization.

Shifting Value Paradigms: Implications for Practice

It is important to recognize that public administration has been mired in decades of reform rhetoric and experimentation, all aimed at improving efficiency and effectiveness (Denhardt & Denhardt, 2000; Kaufman, 1956). These reforms reflect shifting value priorities over time, driven by the changing political, social, and economic landscapes. To fully understand the role of organizational values, we must explore how these priorities have evolved throughout different periods in public administration history. In this section, we focus on three value paradigms and eras of reform that sought to improve organizational performance and examine the core values that have defined each of these paradigms: Traditional Public Administration, NPM, and NPS. This offers insight into how value prioritization has shaped public administration and continues to influence decision-making and behavior in modern organizations.

Traditional Public Administration

The earliest period, referred to as traditional public administration, was designed around core values, characterized by Weberian bureaucracy, focusing on hierarchical structures, efficiency, rationality, impartiality, formal rules and procedures, and centralized control (Weber, 1978). Within this period, bureaucratic ethos emphasized external control mechanisms such as laws and regulations and was associated with "efficiency, efficacy, expertise, loyalty, and accountability"

(Bowman, 2000, p. 674; Van Wart, 1998). A common critique of traditional public administration is that they ignore marginalized "citizens, shunning innovation, and serving their own needs" (Denhardt & Denhardt, 2002, p. 551) rooted in the utilitarian model of Bentham and Mills. The primary values in this paradigm were efficiency, neutrality, rationality, and impartiality. Public servants were expected to follow standardized procedures and deliver services in a consistent manner in accordance with established policies. During the mid-20th century, the human relations movement introduced a shift in focus toward the well-being of employees (McGregor, 1960). This period highlighted values such as employee satisfaction, motivation, and the importance of human interactions within organizations. This shift was influenced by the Hawthorne Studies, which demonstrated that employee productivity could be increased by improving working conditions and fostering a supportive environment. Traditional public administration gradually gave way to NPM and other contemporary approaches to public sector management (Lynn, 2006).

New Public Management (NPM)

NPM emerged as a response to the perceived inefficiencies of traditional public administration. The transition was not always straightforward, with elements of both old and new approaches coexisting and interacting in many organizations. It introduced values from the private sector, such as performance measurement, customer service orientation, and accountability (Denhardt & Denhardt, 2002). NPM emphasized results-oriented management, market-oriented values, decentralization, and the adoption of market mechanisms within public service (Denhardt & Denhardt, 2002). It emphasized rationality and customer service (Lynn, 2006). This paradigm shift brought about a redefinition of public service and organizational values prioritizing values of efficiency and effectiveness and achieving measurable outcomes. The result was a conflict between traditional public service and organizational values, such as equity and public interest, and the new managerial values. It bred chaos as agencies pursued contradictory policies with limited oversight and a lack of accountability (Kaufman, 1956). Public organizations were encouraged to adopt private sector management techniques and focus on achieving measurable outcomes (Maesschalck, 2004).

New Public Service

The limitations of NPM gave way to new paradigms that sought to balance traditional and managerial values. Remnants of previous paradigms reside within the current paradigm and continue influencing practice (Denhardt & Denhardt, 2015). Denhart and Denhardt (2002) argue that in our efforts to be efficient, our discipline has forgotten who they serve and recommends a shift to a more inclusive approach (see also Meyer et al., 2022). Transparency, inclusiveness, equity, and participatory governance have gained prominence in contemporary scholarship on values in public organizations. Digital transformation has also introduced values such as innovation, agility, and data-driven decision-making blurring lines in practice (Denhardt & Denhardt, 2015). Public organizations are now expected to be more responsive, adaptive, and transparent. As public organizations continue to leverage technology to improve service delivery, enhance transparency, and engage citizens, they will need to continually balance consciousness—awareness of disparate outcomes, humanism, and value inculcation. Table 7.2 illustrates the changing values across three periods of paradigm shifts in public administration.

As new standards were pursued, new values were prioritized, often resulting in tensions and contradictions across public administration paradigms. Each

Table 7.2 Shifting Value Paradigms

Periods	Values Categories	Values	Economic, Social, and Political Factors
Traditional Public Service	Classical Regime values	Neutral competence, efficiency, effectiveness, accountability, rationality, impartiality	Politics (post-Watergate—higher expectations and standards) Transactional and rigid
New Public Management (NPM)	Private sector values Reinventing government and political power	Entrepreneurship, innovativeness, profitability, performance-based management, market efficiency, benchmarking, measuring productivity	Growing population Financial pressures Collaboration between and across sectors Sharing system of decision-making, service delivery Profound commitment to new ideas, values, and roles
New Public Service (NPS)	Democratic governance Human values Participatory governance Behavioral	Humanism, equity, engagement, ethics, citizen participation, service over efficiency, social equity, social responsibility, accountability, transparency, inclusiveness	Cultural transformation Shifts to focus on involvement and needs of people— response to Civil Rights movements and social change in the 1960s and 1970s Shift from managerialism to citizenship engagement focusing on collaborative governance

paradigm, in its efforts to improve efficiency and effectiveness, was often blind to realities that did not fit within its framework (Kaufman, 1956). A prime example is educational institutions prioritizing performance measurement focused on short-term outcomes, which can come at the expense of long-term educational gains. These shifts in value paradigms have had far-reaching implications for public life and employee behavior, as organizations and their decision-makers are often inert to change (Denhardt & Denhardt, 2002).

Throughout this chapter, we have examined and discussed how values guide how individuals respond to external pressures, cues, and organizational demands. Adams (2011) cautions individuals to take stock of the values they are practicing as they may blindly adhere to values that mask unethical behavior, as seen in historical tragedies like the Holocaust, where individuals carried out harmful actions under the guide of professional duty. This phenomenon can be interpreted as compliance with orders; adherence to and respect for established protocols, policies, or procedures; and the maintenance of perceived standards of efficiency or effectiveness. This cautionary perspective is echoed in recent events, such as the treatment of immigrant detainees, demonstrating how value prioritization can sometimes obscure moral responsibility.

Across different periods, value tensions continue to shape decision-making based on the environment, culture, and socialized norms. The traditional period emphasized accountability and efficiency. NPM focused on measuring productivity and adopting a competitive market-based model, while NPS prioritized cultural transformation, creating a government that works for and serves the people. These periods, however, are not fixed; organizations continuously seek value-congruence, balancing how employees are socialized and prioritize values based on their cultural and social contexts. Dowling and Pfeffer (1975) argue that "[l]egitimacy can be assessed by an examination of the values and norms prevalent in society. . . . Norms and values are visible in the communications of a culture" (pp. 124–125).

Value-Based Management: Making a Difference

Researchers have contended that management by values (MBV) is a modern public sector management approach (Bryson et al., 2014; Katsamunska, 2012), a new leadership tool (Dolan & Garcia, 2000) complementing the NPM (Vigoda-Gadot & Meiri, 2008), reinventing government (Fallows, 1992) and, where employees in an organization subscribe to and endorse the organization's system of beliefs and expected ways of behaving (Garti & Dolan, 2019). In addition to enhancements to government-established long-standing traditions, NPM equips public service administrators with tools to merge new public service approaches contributing to the alleviation of rigid bureaucratic norms (Pedersen & Rendtorff, 2004). With its focus on instilling company-wide ethical principles and values, value-based management induces public value creation (Meynhardt, 2009) by optimizing value frameworks and ethical reform above bureaucratic practices and structures. In keeping with its genesis in private organizations, values-based management (VBM) supports alignment with the organization's strategic vision, which according to Plunkett et al. (2008) is the platform on which organizational decision-making, employee intents, and a value-based culture are erected. As public sector organizations grow and change values become engrained by way of the organizational culture, and overtime it becomes a standard for employee behavior.

Leadership plays a crucial role in shaping and sustaining organizational values and must recognize their role in communicating, perpetuating, and conveying value prioritization either directly or indirectly. Leaders and managers sometimes get stuck in dogmatic principles where they convey and practice values, based on their personal assessments and ways of thinking (refer to McGreggor's discussion on Theory X and Theory Y). The approach undertaken can significantly influence employees' perceptions of ethical behavior as the ways in which values are communicated can create ambiguity in the organizational culture about which values should be prioritized. Additionally, mechanisms for addressing value conflicts and supporting employees in making value-based decisions are essential. The role of the manager is crucial in cultivating and developing healthy organizations and nurturing employee relationships. Managers meet these aims, according to Neck et al. (2014), through effective and efficient planning, organizing, controlling, and collaborating with individuals, to optimize the distribution of public goods and services. To ensure that organizations are managed well, and their resources are allocated strategically, managers have utilized various techniques including Management by Instructions (MBI) and Management by Objectives (MBO) to convey values. MBI, a top-down decision-making approach has been described as reducing employee control (Dolan & Garcia, 2000; Wallenius, 2002), input, and autonomy (Dolan & Richley, 2006). Drucker's (1954) MBO alternately facilitates employee participation and creativity. Through the process of jointly establishing the organization's goals, the employee and manager can collaborate to set their objectives for accomplishing results for the individual and the organization then in assessment, and compare the objectives with the actual results. According to Dolan and Richley (2006), VBM emerged from MBI and MBO.

Leaders often contend with a cost-benefit analysis focusing on the extent to which they need to be transparent, responsible, or accountable. Full transparency and value prioritization of honesty and accountability are often perceived as having undesirable consequences (Molina & McKeown, 2012). Individuals may evaluate behaviors from different value prioritizations; therefore, asymmetric power relationships will influence value salience and the extent to which a meaningful sense of shared values is achieved. Webster and Cokins (2020) point out that though, historically, VBM was rooted in the private sector, it has expanded to cover diverse scopes. The broader concept, they claim, "seeks to integrate considerations of results to be achieved, resources to be effectively and efficiently consumed, and risks to be appropriately accepted" (p. xiv). Methods for managing employee behavior may vary and may involve interventions such as: close supervision, tight controls, threats, or managers can practice values as motivators for behavior. This is consistent with the argument of Hartley et al. (2013) and Waldo (1984) who discuss collaborative innovation as a value addition to stakeholders demonstrated in creative solutions and enhanced public service delivery.

Reputation credibility, public accountability, employee commitment, and improved organizational performance (Hood, 1995) become more evident in the organizations where VBM is practiced. The command-and-control management characteristic of traditional management practices and decision-making is being replaced by employee/employer compromises and cooperation representative of VBM (Begley & Boyd, 2000; Bovaird, 2007). To manage based on values means that the decision-makers in an organization have a built-in mechanism to evaluate themselves and to prevent them from making decisions that do not serve the best interest of the organization.

Evolving Expectations: Adapting to Change

Values are fluid, iterative, and often messy, motivating behavior in ways that can sometimes be ignored in conventional management approaches. The complexity of prioritizing values in public administration presents significant challenges. Public administration encompasses a very expansive range of professions, each influenced by geographic, political, and economic factors, all of which shape the values that are prioritized. As an applied field, public administration has historically adopted different values in response to shifting social, political, and economic conditions. While paradigm shifts are often proposed to improve public sector performance, one enduring strength of the bureaucracy is its embrace of VBM.

Throughout this chapter, we have explored how organizational and public service values are drawn from a range of historical, social, and situational contexts. These values are shaped not only by individual and organizational factors but also by broader societal influences. Values are formalized in key organizational documents such as mission statements and code of ethics. As discussed throughout, leadership plays a pivotal role in sustaining and reinforcing the values, culture, and ethical standards that are upheld in an organization.

Ouchi (2019) agrees that VBM may facilitate efficiency, organization, coordination, and accountability (see also Fallows, 1992). As shifts in administration and management have occurred over different periods, they necessitate adaptation to new values, requiring continuous learning, training, and development to keep pace with evolving public service demands. While traditional values such as efficiency and rationality remain relevant, contemporary public organizations now emphasize humanism, social equity, and justice. As discussed earlier, leaders must clarify, support, and uphold organizational values while providing systems for reflection, oversight, and ongoing training. Amos and Weathington (2008) contend that person-organization fit is essential for achieving positive outcomes like employee satisfaction, commitment, and retention. Similarly, Molina and McKeown (2012) highlight that decision-making authority influences value-based choices, whether personal or aligned with public service values.

Through VBM, organizations can foster positive employee-organization fit, creating a culture where performance, decision-making, and ethical conduct align with organizational values (Quinn, 2011). However, the complexity of managing organizational values is not a new challenge. As highlighted in this chapter, compliance with orders and respect for established protocols can obscure unethical practices, showing that merely espousing values is insufficient. Training and professional development are crucial interventions to address this challenge.

While values may appear fragmented or scattered, and perceptions may conflict with stated organizational values, this chapter has provided a comprehensive framework for understanding how values are categorized, prioritized, and operationalized. We have explored the mechanisms for value delivery, the expectations placed on employees, and the importance of building accountability structures.

This chapter has cataloged and categorized values in different ways with insight into value prioritization, mechanisms for delivery, value expectations, and building accountability structures. Moving forward, public administration stands to benefit from a more nuanced understanding of how values are not only espoused, but also interpreted, and experienced by employees, guiding their behaviors in meaningful ways. Organizations must be intentional about ensuring that their values are more than just written statements—they must be woven into the daily practices of the organization and embodied in the actions of employees.

References

Adams, G. (2011). The problem of administrative evil in a culture of technical rationality. *Public Integrity*, *13*(3), 275–285.

Argandoña, A. (2003). Private-to-private corruption. *Journal of business ethics*, *47*, 253–267.

Bansal, P. (2003). From issues to actions: The importance of individual concerns and organizational values in responding to natural environmental issues. *Organization Science*, *14*(5), 510–527.

Barnard, C. I. (1938). *The functions of the executive*. Harvard University Press.

Barry, D. (2024, September 28). The not-so-brief history of scandal among New York City mayors. *New York Times*. Retrieved from www.nytimes.com/2024/09/28/nyregion/nyc-mayor-adams-corruption-history.html

Begley, T. M., & Boyd, D. P. (2000). Articulating corporate values through human resource policies. *Business Horizons*, *43*(4), 8–12.

Bourne, H., & Jenkins, M. (2013). Organizational values: A dynamic perspective. *Organization Studies*, *34*(4), 495–514.

Bovaird, T. (2007). Beyond engagement and participation: User and community coproduction of public services. *Public Administration Review*, *67*(5), 846–860.

Bowman, J. (1990). Ethics in government: A national survey of public administrators. *Public Administration Review*, *50*(3), 345–353.

Bowman, J. (2000). Toward a professional ethos: From regulatory to reflective codes. *International Review of Administrative Sciences*, *66*(4), 673–687.

Box, R. C. (2015). *Public service values*. Routledge.

Bozeman, B. (2007). *Public values and public interest: Counterbalancing economic individualism*. Georgetown University Press.

Bryson, J. M., Crosby, B. C., & Bloomberg, L. (2014). Public value governance: Moving beyond traditional public administration and the new public management. *Public Administration Review*, *74*(4), 445–456.

Daft, R. L. (2010). *Organization theory and design* (10th ed.). South-Western Cengage Learning.

Denhardt, J. V., & Denhardt, R. B. (2015). The new public service revisited. *Public Administration Review*, *75*(5), 664–672.

Denhardt, R. B., & Denhardt, J. V. (2002). The new public service: Serving rather than steering. *Public Administration Review*, *60*(6), 549–559.

Detert, J. R., & Burris, E. R. (2007). Leadership behavior and employee voice: Is the door really open? *Academy of Management Journal*, *50*(4), 869–884.

Dickson, M. W, Smith, D. B. Grojean, M. W., & Ehrhart, M. (2001). An organizational climate regarding ethics: The outcome of leader values and the practices that reflect them. *The Leadership Quarterly*, *12*(2), 197–217, ISSN 1048-9843

Dolan, S. L., & Garcia, S. (2000). Managing by values in the next millennium: Cultural redesign for strategic organizational change. http://doi.org/10.2139/ssrn.237628

Dolan, S. L., & Richley, B. A. (2006). Management by values (MBV): A new philosophy for a new economic order. *Handbook of Business Strategy*, *7*(1), 235–238.

Dose, J. J. (1997). Work values: An integrative framework and illustrative application to organizational socialization. *Journal of Occupational and Organizational Psychology*, 70, 219–240.

Dowling, J., & Pfeffer, J. (1975). Organizational legitimacy: Social values and organizational behavior. *Pacific Sociological Review*, *18*(1), 122–136.

Drucker, P. (1954). *The practice of management*. Harper.

Durand, R., Hawn, O., & Ioannou, I. (2019). Willing and able: A general model of organizational responses to normative pressures. *Academy of Management Review*, *44*(2), 299–320.

Fallows, J. (1992). Reinventing government: How the entrepreneurial spirit is transforming the public sector, from schoolhouse to statehouse, city hall to Pentagon. *Atlantic*, *269*(6), 119–124.

Finegan, J. E. (2000). The impact of person and organizational values on organizational commitment. *Journal of Occupational and Organizational Psychology*, *73*(2), 149–169.

Garti, A. N. A. T., & Dolan, S. L. (2019). Managing by values (MBV). *European Business Review*, 46–52.

Goodsell, C. (1989). Balancing competing values. In J. Perry (Ed.), *Handbook of public administration* (pp. 575–584). Jossey-Bass.

Hartley, J., Sørensen, E., & Torfing, J. (2013). Collaborative innovation: A viable alternative to market competition and organizational entrepreneurship. *Public Administration Review*, *73*(6), 821–830.

Herold, T., & Schlegel, F. (2023). Value-based compliance: Integrating integrity and compliance management. In *Value-oriented leadership in theory and practice: Concepts-study results-practical insights* (pp. 111–126). Springer International Publishing.

Hood, C. (1995). The "new public management" in the 1980s: Variations on a theme. *Accounting, Organizations and Society, 20*(2–3), 93–109. https://doi.org/10.1016/S1048-9843(01)00069-8

Jannat, T., Alam, S. S., Ho, Y. H., Omar, N. A., & Lin, C. Y. (2022). Can corporate ethics programs reduce unethical behavior? Threat appraisal or coping appraisal. *Journal of Business Ethics, 176*(1), 37–53.

Katsamunska, P. (2012). Classical and modern approaches to public administration. *Economic Alternatives, 1*, 74–81.

Kaufman, H. (1956). Emerging conflicts in the doctrines of public administration. *American Political Science Review, 50*(4), 1057–1073.

Kroeger, N. W. (1995). Person-environment fit in the final jobs of retirees. *The Journal of Social Psychology, 135*(5), 545–551.

Loyens, K., & Maesschalck, J. (2010). Toward a theoretical framework for ethical decision making of street-level bureaucracy: Existing models reconsidered. *Administration & Society, 42*(1), 66–100.

Lynn Jr, L. E. (2006). *Public management: Old and new*. Routledge.

Maesschalck, J. (2004). The impact of new public management reforms on public servants' ethics: Towards a theory. *Public Administration, 82*(2), 465–489.

Maidment, F., & Elderidge, W. (2000). *Business in government and society: Ethical, international decision-making*. Prentice Hall.

McGregor, D. (1960). *The human side of enterprise*. McGraw-Hill.

McHugh, C. (2024, September 27). What's wrong with New York's mayors? *Politico*. Retrieved from www.politico.com/news/magazine/2024/09/27/whats-wrong-with-new-yorks-mayors-00181400

Meyer, S. J., Johnson III, R. G., & McCandless, S. (2022). Moving the field forward with empathy, engagement, equity, and ethics. *Public Integrity, 24*(4–5), 422–431.

Meynhardt, T. (2009). Public value inside: What is public value creation? *International Journal of Public Administration, 32*(3–4), 192–219.

Molina, A. D. (2015). The virtues of administration: Values and the practice of public service. *Administrative Theory & Praxis, 37*(1), 49–69.

Molina, A. D., & McKeown, C. (2012). The heart of the profession: Understanding public service values. *Journal of Public Affairs Education, 18*(2), 375–396.

Moynihan, D. (2009). "Our usable past": A historical contextual approach to administrative values. *Public Administration Review, 69*, 813–821.

Neck, C. P., Lattimer, C. L. & Houghton, J. D. (2014). *Management: Think, decide, act*. Wiley Publishing.

Ouchi, W. G. (2019). Markets, bureaucracies, and clans. In *Management control theory* (pp. 343–356). Routledge.

Paine, L. S. (1994). Managing organizational integrity. *Harvard Business Review*, 105–118.

Pedersen, S. J., & Rendtorff, D. J. (2004). Value-based management in local public organizations: A Danish experience. *Cross Cultural Management: An International Journal, 11*(2), 71–94.

Perlman, B. J., Reddick, C., & Demir, T. (2023). A compliance—integrity framework for ethics management: An empirical analysis of local government practice. *Public Administration Review, 83*(4), 823–837.

Plunkett, W., Attner, R. F., & Allen, G. (2008). *Management: Meeting and exceeding customer expectations* (International ed.). South-Western Cengage Learning.

Quinn, R. E. (2011). *Diagnosing and changing organizational culture: Based on the competing values framework*. Jossey-Bass.

Roberts, R. (2009). The rise of compliance-based ethics management. *Public Integrity, 11*(3), 261–277.

Schein, E., & Schein, P. (2017). *Organizational culture and leadership.* John Wiley & Sons, Inc.

Schermerhorn, J. (2013). *Management* (12th ed.). John Wiley & Sons.

Sisak, M. R., Peltz, J. Tucker, E., Price, M., & Colvin, J. (2024, May 31)). Guilty: Trump becomes first former US president convicted of felony crimes. *U.S. News.* Retrieved from https://apnews.com/article/trump-trial-deliberations-jury-testimony-verdict-85558c6d08efb434d05b694364470aa0

Spicer, M. (2009). Value conflict and legal reasoning in public administration. *Administrative Theory & Praxis, 31,* 537–555.

Stevens, B. (1999). Communicating ethical values: A study of employee perceptions. *Journal of Business Ethics, 20,* 113–120.

Sweeting, K. D. (2022). Strategies to foster engagement, empathy, equity, and ethics in public service: A conceptual model for public and nonprofit administrators. *Public Integrity, 24*(4–5), 432–447.

Van der Wal, Z., & Huberts, L. (2008). Value solidity in government and business: Results of an empirical study on public and private sector organizational values. *The American Review of Public Administration, 38*(3), 264–285.

Van Wart, M. (1998). *Changing public sector values.* Garland Publishing.

Vigoda-Gadot, E. R. A. N., & Meiri, S. (2008). New public management values and person-organization fit: A socio-psychological approach and empirical examination among public sector personnel. *Public Administration, 86*(1), 111–131.

Waldo, D. (1984). *The administrative state.* Holmes & Meier.

Wallenius, K. (2002). A generic model of management and command and control. In *7th International Command and Control Research and Technology Symposium* (pp. 16–20). Retrieved from http://www.dodccrp.org/events/7th_ICCRTS/Tracks/pdf/058.PDF.

Weber, M. (1978). *Economy and society.* Berkeley.

Webster, D. W., & Cokins, G. (2020). *Value-based management in government.* John Wiley & Sons.

Weston, A. (2021). *A practical companion to ethics.* Oxford University Press.

8 Public Sector Ethics in the Americas

The Brazilian Public Ethics Management Case Study

*Temístocles Murilo de Oliveira Júnior
and Joaquim Manuel Croca Caeiro*

Introduction

Public ethics has been a relevant topic since the rise of good governance in the 1990s with the global diffusion of NPM and post-NPM reforms, which recommended shifts in the role of States and new forms of relations between governments, the private sector, and civil society (Heywood, 2012; Menzel, 2015; Scapin, 2016). This diffusion occurred alongside the exposure of corruption and widespread distrust in different countries, increasing concern about public officials' ethical dilemmas and behaviour, especially in decision-making regarding public-private boundaries (Bowler & Karp, 2004; Ian & Ting, 2015; Scapin, 2016).

In this scenario, initiatives to formulate and provide definitions, prescriptions, and standards for ethics in the public sector have emerged, aiming to preserve trust in government by preventing and combatting corruption and other malad-ministration-related behaviours. Ethics management has emerged from these initiatives as a framework for implementing public ethics policies, with a focus on balancing culture- and compliance-based policies (Choi, 2023; Heywood, 2012; Menzel, 2015; Mills, 1999; Perlman et al., 2023; Tremblay et al., 2017).

This chapter aligns with the volume's purpose for regional analyses by exploring the Brazilian case as a significant experience in the Americas. It focuses on the Ethics Management System of the Executive Federal Branch (SGEP), the only system of its kind at the national level. This system is led by the Public Ethics Commission (CEP) and comprises both culture- and compliance-based mechanisms in all federal executive bodies. Over the past 30 years since the enactment of the Code of Professional Ethics of Civil Servants in 1994—a period marked by anti-corruption-related reforms, cycles of scandals, and a passionate debate on public ethics—critical work on ethics management in Brazil remains nascent.

The theoretical proposal is founded on three interrelated issues that emerge from the literature and experiences of reforms of ethics management and other anti-corruption policies. First, international influence and the anti-corruption

DOI: 10.4324/9781003416258-9

appeal are key drivers for these reforms (Andersson & Ekelund, 2021; Daniel, 2020; Pereyra, 2019; Scott, 2016; de Sousa & Coroado, 2023). Second, although such reforms are generally justified by discourses advocating for politics-free public policies, these drivers have produced policies that are heavily oriented towards political interests (Dâmaso, 2024; Da Ros & Taylor, 2022; Demmke et al., 2023; Oliveira Júnior & Fonseca, 2024; Morris & Blake, 2009; de Sousa & Coroado, 2023). Finally, ethics management systems are marked by these previous issues, resulting in complexity, fragmentation, and imprecisions, which create obstacles to coordination and balance (Demmke et al., 2023; Heywood, 2012; Prayote, 2016; Roberts, 2023; Scapin, 2016).

This chapter argues that the first two general issues provide a basis for exploring the causality of the challenges faced by ethics management systems identified in the third issue. It assumes that a "political-institutional" dynamic of strategies oriented towards power interests mediated by international influence and anti-corruption appeal, as well as by ambiguities in the ethics management domain, is relevant to the ethics management systems' trajectories. By focusing on this dynamic as a causal mechanism, this chapter provides a theoretical proposal and a research design for exploring the case study and drawing inferences on how it has been shaped, resulting in the aforementioned challenges.

The theoretical proposal combines the Institutional Analysis and Development (IAD) perspective with a theory-testing causal (TTC) scheme (Beach & Pedersen, 2013; Schimmelfennig, 2015; van der Heijden et al., 2019). The IAD framework emphasises the importance of power and ambiguity in policymaking, arguing that not only "institutions (in a strict sense) matter," but also key actors' political interests and ambiguities in the target policy domains (Allison & Zelikow, 1999; Jackson, 2005; Mahoney & Thelen, 2010). In turn, the TTC scheme adapts the causal *mechanismic* lens proposed by Oliveira Júnior and Fonseca (2024), based on the work of Beach and Pedersen (2013), Falleti and Lynch (2009), and Mahoney (2016), to explore through process tracing the presence and relevance of the theorised political-institutional dynamic as a causal mechanism in the case study's trajectory.

The research design aligns with the TTC scheme and is based on content analysis using documentary techniques (Bardin, 2013; Cellard, 1997; Gerring & Cojocaru, 2016; Weller & Barnes, 2014). Since the case study pertains to a formal system of rules, structures, and instruments, the documentary corpus was initially composed of SGEP regulations, which represent key milestones in the system's development, followed by assessment reports of this system. As this chapter's goal extends beyond merely explaining formal institutions and highlighting assessments, it includes documents from the formulation processes and news published by both the free press and official media, shedding light on the context, motivations, and debates that surrounded the formulation of SGEP regulations. Additionally, international standards and other documents cited as justifications were also collected.

The Brazilian SGEP is a fruitful case study for this chapter's theoretical proposal and research design for reasons that go beyond the fact that it has three
decades of history and the incipience of critical studies. First, Brazil has been
marked by cycles of scandals and a strong anti-corruption appeal that leads key
actors to adopt strategies for power and expose weak points in the anti-corruption
policy domains, resulting in complex, unbalanced, and ambiguous institutional
arrangements (Da Ros & Taylor, 2022; Oliveira Júnior & Fonseca, 2024; Oliveira
Júnior, 2019). Second, national and international assessment reports published in
the last two decades have indicated challenges for SGEP related to miscoordination, lack of monitoring, and overlaps with two other related federal executive
systems: the Public Integrity System—SITAI—and the Administrative Disciplinary System—SICOR (docs. ID # 46, 59, 64, 68, and 90 in the spreadsheet at
http://tiny.cc/document_index and files at http://tiny.cc/documents_repository).

   This chapter is divided into six sections besides this introduction and its conclusion. The first explores the literature to outline a minimum common understanding of ethics management systems' definitions, boundaries, scope, and
components. The second discusses the three general issues that emerge from the
literature and experiences of ethics management and anti-corruption reforms.
The third develops the theoretical proposal of the political-institutional dynamic
to infer causal chains for the indicated challenges in the case study. The fourth
refers to the research design adopted for gathering, reviewing, treating, and analysing evidence of the presence and relevance of the theorised causal mechanism.
The fifth section traces the SGEP's trajectory by narrating the key actors' strategies, the international influences, corruption scandals, soft spots in the ethics
management domain, and other acts and facts of interest that influenced ethics
management regulations and the aforementioned challenges. The sixth presents
the results of the analysis of evidence, drawing inferences about the presence and
relevance of political-institutional dynamics in the SGEP's trajectory.

Ethics Management Background

Public ethics has been a relevant topic since the rise of good governance in the
1990s with the global diffusion of NPM and post-NPM reforms, which recommended shifts in the role of states and new forms of relations between governments, the private sector, and civil society (Heywood, 2012; Menzel, 2015;
Scapin, 2016). This diffusion took place in parallel with the exposure of corruption and widespread distrust in various countries, which increased concerns
about public officials' ethical dilemmas and behaviour, especially in decision-
making on public-private boundaries (Bowler & Karp, 2004; Ian & Ting, 2015;
Scapin, 2016).

   In response to this, initiatives to formulate and provide definitions, prescriptions, and other standards for ethics in the public sector have emerged, aiming
to preserve trust in government by preventing and combatting corruption and

other maladministration-related behaviours. Ethics management emerged from these initiatives as a framework for implementing public ethics policies, with a focus on the balance between culture- and compliance-based policies (Choi, 2023; Heywood, 2012; Menzel, 2015; Mills, 1999; Perlman et al., 2023; Tremblay et al., 2017). Ethics management has been conceptualised in diverse ways. This term is sometimes associated with anti-corruption policies focused mostly on conflicts of interest and ethical dilemmas. Other times, it is treated as a function, a synonym, or even a subvariant of integrity management (see Heywood, 2012; Heywood & Kirby, 2020; Menzel, 2015; Perlman et al., 2023; Roberts, 2023; van Steden, 2020; Tremblay et al., 2017).

Due to this diversity and overlap with integrity, it is difficult to propose a general inventory of ethical violations that should come under the scope of ethics management. However, it is possible to suggest that they be categorised into two types. The first relates to inappropriate behaviour by public officials in their interactions with other people and in public communications, such as intimidation, harassment, discriminatory treatment, and conduct that damages the image of people and institutions. The second type involves situations that potentially indicate or increase conflicts of interest, such as lobbying, revolving doors, misuse of privileged information, acceptance of gifts and hospitality, prioritisation of private interests, participation in private conflicting activities, disproportionate accumulation of assets, and nepotism (see Boyce & Davids, 2009; Huberts, 2018; Mafunisa, 2003; Menzel, 2015; Palidauskaitė, 2015).

Despite the relative complexity of defining boundaries and the scope of ethics management systems, there is some common understanding. They are primarily associated with institutional arrangements for implementing and balancing culture- and compliance-based policies to promote positive and negative inducement measures aimed at public officials' behaviour and ethical dilemmas. While cultural-based components include consultation services, leadership development, training, participation mechanisms, and merit programmes, those based on compliance refer to codes of conduct, rules, reporting channels, investigation procedures, ethics risk control schemes, lobbying transparency, and quarantine rules (see Andersson & Ekelund, 2021; Choi, 2023; Menzel, 2015; Perlman et al., 2023; Tremblay et al., 2017).

Issues on Ethics Management Reforms

Ethics management reforms have taken place in diverse countries through processes in which international influence represents one of the key drivers. This influence has been materialised through strategies implemented by intergovernmental and non-governmental organisations at both global and regional levels, including the United Nations (in particular its UN Office on Drugs and Crime [UNODC]), The World Bank, the European Council, the Organization of American States (OAS), the Global Coalition for Africa (GCA), and Transparency

International (Andersson & Ekelund, 2021; Cooper & Yoder, 2002; Dyer, 1998; Mills, 1999; Scapin, 2016).

Among these international actors, the Organization for Economic Co-operation and Development (OECD) has been the most influential for its member and non-member countries, which have adopted its ethics and integrity management standards. This adoption movement has been driven by the OECD's continuous efforts to formulate and update resolutions and prescriptions, provide training, form working groups, and hold meetings on public ethics and related topics, always reinforced by extensive communication initiatives (D'Alterio, 2017; Mills, 1999; Scapin, 2016).

In addition to international influence, the anti-corruption appeal is another key driver for the promotion and adoption of ethics management and other corruption-fighting policies. Therefore, the spread of ethics management has also been fuelled by the ongoing exposure of corruption cases, most of which are linked to conflicts of interest involving public officials. In response to these exposures and growing concerns about public ethics, national governments have implemented ethics management and other anti-corruption reforms, adopting international standards (primarily provided by the OECD) based on the legitimising argument that they represent "best practices" (see Andersson & Ekelund, 2021; Daniel, 2020; Luk, 2012; Pereyra, 2019; Scapin, 2016; Scott, 2016; de Sousa & Coroado, 2023; Vyas-Doorgapersad, 2022).

However, these drivers have not only promoted reforms but also had other effects on them. The convergence of national governments towards anti-corruption agendas, combined with the pressure for more integrity and ethics framed as the "absence of corruption," and the "unquestionable moral ideal" of good governance, can lead to an uncritical adoption of these standards (Heywood & Kirby, 2020, p. 18; Huberts, 2014; Oliveira Júnior & Lustosa da Costa, 2020). In this context, despite public ethics and anti-corruption policies generally being justified by discourses for politics-free public policies and the need for mechanisms to guarantee neutral-technical and public-interest-driven decision-making, such reforms can generate increased power, discretion, and prestige, leading them to be significantly shaped by the political interests of actors who guide or influence the formulation and implementation of anti-corruption policies (Dâmaso, 2024; Da Ros & Taylor, 2022; Demmke et al., 2023; Oliveira Júnior & Fonseca, 2024; Morris & Blake, 2009; de Sousa & Coroado, 2023).

Ethics management standards, and not only national systems, have also emerged from contexts and processes shaped by these two issues. These standards, developed over the course of three decades, represent approaches, definitions, and recommendations regarding ethical violations and compliance-based (the "'old' ethics management") and culture-based (the "new ethics management") components (see Cooper & Yoder, 2002; Dyer, 1998; Menzel, 2015, p. 354; Mills, 1999; Scapin, 2016; Topchii et al., 2021).

Focusing on the OECD standards, various legal instruments, policy papers, drafts, reports, and records of symposiums and meetings on public ethics, public integrity, conflict of interests, and transparency in lobbying have been published since the mid-1990s. Over time, ethics management standards have become complex and sometimes ambiguous. A key example of this complexity is the connection between public ethics and public integrity (see Bergue, 2022; van Steden, 2020).

Seminal OECD guidelines on public ethics first appeared in 1998 with the "12 Principles of the Recommendations on Improving Ethical Conduct in the Public Service," which made four brief references to integrity as a feature of public services (see OECD, 1998). Nineteen years later, these guidelines were replaced by the "Recommendations on Public Integrity" based on the justification that "violations of integrity standards . . . have become increasingly complex" (OECD, 2017). Public integrity is now addressed as a strategy for aligning and sharing ethical values, principles, and norms, while ethics is only mentioned in terms of standards of conduct, investing in leadership, providing training and advice, and fostering an open culture (see OECD, 2017).

Another example of the growing complexity of ethics management international standards over time is the emergence of the theme of conflict of interest. This concept has not even been mentioned under this name in the aforementioned 12 principles of 1998 (see OECD, 1998), but in later years it became a central topic in the standards of the OECD and other inter-government organisations. The emergence of this subject resulted in a large series of interrelated standards on lobbying transparency, revolving door regulations and misuse of privileged information, rules of gifts and hospitalities, declarations of private interests and assets, and consultations and authorisations for private activities (see OECD, 2003, 2010a, 2010b) and The World Bank (2020).

National ethics management systems have followed this path through non-linear convergence and formulation processes, which are sometimes still "under construction." In other words, the trajectory of national systems has unfolded in parallel with the construction of ethics management international standards, mirroring their complexity and ambiguity. In addition, as discussed earlier, many cases have been shaped by the context of the anti-corruption appeal, which may have increased the possibility that ethics management has been influenced by the power interests of key actors involved in these processes.

Case studies indicate that ethics management systems comprising culture- and compliance-based codes, rules, programmes, and instruments have expanded to prevent and address various behaviours by public officials that pose potential risks or constitute ethical violations. This expansion has multiplied the number of structures, which may both result from and reinforce power struggles, as actors exploit ambiguities in the ethics management domain. This situation has caused many national systems to become fragmented, with complexities, imprecise boundaries, and challenges regarding coordination and balance, leading to overlaps and gaps (see Basinger, 2016; Demmke et al., 2023; Heywood, 2012; Luk, 2012; Menzel, 2015; Scapin, 2016; Vyas-Doorgapersad, 2022).

Theoretical Proposal

This chapter's theoretical proposal is based on the three interrelated issues that emerge from reforms in ethics management and other anti-corruption policies, as discussed in the previous sections. It presumes that through the lens of the first two issues, which refer to the indications that international influence and anti-corruption appeal represent key drivers for ethics management reforms—what, in turn, has led these reforms to be notably influenced by political interests—it is possible to explore the causality of the challenges in resulting systems, described in the third issue.

Here, it is assumed that a "political-institutional dynamic" of strategies oriented towards power interests mediated by international influence and anti-corruption appeal, as well as ambiguities in the ethics management domain, is relevant to the ethics management systems' trajectories. By focusing on this dynamic as a causal mechanism, this chapter provides a theoretical proposal (and a research design) for exploring the case study and drawing inferences on how it has been shaped, resulting in the aforementioned challenges.

This proposal combines the IAD perspective with a TTC scheme (Beach & Pedersen, 2013; Schimmelfennig, 2015; van der Heijden et al., 2019). The IAD perspective focuses on power and ambiguity in policymaking. It first draws on the idea of policy diffusion and convergence as a result of isomorphic forces, based on the legitimacy of shared beliefs, structures, and practices in a particular organisational field, all of which impose a "logic of appropriateness" (DiMaggio & Powell, 1991; Marsh & Sharman, 2009; Radaelli, 2000). Second, it incorporates approaches that emphasise the central role of politics in policy processes, implying that not only "institutions (in a strict sense) matter," but also political contexts, power struggles, and ambiguities within policy domains (Allison & Zelikow, 1999; Jackson, 2005; Mahoney & Thelen, 2010).

In this context, ethics management represents a policy framework that has been diffused through the convergence of national governments towards international standards, legitimised by the appeal of ethics, integrity, and anti-corruption efforts since the rise of the good governance agenda, especially in the context of cycles of scandals (Da Ros & Taylor, 2022; Heywood & Kirby, 2020, p. 18; Huberts, 2014; Oliveira Júnior & Lustosa da Costa, 2020). However, multiple factors influence convergence processes linked to the natural tensions between international norms and domestic institutions, which are shaped by power strategies mediated by political and institutional factors. Thus, even policy systems resulting from policy diffusion and isomorphic convergence are likely to reflect these tensions (DiMaggio & Powell, 1991; Marsh & Sharman, 2009; Radaelli, 2000).

In the case of ethics management, it is notable that the sources of these international standards display complexity and weaknesses. National systems are shaped not only by international influence but also by scandals, which increase the likelihood that political actors will exploit ambiguities in pursuit of their own interests, as is described in the second and third issues. As a result, the complexity and ambiguity resulting from international standards, when diffused according to the logic of appropriateness and combined with political strategies in the context of scandals, can explain why national systems face challenges regarding coordination and balance, often with gaps and overlaps (see Basinger, 2016; Demmke et al., 2023; Heywood, 2012; Luk, 2012; Menzel, 2015; Scapin, 2016; Vyas-Doorgapersad, 2022).

The TTC scheme views the policymaking process as the unit of analysis, using process tracing to investigate the presence and relevance of theorised causal chains in order to infer the causality of specific outcomes (Beach & Pedersen, 2013; Schimmelfennig, 2015; van der Heijden et al., 2019). For this chapter, the TTC scheme uses political-institutional dynamics as a causal mechanism to explore how reforms in ethics management have been shaped, potentially shedding light on the challenges regarding coordination and balance within many national systems.

Adapting the framework proposed by Oliveira Júnior and Fonseca (2024) for analysing political dynamics in anti-corruption reforms, based on Beach and Pedersen (2013), Falleti and Lynch (2009), Mahoney (2016), and Zittoun (2014), this chapter's TTC scheme can be represented by "I (international standards and corruption scandals as input) → M (political-institutional dynamics as causal mechanism) → O (challenges regarding coordination and balance as outcome)."

Delving deeper, the causal mechanism "M" comprises the political context conducive to anti-corruption gains (C), the specific features of the ethics management domain (F), and the strategies of key actors seeking power (S). Therefore, it is not only international influence and the exposure of corruption (I) that explain the outcomes. The strategies (S) adopted in response to the public ethics appeal (C) and weaknesses in the ethics management domain (F) also play a significant role. The final formula is "I → (C + F → S) → O."

Research Design

For this chapter, the Brazilian ethics management system at the national level was chosen as the case study, considering its relevance within the Americas. It is supposed that this system has been significantly shaped by the political-institutional dynamic, resulting in complexities and fragmentation that have imposed challenges for coordination and balance. The research design was therefore structured to allow an examination of the system's trajectory, which serves as the unit of analysis.

The focus is on the SGEP (Sistema de Gestão da Ética Pública), whose scope is limited to the Federal Executive Branch, as it is the only ethics management system at the upper levels of government. This system is led by the CEP (Comissão de Ética Pública) and comprises a series of culture- and compliance-based policies implemented by ethics commissions in all federal executive bodies. After 30 years since the enactment of the Public Servant Code of Ethics in 1994—the first regulation on the public ethics management domain in Brazil—critical work on this topic remains limited.

The SGEP is a valuable case study for this chapter's theoretical proposal for reasons that extend beyond its three decades of history and the scarcity of critical studies. First, Brazil is marked by cycles of scandals and a strong focus on fighting corruption, which leads key actors to adopt power strategies and exploit weaknesses in the anti-corruption policy domains, resulting in complex, unbalanced, and ambiguous institutional arrangements (Da Ros & Taylor, 2022; Oliveira Júnior & Fonseca, 2024; Oliveira Júnior, 2019). Second, national and international assessment reports published in the past two decades have highlighted challenges for the SGEP regarding miscoordination, lack of monitoring, and overlaps with two other federal executive systems: the Public Integrity System—SITAI—and the Administrative Disciplinary System—SICOR (docs. ID # 46, 59, 64, 68, and 90—see the spreadsheet available at http://tiny.cc/document_index).

The research design aimed to gather evidence of the presence and relevance of the political-institutional dynamic in the SGEP's evolution, allowing inferences to be drawn regarding the causal chains between this dynamic and the challenges regarding coordination and balance within the system. The design followed the TTC scheme, based on content analysis using documentary techniques that would support process tracing of the SGEP's trajectory (Bardin, 2013; Cellard, 1997; Gerring & Cojocaru, 2016; Weller & Barnes, 2014).

The collection, review, treatment, and analysis of documents were carried out in five steps. At each stage, the gathered documents informed the scope of the subsequent steps. Given that the case study focuses on a formal policy domain, SGEP regulations that established high-level rules, structures, and policies regarding ethics management were considered milestones in its trajectory. Thus, these regulations formed the basis of the first step. Subsequently, given the need for information on the challenges faced by the SGEP, the aforementioned assessment reports were included in the second step.

Since the chapter's goal goes beyond exploring such formal components and assessment reports, documents related to the formulation processes of SGEP legal milestones were collected in the third step. News articles published by the free press and official media, which shed light on the context, motivations, and debates surrounding the SGEP and its legal milestones, comprised the fourth step. Finally, international standards and other documents referenced in the formulation processes, or that provide further insight into the SGEP's trajectory and challenges, were included in the fifth step.

The SGEP regulations from the first step were obtained from the CEP website (www.gov.br/planalto/pt-br/acesso-a-informacao/acoes-e-programas/govern-anca/etica-publica/cep), which also contains lower-level regulations, such as resolutions and implementation rules, as well as meeting minutes, event outcomes, and official news, all included in the fourth and fifth steps. Assessment reports collected in the second step were obtained from the Brazilian Federal Court of Accounts—TCU—website (https://portal.tcu.gov.br), the external control body responsible for assessing government policies and programmes, and from the OECD, OAS, and UNODC websites, as these organisations are responsible for evaluating the implementation of anti-corruption conventions to which Brazil has adhered.

The documents in the third step, related to formulation processes of SGEP regulations, were obtained through information requests made via the Federal Executive Branch's Freedom of Information service, called Fala.BR (https://falabr.cgu.gov.br/). A total of 28 requests were sent, as multiple bodies and several commissions and working groups were involved in these processes. The list of requests and documents shared in response are available at http://tiny.cc/Requests_For_Information. In the case of the only ordinary legislation that constitutes a legal milestone, Act no. 12,813, of 16 May 2013, documents from its legislative process were obtained from the websites of the National Congress (www.camara.leg.br and www.senado.leg.br).

In the fourth step, official media coverage was sourced from the websites of the CEP and the Office of the Comptroller General—CGU (www.gov.br/cgu/pt-br), the Federal Executive Branch's anti-corruption body that represents Brazil in the implementation of conventions on this subject and which is mentioned in the SGEP regulations, assessment reports, and formulation processes. News articles from the free press were gathered using internet search engines, using keywords related to ethics management, focusing on reports published around the time of SGEP regulation proposals, approvals, and relevant scandals that could affect the public ethics debate.

International recommendations and publications referenced in SGEP proposals and justifications were obtained from the OECD website during the fifth step, given that its standards represented the primary source referenced in the proposals and justifications that appear in the formulation processes and news in the official media. This step also included the text of the United Nations Convention against Corruption (UNCAC), ratified by Brazil in 2006, a publication by the State Reform Council of 1997, and a collection of texts from a CEP event in 2001, all of which were referenced as sources and provide information on the formulation of the SGEP regulation process.

To ensure that the research design would capture evidence of the political-institutional dynamic shaping the SGEP's trajectory, enabling inferences about causality, a final review and treatment of documents was carried out. The remaining documents contained useful information for the proposed formula "I → (C + F → S) → O" in the TTC scheme, related to:

- international standards and commitments and corruption scandals that drove ethics management novelties (I);
- political context of the anti-corruption appeal resulting from international pressures and cycles of scandals that increased the returns on ethics management policies (C);
- features of the ethics management domain that resulted in ambiguities that were exploited for power gains (F);
- actions undertaken by key actors to propose or enact regulations that provided them power, including at the expense of other actors, taking advantage of the favourable context and ambiguities (S); and
- challenges indicated by the aforementioned national and international assessment reports produced by the TCU, OAS, and OECD (O).

After the treatment and analysis stage, each document was indexed, and its key information was highlighted, along with comments on its importance for understanding the political-institutional dynamics. The final corpus comprises 103 documents stored in a file repository available at http://tiny.cc/documents_repository. With the exception of international standards and OECD assessment reports, all other documents are in Portuguese. The documents are identified by their respective IDs, and the results of their treatment and analysis (in English) can be found in the spreadsheet available at http://tiny.cc/document_index. Downloadable documents are available in PDF format, and for those with download restrictions, a TXT file with the access link has been provided.

Case Study Process Tracing

This process tracing focuses on evidence of the presence and relevance of the political-institutional dynamic in the SGEP's trajectory, aiming to infer causal chains between such a dynamic and the challenges identified in this system. Since the SGEP regulations represent the legal milestones that underpin this analysis, they are presented in the following list:

1. Decree no. 1,171, of 22 June 1994, which established the Code of Professional Ethics for Civil Servants of the Federal Executive Branch and imposed that all federal executive bodies should create their respective Ethics Commissions (doc. ID # 6).
2. Decree of 26 May 1999, which created the Public Ethics Commission of the Presidency of the Republic—CEP (doc. ID # 14).
3. Explanatory Memorandum no. 37, of 18 August 2000, which established the Code of Conduct of the High Federal Administration (doc. ID # 19).

4. Decree no. 6,029, of 1 February 20007, which created the Ethics Management System of the Federal Executive Branch—SGEP (doc. ID # 53).
5. Act no. 12,813, of 16 May 2013, which establishes general rules on conflict of interests, quarantine, and declarations of assets and private interests (doc. ID # 61).
6. Decree no. 10,571, of 9 December 2020, which regulates the implementation of declarations of assets and private interests (doc. ID # 83).
7. Decree no. 10,889, of 9 December 2021, which regulates the implementation of rules on gifts, hospitality, and publishing the agenda of public meetings (doc. ID # 93).

The Emergence of the Ethics Management in Brazil

The formulation of Decree no. 1,171 emerged in the political context of the anti-corruption appeal in the early 1990s marked by the massive scandal involving President Collor de Melo (the PC Farias case), which resulted in his impeachment. In 1993, following the exposure of another scandal involving irregularities among congressmen during the budget process, President Itamar Franco created a Special Commission of Investigation (CEI) to examine executive public officials' involvement and propose regulatory improvements (docs. ID # 1, 2, 3, 4, and 9).

The CEI prepared the Explanatory Memorandum no. 001/94-CE of May 1994, proposing the Code of Professional Ethics for Civil Servants of the Federal Executive Branch for low-ranking public officials, related to officials ranking up to general coordinators and equivalent, known as DAS 4. This code, approved by Decree No. 1,171 of June 1994, was justified by arguments about the widespread corruption that reinforced impunity, the lack of ethical and moral values, and disrespect towards public service users. It focused on how lower-ranking officials should treat people in general and public property without addressing ethical dilemmas and conflicts of interest. It also held ethics commissions responsible for advising public officials, investigating violations, and applying ethical sanctions (docs. IDs # 5 and 6).

A few months after Decree no. 1,171, it was established that the technical orientation of ethics commissions would be under the Federal Administration Secretariat—SAF/PR. In January 1995, the SAF was replaced by the Ministry of Administration and State Reform (MARE), highlighting the link between public ethics and the managerial reform agenda in President Fernando Henrique Cardoso's term. In January 1999, the Ministry of Planning, Budget, and Management (MPOG) replaced MARE (docs. ID # 7, 8, and 13).

Decree of 26 May 1999, which created the CEP, and Explanatory Memorandum no. 37 of August 2000, which established the Code of Conduct of the High Federal Administration, were formulated in parallel. Both regulations responded to growing calls for strengthening public ethics to prevent conflicts of interest in the same political context as the aforementioned managerial reform agenda. These initiatives were also influenced by OECD standards on public ethics (1998) and conflict of interest (1999). At the same time, Brazil was in the process of adhering to the OECD Anti-Corruption Convention, ratified in November 2000 (docs. ID # 11, 12, 15, 16, 17, 18, 19, and 26).

The CEP was created within the structure of the Presidency of the Republic as a collegiate body responsible for the final proposal of the Code of Conduct of the High Federal Administration, as well as for reviewing other rules on ethical conduct, and leading the ethics commissions, replacing the MPOG in this regard. The first CEP president was a former member of the State Reform Council—which represented the advisory collegiate for the managerial reform agenda in President Cardoso's term mandate—and led the debate on public ethics focused on ethical dilemmas and conflicts of interest, a stance supported by all CEP members (docs. ID # 10, 15, and 34).

The Code of Conduct of the High Federal Administration proposed for the CEP was justified by two arguments. The first was that OECD studies indicated scepticism towards public administrators and politicians and the need for changes in the role of the State, which should focus on regulating economic activity and public services delegated to private companies. The second was that ethical dilemmas would arise in the grey area that had grown in this new context, challenging the separation between public and private interests.

This new Code was published in August 2000, focusing on high-ranking positions—equal to or greater than DAS 5 as directors, secretaries, and ministers. It addressed conflict of interest as a relevant topic regarding ethics management with rules on declarations of assets and private interests, acceptance of gifts and hospitality, privileged information, private activities, and quarantine regulations, and also on the public opinions that are damaging to the image of institutions or people (docs. ID # 6 and 19).

From 2000 to 2003, the CEP enacted eight resolutions on conflicts of interest and their subtopics, except one, and published a series of notes and guidelines on the topic. During this same period, the OECD published guidelines and policy drafts reinforcing the link between ethics management and conflict of interest. In May 2003, the OECD published its recommendations for managing conflict of interest in the public sector, a document that became widely cited (docs. ID # 20 to 25, 27 to 33, and 35 to 37).

The Entry of the CGU and the Creation of the SGEP

From 2004 onwards, the CGU, which had been legally strengthened during President Lula da Silva's first term, began influencing the trajectory of ethics management, focusing on conflict of interest. That year, at the first meeting of the Public Transparency and Combating Corruption Council (CTPCC), under CGU leadership, its minister proposed drafting a bill on conflict of interest within that collegiate. As stated in the meeting minutes, the CEP representative warned that anti-corruption and public ethics would no longer be interactive and highlighted the delay in measures to improve ethics management, suggesting that the CEP should participate in the monitoring of international commitments made by Brazil (doc. ID # 38).

Between 2005 and 2006, a period marked by massive corruption scandals involving high authorities of the Federal Executive Branch, the CGU led the formulation of a bill's proposal on conflict of interest, as indicated by minutes of CTPCC meetings, documents of a public consultation on the bill, and the resulting explanatory memorandum presenting the proposal. The bill stated that powers should be attributed to the CGU to manage conflicts of interest in low-ranking positions, justified by arguments that they were not covered by the Code of High Federal Administration, being outside the scrutiny of the CEP (docs. ID # 38, 41, 43, 45, and 48 to 51).

At that period, the CGU proposed the establishment of the SISCOR, created by Decree no. 5,480 of July 2005, with no evidence of discussions about this new system in the CTPCC or with the participation of CEP. The CGU became the SISCOR's central body, and internal affairs units were created in all executive federal bodies to investigate and punish public officials for disciplinary violations. In the next year, the OAS assessment report stated the importance of creating an ethics management system and recommended strengthening the CEP to ensure greater institutionalisation. News articles indicated that the CEP faced challenges such as delays in appointing members, lack of support, and institutional insufficiency (docs. ID # 42, 46, 47, and 54).

At the beginning of 2007, the CEP proposed a decree establishing the SGEP without evidence of the CGU's participation. In the explanatory memorandum, the CEP argued for the need to improve the management of conflicts of interest. Decree no. 6,029 of February 2007 makes only one mention of the CGU, in a provision that deals with the referral of cases where, after investigating ethical transgressions, there are indications of disciplinary violations. The following year, the CEP enacted Resolution no. 8 on investigations of ethical violations (docs. ID # 52, 53, and 55).

Between 2009 and 2012, the conflict of interest bill progressed slowly through the National Congress, and there were no significant changes related to ethics management, except for a new decree on nepotism. The CGU led the formulation process of this regulation, and there is no evidence of the CEP's participation. At that time, the OECD expanded its ethics management guidelines with new conflict of interest standards, specifically on lobbying transparency and best practices on post-public employment (docs. ID # 56 to 58).

In November 2012, the OECD published an assessment report that included SGEP and SICOR in its scope, in which challenges regarding coordination and balance were the main focus. The report suggested that the Code of High Federal Administration be broader, reaching at least the general coordinators (DAS 4) and that the CEP should adopt ethical risk management. All other recommendations were addressed to the CEP and the CGU, alleging that the SGEP and SISCOR had similar goals and presented vague boundaries and overlaps, implying challenges for balance and dual recommendations for coordination, monitoring, and assessment (doc. ID # 59).

The CGU's entry with SISCOR, along with the formal creation of the SGEP, resulted in the existence of two parallel systems focused on public officials' behaviour. On the one hand, the SGEP, led by the CEP as its central body and comprised of ethics committees, was responsible for preventing and addressing administrative ethical violations. On the other hand, SICOR, led by the CGU and comprised of internal affairs units, was responsible for preventing and addressing administrative disciplinary violations. Therein lies a central challenge: some public officials' maladministration practices represent ethical and disciplinary violations at the same time. This is worsened by the unclear separation of responsibilities or rules on concomitances. It is notable that the CGU was not included in the SGEP as a co-central body in any other capacity (docs. ID# 53 and 90).

The Legal Rise of Conflict of Interest and Integrity Management

In April 2013, the bill on conflicts of interest was sent for approval by the Senate plenary, but the bill rapporteur proposed excluding the CGU's powers. He argued that they would cause confusion and overlap of the CEP's powers, hinder the SGEP, and undermine the ethics commissions' education and prevention efforts. Despite this, Act no. 12,813 of May 2013 maintained the CGU's powers, establishing a dual system of coordination in ethics management. The CEP remained responsible for preventing conflicts of interest and their subtopics among high-ranking positions, and the CGU officially became responsible for preventing conflicts of interest in low-ranking positions (docs. ID # 60 and 61).

Four months after the approval of Act no. 12,813, the CGU, with the MPOG, enacted the Joint Ordinance no. 333, which regulates consultations on possible conflicts of interest and requests for authorisation to engage in private activities for low-ranking public officials. There is no evidence that the CEP participated in its formulation, although it established that the ethics commissions, units of the SGEP led by the CEP, could assume new responsibilities. From then on, all low-ranking public officials would make consultations or requests through the Electronic System for the Prevention of Conflicts of Interest (SeCI), under the CGU's coordination and guidance. Since this regulation and the SeCI did not apply to high-ranking officials, a situation emerged in which consultations or requests to prevent conflicts of interest of each executive body have been processed, coordinated, guided, and regulated by different central bodies (docs. ID # 62 and 63).

In November 2013, the TCU developed its first assessment report of ethics management, indicating that 25% of federal executive bodies did not adopt any codes of ethics, 49% did not monitor compliance with the codes of ethics, and

53% did not carry out periodic efforts to disseminate such codes. In the second report from March 2017, the TCU presented an overview of ethics management across all federal branches. The findings regarding the SGEP highlighted the role of ombudsmen as reporting channels and internal affairs units, considering the duality between ethics and discipline (docs. ID # 64 and 68).

Regarding the trajectory of the CEP and the SGEP, between 2014 and 2020, four resolutions, one guidance note, and one jointly normative guidance with the CGU were enacted, all on conflicts of interest and their subtopics. However, the CEP still does not have an IT system similar to the SeCI. Therefore, consultation on potential conflicts of interest and requests for authorisation of private activities by high-ranking public officials are received through the CEP mail protocol service (docs. ID # 65, 67, 71 to 78).

Regarding the CGU's role, in 2016, it began pursuing a new "competing" system by investing heavily in the public integrity management agenda. This effort involved the issuance of ordinances published in April 2016, August 2017, April 2018, and January 2019, followed by decrees in July 2021 and May 2023, which created the SITAI. Public ethics and conflict of interest were treated as integrity measures or functions, being organised and monitored based on organisational integrity programmes, guided and supervised by the CGU, indicating a sense of subordination of integrity management over ethics management (docs. ID # 66, 70, 73, 77, 87, and 102).

The political context of anti-corruption appeal driven by the Car Wash scandal, along with debates on strengthening public and private compliance, influenced the discussions and formulation processes of the integrity regulations. These discussions were followed by calls to expand the focus beyond merely preventing corruption and bribery to addressing other maladministration practices. These justifications were reinforced by OECD standards, which were frequently cited. Documents of such processes indicate that the CEP would only have been formally called upon to provide contributions on the decree published in 2021 that instituted the Integrity System of the Federal Executive Branch (SIPEF), renamed as SITAI in 2023 (docs. ID # 69, 72, 83, 84, and 100).

Decrees nos. 10,571 and 10,889 of December 2020 and 2021, related to conflicts of interest, were formulated under the leadership of the CGU and their publication was accompanied by the launch of two new IT systems. The first decree addresses the declaration of assets and situations that may constitute a conflict of interest, and the IT system was the e-Patri. The second decree addresses the transparency of meetings and the acceptance of gifts and hospitality related to high-ranking public officials, and the corresponding IT system is the e-Agendas. There is evidence of the CEP's participation, though only in the formulation process of the second decree as a co-leader (docs. ID # 79, 82, 85, and 91 to 93).

In December 2021, the OECD published a second assessment report, including SITAI, SICOR, and SGEP. This report indicated four challenges. First, the coexistence of SGEP and SITAI would create complexity, opacity, and overlaps, especially for training and guidance on values, ethical dilemmas, and situations of conflict of interest, resulting in misunderstandings and confusion among public officials. Second, federal bodies' ethics commissions are composed of public officials with short office terms, making it difficult to gain proper training and experience. Third, these commissions struggled to gain the trust of public officials in their respective bodies, given that they conducted investigations and applied sanctions, which would create tensions within their advisory role. Fourth, there would be overlaps between the ethics management and the disciplinary regime of SISCOR and its internal affairs units (doc. ID # 90).

Returning to the CEP, between 2021 and 2023, due to the decrees on assets and situations of conflict of interest and transparency in meetings and the acceptance of gifts and hospitality, the CEP enacted three new resolutions that amended or revoked previous resolutions. Finally, in 2023, the CEP published three additional resolutions focusing on the SGEP, amending its internal regulations, defining the disclosure of information on ethical sanctions, and formalising the sharing of information between ethics commissions and oversight bodies (docs. ID # 89, 94 to 99, and 103).

Results and Discussions

The narrative of the case study provided diverse evidence of the presence and relevance of political-institutional dynamics in the development of ethics management in Brazil. The three-decade path and the system resulting from this trajectory were marked not only by international standards and corruption scandals. The process tracing made it possible to demonstrate the relevance of CEP's and CGU's strategies based on these standards and scandals that legitimised their proposals of new regulations, which, in turn, increased these key actors' powers— sometimes with disputes and compromises. These strategies, thus, resulted from the political context of international influence and anti-corruption appeal, combined with exploring weaknesses of the ethics management domain, which was marked by soft spots in international recommendations and domestic institutions.

International standards and corruption scandals affected the SGEP's trajectory in multiple ways. In addition to representing drivers (as inputs "I"), they also facilitated the approval of ethics management regulations, reducing possible veto points, and increasing the likelihood of political actors seeking a leadership role for power-positive feedback (as the political context "C"). It is worth indicating that OECD standards have created ambiguities in the ethics management domain in Brazil (as the first part of features of policy domain "F") due to their complexities and imprecisions, especially related to the rise of conflicts of interest and vague boundaries with integrity management.

Such ambiguities in the ethics management domain also resulted from weaknesses in Brazilian institutions (as the second part of features of policy domain "F"), characterised by a lack of rules, structures, and instruments, especially in responsibilities for preventing conflict of interest between high- and low-ranking positions. In the development of the SGEP, numerous proposals and actions undertaken by the CEP and the CGU in favourable contexts and by exploiting these ambiguities resulted in more legal prerogatives for these same key actors (as strategies for power "S").

On the one hand, the CEP proposed the Code of High Federal Administration and the SGEP, which guaranteed and reinforced its prerogatives on preventing conflict of interest in high-ranking positions and its leadership role over ethics commissions in federal executive bodies. On the other hand, the CGU led and sometimes monopolised formulation processes of ethics-management-related regulations in arenas and channels under its control, justifying its role as the Federal Executive Branch anti-corruption agency, combined with efforts to expand systems that compete with the SGEP.

These findings allow us to infer that the aforementioned challenges in coordination and balance in ethics management in the Federal Executive Branch were also caused by the coexistence of three systems (SGEP, SISCOR, and SITAI) led by two different central bodies (CEP and CGU). Each of these systems focuses on public officials' behaviour, ethical dilemmas, and conflicts of interest, resulting in complexity, fragmentation, and overlaps that represent the challenges identified by this chapter's causal mechanism as the outcomes of interest "O" from the analysis of the political-institutional dynamic.

This chapter's results go beyond merely addressing gaps in the critical debate and research on ethics management in Brazil. Given that the assumptions supporting the political-institutional dynamics proposal relate to broader anti-corruption reforms, the theoretical proposal and research design can be adapted to explore other case studies. Furthermore, since these assumptions address general issues regarding ethics management reforms, this chapter's theoretical proposal and findings can contribute to the literature on this subject in the Americas and other regions worldwide.

Conclusion

This chapter aligns with the volume's purpose for regional analyses by exploring the Brazilian case as a significant experience in the Americas. It focused on the Ethics Management System of the Executive Federal Branch—SGEP—which is the only one of its kind at the national level. Assessment reports indicate that such a system has presented challenges for coordination and balance. Over the past 30 years since the first regulation on ethics management in Brazil, critical work on this topic remains timid.

The theoretical proposal was grounded in three general issues. First, the international standards and corruption scandals represent key drivers for ethics management reforms. Second, these drivers have led to policies significantly oriented towards political interests to the extent they generate power gains. Finally, national ethics management systems produced from these reforms have been shaped by ambiguous standards and non-linear power-driven processes, resulting in complexity, fragmentation, and overlaps.

This way, this chapter proposes that a political-institutional dynamic of strategies oriented towards power interests mediated by a political context of international influence and anti-corruption appeal, as well as by ambiguities in the ethics management domain, is relevant to the ethics management systems' trajectories. By focusing on this dynamic as a theorised causal mechanism, this chapter explored the case study for drawing inferences on how it has been shaped, resulting in the aforementioned challenges.

The case study process tracing clarified key actors' strategies for approving SGEP regulations. These strategies took place in a political context marked by international influence and anti-corruption appeals, creating expectations of power gains from resulting ethics policies. These actors also explored ambiguities in the ethics management domain, marked by weak points in both international standards and domestic institutions. These findings suggest that challenges in the ethics management of the Brazilian Federal Executive Branch stem from the presence and relevance of the theorised political-institutional dynamic.

This chapter builds on and innovates from previous studies on the balance between cultural- and compliance-based policies in public ethics. If political interests, combined with the vagueness of international standards and weaknesses in national institutions, may constitute a general causality of challenges in ethics management systems, the theorised political-institutional dynamic can also be applied to analyse other systems and help explain the blurred boundaries between ethics and integrity. In this sense, its theoretical proposal and research design can be adapted to explore other cases of ethics management reforms in the Americas and other regions worldwide.

Furthermore, from the institutionalism and causal mechanisms perspective, this chapter suggests that power and ambiguity can represent significant causal components, even in reforms justified by discourses advocating politics-free public policies through mechanisms designed to ensure neutral and technical decision-making. Since these issues emerge from the broader anti-corruption literature, this chapter can contribute to future studies by highlighting opportunities for a research agenda that addresses the centrality of power and ambiguity in reforms of public ethics and other related topics.

Disclosure Statement

The authors reported no potential conflict of interest.

Acknowledgements

This work is supported by Portuguese national funds through FCT—Fundação para a Ciência e a Tecnologia—under project UIDP/00713/2020.

Notes on Contributors

Temístocles Murilo de Oliveira Júnior is a Collaborative and PostDoc Researcher at the Centre for Public Administration and Public Policies of the Institute of Social and Political Sciences of the *Universidade de Lisboa* (CAPP/ ISCSP/ULisboa). He holds a doctorate in Public Policies by the *Universidade Federal do Rio de Janeiro* (UFRJ). Oliveira Júnior is Integrity Coordinator and Ethics Commission's Executive-Secretary at the Brazilian Ministry of Racial Equality (MIR). E-mail: tmurilo@edu.ulisboa.pt.

Joaquim Manuel Croca Caeiro is Associate Professor with Aggregation and integrated researcher at the Centre for Public Administration and Public Policies of the Institute of Social and Political Sciences of the *Universidade de Lisboa* (CAPP/ ISCSP/ULisboa). He holds a doctorate in Social Sciences by the Institute of Social and Political Sciences of the University of Lisbon. E-mail: jcaeiro@iscsp.ulisboa.pt.

References

Allison, G., & Zelikow, P. (1999). *Essence of decision: Explaining the cuban missile crisis*. Longman.

Andersson, S., & Ekelund, H. (2021). Promoting ethics management strategies in the public sector: Rules, values, and inclusion in Sweden. *Administration & Society*, *54*(6), 1089–1116. https://doi.org/10.1177/00953997211050306

Bardin, L. (2013). *L'analyse de contenu*. Universitaires de France.

Basinger, S. J. (2016). Scandals and ethics reform in the U.S. house of representatives. *Public Integrity*, *18*(4), 359–375. https://doi.org/10.1080/10999922.2016.1172932

Beach, D., & Pedersen, R. B. (2013). *Process-tracing methods: Foundations and guidelines*. The University of Michigan Press.

Bergue, S. T. (2022). Ethics, codes of conduct and integrity in the Brazilian public administration. *Administração Pública e Gestão Social*, *14*(4). https://doi.org/10.21118/apgs. v14i4.13459

Bowler, S., & Karp, J. A. (2004). Politicians, scandals, and trust in government. *Political Behavior*, *26*(3), 271–287. https://doi.org/10.1023/B:POBE.0000043456.87303.3a

Boyce, G., & Davids, C. (2009). Conflict of interest in policing and the public sector. *Public Management Review*, *11*(5), 601–640. https://doi.org/10.1080/14719030902798255

Cellard, A. (1997). L'analyse documentaire. In J. Poupart, J. P. Deslauriers & L. H. Groulx (Eds.), *La recherche qualitative: Enjeux épistémologiques et méthodologiques* (pp. 275–296). Gaëtan Morin.

Choi, J.-W. (2023). *Ethics management in the public sector: Implications for performance and productivity*. (Vol. 3–7), *Productivity Talk (P-Talk)*. Asian Productivity Organization.

Cooper, T. L., & Yoder, C. (2002). Public management ethics standards in a transnational world. *Public Integrity*, *4*(4), 333–352. https://doi.org/10.1080/15580989.2002.11770926

D'Alterio, E. (2017). Integrity of the public sector and controls: A new challenge for global administrative law? *International Journal of Constitutional Law*, *15*(4), 1013–1038. https://doi.org/10.1093/icon/mox077

Da Ros, L., & Taylor, M. (2022). *Brazilian politics on trial: Corruption and reform under democracy*. Lynne Rienner Publishers.

Dâmaso, E. (2024). *Corrupção: Breve história do crime que nunca existiu*. Objectiva.

Daniel, L. F. (2020). The efficacy of anti-corruption institutions in Italy. *Public Integrity*, *22*(6), 590–605. https://doi.org/10.1080/10999922.2020.1739362

de Sousa, L., & Coroado, S. (2023). Political corruption in portugal. In J. M. Fernandes, P. C. Magalhães & A. C. Pinto (Eds.), *The oxford handbook of portuguese politics* (pp. 589–603). Oxford University Press.

Demmke, C., Autioniemi, J., & Lenner, F. (2023). Explaining the popularity of integrity policies in times of critical governance—the case of conflicts of interest policies for ministers in the EU-member states. *Public Integrity*, *25*(1), 1–14. https://doi.org/10.10 80/10999922.2021.1987056

DiMaggio, P., & Powell, W. (1991). Introduction. In W. Powell & P. DiMaggio (Eds.), *The new institutionalism in organizational analysis*. The University of Chicago Press.

Dyer, J. L. (1998). International ethics initiatives [abstract]. *The Government Accountants Journal*, *47*(24).

Falleti, T. G., & Lynch, J. F. (2009). Context and causal mechanisms in political analysis. *Comparative Political Studies*, *42*(9), 1143–1166. https://doi.org/10.1177/0010414009331724

Gerring, J., & Cojocaru, L. (2016). Selecting cases for intensive analysis. *Sociological Methods & Research*, 45(3), 392–423. https://doi.org/10.1177/0049124116631692

Heywood, P. M. (2012). Integrity management and the public service ethos in the UK: Patchwork quilt or threadbare blanket? *International Review of Administrative Sciences*, *78*(3), 474–493. https://doi.org/10.1177/0020852312445172

Heywood, P. M., & Kirby, N. (2020). Public integrity: From anti-corruption rhetoric to substantive moral ideal. *Etica Pubblica. Studi su legalità e Partecipazione*, *2*, 11–31. https://doi.org/10.1400/281574

Huberts, L. W. J. C. (2014). Placing integrity of governance in context. In L. Huberts (Ed.), *The integrity of governance: What it is, what we know, what is done, and where to go* (pp. 198–229). Palgrave Macmillan.

Huberts, L. W. J. C. (2018). Integrity: What it is and why it is important. *Public Integrity*, *20*(1), 518–532. https://doi.org/10.1080/10999922.2018.1477404

Ian, S., & Ting, G. (2015). Integrity management in the public sector: Organizational challenges and public perceptions. *International Public Management Journal*, *18*(3), 386–389. https://doi.org/10.1080/10967494.2015.1057789

Jackson, G. (2005). Contested boundaries: Ambiguity and creativity in the evolution of German codetermination. In W. Streeck & K. Thelen (Eds.), *Beyond continuity: Institutional change in advanced political economies* (pp. 229–254). Oxford University Press.

Luk, S. C. Y. (2012). Questions of ethics in public sector management: The case study of Hong Kong. *Public Personnel Management*, *41*(2), 361–378. https://doi.org/10.1177/009102601204100207

Mafunisa, J. (2003). Conflict of interest: Ethical dilemma in politics and administration. *South African Journal of Labour Relations*, *27*, 4–22.

Mahoney, J. (2016). Mechanisms, Bayesianism, and process tracing. *New Political Economy*, *21*(5), 493–499. https://doi.org/10.1080/13563467.2016.1201803

Mahoney, J., & Thelen, K. (2010). A theory of gradual institutional change. J. Mahoney & K. Thelen (Eds.), In *Explaining institutional change: Ambiguity, agency, and power* (pp. 1–37). Cambridge University Press.

Marsh, D., & Sharman, J. C. (2009). Policy diffusion and policy transfer. *Policy Studies*, *30* (3), 269–288. https://doi.org/10.1080/01442870902863851

Menzel, D. C. (2015). Research on ethics and integrity in public administration: Moving forward, looking back. *Public Integrity*, *17*(4), 343–370. https://doi.org/10.1080/1099 9922.2015.1060824

Mills, A. (1999). Ethics goes global: The OECD council recommendation on improving ethical conduct in the public sector. *Australian Journal of Public Administration, 58*(2), 61–69. https://doi.org/https://doi.org/10.1111/1467-8500.00089

Morris, S., & Blake, C. (2009). Political and analytical challenges of corruption in Latin America. In C. Blake & S. Morris (Eds.), *Corruption and democracy in Latin America* (pp. 1–24). University of Pittsburgh Press.

OECD. (1998). *Recommendation of the council on improving ethical conduct in the public aervice including principles for managing ethics in the public service.* Retrieved from https://legalinstruments.oecd.org/en/instruments/OECD-LEGAL-0298

OECD. (2003). *Recommendation of the council on guidelines for managing conflict of interest in the public sector.* Retrieved from https://legalinstruments.oecd.org/public/doc/130/130.en.pdf

OECD. (2010a). *Post-public employment: Good practices for preventing conflict of interest.* Retrieved from https://www.oecd.org/en/publications/post-public-employment_9789264056701-en.html

OECD. (2010b). *Recommendation of the council on principles for transparency and integrity in lobbying.* Retrieved from https://legalinstruments.oecd.org/public/doc/256/256.en.pdf

OECD. (2017). *Recommendation of the council on public integrity.* Retrieved from https://legalinstruments.oecd.org/en/instruments/OECD-LEGAL-0435

Oliveira Júnior, T. M. (2019). Cultura do escândalo e a ortodontia da accountability em democracias recentes: Estudo sobre reformas anticorrupção no Brasil na era Lava Jato. *Revista da CGU, 11*(18). https://doi.org/10.36428/revistadacgu.v11i18

Oliveira Júnior, T. M., & Costa, F. L. (2020). Reforma do estado e política de acesso à informação no Brasil. In *Reformas do Estado no Brasil: Trajetórias, inovações e desafios.* (pp. 365–390). IPEA.

Oliveira Júnior, T. M., & Fonseca, C. M. (2024). Political dynamics in policymaking of freedom of information in Brazil. *Brazilian Journal of Public Administration, 58*(1). https://doi.org/10.1590/0034-761220230069x

Palidauskaitė, J. (2015). Lithuanian experience regulating conflict of interest: Balancing on private and public edge. *Politologija, 57*(1), 3–39. https://doi.org/10.15388/Polit.2010.1.8318

Pereyra, S. (2019). Corruption scandals and anti-corruption policies in Argentina. *Journal of Politics in Latin America, 11*(3), 348–361. https://doi.org/10.1177/1866802x19894791

Perlman, B. J., Reddick, C., & Demir, T. (2023). A compliance—integrity framework for ethics management: An empirical analysis of local government practice. *Public Administration Review, 83*(4), 823–837. https://doi.org/https://doi.org/10.1111/puar.13610

Prayote, S. (2016). Managing ethics in public sector: Integrity approaches. *Jurnal Studi Pemerintahan, 7*(4), 578–593. https://doi.org/10.18196/jgp.2016.0043.578-593

Radaelli, C. (2000). Policy transfer in the European union: Institutional isomorphism as a source of legitimacy. *Governance: An International Journal of Policy and Administration, 13*(1), 25–43.

Roberts, R. (2023). The new public integrity management and the protection of the impartiality of bureaucratic decision-making. *Public Integrity, 1*–24. https://doi.org/10.1080/10999922.2023.2297118

Scapin, T. (2016). The ambiguous meaning of the ethical issue in a context of NPM reforms: Insights from the OECD, Canada and France. *The NISPAcee Journal of Public Administration and Policy, IX*(2), 93–119. https://doi.org/https://doi.org/10.1515/nispa-2016-0016

Schimmelfennig, F. (2015). What makes process tracing good? Causal mechanisms, causal inference, and the completeness standard in comparative politics. In A. Bennett & J. T.

Checkel (Eds.), *Process tracing: From metaphor to analytic tool* (pp. 98–125). Cambridge University Press.

Scott, J. B. (2016). Scandals and ethics reform in the U.S. House of representatives. *Public Integrity, 18*(4), 359–375. https://doi.org/10.1080/10999922.2016.1172932

Topchii, V., Zadereiko, S., Didkivska, G., Bodunova, O., & Shevchenko, D. (2021). International anti-corruption standards. *Linguistics and Culture Review*. https://doi.org/10.21744/lingcure.v5ns4.1866

Tremblay, M., Martineau, J. T., & Pauchantm, T. C. (2017). Managing organizational ethics in the public sector: A pluralist contingency approach as an alternative to the integrity management framework. *Public Integrity, 19*(3), 219–233. https://doi.org/10.1080/10999922.2016.1230688

van der Heijden, J., Kuhlmann, J., Lindquist, E., & Wellstead, A. (2019). Have policy process scholars embraced causal mechanisms? A review of five popular frameworks. *Public Policy and Administration, 36*(2), 163–186. https://doi.org/10.1177/0952076718814894

van Steden, R. (2020). Blind spots in public ethics and integrity research: What public administration scholars can learn from Aristotle. *Public Integrity, 22*(3), 236–244. https://doi.org/10.1080/10999922.2020.1714412

Vyas-Doorgapersad, S. (2022). Organisational ethics management to combat corruption in the South African public sector. *Business Ethics and Leadership, 6*, 14–22. https://doi.org/10.21272/bel.6(3).14–22.2022

Weller, N., & Barnes, J. (2014). Pathway analysis and the search for causal mechanisms. *Sociological Methods & Research, 45*(3), 424–457. https://doi.org/10.1177/0049124114544420

The World Bank. (2020). *Preventing and managing conflicts of interest in the public sector: Good practices guide*. Retrieved from www.unodc.org/documents/corruption/Publications/2020/Preventing-and-Managing-Conflicts-of-Interest-in-the-Public-Sector-Good-Practices-Guide.pdf

Zittoun, P. (2014). *The political process of policymaking: A pragmatic approach to public policy, studies in the political economy of public policy*. Palgrave Macmillan.

9 Preconditions for Anti-Corruption Reform

The Post-1989 Italian Experience and Lessons

Daniel L. Feldman and Jason D. Rivera

Introduction

In November 2023, hundreds of people were sentenced to prison in Italy for their participation in corrupt activities. Although a number of these individuals had ties to the Mafia in Southern Italy, many of the people sentenced were part of the national and local public administration system (Pianigiani, 2023). Among them were members of the financial police, a regional councilor, and a former member of the Democratic Party's national assembly. These convictions come after a recent wave of anti-corruption legislation within the country that culminated with the passage of Law No. 3/2019 in January 2019. This new law amends and extends criminal and civil laws and penalties associated with corruption of public administration and its personnel. Along these lines, the law has been nicknamed the "bribe destroyer law" and seeks to strengthen activities related to the prevention, detection, and repression of crimes against the "public administration" (OHCHR, 2019; Maggio, 2021).

However, despite the passage of this law and the wave of mass arrests, Italy ranked 42 out of 180 countries in relation to its level of corruption and had a score of 56 out of 100 on the Corruption Perceptions Index (CPI) in 2023 (Transparency International, 2024). Although far from the most corrupt country in the world, Italy has exhibited a long history of corruption that can be attributed, in various ways, to its national and economic development, social or cultural norms, and decentralization stemming from the countries' administration under various regimes (i.e., Papal States, the Spanish, and/or the Normans) (Banfield, 1958; Putnam, 1993; Di Liberto & Sideri, 2015). As a result, Italy provides an example of how preconditions, in some cases present within the country's central government for more than 150 years, and more recent administrative trends have contributed to the persistent role of corruption.

Despite the preconditions to corruption (discussed in the following sections), several events in Italy, especially the Clean Hands investigations and the assassinations of anti-Mafia prosecutors in 1992, have had a positive impact on the development of anti-corruption institutions within Italy (Feldman, 2020). These

DOI: 10.4324/9781003416258-10

young anti-corruption institutions are just starting to have an impact on the practice of corruption within the country, as exemplified by the arrests earlier in 2023. But despite important institutional progress, Italy still has a long way to go to combat corrupt practices and thereby lighten the administrative burden they impose (Maggio, 2021; Batohi & Stone, 2023).

This chapter therefore explains some particularly Italian factors that nurture the presence of corruption, but many of the key factors have global impact. The chapter then describes how three events, *Mani Pulite*—sarcastically dubbed the "clean hands" scandal, assassinations of two anti-Mafia prosecutors in 1992, and the fall of the Soviet Union—inspired anti-corruption initiatives in Italy. Along these lines, it discusses various laws recently passed by the Italian government to fight corruption as examples of the country's current efforts. Finally, the chapter concludes with recommendations for institutional change in Italy and other governments that might further reduce the presence and practice of corruption.

Italy's progress, such as it is, reflects some idiosyncratic elements, like the need to overcome the persistence of significant Communist party influence well past its significance in other Western democracies. However, Italy's real advances in public integrity in recent decades did not come without effort. The history of those advances holds lessons for anti-corruption reformers in Italy's European neighbors, as this chapter will show.

Operationalizing Public Sector Corruption

Feldman and Alibašić (2019) define corruption as the exchange or use of governing power for private gain. However, Mugellini et al. (2021) maintain that the concept of corruption is relatively broad, with no consensus on a standard definition. To this end, Mugelinni (2020) argues that understanding corruption requires a multidisciplinary approach observing various aspects of the concept individually. It also requires knowing what mechanisms are used or abused to engage in the activity (Mugelinni, 2020). However, in the interest of brevity and clarity, here we use the World Bank (1997) approach, defining corruption as the use of one's public office for personal or private gain.

This general definition of corruption encompasses two important variations, political and administrative. For our purposes it is important to distinguish them. Political corruption typically refers to acts that affect legislators and influence the creation of laws, regulations and policies (OECD, 2015; Mugelinni et al., 2021). This type of corruption has profound influence on the governance of society and how actors are held accountable to superiors in addition to the public more broadly. Administrative corruption refers to acts that involve civil servants or bureaucrats in their interactions with their superiors during the implementation of public policies or with the general public in the context of service delivery (Khan, 2004; Mugelinni, 2020). This may take the form of civil servants bribing their superiors for career advantage or charging individuals of the public extra fees for services. Both political and administrative corruption reduce administrative and fiscal efficiency and also detrimentally impact public trust in governing actors (Çera et al., 2019; Mazzanti et al., 2020; Androniceanu et al., 2022). As a byproduct, political and administrative corruption reduce the ability of governments to provide public services and worsen the environment for international and domestic investments in the development of the private sector (Mircica, 2020).

General Factors Affecting the Presence of Corruption

Although corruption can be attributed to the individual choices that people make in their pursuit of both personal and career goals, several studies have identified macro-level factors that influence the predominance of the phenomenon in certain geographic areas. Along these lines, social and administrative norms, as well as institutional arrangements/governance approaches, contribute to the pervasiveness of corruption in a society (Del Monte & Papagni, 2007; Acemoglu & Robinson, 2012; Campante & Do, 2014; Di Liberto & Sideri, 2015; De Angelis et al., 2020). Each factor buttresses the others in various ways. It is helpful to consider their potential compounding impact when deconstructing environments in which corruption can occur and when assessing its extent.

Administrative Norms and Social Dynamics

In many respects, the United States and Western European counties exhibit similar political institutions and economic structures. However, some counties, such as Italy, are characterized by relatively higher levels of corruption. Del Monte and Papagni (2007), Putnam (1993), and Di Liberto and Sideri (2015) maintain that this difference can be explained through cultural dynamics indicative to specific nations, and various regions within respective countries. According to Di Liberto and Sideri (2015), in Europe, provinces or countries that were at one time maintained by Spanish, Papal State or Norman regimes, like most of Italy, exhibit relatively heightened levels of corruption. They attribute this relationship to the ways in which those countries administrated their provinces in relation to their central governments. Specifically, those powers concentrated their attention on highly centralized governance structures, leaving peripheral or territorial areas with a great deal of autonomy (Flora et al., 1999; La Porta et al., 1999). Moreover, many of the peripheral locations' administrators lacked the interest and/or ability to enforce rules of the central government (Melis, 1996). Because of the lack of enforcement, provinces developed cultural norms shaping their efforts to best achieve administrative goals while remaining somewhat accountable to the central authority. In this way administrative and political corruption offered relatively efficient, short-term means of pursuing and achieving goals. These cultural and administrative norms, reinforced over the centuries, provided the opportunity for corruption to perpetuate, and often to be accepted as a pragmatic solution to achieving administrative goals (Cavazza & Graubard, 1974; Del Monte & Papagni, 2007; Di Liberto & Sideri, 2015).

However, this administrative culture affected social ties between members of society. Del Monte and Papagni (2007) and Putnam (1993) maintain that as these types of pragmatic administrative mechanisms were used by government officials and private citizens, the broader society's sense of loyalty to official government actors weakened. Moreover, society's overall interest and appreciation for government offices and politics diminished (Tabellini, 2010). Putnam (1993) maintains that this also weakened people's social capital, which ultimately makes populations less civically oriented. Putnam's insight led a number of other scholars to identify the relationship between a nation's relative level of social capital and the presence of corruption (Della Porta, 2000; Graeff, 2004; Pena López & Sánchez Santos, 2014; Wachs et al., 2019). These cultural norms and weak social ties, compromised by the debased administrative norms, partially contributed to Italy's environment of corruption until the early 1990s (Golden, 2000), at which point a number of important events occurred to alter the political and social situation.

Institutional Arrangements and Governance

Administrative and social norms impinge on the political and economic dynamics of the administrative state. As noted earlier, corruption tends to thrive when greater autonomy makes environments more difficult to regulate. However, other scholars have argued that increasing the presence of the state (i.e., further centralization) also has the effect of increasing corruption (Del Monte & Papagni, 2007). Along these lines, Becker and Stigler (1974) and Shleifer and Vishny (1993) maintain that as state regulation increases, traditional management and entrepreneurial skills that typically yield individual rewards become less valuable. As a result, corruption becomes a more profitable avenue for achieving personal ambitions when states increase the regulatory environment. To counter this, Becker and Stigler (1974), Acemoglu and Verdier (2000), and Aidt (2003) argue that as it becomes more difficult to control or provide oversight to bureaucrats, individuals should receive higher wages or salaries and government intervention in their affairs should decrease. Moreover, if governmental intervention continues to be needed or expanded, the number of bureaucrats and their wages should be dramatically increased (Acemoglu & Verdier, 2000). Although the notion of increasing bureaucrats' wages or salaries as a means of reducing the temptation of corruption is plausible, it may not be practical due to decreasing public budgets and increasing interest in the further decentralization of the state (Everett et al., 2006).

The emphasis on further decentralization as a means of reducing corruption stems from neoliberal perspectives urging limited governmental intervention and favoring privatization, outsourcing, deregulation, and downsizing. Advocates of this approach argue that outsourcing the interaction between government and public procurement reduces corruption (Berrios, 2006; Lessig, 2011). In this way, inefficiencies manifested through corrupt practices would be reduced because market dynamics would push out such practices for more efficient, profit-maximizing, administration and service provision/procurement. Two governance paradigms in public administration, new public management and new public governance, further inform this approach. New public management is most directly tied to this perspective. It assumes that private sector influences and styles of management will improve the efficiency and effectiveness of the public sector (Morales et al., 2014; Grossi & Pianezzi, 2018). New public governance emphasizes the role of the hollow state, transferring governmental functions to third-party contractors (Foster & Plowden, 1996; Agranoff, 2008). Thus, problems and/or inefficiencies (such as corruption) are solved within networks of actors that hold themselves accountable to one another (Klijn, 2012; Almquist et al., 2013), because service providers are not directly accountable to the public through political dynamics, but to their customers.

However, although decentralization is a relatively popular approach to dealing with both corruption and other market "inefficiencies," the approach has drawn criticism. For example, the new public management perspective assumes that the private sector operates with perfect market dynamics and its personnel are immune to corruption. In response, Frederickson (1999) and Morales et al. (2014) argue that this approach with its underlying assumptions actually increases opportunities for corruption by encouraging public officials to engage in otherwise "selfish" behaviors. Other authors have indicated that decentralization provides more opportunities for corruption because it weakens control by central agencies (Tanzi, 1995) and brings bureaucrats into larger numbers of interactions with potential investors/contractors seeking their own benefits (Shleifer & Vishny, 1993; Blanshard & Schleifer, 2000). However, proponents of decentralization argue that it creates greater accountability of the bureaucracy to the public (Arikan, 2004; Ivanyna & Shah, 2010; Grossi & Pianezzi, 2018; Rivera & Knox, 2023), arguably because citizens have a closer view of government at the local level.

Dynamics of Corruption in Italy Between World War II and 1991

As previously pointed out, corruption within the Italian context is not a recent manifestation, but a byproduct of hundreds of years of public administrative, political, cultural, and social development (Cavazza & Graubard, 1974). According to Cavazza and Graudbard (1974), after World War II, the country's political institutions suffered from inefficient public administration, but also stable political systems. These relatively stable political systems were the byproduct of *clientelismo* or political patronage. This political patronage system provided groups of people to directly link themselves to politicians, which allowed them to reap personal rewards through the development of special laws (*leggine*) or through political appointments (Cazzola, 1988). According to Del Monte and Papagni (2007), these appointments or bestowed rewards were in no way directed at recruiting professional skills or enhancing bureaucratic efficiency but developing and perpetuating political power bases. However, even up through much of the 1980s these patronage systems were not perceived as political corruption as we think of it today (Cazzola, 1988; Del Monte & Papagni, 2007). They were viewed as the normal way of conducting business and earning political support.

The problem with the system, however, arose in the eventual culmination of the factors previously described—relatively lower social capital across the country, a depressed trust in government institutions and actors, weakened legality in imposing regulations and laws in isolated/remote provinces—and those that took advantage of the political patronage system—in this case, organized crime. According to LaSpina (2014, p. 608), "administrative inefficiency, clientelism, ineffective development policies, weak legality," in combination with a political system that was culturally accepting of patronage, provided organized crime the ability to legitimize itself. The system and the social environment almost encouraged political and administrative corruption (Feldman, 2019). Although bribery had always been present, it became so widespread in the 1970s and 1980s that a significant number of citizens became intolerant of the political corruption and demanded that the government do something. However, what also became more prominent in certain areas of the country was the growing use of violence in relation to political and administrative corruption.

Ruggiero (2016, p. 102) maintains that the deeply entrenched tradition of corruption in parts of Italy, as was previously pointed out, is a byproduct of historic legacies of governance practices:

> [T]he ruling class has never managed to make the transition from a system based on wild and violent accumulation to a social order respectful of legality based on shared values. The elite in Italy has never really renounced violence. See the example of state terrorism scattered along the history of the country.

Feldman (2019) maintains that organized crime and the corrupt practices they have engaged in were a byproduct of a political environment and governance structures that were ill-equipped to provide necessary services to the citizenry. Because of these organizations' ability to provide services through corrupt means, they often enjoyed a great deal of political support from the populations in which they operated (Paoli, 2014; LaSpina, 2014). However, although organized crime received a great deal of attention in reference to political and administrative corruption in Italy, and in other national contexts, these organizations were not and are not the only perpetrators. Moreover, Del Monte and Papagni (2007) maintain that there were also regional differences in the concentration of corruption in Italy—with higher levels of corruption occurring in the southern part of the country in comparison to the north.

Events Leading to Change in Italian Approaches to Corruption

Various authors have argued that geopolitical changes in the powers of Europe, specifically the fall of the USSR and political changes among its former member states, ushered in a new public acknowledgement and perspective on administrative and political corruption (Wheaton, 1992; Rose, 2001; Lanskoy & Suthers, 2019; Simonyan & Shultz, 2023). To this end, corruption was in some way tolerated, not only in Italy but in other countries of western Europe as long as it off-set the spread of communism (Rose, 2001; Del Monte & Papagni, 2007). However, this toleration of administrative and political corruption within continental western European counties ended after the fall of the Berlin Wall. Although these changes in world politics had profound implications for the way in which democracies would function throughout Europe, there were triggering events within Italy that changed the way the nation perceived and responded to corruption—*Mani Pulite* and the assassinations of Falcone and Borsellino.

Mani Pulite

Mani Pulite, or Clean Hands, was a corruption investigation that altered the perception of the breadth of administrative and political corruption in Italy. In 1992, Mario Chiesa, a Milanese nursing home director, was arrested for accepting a kickback in relation to a cleaning contract. However, he interestingly also somehow gained control over a minimum of $5 million worth of property. As a means of seeking leniency, Chiesa cooperated with prosecutors to bring two former mayors of Milan under investigation for the receipt of stolen goods. Moreover, Chiesa also identified various local business owners, who accused various members of the Milan City Council of accepting bribes from them for various reasons (Cowell, 1992). Soon after, leaders in some of Italy's largest firms, such as Fiat, Olivetti, and ENI, were also implicated in engaging in corrupt practices. These business leaders, in turn, implicated numerous politicians across the country belonging to all political parties and working in various levels of government (Nelken, 1996). To this end, Vannucci (2009, pp. 233–234) states:

> Six former prime ministers, more than five hundred members of Parliament and several thousand local and public administrators had become caught up in the investigations. The scandal they produced led to a dramatic crisis of the political system: in a few months, most leading political figures had been forced to resign or go into exile; the major parties disappeared or underwent radical transformation; new parties emerged on the scene to fill the political vacuum left by the old.

As a result, Vannucci (2016) maintains that the *Mani Pulite* investigations signaled the end of the "First Republic" of Italy. However, laws and other regulations to curb corruption in the Italian public administrative system did not occur until around 1996 under the center-left government of Romano Prodi (Vannucci, 2009). But, even with new regulations, it was argued by some government officials and prosecutors that subsequent to the investigations, corruption just got worse and more sophisticated (Day, 2015; Locatelli et al., 2017; Vannucci, 2009). Despite this, the *Mani Pulite* investigations brought to light the deep entrenchment of political and administrative corruption, which forced Italian political leadership to begin addressing it.

The Assassinations of Falcone and Borsellino

As was previously pointed out, while the Soviet Union was in power and the Iron Curtain remained, political entities in Italy were tolerant of organized crime because it helped stall the spread of communism. Specifically, the Christian Democratic party blocked prosecutions of the Mafia in Italy in exchange for southern Italian votes (Drozdiak, 1993). The political corruption was so widespread among appellate judges, in addition to loopholes in the justice system, that after 360 individuals were convicted of various things related to organized crime in 1987, many of them were quickly released. As a result of this obvious perversion of the law, two prosecutors emerged that would help to change the public's perception of organized crime in Italy as it related to corruption, Giovanni Falcone and Paulo Borsellino (Kleinfeld, 2018; Ser, 2007). By 1992, these two prosecutors were able to return most of the individuals convicted but released in 1987 back to prison. As a result of what they believed to be a betrayal by the political system, organized crime arranged for the assassination of Falcone and Borsellino in July and August of 1992 (Bohlen, 1997). Moreover, the Mafia bombed several well-known churches throughout Italy, the Uffizi Museum in Florence, and also arranged the murder of Sicilian Father Pino Puglisi who had renounced the Mafia (Cayli, 2017; Ser, 2007). These drastic and extremely conspicuous actions altered the public's attitudes toward organized crime and its associations with political and administrative corruption.

Legal Advancements and Challenges to Anti-corruption in Italy

These incidents generated an interest in change and even some recognition of the role of entrenched norms in perpetuating corrupt practices. Although relatively slowly, Italy began to adopt a variety of laws and decrees to curb administrative and political corruption. For example, Law No. 300/2000 ratified the 1997 European Union (EU) Convention against the corruption of European Community actors, in addition to the 1997 Organization for Economic Co-operation and Development (OECD) Convention against the corruption of foreign public officers and representatives. Law No. 97/2001 linked penal sanctions and disciplinary sanctions for public officials involved in corruption activities and other types of crimes. Additionally, Law No. 190/2012 institutionalized the Italian National Anti-Corruption Authority (ANAC) (ANAC, n.d.).

In 2001, Legislative Decree 231/2001 broadened the scope of who and what (i.e., organizational entities) could be held accountable in criminal and civil court for direct engagement in corrupt activities or that of individuals representing a respective organization or office. Specifically, according to Maggio (2021, p. 514), Decree 231/2001 holds organizations and individual liable for offences committed in their interests or to the "advantage of directors, executives and their subordinates, agents and other individuals acting on behalf of the legal entity." Along these lines, the decree also provides protections to whistle-blowers against retaliation or discrimination. Bernardo Georgio Mattarella and Antonino Gullo (personal communication, October 28, 2008), Quattrocolo (2016), and Maggio (2021) also maintain that the decree stipulates that organizations that fail to prevent corruption by these same actors or representatives can result in criminal conviction of the organization itself, which is consistent with the broader political environment of the EU and the OECD. Organizations that fail to identify and eliminate their own internal corruption can be penalized with fines, the seizure of assets, the loss of licenses, and the right to conduct business (De Nigris et al., 2016). To this end, the Italian Criminal Code provides judges with wide discretion in the application of criminal penalties that range between one and 12 years of imprisonment for engaging in corrupt practices (Maggio, 2021).

In 2019, Italy passed a new law (Law No. 3/2019) that introduced a variety of criminal changes to how the country deals with corruption, in addition to changes to civil codes. The Law also amends Decree 231/2001 in respect to the extent of corporate liability related to corruption. As such, the law has been nicknamed the "bribe destroyer law," and seeks to better prevent, detect, and repress administrative and political corruption (OHCHR, 2019; Maggio, 2021). In reference to the criminal law, the new legislation provides for the following:

- Increases penalties for general corruption with the minimum penalty increased from one to three years of imprisonment and a maximum penalty increase from six to eight years;
- Provides for life-long prohibition of dealing with governing administrations and disqualification from holding public office;
- Suspends the statute of limitations from the judgment of the first instance of corruption (whether the charge led to a conviction or acquittal) until the final judgment becomes enforceable, and that the statute of limitations will begin at which time the most recent crime has been shown to have ended; and
- Extends the prohibition of dealing with governing administrations and disqualification from holding public office for crimes of embezzlement, corruption in judicial proceedings, and trafficking in illegal influence.

Although this is not a comprehensive list of criminal extensions to the law, these examples highlight the government's interest in curbing corruption practices with the threat of imprisonment and restrictions on perpetrators' interactions with government after conviction. Finally, the law amends the Italian Civil Code by providing for the possibility of prosecuting *ex officio* private-to-private corruption (Maggio, 2021).

In addition to these new expansions to the criminal and civil law, Law No. 3/2019 also amends Decree 231/2001 in a variety of ways. Most significant among its amendments are: (1) it extends the list of predicate crimes to include illegal influence (i.e., influence peddling); (2) it increases restraining measures to certain crimes against public administration to a minimum of four years and not to exceed seven, in addition to crimes committed by top-level managers in public and private organization or individuals that commit crimes based on a superior's directions; and (3) it reduces restraining measures for extortion and improper inducement to bribery when a company or organization attempted to stop the illegal activity, cooperated with authorities, and remediated organizational structures that might provide future opportunities of criminal activity (Maggio, 2021). As such, these amendments provide legal incentives and justifications for making internal organizational changes that would potentially reduce the occurrence of administrative and political corruption from individuals working in their respective organizations. However, Maggio argues that these legal measures are not sufficient and do not address the engrained cultural and social dynamics in Italy that contribute to the perception that corruption is not a crime (2021).

Dealing With Engrained Dynamics to Reduce Corruption

As we have indicated throughout this chapter, the practice of administrative and political corruption in Italy is a phenomenon that has been reinforced over the centuries through administrative structures and the development of cultural and social norms that have often tolerated and perpetuated the illegal behavior. Although the focus of this chapter has been on the Italian experience with these types of corruption, these practices are by no means isolated or confined to this country. According to Transparency International (2024), of all 180 countries that the organization monitors for corruption, none are totally devoid of corruption, but neither is any country "totally" corrupt. In Europe, Denmark ranks as the least corrupt nation. Nations with higher levels of corruption than Italy include, among others, Bosnia and Herzegovina, Albania, Serbia, Belarus, and Russia (Transparency International, 2024). In many ways, those countries have experienced the development of similar cultural and political norms associated with corruption that have provided opportunities for the practices to persist. As such, understanding how to reduce corruption is important well beyond the Italian example.

Italy and many other nations throughout Europe have enacted legislation intended to curb administrative and political corruption through criminal prosecutions and civil procedures. Batohi and Stone, however, point to South Africa as a nation that has pursued what is arguably a more sophisticated approach, attempting to change cultural norms surrounding this phenomenon at the national level as opposed to within individual institutions (2023). They regard as ineffective the legal strategy of deterrence through prosecution for three reasons. First, prosecutions are long uncertain processes in which the slower the process the less likely the case will result in a conviction. Because of the dynamics of political and administrative corruption, the more severe the corrupt offence the longer it takes to build a case and prosecute violators of the law, which has been observed to lower the likelihood of convictions (Gordon, 2009; Alldridge, 2013). Moreover, these processes are often further prolonged through the use of highly paid defense counsel that often has more experience than the prosecutors (Batohi & Stone, 2023).

Second, prosecutions of top officials typically focus on specific illegal acts engaged in by individuals as opposed to systematic reforms to organizations or institutions (Batohi & Stone, 2023). Because of the lack of institutional reform, other individuals take advantage of the continuing opportunities for corruption. In Italy, Vannucci (2009) maintains, in the aftermath of the *Mani Pulite* investigations, even though the prosecutions brought a massive change of personnel within the administrative and political system, they only temporarily stemmed corruption. Although the *Mani Pulite* brought enhanced attention to the entrenchment of corruption within Italy and its punishment, it did not produce institutional stakeholders that could change political party financing processes and political patronage, which continued to provide opportunities for people and organizations to take advantage of (Batohi & Stone, 2023).

Third, and much related to the second point, Batohi and Stone (2023) argue that prosecutors' ability to make systematic institutional changes is diminished because they typically operate outside the organizations that are corrupt. Alternatively, Burke (2009) also points out that sometimes these same prosecutions lack moral authority due to the presence of corruption within the legal organizations behind the prosecutions. As such, they lack the opportunity and access to processes that would change the organizational cultures and structures within government and private organizations that contribute to persistence of corruption (Koudelková et al., 2015; Jávor & Jancsics, 2016; Mendelski, 2021). This subsequently has the potential to inhibit lasting change, not only within both public and private organizations, but also within the broader administrative system in which they operate.

As a result of these shortcomings, Batohi and Stone (2023) argue that governments should engage in four interrelated steps that include the prosecution of illegal practices, but emphasize impactful institutional reforms that reduce the opportunities for corruption:

1. Build integrity and measure progress department-by-department.
2. Reconcile institutional independence with interdependence.

3. Delegate authority to protect against capture.
4. Put the "public" back in public integrity.

Along these lines, these authors emphasize that focusing only on corruption at the national level obscures not only our understanding of the presence of corruption but also the successes and challenges that are experienced by entities at all levels of government that are combatting the issue. Moreover, although law enforcement should be devoid of political interference, these two spheres need to work collaboratively to accomplish their mutual goals of reducing corruption and other illegal acts hindering broader administrative and political efficiency. To this end, Batohi and Stone (2023) see the public as an asset in this regard. Specifically, the public, through its support of anti-corruption efforts, can provide politicians and public servants the needed will to pursue the systematic reform efforts, in conjunction with legal prosecutions, that might lead to reducing corruption. Finally, this approach also supports notions of decentralization, which they believe makes it more difficult for entities to engage in practices of state capture.

Conclusion

Mani Pulite left a political vacuum as its revelations discredited all the major Italian political parties. In its wake, a media mogul—Silvio Berlusconi—created a brand-new political party, Forza Italia, and in alliance with other right-wing parties it came to dominate the political scene. Belusconi's deep record of dishonesty and illegality gave support to sophisticated critics like Batohi and Stone (2023), who then question whether the *Mani Pulite* prosecutions had any meaningful sanitizing effect. We recognize the considerable value of the Batohi and Stone (2023) approach. But they may overstate their case. Italy's national government broke from its long history of tacit toleration of corruption when it adopted strong anti-corruption laws in the aftermath of Mani Pulite (and the assassinations of 1992). That change both reflected and encouraged some change in Italy's traditional cultural norms, despite the sorry spectacle of Berlusconi's political successes. Victory against corruption is never total, and Italy still has a long way to go. But it has surely made progress, and its history in that regard holds useful lessons for others.

This history holds some meaningful lessons for other European democracies. First, public opinion matters. Increasing and informing the public's focus may well be contingent upon large scandals that are prominent enough to command attention and alter perceptions. Anti-corruption campaigns that focus on the use of media, as opposed to only legislation and litigation, are possibly a more time-efficient approach that can be used in a variety of nations, such as Hungary, Estonia, Portugal, Malta, and Slovakia, to name a few. But anti-corruption activists must be ready to take advantage of such contingencies as Italian reformers did in the years after 1992. In a democracy, public outrage can strength the resolve of legislators to enact anti-corruption measures and judges to impose meaningful sentences on perpetrators.

Second, such scandals can generate unanticipated negative consequences, such as the political vacuum exploited by Berlusconi, as a result of the very same 1992 scandals. Should such conditions arise that offer credible hope for renewed support for integrity in government, as they did for Pashinyan in Armenia (Feldman & Alibašić, 2019), activists should be ready to initiate and support a movement for political reform. However, political vacuums can emerge for a number of other reasons as well. In any event, they provide opportunities for anti-corruption campaigns to take fruit if actors are able to take fast advantage of the situation. Places like Bosnia, in addition to more local-level jurisdictions such as cities and regions of Ukraine liberated from Russian occupation, provide opportunities for anti-corruption initiatives to be successful. But as the Italian case illustrates, these political vacuums can also be exploited by deeply entrenched practices that lead to further corruption.

Finally, and related to the last point, prosecution and harsh statutory penalties do not suffice. Cultural norms have profound influences on the way people act and, in turn, perceive the actions of others. This is especially true when cultural norms have been ingrained over centuries. As such, in contexts such as these, socialization processes need to be taken to reorient people, especially at the local level, to reconceive of the appropriateness of centuries-long behaviors that contribute to corrupt practices. Moreover, socialization also should occur across sectors as opposed to just within the public sphere, for example, in the way Italy has now forced corporations to install internal integrity officers. However, these types of social and cultural perception changes are not confined to Italy. Places like France, Slovenia, and Macedonia also have deep rooted cultural legacies of political corruption tied to cultural norms that are in the process of changing. In the case of France, the criminal conviction of former president Nicholas Sarkozy in 2023 for influence peddling and attempted bribery of a judge exposed corruption at the top (Hummel, 2023). However, the French strategy for anti-corruption reform does not appear to include institutional change at the corporate level (see Ministry for Europe and Foreign Affairs, 2021; see also Agence Française Anti-corruption, n.d.). In this respect, France could learn from the Italian example.

Whatever the approach, action on this issue is required. Although a multi-pronged approach to curbing corruption in Italy and throughout Europe is most appropriate, it starts with individuals taking charge. This is not a short-term endeavor. Altering deep-seated cultural norms and assumptions that can eventually limit the tolerance for corruption (and the failure to recognize corrupt behavior as corruption) only occurs over relatively long periods of time. However, now is the time for a renewed sense of motivation. We cannot allow administrative corruption the opportunity to perpetuate itself throughout Europe. If we do, we also provide encouragement of the like to flourish in other places throughout the world.

References

Acemoglu, D., & Robinson, J. A. (2012). *Why nations fail: The origins of power, prosperity, and poverty*. Random House.

Acemoglu, D., & Verdier, T. (2000). The choice between market failure and corruption. *American Economic Review, 90*(1), 194–211.

Agence Française Anticorruption. (n.d.) www.agence-francaise-anticorruption.gouv.fr/fr

Agranoff, R. (2008). Intergovernmental and network administration, accountability and performance: Symposium introduction. *Public Performance & Management Review, 31*(3), 315–319.

Aidt, T. (2003). Economic analysis of corruption: A survey. *The Economic Journal, 113*(491), F632–F652.

Alldridge, P. (2013). Bribery and the changing pattern of criminal prosecution. In J. Horder & P. Alldridge (Eds.), *Modern bribery law: Comparative perspectives* (pp. 219–250) Cambridge University Press.

Almquist, R., Grossi, G., van Helden, G. J., & Reichard, C. (2013). Public sector governance and accountability. *Critical Perspectives on Accounting, 24*(7–8), 479–487.

Androniceanu, A., Georgescu, I., & Kinnunen, J. (2022). Public administration digitalization and corruption in the EU member states: A comparative and correlative research analysis. *Transylvanian Review of Administrative Sciences, 65*, 5–22.

Arikan, G. (2004). Fiscal decentralization: A remedy for corruption? *International Tax and Public Finance, 11*, 175–195. https://doi.org/10.1023/B:ITAX.0000011399.00053.a1

Autorità Nazionale Anticorruzione (ANAC). (n.d.) *The Italian national anti-corruption authority*. Retrieved May 9, 2024, from www.anticorruzione.it/documents/91439/560ea10b-2308-4877-d60h-6e3242eca017.

Banfield, E. G. (1958). *The moral basis of a backward society*. Free Press.

Batohi, S., & Stone, C. (2023). The world's anti-corruption efforts need a reset. *The Chandler Session Papers, University of Oxford*. Retrieved from www.bsg.ox.ac.uk/sites/default/files/2023-11/The%20Chandler%20Papers%20%E2%80%93%20The%20world%E2%80%99s%20anti-corruption%20efforts%20need%20a%20reset.pdf.

Becker, G. S., & Stigler, J. (1974). Law enforcement, malfeasance and the compensation of enforcers. *Journal of Legal Studies, 3*(1), 1–18.

Berrios, R. (2006). Government contracts and contract behavior. *Journal of Business Ethics, 63*, 119–130. https://doi.org/10.1007/s10551-005-3969-8

Blanshard, O., & Schleifer, A. (2000). *Federalism with and without political centralization: China versus Russia*. WP 7617. National Bureau of Economic Research.

Bohlen, C. (1997, September 27). 24 Top mafia figures get life sentences in Sicily. *The New York Times*. Retrieved May 7, 2024, from www.nytimes.com/1997/09/27/world/24-top-mafia-figures-get-life-sentences-in-sicily.html.

Burke, R. J. (2009). Corruption in organizations: Causes, consequences, and choices. In R. J. Burke & C. Cooper (Eds.), *Research companion to corruption in organizations* (pp. 1–31). Edward Elgar Publishing.

Campante, F. R. & Do, Q. A. (2014). Isolated capital cities, accountability and corruption: Evidence from US state. *American Economic Review, 104*(8), 2456–2481.

Cavazza, F. L. & Graubard, S. R. (1974). *Il caso italiano*. Garzanti.

Cayli, B. (2017). The relationship between power and perception of identity: The case of the Italian Mafioso. In A. Mateos-Aparicio Martin-Albo & E. de Gregorio Godeo (Eds.), *Identity and identification* (Vol. 27–34). Ediciones de la Universidad de Castilla-La Mancha.

Cazzola, F. (1988). *Della corruzione*. Il Mulino.

Çera, G., Meço, M., Çera, E., & Maloku, S. (2019). The effect of institutional constraints and business network on trust in government: An institutional perspective. *Administratie si Management Public*, *33*, 6–19.

Cowell, A. (1992, May 5). Scanal in Italy hurts socialists. *The New York Times*. Retrieved May 2, 2024, from www.nytimes.com/1992/05/05/world/scandal-in-italy-hurts-socialists.html.

Day, M. (2015, March 20). Scandal in Italy 'worse than ever' as minister quits over links with gang accused of bribery. *The Independent*. Retrieved May 7, 2024, from www.independent.co.uk/news/world/europe/corruption-in-italy-worse-than-ever-as-minister-quits-over-links-with-gang-accused-of-bribery-10124024.html.

De Angelis, G., de Blasio, L., & Rizzica, L. (2020). Lost in corruption: Evidence from EU funding in southern Italy. *Italian Economic Journal*, *6*(2), 355–377.

De Nigris, M., Laternini, A. S., & Arrotino, A. (2016). The legislative decree No. 231/01, the test of the international law. *Il diritto penale della globalizazion*. Pacini Editore. Retrieved May 9, 2024, from www.dirittopenaleglobalizzazione.it/the-legislative-decree-no-23101-the-test-of-the-international-law/.

Del Monte, A., & Papagni, E. (2007). The determinant of corruption in Italy: Regional panel data analysis. *European Journal of Political Economy*, *23*(2), 379–396.

Della Porta, D. (2000). Social capital, beliefs in government, and political corruption. In S. J. Pharr & R. D. Putnam (Eds.), *Disaffected democracies: What's troubling the trilateral countries?* (pp. 202–228). Princeton University Press.

Di Liberto, A., & Sideri, M. (2015). Past dominations, current institutions and the Italian regional economic performance. *European Journal of Political Economy*, *38*, 12–41. https://doi.org/10.1016/j.ejpoleco.2014.12.006

Drozdiak, W. (1993, April 5). Italy probes possible mafia link with ruling party since 1940's. *The Washington Post*. Retrieved May 7, 2024, from www.washingtonpost.com/archive/politics/1993/04/06/italy-probes-possible-mafia-link-with-ruling-party-since-1940s/973bd3dc-d324-4661-b32d-096a4c6d2d5b.

Everett, J., Neu. D., & Rahaman, A. S. (2006). The global fight against corruption: A foucaultian, virtues-ethics framing. *Journal of Business Ethics*, *65*, 1–12. https://doi.org/10.1007/s10551-005-8715-8

Feldman, D. (2019). Corruption in Italy: Indigenous impediments to reform. In C. L. Jurkiewicz (Ed.), *Global corruption and ethics management: Translating theory into action* (pp. 53–62). Rowman & Littlefield.

Feldman, D. (2020). The efficacy of anti-corruption institutions in Italy. *Public Integrity*, *22*(6), 590–605.

Feldman, D., & Alibašić, H. (2019). The remarkable 2018 "Velvet Revolution": Armenia's experiment against political corruption. *Public Integrity*, *21*(4), 420–432.

Flora, P., Kuhnle, S., & Urwin, D. (1999). *State formation, nation building and mass politics in Europe*. Oxford University Press.

Foster, C. D., & Plowden, F. J. (1996). *The state under stress: Can the hollow state be good government?* Open University Press.

Frederickson, H. G. (1999). Ethics and the new managerialism. *Public Administration & Management*, *4*(2), 299–324.

Golden, M. (2000). Political patronage, bureaucracy and corruption in post-way Italy. Unpublished Paper. Department of Political Science, University of California at Los Angeles. Retrieved from https://www.russellsage.org/sites/all/files/u4/Golden_Political%20Patronage,%20Bureaucracy,%20&%20Corruption%20in%20Postwar%20Italy.pdf

Gordon, S. C. (2009). Assessing partisan bias in federal public corruption prosecutions. *American Political Science Review*, *103*(4), 534–554.

Graeff, P. (2004). Why should one trust in corruption? The linkage btween corruption, norms and social capital. In J. Graf Lambsdorff, M. Taube & M. Schramm (Eds.), *The new institutional economics of corruption* (pp. 54–72). Routledge.

Grossi, G., & Pianezzi, D. (2018). The new public corruption: Old questions for new challenges. *Accounting Forum, 42*(1), 86–101.

Hummel, T. (2023, May 17). France's Sarkozy loses corruption appeal, to challenge at highest court. *Reuters*. Retrieved from www.reuters.com/world/europe/frances-sarkozy-defending-his-honour-awaits-corruption-appeal-verdict-2023-05-17/.

Ivanyna, M., & Shah, A. (2010). Decentralization and corruption: New cross-country evidence. *Environment and Planning C: Government and Policy, 29*, 344–362. Retrieved from https://www.researchgate.net/publication/46444045_Decentralization_and_Corruption_New_Cross-Country_Evidence

Jávor, I., & Jancsics, D. (2016). The role of power in organizational corruption: An empirical study. *Administration & Society, 48*(5), 527–558.

Khan, M. M. (2004). Political and administrative corruption: Concepts, comparative experiences, and Bangladesh case. *Paper Prepared for Transparency International*. Retrieved April 23, 2024, from www.academia.edu/download/51359133/Political_administrative_corruption.pdf.

Kleinfeld, R. (2018). *A savage order*. Pantheon Books.

Klijn, E. H. (2012). New public management and governance: A comparison. In D. Levi-Faur (Ed.), *Oxford handbook of governance* (pp. 201–214). Oxford University Press.

Koudelková, P., Strielkowski, W., & Hejlová, D. (2015). Corruption and system change in the Czech republic: Firm-level evidence. *Danube, 6*(1), 25–46.

La Porta, R., Lopez-de-Silanes, F., & Schleifer, A. (1999). The quality of government. *Journal of Law, Economics and Organization, 15*(1), 222–279.

Lanskoy, M., & Suthers, E. (2019). Armenia's velvet revolution. *Journal of Democracy, 30*(2), 84–99.

LaSpina, A. (2014). The fight against the Italian Mafia. In L. Paoli (Ed.), *The Oxford handbook of organized crime* (pp. 593–611). Oxford University Press.

Lessig, L. (2011). *Republic lost*. Twelve.

Locatelli, G., Mariani, G., Sainati, T., & Greco, M. (2017). Corruption in public projects and megaprojects: There is an elephant in the room! *International Journal of Project Management, 35*(3), 252–268.

Maggio, P. (2021). A critical analysis of corruption and anti-corruption polities in Italy. *Journal of Financial Crime, 28*(2), 513–530.

Mazzanti, M., Mazzarano, M., Pronti, A., & Quatrosi, M. (2020). Fiscal policies, public investments and wellbeing: Mapping the evolution of the EU. *Insights into Regional Development, 2*(4), 425–749.

Melis, G. (1996). *Storia dellamministrazione Italiana (1861–1993)*. Il Mulino.

Mendelski, M. (2021). 15 years of anti-corruption in Romania: Augmentation, aberration and acceleration. *European Politics and Society, 22*(2), 237–258.

Ministry for Europe and Foreign Affairs, Republique Francaise. (2021). *France's anti-corruption strategy in its cooperation action 2021–2030*. Retrieved from www.diplomatie.gouv.fr/IMG/pdf/strategie_anticorruption_de_la_fce_ds_son_aciton_de_coop_en_cle81dc7d.pdf

Mircica, N. (2020). Restoring public trust in digital platform operations: Machine learning algorithmic structuring of social media content. *Review of Contemporary Philosophy, 19*, 85–91.

Morales, J., Gendron, Y., & Guénin-Paracini, H. (2014). State privatization and the unrelenting expansion of neoliberalism: The case of the Greek financial crisis. *Critical Perspectives in Accounting, 25*(6), 423–445.

Mugelinni, G. (2020). Corruption. In P. Harris, A. Bitonti, C. Fleisher & A. Skorkjaer (Eds.), *The palgrave encyclopedia of interest groups, lobbying and public affairs*. Palgrave Macmillan. https://books.google.com/books?hl=en&lr=&id=32J2EAAAQBAJ &oi=fnd&pg=PR8&dq=The+Palgrave+Encyclopedia+of+Interest+Groups,+Lobbyin g+and+Public+Affairs&ots=Ngxg3UrfPw&sig=yigSDnLTmbEhzWl5DCBItIK6ol0. Retrieved 4/23/24.

Mugellini, G., Bella, S. D., Colagrossi, M., Isenring, G. L., & Killias, M. (2021). Public sector reforms and their impact on the level of corruption: A systematic review. *Campbell Systematic Reviews*, *17*(2), 1–46. https://doi.org/10.1002/cl2.1173

Nelken, D. (1996). The judges and political corruption in Italy. *Journal of Law and Society*, *23*(1), 95–112.

OECD. (2015). *Consequences of corruption at the sector level and implications for economic growth and development*. https://doi.org/10.1787/9789264230781-en. Retrieved April 23, 2024

Office of the High Commissioner on Human Rights. (2019). *Italy's remarks following UN human rights council resolution 41/9*. Retrieved March 16, 2024, from www.ohchr.org/sites/default/files/Documents/Issues/Corruption/Challenges/Italy.pdf.

Paoli, L. (2014). The Italian mafia, 121–141. In L. Paoli (Ed.), *The Oxford handbook of organized crime*. Oxford University Press. http://doi.org/10.1093/oxfordhb/9780199730445.013.025

Pena López, J. A., & Sánchez Santos, J. M. (2014). Does corruption have social roots? The role of culture and social capital. *Journal of Business Ethics*, *122*, 697–708.

Pianigiani, G. (2023, November 21). Italian mafia takes a blow as hundreds are sentenced. *The New York Times*, p. A10.

Putnam, R. (1993). *Making democracy work: Civic tradition in modern Italy*. Princeton University Press.

Quattrocolo, S. (2016). The role of compliance in Italian counter-corruption policies. *Journal of Civil & Legal Sciences*, *5*(3), 1–6.

Rivera, J. D., & Knox, C. C. (2023). Bureaucratic discretion, social equity, and the administrative legitimacy dilemma: Complications of New Public Service. *Public Administration Review*, *83*(1), 65–77. http://doi.org/10.1111/puar.13550

Rose, R. (2001). How people view democracy: A diverging Europe. *Journal of Democracy*, *12*(1), 93–106.

Ruggiero, V. (2010). Who corrupts whom? A criminal eco-system made in Italy. *Crime, Law and Social Change*, *54*(1), 87–105. https://doi.org/10.1007/s10611-010-9242-9

Ser, S. (2007, May 3). The day the mob fell. *The Jerusalem Post*. Retrieved May 7, 2024, from www.jpost.com/magazine/features/the-day-the-mob-fell.

Shleifer, A. & Vishny, R. W. (1993). Corruption. *Quarterly Journal of Economics*, *108*(3), 599–617.

Simonyan, A., & Schultz, D. (2023). Democracy building and the link between public trust and corruption perception: Comparative analysis before and after the Armenian velvet revolution in 2018. *Central European Journal of Public Policy*, *17*(1), 27–40.

Tabellini, G. (2010). Culture and institutions: Economic development in the regions of Europe. *Journal of the European Economic Association*, *8*(4), 677–716.

Tanzi, V. (1995). Fiscal federalism and decentralization: A review of some efficiency and macroeconomics aspects. In M. Bruno & B. Pleskovic. (Eds.), *Annual World Bank Conference on Development Economics* (pp. 295–316). The World Bank.

Transparency International. (2024). *Corruption Perceptions Index (CPI): Italy*. Retrieved March 16, 2024, from www.transparency.org/en/cpi/2023/index/ita.

Vannucci, A. (2009). The controversial legacy of "Mani Pulite": A critical analysis of Italian corruption and anti-corruption policies. *Bulletin of Italian Politics*, *1*(2), 233–264.

Vannucci, A. (2016). The "clean hands" (Mani Pulite) inquiry on corruption and its effects on the Italian political system. *Belo Horizante, 8*(2), 62–68.

Wachs, J., Yasseri, T., Lengyel, B., & Kertész, J. (2019). Social capital predicts corruption risk in towns. *Royal Society Open Science, 6*(4). https://doi.org/10.1098/rsos.182103

Wheaton, B. (1992). *The velvet revolution: Czechoslovakia, 1988–1991*. Routledge.

World Bank. (1997). Helping counties combat corruption: The role of the World Bank. *The World Bank*. Retrieved April 23, 2024, from http://documents1.worldbank.org/curated/en/799831538245192753/pdf/Helping-Countries-Combat-Corruption-The-Role-of-the-World-Bank.pdf

10 Public Integrity Compliance in Thailand

Amporn Tamronglak, Patthara Limsira, and Tass Pongpisit

Introduction

Government trust, accountability, and successful governance depend on public honesty. Thai public confidence in government institutions and good public service delivery depend on public honesty, as in any country. However, the Thai government must address significant public integrity challenges. Thailand suffers with public honesty despite its importance. Thai government agencies commit bribery, embezzlement, and power abuse. Oversight gaps, transparency difficulties, and political interference in administrative institutions harm public integrity.

Given these challenges, Thailand needs legal reforms, institutional improvements, and a cultural shift toward ethical government to restore public integrity. Addressing these concerns and encouraging honesty and accountability will boost public trust, democratic institutions, and sustainable development for all Thais. Over the previous decade (2014–2023), Transparency International's (TI) Corruption Perception Index (CPI) of Thailand scores have fluctuated between 34 and 38 out of 100, averaging 43 among 180 nations. The recent decline, especially from 38 in 2020 to 35 in 2023, raises questions about corruption and anti-corruption initiatives. Thailand ranked 101 in 2022 and 108 in 2023 in corruption Minimum: 104, maximum: 34 (Transparency International, 2023). The scores may motivate reforming effective policies, laws, regulations, and proactive openness and governance.

The Transparency International Global Corruption Barometer-Asia (GCB) is another popular corruption index. GCB discovered corruption in bribes, personal connections, vote-buying, and sextortion (Transparency International, 2020). It shows that a large section of Asia Pacific views government corruption as a big issue. Nearly 1 in 5 public service users in the past year paid a bribe, or 836 million people in the region. This broad study illuminates important concerns like election vote-buying, sextortion, and using personal connections to gain public services. Despite these obstacles, 62% of respondents believe ordinary people can resist corruption (Transparency International, 2020).

DOI: 10.4324/9781003416258-11

Legal Framework Against Corruption

The legal initiatives on corruption prevention and suppression can be traced back to 1292 on the King Ramkhamhaeng's stone inscription, highlighting the King's dedication to justice (Limsira, 2021, Griswold & Prasert, 1965). Today, Thailand's regulations prevent corruption and encourage ethical public administration. These frameworks combat corruption from minor bribery to high-level graft and provide integrity and accountability standards for public officials.

The 2017 Constitution, which upholds the rule of law, value for money, transparency, accountability, public engagement, and integrity in governance, underpins its anti-corruption initiatives. It promotes public servant ethics and legalizes anti-corruption organizations.

For example, Article 98 outlines the qualifications and prohibitions for candidates running for the House of Representatives, and Article 160 outlines the qualifications for individuals to be appointed as ministers in the government to ensure that candidates uphold high ethical standards and integrity.

The 2018 Organic Act on Counter Corruptions defines corrupt activities and their punishments. This statute sets the legal standards for public officials and mandates corruption investigations and prosecutions as the legal instrument to implement the 2003 United Nations Convention against Corruption (UNCAC).

The Public Sector Anti-misconduct Commission (PACC) was established under the 2008 Executive Measure Act on Anti-Corruption Commission to prevent and suppress the corruption of state officials and agencies. This statute allows the PACC to actively detect and prevent corruption, improving the government's integrity. The law also compels public officials to declare their assets and liabilities at the start of their tenure, frequently during their term, and upon leaving office. This approach makes financial disclosures public and scrutinized by anti-corruption agencies and the public to prevent unlawful enrichment and conflicts of interest.

Thailand has laws protecting whistleblowers, encouraging them to report corruption without repercussions. Legal protection is key to encouraging citizens and officials to disclose wrongdoing.

Despite robust legislative frameworks, Thailand's anti-corruption initiatives generally depend on continuous implementation and political resolve to enforce them. Bureaucratic delay, political intervention, and limited resources might hinder these legal systems. However, Thailand's anti-corruption laws are essential to an open, responsible, and ethical public sector.

Thailand Corruption Category

Corruption involves abusing public or private office for personal benefit and takes several forms depending on the parties and number of persons involved. Bribery, embezzlement, extortion, nepotism, cronyism, patronage, state capture, and others are corruption practices found in Thailand. The direct form of corruption is bribery, while embezzlement involves financial fraud with document fabrication (OECD, 2013). Extortion is the illegal use of one's position to demand payment for an unfair advantage, frequently under fear or force (OECD, 2013). Patronage benefits supporters or political associates, whereas nepotism and cronyism bypass merit or competitive processes in hiring or contract awards (Pozsgai-Alvarez & Varraich, 2023). Finally, economic state capture is a form of corruption in which businesses or individuals manipulate policy formation and state decisions by influencing regulation drafting to benefit their operations (Pozsgai-Alvarez & Varraich, 2023).

Corruption in Thai bureaucracy dates back to its founding. Partisan negotiation to policy corruption has three steps. In the first phase, officials directly contacted businessmen and the public to gain personal and partisan advantage. Accepting bribes from state officials or protection payments for smooth commercial operations, especially in illegal businesses, was included. The second stage involved more complicated interactions between politicians, civil servants, and businesses. They took advantage of legal loopholes to get state project benefits, exclusive rights, or concessions for personal or economic gain. This corruption became a group effort to profit from the law. The final step was to complicate corruption tactics to reduce detection and punishment. A crucial strategy was to include "technocrats" or academics with corruption-related skills. They helped society accept specific policies and regulations by "creating conditions" that legitimized the original group (politicians, civil servants, and entrepreneurs). Policy corruption legitimizes corruption through complicated processes and numerous tactics. It links corruption to "conditions of legitimacy" for policies and regulations, allowing numerous organizations to exploit these instruments for corruption and making detection nearly complicated due to their complexity and legitimization. This latest type of policy corruption was seen in Prime Minister Yingluck Shinawatra's 2011 rice pledging scheme, which guaranteed prices and provided zero-interest loans and cost US$2.6 billion (Sawasdipakdi, 2014; Bangkok Biz News, 2013; Ruengchan, 2016; Thailand Development Research Institute, 2012).

Causes of Corruption

Michael Johnston (2005, 2014) identified four "syndromes of corruption" that explain why many poor countries struggle to grow economically and promote democracy: influence markets, elite cartels, oligarchs, and official moguls. While the wealthy influence policy, elite cartels dominate political and economic spheres and use corruption to cement their status and exclude potential competitors at the expense of weak institutions that prevent elite collusion (Johnston, 2005, 2014). The dominance of powerful individuals or families in the state and market creates public-private conflicts that threaten institutional integrity. The last influential factor of official moguls is inadequate state structures that allow power abusers to profit themselves without consequence (Johnston, 2005, 2014).

Opoku et al. (2022) found that Thai cultural practices and official conduct blur the lines between public service and corrupt behavior, normalizing corrupt practices in the industry by giving a small amount of money for "tip" or "tokens of generosity" (Noisuwan, 2003, Opoku et al., 2022, pp. 308–309). Nepotism in procurement as the "good old boys' network" favors human ties to speed up bureaucracy (Opoku et al., 2022, p. 309). Low pay and fees for Thai architects and engineers, compared to attorneys and doctors, may encourage unscrupulous practices in the building business to supplement their income (Opoku et al., 2022, 309). Greed, organizational system, ineffective legislation, red tapes, strong competitiveness, and meddling caused fraud, bribery, and collusion in Thailand building projects (Opoku et al., 2022, p. 311). According to Opoku et al. (2022, p. 312), the judiciary's inability to control corruption makes it easier for corruption to persist in the construction sector. Corruption is caused by politics, economics, environmental issues, professional ethics, legislative issues, customs, and demographics, according to Dockthaisong and Maharutsakul (2022). Lack of selfless leaders dedicated to the country's welfare and a government that lacks the ability and sincerity to undertake serious reforms are major factors. A unique suggestion is to emphasize transparency and Buddhist ideals alongside legal measures to fight corruption (Dockthaisong & Maharutsakul, 2022, pp. A10–A12).

Administrative Corruption Prevention and Suppression Organizations

Anti-corruption agencies and their regulatory frameworks differ by country due to diverse socio-economic environments and governance types. A nation's corruption fight generally reflects its culture, politics, and public administration. Ora-Orn Poocharoen (2014) outlines global corruption prevention strategies. Japan and Finland, for instance, dissuade corruption by cultural purity and societal transparency, not anti-corruption authorities. Singapore and Sweden use a single, robust anti-corruption agency to develop trust between officials and citizens by emphasizing strict ethical standards and open governance. Thus, different countries tailor anti-corruption policy to their setting and governance needs, using cultural strengths, centralized power, or specialized institutions. Thailand, on the other hand, fights corruption with various specialized authorities, each with specific duties (Table 10.1). On the bright side, each agency can master its expertise in different specialized and incomprehensible cases and also reduce the number of cases to investigate, creating bottleneck in the process.

Other small units that handle anti-corruption issues, such as the Ministry-Level Operation Center Against Corruption (MOCAC), grew more visible in

Table 10.1 Thai Anti-Corruption Agencies' Duties

Agency	Responsibilities	Website
National Anti-Corruption Commission (NACC)	Tackles corruption involving government officials; lacks authority over misconduct or disciplinary violations.	www.nacc.go.th/english
Office of the Auditor General of Thailand (OAG)	Audits government financial expenditures for compliance with regulations.	www.audit.go.th/en/home
Public Sector Anti-Corruption Commission (PACC)	Holds limited jurisdiction over corruption and misconduct by state officials.	www.pacc.go.th/index. php/home
Anti-Money Laundering Office (AMLO)	Focuses on suppressing money laundering and seizing assets derived from illegal activities.	www.amlo.go.th/index. php/en/
Department of Special Investigation (DSI)	Addresses corruption cases not involving state officials; penalizes individuals committing offenses.	www.dsi.go.th/en
Corrective Action Against Corruption (Thai CAC)-private sector coalition	Builds a clean and transparent business community, uplifts compliance standards in private companies, and co-creates changes in public services for better efficiency and transparency.	www.thai-cac.com/ who-we-are/about-cac/
Ombudsmen	Reports corruption or malfeasance in office or criminal offence or discipline violation to the authorities concerned and supervisor in such office to take further legal action.	www.ombudsman.go.th/ new/en/background-of-ombudsman-thailand/

2015 under Prime Minister Prayut, but ministry support has declined. PACC created the National Command Center for Combating Corruption (NCCCC) to coordinate a holistic approach that emphasizes state agency integration. This prime minister chairs a government-appointed committee, although the present government has not appointed it. In 2010, major corporate companies formed Thai-Corrective Action Against Corruption (Thai CAC), a voluntary coalition to support anti-corruption policies and compliance standards for more efficient and transparent public services.

In this chapter, only two distinguished agencies—the National Anti-Corruption Commission (NACC) for high-ranking government officials and PACC for low-ranking civil servants—are discussed as the main units fighting corruption. Other agencies, like AMLO and the Ombudsmen, are also important in fighting money laundering issue in collaboration with international organizations and reporting corruption, and other discipline violation issues to the concerned authorities.

The National Anti-Corruption Commission (NACC)

In 1999, the NACC was established as an independent agency to replace and combine the ONCCC with enlarged responsibilities and investigative capabilities to promote democracy and fight corruption. Political officeholder wrongdoing and public service ethics were investigated. The NACC might sue, investigate, and advise Thai Parliament on anti-corruption measures.

The 2007 Constitution empowered the NACC to investigate political office-holder wrongdoing, safeguarding political integrity and accountability. To guarantee variety and expertise, the NACC has nine commissioners, including a chairperson. Selecting commissioners requires Senate and committee approval. They serve one nine-year term while neutralizing the body. Several NACC bureaus handle anti-corruption investigations, legal matters, asset evaluation, and international collaboration. Secretaries-General oversee everyday operations and strategy. Though independent, the NACC promotes corruption reporting and integrity through public and civil society engagement. This governance paradigm keeps the NACC transparent and independent from the executive, legislative, and judicial departments, retaining its role in fighting corruption in Thailand (National Anti-Corruption Commission, 2023).

The NACC has introduced many corruption suppression methods, enhancing case management and investigation, digital transformation and information systems with digital platform, international cooperation, public awareness campaigns, monitoring system, and so on.

The NACC has enhanced law enforcement and case management for years. Through education and awareness, the NACC boosted claims by 4,468 (84.4%) from 2019 to 2022 as the public became more likely to report wrongdoing online. An excellent operational plan splits cases between the NACC and other organizations to optimize resources and transfer them to the relevant agency. It also participates in international forums, networks, and collaborations to align Thailand's anti-corruption measures with global standards and share corruption reduction expertise and best practices, showing that corruption is a global issue that requires coordinated response.

Educational activities and partnerships with other institutions including the 2020 "Zero Tolerance—Thais Do Not Tolerate Corruption" campaign promoted civic sector cooperation, anti-corruption education, community participation, and corruption awareness. Innovative digital development projects, stakeholder surveys, and integrated corruption combat measures dominated 2021 public awareness. The NACC scored 76.4% in 2022, reflecting high stakeholder satisfaction and public confidence in its anti-corruption initiatives (National Anti-Corruption Commission, 2023).

The Office of Public Sector Anti-Corruption Commission (PACC)

The PACC Committee and its office were established under the 2008 Administrative Sector Corruption Prevention and Suppression Act to investigate and adjudicate corrupt acts by lower-level officials or civil servants; below high-ranking CEOs and civil servants below department directors were not the NACC's or any other entity's responsibility (Public Sector Anti-Corruption Commission (PACC), 2022, pp. 24–25).

In driving government policy, the PACC has deployed and implemented various mechanisms to advance the National Reform Plan in prevention and suppression of corruption and misconduct (Revised Edition). Key reform activities (BIG ROCK) include the "No Gift Policy from the Performance of Duties" and the "Anti-Corruption Campaign Camp Project."

In 2003, the government signed the UN Convention against Corruption (UNCAC) and ratified it on March 30, 2011, to fight corruption and promote morality. Since 2006, the government has considered joining the OECD after a Thailand Development Research Institute (TDRI) research found economic readiness but a need for better capital movement, trade, and service legal and regulatory frameworks. The PACC and the Office of the Civil Service Commission (OCSC) worked with the OECD to prepare actionable plans based on the "Integrity Review of Thailand Phase 2" document to solve these concerns and fulfill OECD standards. By fiscal year 2022, government agency performance improvements were measured against the OECD's anti-corruption guidelines. From OECD analysis and recommendations, the PACC has improved corruption prevention standards by 96%, aiming for OECD membership (Public Sector Anti-Corruption Commission (PACC), 2022, pp. 32–34).

Another PACC project, "Supervision and Monitoring of Public Agencies in the Integrity and Transparency Assessment (ITA)," monitors 146 government departments, of which 126 departments (86.30%) met or above the 85-point assessment level, confirming compliance with the PACC's ITA integrity and transparency standards. PACC projects aim to enhance the CPI.

Due to PACC's efforts, the number of complaints received versus the number of complaints investigated for facts from 2012 to 2022 fluctuated with 37,401 cases for fact-finding. In recent years, rigorous preventive measures have reduced cases.

Compliance and Integrity Approaches

In analyzing public sector ethics and integrity in Thailand, it is crucial to clarify and explore the complex interplay between compliance and integrity, particularly within the realm of Thai politics. The current integration of these concepts inside Thai bureaucracy seems to blur their differences.

Compliance constitutes a rule-based approach. It underscores compliance with existing laws, regulations, and protocols. Public officials are required to adhere to external norms, and noncompliance generally results in sanctions or penalties. This strategy emphasizes the deterrence of unethical activity by enforcement mechanisms such as audits, codes of conduct, and legal sanctions. In nations with robust legal structures, public officials may adhere to regulations to evade legal repercussions rather than from an intrinsic dedication to ethical conduct. David Orozco (2020) provided elucidation on a compliance theory aimed at enhancing the explanation and prediction of compliance-related outcomes. The systems theory of compliance delineates the diverse actors, institutions, and relationships that influence compliance processes. Consequently, compliance is perceived as a procedure, resulting in insufficient explanatory and predictive capability (Orozco, 2020).

Integrity transcends simple adherence to rules. It highlights a value-oriented framework, wherein individuals are directed by internalized ethical standards. The emphasis is on fostering a culture of ethical conduct rooted in moral values, including honesty, fairness, and accountability, rather than reliance on fear of punishment (Rohr, 1998). This approach promotes ethical behavior among public servants, even in the absence of explicit regulations. The approach fosters personal responsibility and moral reasoning, striving for elevated standards of conduct derived from character instead of regulation (Cooper, 2012). From legal perspective, it examined the processes of law, highlighting how prosecution in regulatory enforcement mirrors processes typically seen in the legal system. Hawkins discussed the formation and development of legal cases, their decline, and the procedures involved in prosecution. The theory of decision-making is developed and applied by linking overarching characteristics of the legal bureaucracy's environment to the specifics of decisions in individual cases (Hawkins, 2003).

The Interrelation of Compliance and Integrity in the Thai Public Sector

In Thailand, politicians and public officials often invoke the presumption of innocence when facing allegations of misconduct, reflecting a strong reliance on a compliance-based approach to ethics. This approach, which interprets the absence of legal convictions as adherence to ethical standards, has increasingly converged with the integrity-based framework traditionally rooted in personal values. Consequently, integrity, once seen as a value-driven concept, has been subsumed under legal mechanisms, making ethical behavior subject to legal scrutiny.

While business practitioners and management scholars generally distinguish between compliance and integrity (Michaelson, 2006), the Thai public sector seems to function within a unique contextual framework. The merging of compliance and integrity frameworks complicates the distinction between actions driven by personal values and those mandated by legal requirements. This intricate relationship can be exemplified by the metaphor of a "martini," where gin and vermouth merge indistinguishably, symbolizing the seamless integration of compliance and integrity within the ethical framework of the Thai public sector. Thai officials operate in a context where personal ethical standards and adherence to rules are not separate entities but rather exist within an ambiguous intersection of overlapping principles.

This integration has resulted in ambiguity regarding the distinction between genuine ethical conduct and actions designed solely to circumvent sanctions, thereby raising concerns about the effectiveness of existing ethics management frameworks in fostering true integrity within the Thai public sector.

In Thailand, social media has become a crucial element affecting investigation and adjudication processes, influencing public perceptions and complicating the ethical landscape. The lack of a strong commitment to personal integrity in public sector ethics management can be effectively illustrated by the phrase from Carl Sandburg: "If the facts are against you, argue the law." In the face of legal opposition, present the factual evidence. "When the law and the facts are unfavorable, resort to loud protest and vigorous expression" Smith (2014). This strategy highlights the shortcomings of the integrity approach when it becomes overly idealistic and detached from practical realities.

For instance, the Election Commission is investigating allegations of falsification regarding the educational qualifications of a newly appointed Senator, who secured the position with the highest score. This controversy has captured media headlines, raising concerns about the Senator's integrity. Despite calls for resignation, the Senator has remained silent, opting to await the outcome of the legal proceedings (The Nation, 2024a).

A recent example that demonstrates this dynamic occurred on August 14, 2024, when the Constitutional Court of Thailand ruled that the prime minister breached ethical standards by appointing Phichit, an individual with a criminal conviction, to the prime minister's office. The Court stated that the prime minister's decision showed a lack of "evident integrity," despite Phichit's prior removal from consideration (Thai PBS World, 2024). This landmark ruling sets a precedent for rigorous background checks for future cabinet candidates and led to changes in the cabinet lineup, although some adjustments were merely reshuffling within the same political circle (The Nation, 2024b). This case highlights the growing emphasis on integrating integrity within the compliance framework in Thai public sector ethics management.

Review of Approach to Thailand Anti-Corruption Research

From the investigation, there are prominent studies over the past years as foundation till present research concerning public integrity compliance issue in Thailand, including Fred Riggs theories of the prismatic society and bureaucratic polity, good governance approach, deep democracy approach, principal-agent theory, case study, social network analysis (SNA) approach, and whistleblowing; see Table 10.2 for the summary of their focus.

Table 10.2 Summary of Anti-Corruption Theories in Research

Anti-Corruption Theories and Foundational Discipline	Content Description	Foundational Reference	Research Examples
Principal-agent theory/economics, organizational theory	Focus on the relationships where one party (agent) is supposed to act in the interest of another (principal) but may pursue their own interests due to asymmetric information and misaligned incentives.	Klitgaard, R. (1988). "Controlling Corruption." University of California Press.	Examine the role of oversight mechanisms in government and corporate settings to reduce corruption.
Institutional theory/sociology, political science	Examine how institutional structures, norms, and cultures shape individual and organizational behaviors, and how these institutions can perpetuate or reduce corruption.	North, D. C. (1990). "Institutions, Institutional Change and Economic Performance." Cambridge University Press.	Analysis of how entrenched norms in public sectors contribute to systemic corruption and the impact of institutional reforms.
Social network theory/sociology anthropology	Analyze how social structures and networks influence behaviors and outcomes, including the facilitation or disruption of corrupt practices.	Borgatti, S. P. et al. (2009). "Network analysis in the social sciences." Science, 323(5916), 892–895.	Research on networks of corruption within organizations and how information flows within these networks.
Corrective action theory/economics, political science	Address problems where individuals acting in their own interest rather than the common good lead to suboptimal societal outcomes, emphasizing solutions that encourage collective efforts.	Ostrom, E. (1990). "Governing the Commons: The Evolution of Institutions for Collective Action." Cambridge University Press.	Studies on community-based anti-corruption initiatives and how collective action can mitigate corruption.
Resource-based view (RBV)/business management	Traditionally used in business strategy to understand how organizations can leverage unique resources for competitive advantage, adapted here for analyzing capabilities in fighting corruption.	Barney, J. (1991). "Firm Resources and Sustained Competitive Advantage." Journal of Management, 17(1), 99–120.	Evaluations of how specific capabilities or resources within law enforcement agencies contribute to effective corruption control.

(Continued)

Table 10.2 (Continued)

Anti-Corruption Theories and Foundational Discipline	Content Description	Foundational Reference	Research Examples
Behavioral economics/ criminology, law	Study how psychological and socio-economic factors influence economic decisions, including corrupt behavior, and how interventions can modify these behaviors.	Thaler, R. H., & Sunstein, C. R. (2008). "Nudge: Improving Decisions About Health, Wealth, and Happiness." Yale University Press.	Research on how behavioral nudges can reduce corrupt practices by altering incentive structures.
Deterrence theory/political science, sociology	From criminology, suggests that increasing the costs associated with corrupt acts (through penalties) can deter individuals from engaging in such acts.	Becker, G. S. (1968). "Crime and Punishment: An Economic Approach." In The Economic Dimensions of Crime. Palgrave Macmillan. London.	Empirical studies assessing the effectiveness of stricter laws and penalties in reducing corruption rates.
Grand theory good governance/political science, public administration	Emphasize the integration of transparent, accountable, and participatory practices in governance to ensure effective and equitable management of public affairs and resources, ultimately preventing corruption.	World Bank, OECD, and other international organizations studies	Implementations of governance reforms that include transparent systems, accountability mechanisms, and citizen participation in decision-making to prevent corruption.
Whistleblowing/ organizational theory, law	Examine the role and impact of individuals who report unethical or illegal activities within their organizations, focusing on the mechanisms that protect and encourage whistleblowers to come forward.	Miceli, M. P., & Near, J. P. (1992). "Blowing the Whistle: The Organizational and Legal Implications for Companies and Employees." Lexington Books.	Studies on the effectiveness of whistleblower protections in public and private sectors and their impact on uncovering and reducing corruption.

Bureaucratic and Prismatic Societies

Analyzing Thai corruption requires an examination of bureaucratic behavior and its interactions with various stakeholders. Fred Riggs's works, "The Prismatic Society" (1964) and "Bureaucratic Polity" (2021), offer significant insights into the complex dynamics of corruption in Thailand. This model describes how formal institutions in Thailand, similar to those in more industrialized countries, operate in a framework greatly impacted by traditional, relationship-based practices. The coexistence of these factors can obscure accountability and enable corrupt practices, including nepotism and the exploitation of informal networks within public sectors such as procurement, recruitment, land use, zoning regulations, regulatory compliance, and inspections, as well as recent instances of policy corruption (Riggs, 1964; Tangkitvanich et al., 2023; Rathamarit, 2016).

The bureaucratic polity model, refined by Riggs in 2021, focuses on the powerful role of bureaucracy in Thai governance. It posits that bureaucracy, which is meant to implement policies, often ends up shaping them, blurring the lines between administration and politics. This extensive autonomy and lack of clear demarcation facilitate corruption, including procurement fraud and the misallocation of public resources, particularly when oversight mechanisms are weak (Riggs, 2021).

While Riggs's models can be used to understand Thailand's bureaucratic system's historical development, its impact on politics and society, and its modernization issues, they have limits when applied to contemporary Thailand. These models may not account for corruption's dynamic character or global and regional influences on domestic governance. Transnational money laundering and corporate fraud pose issues that Riggs's paradigm may not fully capture as Thailand becomes more connected with the global economy.

The focus on bureaucracy may result in the role of private sector, civic society, and international organizations in maintaining and fighting corruption being overlooked. Knowing corruption techniques requires knowing these players' interactions with the bureaucracy.

Good Governance Approach

The economic crisis during 1994 has forced Thai government, like most other countries in Asia, to unwillingly take a loan from the World Bank and with it the enforcement of the "good governance" concept and implementation of New Public Management to eradicate corruption in the administrative reform. Legislations for the reform based on good governance practices have been embedded in the people's constitution in 1997 to the present 2017 constitution. It can be said that good governance has been the dominant paradigm in fighting corruption in Thai bureaucracy, emphasizing the importance of six principles of efficiency, transparency, participation, accountability, integrity, and rule-based governance systems as key mechanisms for preventing corruption. The good governance approach is aimed at strengthening institutions, enhancing transparency, promoting accountability, and ensuring the rule of law, with the expectation that these measures will collectively reduce opportunities for corrupt practices.

As a result of the reform in 1997, the government has issued a series of laws in accordance with the constitution in suppressing corruption through the good governance mechanisms (Table 10.3). The Public Sector Management and Governance Act 1999 has been revised and updated five times to date. The 20-year National Strategic Plan (2018–2037) and the National Economic and Social Development Plan (NESDP) also embrace the good governance practice from the World Bank and the United Nations (UN), with the emphasis on ensuring transparency, accountability, participation, and adherence to the rule of law, aimed at fostering a peaceful, just, and sustainable society. Thus, good governance has become "grand paradigm" to all agencies' public services, business civil society, and academic community.

In promoting good governance practices in Thai public agencies from national to local administration, several good governance rewards have been initiated to best practice agencies. The Office of the Public Sector Development Commission (OPDC), for instance, is a leading central government unit to reward "Public Sector Excellence Awards" to recognize outstanding performance and

Table 10.3 Examples of Good Governance Principles–Related Laws and Significance in Thailand

No.	Law	Year	Significance
1	1997 Constitution of Thailand	1997	Comprehensive governance reforms emphasizing transparency, accountability, and public participation.
2	Organic Act on Counter Corruption	1999	Combat corruption within public and private sectors, establishing disclosure measures.
3	Bankruptcy Act (Amendment)	1997	Facilitate the restructuring of businesses and financial institutions.
4	Financial Institution Act	1998	Strengthen financial sector with rigorous regulatory and supervisory frameworks.
5	Securities and Exchange Act (Amendment)	1997	Introduce stricter regulations for the stock market and securities trading to protect investors.
6	Anti-Money Laundering Act	1999	Combat money laundering activities and align with international standards.
7	Establishment of the Thai Financial Restructuring Authority	1997	Stabilize and restructure the financial sector post-crisis.
8	Public Sector Management and Governance Act (with many revisions)	1999	Improve efficiency and accountability in public sector management.

adherence to principles of good governance in three categories, that is, public service excellence, public sector management quality, and participatory governance (opdc.go.th). At the local administration level, the Office of the Decentralization of the Local Government Organization Committee (DLGO) also allocates grants as rewards for local government organizations that exhibit good management. This policy aims to stimulate and encourage competition in development, as well as to enhance the efficiency, effectiveness, and responsiveness of local management according to the principles of good governance and proper urban management since 2003 (odloc.go.th). Winners of the awards are supported by the government to compete at the global level for the United Nations Public Service Awards (UNPSA), starting in 2003 to promote and support innovations in public service delivery and to highlight the pivotal role of public administration in the implementation of the sustainable development goals (SDGs). In all, there are at least 13 awards for best practices in good governance in different categories and government levels, and their effects on improving governance of the public and private sectors can be said to be intriguing.

However, while good governance initiatives are important, they were criticized for often falling short of addressing deeper systemic and political issues that enable corruption (Johnston & Fritzen, 2020). It is suggested that focusing solely on technocratic solutions and institutional reforms, without engaging with the underlying power dynamics and social injustices that give rise to corruption, limits the effectiveness of anti-corruption efforts. There are numbers of criticisms on the "grand theory of good governance" forcefully injected into the developing countries during the economic crisis by the international organizations "Big Six" (the World Bank, the International Monetary Fund [IMF], the Organization for Economic Co-operation and Development [OECD], TI, the UN, and the European Union [EU]). First, for instance, major criticism is the assumption of the one-size-fits-all approach, applying a standardized set of anti-corruption strategies across diverse political, economic, and cultural contexts. The uniform approach fails to consider the specificities and complexities of individual countries, leading to ineffective or counterproductive outcomes. Second, it focuses on fine-tuning bureaucracy with technical solutions, resulting in creating many measurement indices with technical fixes, such as improving public sector management, enhancing transparency, and strengthening legal frameworks while often overlooking deeper political and economic power structures that enable corruption. Third, it frequently ignores issues of social justice and equity. Fourth, the attack is particularly on TI, developing the corruption measure based on perception indices, is highly subjective, and fails to capture the multifaceted nature of corruption, potentially misguiding policy priorities. Last, the top-down approach to combating corruption does not allow local actors, civil society, local communities, and grassroots organizations to engage in designing and implementing anti-corruption measures (Johnston, 2014; Johnston & Fritzen, 2020, pp. 25–48; Table 10.4).

Table 10.4 Summary of Big Six Strategies, Its Pros and Cons

Strategy	Details	Pros	Cons	Examples
Crime Prevention	Techniques for detecting, punishing, and preventing corruption, including independent anti-corruption agencies.	Focus on actionable legal frameworks and tangible penalties.	Overly dependent on an effective rule of law; may struggle in compromised judicial systems.	Anti-corruption agencies like Singapore's Corrupt Practices Investigation Bureau (CPIB), NACC and PACC in Thailand.
Incentives	Offering higher pay and rewards for good performance alongside penalties for corruption.	Encourage better behavior through rewards and disincentives.	Can overlook ethical and cultural factors; focuses mainly on material benefits.	Performance-based pay in government jobs in countries like Canada, which aims to reduce bureaucratic corruption.
Civil Society Action	Mobilizing public demand for reform and enabling citizens to monitor government performance.	Engage the public directly in anti-corruption activities.	Faces challenges without strong civic engagement; may be suppressed by powerful corrupt entities.	Transparency International's use of Corruption Perceptions Index to mobilize and inform public opinion.
Transparency	Making information about institutional activities available to public scrutiny.	Empower citizens to hold institutions accountable.	Information alone may not be effective without the capability and willingness to use it.	The Open Government Partnership, promoting transparency through public access to government activities.
Liberalization	Reducing government's role in the economy to decrease corruption opportunities by minimizing discretion.	Reduce the interface where corruption can occur.	May lead to less regulation and oversight, potentially increasing other forms of corruption.	Privatization of previously state-controlled industries in Eastern Europe to reduce bureaucratic corruption.
International Treaties and Conventions	Establishing international standards and cooperation to combat corruption across borders.	Facilitate global standards and collaborative enforcement.	Enforcement can vary greatly and depends on political will and stability in participant countries.	The United Nations Convention against Corruption (UNCAC), facilitating international legal frameworks.

Source: Adapted from Johnston and Fritzen, 2020, pp. 33–42.

Other criticisms on "good governance" solution to anti-corruption are from Drake et al. (2001–2002) that the World Bank's approach is market-centric, emphasizing market efficiency and private-sector-led development. If limiting government intervention minimizes corruption, deregulation and privatization are prioritized. However, it may ignore state capacity and the need for strong public institutions to guarantee that governance reforms are effective and inclusive, underestimating the complexity of developing institutions that can oversee market activities and protect public interest. Warsta (2004) observed a gap between corruption laws and their execution due to a lack of political will among those in power, who are often deeply involved in the corruption they denounce. Thailand's traditional history contrasts with modern legal systems and democracy, causing corruption. Some of the persistent problems in anti-corruption efforts are powerful individuals and media influence preventing transparency and accountability essential for meaningful government reforms. Political personalities' media control highlights the challenges of maintaining a free press, a cornerstone of democracy and important to exposing and combating corruption (Warsta, 2004).

Deep Democracy Approach

Given the grand theory's limitations and the system's persistent "syndromes or patterns of corruption," curbing it requires a long-term gradual dynamic process of "deep democracy" where citizens participate in elections, decision-making, oversight, and holding officials accountable. Deep democratization illuminates each society's intricate economic and political history. Corruption, money in politics, social justice, and inequality can be explained by political and economic causes. Corruption causes social divisions and distrust. Lowering disparities and supporting equitable growth reduce corruption risks. Johnston advises on institutional governance and corruption resistance, including anti-corruption institutions, courts, law enforcement, and public administration. Institutions should promote honesty, competence, and autonomy. This approach emphasizes grassroots and civil society anti-corruption movements (Johnston, 2014; Johnston & Fritzen, 2020). Local recognition and global anti-corruption cooperation are stressed. Collaboration on global corruption issues like money laundering and offshore tax havens, sharing best practices, and supporting transnational investigations and prosecutions are examples.

Expanding stakeholders and incorporating political and economic concerns are important, but deep democracy has several drawbacks. Practical implementation is challenging when corruption syndromes are difficult to diagnose and may not be actionable. This complexity and the need for political will and collaboration from individuals who may be entrenched in and benefiting from corrupt institutions make his recommendations politically tough, especially in Thailand, where "networking of nepotism and favoritism" is strong. To analyze the techniques' viability and success in varied political and cultural environments, one must understand corruption's multidimensional nature and the possibility for unexpected consequences, such as political instability in Thailand or new corrupt behaviors.

Principal-Agent Theory

Limsuthiwanpoom, T. (2020) formed the "corruption tree" to represent the root causes and branching out of corruption by focusing on a few main actors in the corruption cycle: merchants, civil servants, politicians, and the public. The model stresses the stability and strength of participants, showing how entrenched corruption gets with strong interpersonal connections and actions that foster corruption. The principal-agent theory is discussed in relation to how corruption is regarded through various theoretical frameworks. The principal-agent (P-A) model defines corruption as an agent's divergence from a principal's goals and wants. This departure is frequently fostered by institutional factors such as unequal or restricted information available to the principal regarding the agent's conduct, or problems with enforcement procedures.

In circumstances where principals are government leaders, the argument holds that they may be unable to confront corruption at lower levels of the system, particularly if they are not involved in misconduct. Alternatively, the principal can be viewed figuratively as the citizens of a democracy, whose democratic intents and best interests are obstructed by corrupt principals and agents at all levels of command.

This model influenced anti-corruption practices, particularly through strategies developed by Robert Klitgaard (1988), who proposed approaches such as selecting more honest agents, establishing rational rewards and penalties, improving information and monitoring systems, restructuring principal-agent relations to reduce monopoly and limit discretion, and raising the moral costs of corruption.

Case Study Approach

Most Thai research uses case studies, analyzing notorious cases. Chuenjitsiri, J. et al. (2022), for instance, used the case study approach to analyze government socio-economic development and intervention policies, programs, and projects in various sectors for the NACC. The study identified opportunities and risks for corruption in these initiatives, analyzed all forms of corruption processes, estimated the scope and magnitude of damages through case studies, and recommended good governance models to prevent or minimize corruption among public officials, politicians, and related external parties. The findings showed that Yingluck Shinawatra and General Prayut Chan-o-cha faced challenges that fostered corruption. The study identified high-risk policy-driven corruption schemes and evaluated financial damages. It also noted the lack of openness, account-ability, equity, and corruption in project implementation and public participation in decision-making, especially during COVID-19 economic stimulus initiatives.

The report shows that South Korea, Denmark, and Singapore prevent corrup-tion with political will, comprehensive and integrated anti-corruption measures, independent and capable anti-corruption agencies, strict law enforcement, pub-lic service development, financial system transparency, parliamentary scrutiny, and public empowerment. Specific proposals to strengthen policymaking and project execution corruption surveillance and prevention conclude the docu-ment. It emphasizes transparency, public involvement, legislative framework strengthening, judicial process development, public service efficiency, political determination against corruption, and governance-principles-based transparent and beneficial policies. To establish a transparent, clean society with increased public trust in state operations in Thailand, the research analyzes, understands, and develops solutions to fully monitor and prevent corruption in government policies and programs.

Social Network Analysis Approach

This approach was recently proposed to explore the dynamics and efficiency of information distribution in Thai anti-corruption networks by Yomnak et al. (2024). The study examines how anti-corruption agencies and stakeholders com-municate information. A SNA method was used to map and analyze communica-tion and information flow in these networks. Though not exhaustive, the study developed the SNA based on network structure, dynamics, and information dif-fusion within networks, such as those by Borgatti et al. (2009), Newman et al. (2006), and Hambrick et al. (2012).

Thailand's specialized agencies' anti-corruption networks are highly dispersed, lacking defined central nodes or entities to coordinate information flow. This structure promotes extensive distribution but slows information flow and raises the danger of losing crucial information. The report recommends reorganizing networks to increase systematic and efficient communication to combat corrup-tion. It suggests social network analysis to understand and optimize information communication dynamics in these networks. A more organized and successful corruption fight is the goal. The SNA included stakeholders in the models, but left out business partners and politicians, who are vital outside bureaucracy. The SNA model helps evaluate bureaucratic governance's corruption control. It overlooks corruption's complexity. To depict Thailand's multifaceted corruption practices, iron-triangle relationship, and deep democracy approach, the modified model includes all parties involved in the exchanges. Additionally, the statistical analysis of network effectiveness includes a basic frequency of networks sharing infor-mation on anti-corruption funding, technology, activities, and an overview. No consideration is given to network information exchange effectiveness and impact.

Whistleblowing

For politicians, bureaucrats, business or labor leaders, and regular citizens, corruption is a daily choice influenced by immediate social, economic, and political forces (Morris, 2022, p. 121). Whistleblowing puts people at the crossroads of ethics and risk. Witnesses of corruption must decide whether to report it and risk retaliation or keep quiet to protect their personal and professional interests. Morality and probable implications complicate this option (Morris, 2022, pp. 121–144). Organizational transparency and corruption prevention depend on whistleblowing. Many people fear reprisal or distrust the system and don't disclose corruption (Warsta, 2004). The 2018 OECD Integrity Review of Thailand found no whistleblower protection law. Recent whistleblower protection laws are scattered and unsystematic, which may not provide enough protection or clarity for future whistleblowers. Lack of a cohesive legal framework can deter whistleblowers owing to legal ambiguity, retribution, or inadequate protection (Taweejamsup et al., 2021). Legal reforms to protect whistleblowers' employment, anonymity, remedies, and incentives, including more reliable and systematic report handling, are urgently needed (OECD, 2018; Taweejamsup et al., 2021). In the digital age, civic engagement is as fundamental as legal reform. Technology has enabled anonymous and safe corruption reporting. Facebook, Twitter, and LINE are increasingly used to denounce wrongdoing and promote awareness in Thailand. Individuals can safely share information and expose corrupt activities on these platforms without fear of retaliation. The 2011-founded private collaborative Anti-Corruption Organization of Thailand (ACT) uses social media to promote whistleblowing and disclose corruption situations. Nonprofits like @watchdog.act and Youth2020 use social media for similar goals. It's exciting to gauge public opinion on utilizing social media to disclose wrongdoing, signaling a major change in whistleblowing.

The Theory of Planned Behavior (TPB)

Whistleblowing intents, attitudes, subjective norms, and perceived behavioral control have been examined using the theory of planned behavior (TPB). Park and Blenkinsopp (2009) surveyed South Korean police officers about whistleblowing as planned behavior. Positive attitudes and peer or superior approval boost misconduct reporting. When they feel in control of the whistleblowing process without repercussions, people are more likely to act. Organizational support and moral norms also moderate these associations, increasing whistleblowing intentions (Park & Blenkinsopp, 2009).

In another study, Owusu et al. (2020) surveyed 524 accounting students at the University of Ghana Business School and used structural equation modeling. Students are more likely to report misconduct within than externally. Whistleblowing attitudes and perceived social norms strongly favor internal reporting, but perceived control favors external reporting (Owusu et al., 2020).

Tuan Mansor et al. (2022) used a moderated multicomponent model of TPB to evaluate external Malaysian auditors' whistleblowing intents, including perceived organizational support (POS) and moral norms. Perceived behavioral control and POS positively connect with whistleblowing intentions, whereas attitudes and subjective norms do not. The TPB model is partially supported by moral standards' moderating effect on attitudes and whistleblowing intentions (Tuan Mansor et al., 2022). See Table 10.5 for the summary of investigation on whistleblowing intentions.

Modeling Social Media's Effect on Whistleblowing Intention

Social media is essential for personal networking and employment. Facebook and LINE dominate Thai social media use in 2023. A large share of internet users utilizes Facebook. However, LINE is popular in Thailand for its messaging services. TikTok has grown and become popular for its short videos (DataReportal, 2023). TikTok dominates Thai social media in 2023 with 49.3% usage. This high adoption rate shows that younger people prefer TikTok. Businesses advertise on Facebook, which has 48.1 million users. With 19.65 million users, Instagram is popular among 25- to 34-year olds. Additionally, 51.83 million Thais—73.8% of the population—use Messenger (Norcross, 2023, NapoleonCat, 2023). The Senate Commission on Political Development and Public Participation found in 2024 that most Thais care about corruption and government misconduct scandals and new technology research and development. Social media should be considered as an external element in the TPB model to understand Thai whistleblowing. Due to its anonymity and visibility, Thai people may view social media as a safer medium to secure their identity. Introducing social media factor to the model for the first time enhances these frameworks' analysis of the TPB in the modern day. It is assumed to have mediate effect on attitudes (favorable or unfavorable views of whistleblowing through social media), subjective norms (influence of peers and public opinion online), perceived behavioral control (ease of use and potential anonymity on social media), and POS. As shown in Figure 10.1, incorporating social media within these models can reveal its role as a whistleblower facilitator and barrier. It allows us to study how digital platforms alter the psychological and social components of reporting misconduct, improving our theoretical and empirical understanding of whistleblowing in the digital age.

Empirical Results

A random 250-person online survey was conducted in April 2024. The demographic analysis indicated that majority of respondents were female (57.6%), 38.8% male, and the rest other. The largest age group (40.8%) was 43–58, followed by 27–42 (30.8%). Over half of the participants had bachelor's degrees (29.6%) or higher (37.6%). Most respondents (48.45%) were government

Table 10.5 Summary of Whistleblowing Studies

Paradigm or Theory	Details	Strengths	Weaknesses	Reference Work
Scenario Studies	Participants respond to hypothetical situations involving ethical dilemmas to assess their intentions.	Controlled and versatile Useful for testing theoretical models Easy to manipulate variables	May not predict actual behavior Responses can be influenced by social desirability bias	Miceli, M. P. and Near, J. P. (1984). The relationships among beliefs, organizational position, and whistleblowing status: A discriminant analysis. Academy of Management Journal.
Autobiographical Recall	Participants recall and report past instances where they observed or reported unethical behavior.	Provides insights into actual behaviors Can reveal historical patterns and decision-making processes	Susceptible to memory bias and selective recall Participants may alter stories to appear more ethical	Near, J. P. and Miceli, M. P. (1996). Whistleblowing: Myth and reality. Journal of Management.
Immersive Behavioral	Participants engage in simulated environments that mimic real-life scenarios to observe their behavior.	Observes real behaviors in simulated environments Dynamic and interactive	High cost and complexity in setup May not ensure natural behavior due to awareness of being studied	Dworkin, T. M. and Baucus, M. S. (1998). Internal vs. External Whistleblowers: A Comparison of Whistleblowing Processes. Journal of Business Ethics.
Economic Games	Structured tasks where participants make decisions involving ethical considerations within a game setting.	Clear, measurable outcomes Can simulate costs and benefits Useful for studying decision-making	May not capture the emotional/social complexities of real-world whistleblowing Players may behave differently due to game environment	Mazar, N. and Aggarwal, P. (2011). Greasing the Palm: Can Collectivism Promote Bribery? Psychological Science.

(Continued)

Table 10.5 (Continued)

Paradigm or Theory	Details	Strengths	Weaknesses	Reference Work
Theory of Planned Behavior	Analyze whistleblowing through the lens of attitudes, subjective norms, and perceived behavioral control.	Provides a structured framework to predict whistleblowing behavior Integrates psychological and social factors	May lack direct observational validation in real-world scenarios Theoretical predictions may not always align with actual behavior	Park, H. and Blenkinsopp, J. (2009). Whistleblowing as Planned Behavior—A Survey of South Korean Police Officers. Journal of Business Ethics.
Social Learning Theory	Examine whistleblowing as a behavior learned through observing and mimicking others in social contexts.	Highlights the role of social influences and prior experiences Useful for understanding group dynamics affecting whistleblowing	Less focus on individual decision-making autonomy May not account for spontaneous whistleblowing events	Vadera et al. (2009). Making sense of whistle-blowing's antecedents: Learning from research on identity and ethics programs. Academy of Management Review.
Social Media Influence Theory	Explore how social media platforms facilitate or inhibit whistleblowing through visibility and community feedback.	Addresses the modern digital context of whistleblowing Examines the role of public and peer influence via digital platforms	Potential bias in data from self-reporting on social media Difficulties in isolating social media's effect from other influences	Breit et al. (2015). Critiquing Corruption: A turn to theory. Ephemera: Theory & Politics in Organization.

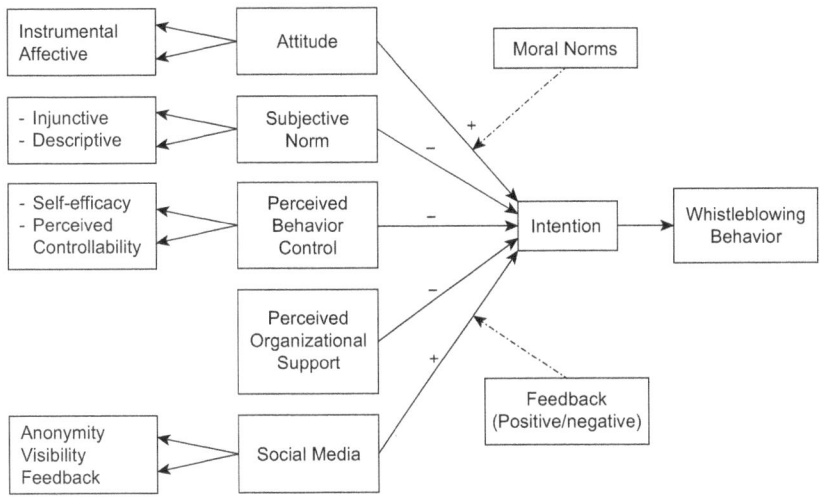

Figure 10.1 Social Media's Effect on Whistleblowing Intention Model.

workers and 27.2% self-employed. Facebook (83.6%), LINE (71.2%), and YouTube (47.2%) were the most popular social media networks. Facebook was favored for reporting wrongdoing at 73.2%, followed by LINE at 61.2%, government responsible units at 32.8%, TV influencers at 27.2%, and TikTok at 24%.

By employing SEM statistical analysis to test the model fit of social media factor on the original and expansion whistleblowing intention model in Figure 10.1, the results assured that each factor is statistically significant (p value = < 0.05) affecting whistleblowing intention, with social media factor being the most influential. Also, all five factors confirm to have explained the relationships among all exogenous variables in explaining the whistleblowing intention. The SEM results indicate a reasonable model fit based on various indices (CFI = 0.936, TLI = 0.908, RMSEA = 0.070, SRMR = 0.054); see Tables 10.6 and 10.7. Of particular interest is the significant positive influence of social media on whistleblowing intention (coefficient = 1.195, p = 0.004). This relationship highlights the potential role of social media in shaping users' intentions to report misconduct. Other factors such as attitude, subjective norms, perceived behavioral control, and organizational support did not show statistically significant effects on whistleblowing intention. Though this attempt may not find the best fit of the hypothesized model, it would be interesting to further investigate the crucial impact of social medial factor on whistleblowing intention. Open-ended surveys from respondents revealed that other motives to use social media to report wrongdoing practices are the legal efficacy, the capacity to raise public awareness, the assurance of secrecy, the rapid dissemination of information, and the ease of accessibility.

Table 10.6 Goodness of Fit Result (*N* = 250)

Fit Index	Value	Acceptable Range	Interpretation
Chi-Square (χ^2)	163.194	Non-significant	Significant, indicating some discrepancy (sensitive to sample size)
Degrees of Freedom	73	N/A	N/A
CFI (Comparative Fit Index)	0.936	≥ 0.90	Good fit
TLI (Tucker-Lewis Index)	0.908	≥ 0.90	Acceptable to good fit
RMSEA (Root Mean Square Error of Approximation)	0.070	≤ 0.08	Acceptable fit
SRMR (Standardized Root Mean Square Residual)	0.054	≤ 0.08	Good fit

Table 10.7 Structural Model Results

Hypothesized Paths	Coefficients	p value
Attitude → Whistleblowing Intention	1.017	0.378
Subjective Norm → Whistleblowing Intention	−0.248	0.309
Perceived Behavioral Control → Whistleblowing Intention	−0.520	0.508
Perceived Organizational Support → Whistleblowing Intention	−0.315	0.146
Social Media Influence → Whistleblowing Intention	1.195	0.004*

Model Fit: χ^2 = 163.194, df = 73, p value = 0.000, CFI = 0.936, RMSEA = 0.070, SRMR = 0.054.

*p-value is statistically significant ($p < 0.05$)

Research Prospects

The modified TPB model of whistleblowing intention enables exploration within local administration agencies characterized by a high prevalence of corruption across various sectors. A comparative study of social media influence could confirm the model that best fits the mediating role of social media in whistleblowing behavior. Furthermore, increasing the sample size would enhance the critical analysis of SEM, econometrics, and any statistical modeling that necessitates the definition of relationships and causal structures among various factors. Furthermore, enhancing the measurement model to optimize construct measurement can yield a more precise evaluation of the impact of social media on whistleblowing intention.

Multiple research inquiries can be explored concerning good governance practices in Thailand from various perspectives. The research team at King Prajadhipok Institute (KPI) has established measurement indices for the six principles of good governance (Bureekul et al., 2002, 2019). Numerous studies have examined factors influencing good governance at both national and local levels. However, a comprehensive assessment of the effectiveness of implementation and enforcement by agencies utilizing SNA to encompass public, private, international organizations, non-profit entities, and civil society necessitates further investigation (Yomnak et al., 2024; Arya Brata, 2009). To investigate the research question regarding the effectiveness of anti-corruption efforts in Thailand, it is essential to analyze the factors contributing to the success or failure of current measures and to consider innovative solutions that may improve compliance with public integrity (Warsta, 2004). Additionally, research should examine the contributions of each stakeholder and agency in combating corruption and enhancing transparency.

Examining various court rulings in notable cases of politicians accused of corruption through the case study method offers valuable insights into public integrity compliance. The 2017 Constitution establishes four entities that exercise judicial authority: the Constitutional Court, the Administrative Court, the Military Court, and the Court of Justice (Satayanurug & Nakornin, 2014). Nonetheless, a single case may fall under the jurisdiction of multiple courts, leading to conflicting rulings. The proliferation of judgments concerning political matters includes, among others, the Thai rice pledging system cases (Online Reporters, 2021) and the proceedings regarding the transfer of the secretary-general of the National Security Council (Post Reporter, 2023). A thorough examination of the consistent rulings issued by different courts in these cases will provide public officials with a basis for effective policy implementation and governance.

Another potential concern is the excessive emphasis on the grand strategy of good governance. Examining each element of good governance individually is essential for assessing the effectiveness of agencies in delivering services to the public. Additionally, investigating how these principles facilitate the development of trust in government is significant. It is essential to develop a structural model that demonstrates their interactions. Additional empirical research is required to determine the extent to which a transparency or open governance strategy may effectively encourage whistleblowing and subsequently decrease corruption.

Multiple strategies for addressing corruption are examined in Table 10.2. A synthesis of these strategies may facilitate a more nuanced understanding of human behavior. The advancement of Artificial Intelligence (AI) may lead to complex cases of fraud and falsification that are undetectable by human capabilities and current legal standards. Anticipating possible corruptions in the digital wallet policy implemented by the current Thai government may aid in mitigating policy corruption in the digital age.

Research should investigate the role of technology in improving transparency and accountability, including the utilization of digital platforms for corruption reporting and the implementation of e-governance systems. Furthermore, research must examine the significance of international cooperation and collaboration in addressing corruption, along with the effects of regional and global anti-corruption initiatives on the Thai public sector (Brata, 2009).

Conclusion

This chapter has emphasized the challenges and complexities associated with managing public integrity and compliance in Thailand's governance system. Despite extensive legislative frameworks, including the 2017 Constitution and various anti-corruption laws, along with the establishment of multiple anti-corruption agencies, corruption persists as a pervasive issue. The ongoing nature of these issues highlights the shortcomings of an exclusively compliance-oriented strategy in public ethics management, which depends significantly on rule enforcement and external oversight.

The chapter examined the integration of compliance and integrity approaches in the management of public sector ethics. Compliance entails following established rules and regulations, typically enforced through deterrent measures like sanctions and penalties. Integrity fosters a value-oriented framework that motivates public officials to engage in ethical behavior driven by an internalized sense of duty and responsibility. In Thailand, the integration of these two frameworks frequently leads to ambiguities, rendering actions driven by personal values and those mandated by regulations indistinguishable.

Although there are strong institutional frameworks, including the NACC, PACC, and Anti-Money Laundering Office (AMLO), the enforcement of integrity and compliance measures is compromised by systemic issues, including political interference, bureaucratic inertia, and inadequate resources. The findings indicate that successful anti-corruption initiatives necessitate more than the mere enactment of laws and the creation of agencies; they must also cultivate a culture of ethical conduct and encourage a comprehensive societal shift toward the principles of integrity, transparency, and accountability.

This chapter identifies gaps in the literature and outlines several considerations for future research. Deeper exploration of the socio-cultural dimensions of corruption is necessary, especially regarding the influence of traditional values and power structures on the persistence of unethical practices. Furthermore, empirical research on the effectiveness of whistleblowing policies and the influence of social media in enhancing transparency and civic engagement remains limited. Future research should evaluate the long-term impact of anti-corruption policies, assess the effectiveness of technological solutions such as digital platforms for reporting corruption, and explore the potential of cross-sector collaborations in mitigating corruption.

Subsequent research may investigate the incorporation of behavioral theories, including the TPB, alongside emerging digital tools to enhance the understanding and prediction of whistleblowing intentions. This chapter proposes the inclusion of social media as a factor in the TPB model, indicating that digital platforms can significantly affect individuals' willingness to report misconduct. Future research may enhance this model by investigating the impact of additional emerging technologies on public ethics and integrity management.

In conclusion, attaining public integrity in Thailand necessitates a comprehensive and adaptive strategy that transcends mere adherence to rules and regulations. Strong legal frameworks, independent institutions, societal engagement, and cultural transformation are essential components. A balanced approach that emphasizes integrity and compliance can enhance public trust and foster sustainable governance, resulting in a more transparent, accountable, and ethical public sector.

Acknowledgements

The authors would like to express their gratitude to Mananya Techalertkamol for her prompt and efficient assistance in conducting the SEM statistical analysis. Our appreciation goes to Maneechatchavan Maneesri for her invaluable assistance in efficiently disseminating the online survey, which enabled us to collect a sufficient sample size for our study. Finally, our sincere gratitude to Chris Reddick and the editorial team for giving us the opportunity to contribute to this project.

References

Bangkok Biz News. (2013, June 7). *Yan rattaban khadtoon chamnam khao 2.6 san laan [Confirmed, the Government Lost 260 billion in the Rice-pledging Scheme].* Retrieved from www.bangkokbiznews.com/news/509898

Barney, J. B. (1991). Firm resources and sustained competitive advantage. *Journal of Management, 17*(1), 99–120. https://doi.org/10.1177/014920639101700108

Becker, G. S. (1968). Crime and punishment: An economic approach. In G. S. Becker & W. M. Landes (Eds.), *Essays in the economics of crime and punishment* (pp. 1–54). National Bureau of Economic Research.

Borgatti, S. P., Mehra, A., Brass, D. J., & Labianca, G. (2009). Network analysis in the social sciences. *Science, 323*(5916), 892–895.

Brata, R. A. (2009). Chapter 6 Why did anticorruption policy fail? Implementation of the anticorruption policy of the authoritarian new order regime in Indonesia, 1971–1998. In C. Wescott, B. Bowornwathana & L. R. Jones (Eds.), *The many faces of public management reform in the Asia-Pacific region* (Research in Public Policy Analysis and Management, Vol. 18, pp. 123–153). Emerald Group Publishing Limited. https://doi.org/10.1108/S0732-1317(2009)0000018008

Breit, E., Lennerfors, T. T., & Olaison, L. (2015). Critiquing corruption: A turn to theory. *Ephemera: Theory & Politics in Organization, 15*(2), 319–336.

Bureekul, T., Tamronglak, A., & Others. (2002). *A research project to develop an index for measuring the outcomes of good governance development.* King Prajadhipok's Institute.

Bureekul, T., Tamronglak, A., & Others. (2019). *Principles of good governance: From concepts to practices in Thai society.* King Prajadhipok's Institute.

Chuenjitsiri, J. P., Rinthisong, I., Chongcheawchamnan, M., Arunbeikfa, N., & Isaro, S. (2022). *Surveillance and prevention of corruption projects from government policies and projects. Final report.* Office of the National Anti-Corruption Commission.

Cooper, T. L. (2012). *The responsible administrator: An approach to ethics for the administrative role* (6th ed.). Jossey-Bass.

DataReportal. (2023). *Digital 2023: Thailand*. Retrieved from https://datareportal.com/reports/digital-2023-thailand

Dockthaisong, B., & Maharutsakul, P. (2022). Enhancing transparency and the ability of Thai government to manage in the era of the new imperialist competition. *Journal of MCU Social Science Review*, *11*(6), 1–14. Mahachulalongkornrajavidyalaya University.

Drake, E., Malik, A., Xu, Y., Kotsioni, I., El-Habashy, R., & Misra, V. (2001–2002). *Good governance and the world bank*. In V. Collingwood (Ed.), *Nuffield College, University of Oxford*.

Dworkin, T. M., & Baucus, M. S. (1998). Internal vs. external whistleblowers: A comparison of whistleblowing processes. *Journal of Business Ethics*, *17*(12), 1281–1298.

Griswold, A. B., & Prasert, na Nagara. (1965). The inscription of King Ramkhamhaeng of Sukhodaya (1292 A.D.). *The Journal of the Siam Society*, *59*(2), 181–203.

Hambrick, M. E., Simmons, J. M., & Mahoney, T. Q. (2012). An analysis of Internet media coverage of professional athletes. *International Journal of Sport Management*, *13*(1), 1–17.

Hawkins, K. (2003). *Law as last resort: Prosecution decision-making in a regulatory agency*. Oxford University Press.

Johnston, M. (2005). *Syndromes of corruption: Wealth, power, and democracy*. Cambridge University Press.

Johnston, M. (2014). *Corruption, contention, and reform: The power of deep democratization*. Cambridge University Press. https://doi.org/10.1017/CBO9781139540957

Johnston, M., & Fritzen, S. A. (2020). *The conundrum of corruption: Reform for social justice*. Routledge.

Klitgaard, R. (1988). *Controlling corruption*. University of California Press.

Limsira, P. (2021). History & theoretical approach of Thailand in international law. In S. Lee (Ed.), *Encyclopedia of public international law in Asia online*. Brill | Nijhoff. https://doi.org/10.1163/2772-8161_EPIL_COM_2086

Limsuthiwanpoom, T. (2020). Models and guidelines for preventing corruption in Thai government agencies. *Rajapark Journal*, *14*(35), 1–8.

Mazar, N., & Aggarwal, P. (2011). Greasing the palm: Can collectivism promote bribery? *Psychological Science*, *22*(7), 843–848. https://doi.org/10.1177/0956797611412389

Miceli, M. P., & Near, J. P. (1984). The relationships among beliefs, organizational position, and whistle-blowing status: A discriminant analysis. *Academy of Management Journal*, *27*(4), 687–705. https://doi.org/10.2307/255873

Miceli, M. P., & Near, J. P. (1992). *Blowing the whistle: The organizational and legal implications for companies and employees*. Lexington Books.

Michaelson, C. (2006). Compliance and the illusion of ethical progress. *Journal of Business Ethics*, *66*(2–3), 241–251.

Morris, S. D. (2022). *The corruption dilemma: Controlling the power of the powerful*. Lynne Rienner Publishers.

NapoleonCat. (2023). *Social media users in Thailand—2023*. Retrieved from https://napoleoncat.com/stats/social-media-users-in-thailand/2023/

The Nation. (2024a, July 17). EC to probe authenticity of doctorate from US claimed by new senator. *The Nation Thailand*. Retrieved from www.nationthailand.com/news/politics/40039756

The Nation. (2024b, September 3). Chada bows out from next Cabinet to make way for his daughter. *The Nation Thailand*. Retrieved from www.nationthailand.com/news/politics/40041144

National Anti-Corruption Commission. (2023). *Annual report 2023*. Office of the National Anti-Corruption Commission. https://www.nacc.gov.au/sites/default/files/documents/2024-11/annual_report_2023-24.pdf

Near, J. P., & Miceli, M. P. (1996). Whistle-blowing: Myth and reality. *Journal of Management*, *22*(3), 507–526. https://doi.org/10.1177/014920639602200306

Newman, M. E. J., Barabási, A.-L., & Watts, D. J. (Eds.). (2006). *The structure and dynamics of networks*. Princeton University Press. https://doi.org/10.1515/9781400841356

Noisuwan, T. (2003). Culture corruption in Thai society: The case of Thai journalist. *Thammasat Review*, 8(1), 170–202.

North, D. C. (1990). *Institutions, institutional change, and economic performance*. Cambridge University Press. https://doi.org/10.1017/CBO9780511808678

Norcross, David. (2023). *Social media trends in Thailand 2023*. Retrieved from https://lexiconthai.com/blog/social-media-trends-in-thailand-2023/

OECD. (2013). What are bribery and corruption?. In *Bribery and corruption awareness handbook for tax examiners and tax auditors*. OECD Publishing. https://doi.org/10.1787/9789264205376-en

OECD. (2018). *OECD integrity review of Thailand: Towards coherent and effective integrity policies*. OECD Public Governance Reviews, OECD Publishing. https://doi.org/10.1787/9789264291928-en

Ostrom, E. (1990). *Governing the commons: The evolution of institutions for collective action*. Cambridge University Press.

Office of the Public Sector Anti-Corruption Commission. (PACC). (2022). *Annual Report* 2022.

Online Reporters. (2021, April 2). Yingluck freed of B35bn rice compensation order. *Bangkok Post*. Retrieved from www.bangkokpost.com/thailand/politics/2093923/yingluck-freed-of-b35bn-rice-compensation-order.

Opoku, A., Poshyanand, M., Elmualim, A., Kavishe, N., Mushtaha, E. S. N., & Abdalla, S. B. (2022). Corruption in the construction industry: An insight from the Thai construction sector. In A. Tutesigensi & C. J. Neilson (Eds.), *Proceedings of the 38th Annual ARCOM Conference, 5–7 September 2022, Glasgow, UK* (pp. 307–316). Association of Researchers in Construction Management.

Orozco, D. (2020). A systems theory of compliance law. *University of Pennsylvania Journal of Business Law*, 22(2), 244–302.

Owusu, G. M. Y., Bekoe, R. A., Anokye, F. K., & Okoe, F. O. (2020). Whistleblowing intentions of accounting students: An application of the theory of planned behaviour. *Journal of Financial Crime*, 27(2), 477–492.

Park, H., & Blenkinsopp, J. (2009). Whistleblowing as planned behavior—a survey of South Korean police officers. *Journal of Business Ethics*, 85(3), 545–556. https://doi.org/10.1007/s10551-008-9788-y

Poocharoen, O. (2014). Collaboration in anti-corruption work: Who to work with and how? *Lee Kuan Yew School of Public Policy Research Paper* No. 14–12, Available at SSRN: https://ssrn.com/abstract=2461597 or http://dx.doi.org/10.2139/ssrn.2461597

Post Reporter. (2023, December 26). Supreme Court acquits ex-PM Yingluck in one case. *Bangkok Post*. Retrieved from www.bangkokpost.com/thailand/politics/2713371/supreme-court-acquits-ex-pm-yingluck-in-one-case.

Pozsgai-Alvarez, J., & Varraich, A. (2023, November). Are different types of corruption tolerated differently? *Working Paper Series 2023:15*. The Quality of Government Institute, Department of Political Science, University of Gothenburg. ISSN 1653-8919.

Public Sector Anti-Corruption Commission (PACC). (2022). *Annual report 2022*. Office of Public Sector Anti-Corruption Commission. https://www.pacc.go.th/pacc_2015/uploads/files/annual_report/annual_report2022.pdf

Rathamarit, U. (2016). *Policy corruption project: Legal measures to control and prevent policy corruption problems in Thailand: Final report*. Office of the Board for the Promotion of Science, Research, and Innovation.

Riggs, F. W. (1964). *Administration in developing countries: The theory of prismatic society*. Houghton Mifflin.

Riggs, F. W. (2021). *Thailand: The modernization of a bureaucratic polity*. University of Hawaii Press. https://doi.org/10.1515/9780824885458

Rohr, J. A. (1998). *Public service, ethics, and constitutional practice*. University Press of Kansas.

Ruengchan, S. (2016, October). [Preliminary summary]. In Siamwala, A., et. al., *Corruption case study: The rice pledging scheme for every grain*. (Presented to the Office of the Higher Education Commission Research Fund, August 2014).

Satayanurug, P., & Nakornin, N. (2014). Courts in Thailand: Progressive development as the country's pillar of justice. In J.-R. Yeh & W.-C. Chang (Eds.), *Asian courts in context* (pp. 407–446). Cambridge University Press. https://doi.org/10.1017/CBO9781110 7588813.014

Sawasdipakdi, P. (2014). The politics of numbers: Controversy surrounding the Thai rice-pledging scheme. *The SAIS Review of International Affairs, 34*(1), 45–58. The Johns Hopkins University Press. www.jstor.org/stable/10.2307/27000939

Senate Commission on Political Development and Public Participation. (2024). *Development of political parties and citizen engagement in the digital age: Problems and solutions*. Office of the Secretary-General of the Senate.

Smith, J. L. (2014). Law, fact, and the threat of reversal from above. *American Politics Research, 42*(2), 226–256.

Tangkitvanich, Somkiat et. al. (2023). *Final report on public construction procurement law reform*. Institute for the Development of Thailand, Thai Construction Industry Association.

Taweejamsup, S., Jittirat, N., Eiamchamroonlarp, P., & Rajpradit, W. (2021). Assessment of whistleblowing's efficiency. *Chulalongkorn Law Journal, 39*(1). Chulalongkorn University, Faculty of Law.

Thai PBS World. (2024, August 14). Srettha lacks evident integrity, says Constitutional Court. *Thai PBS World*. Retrieved from https://world.thaipbs.or.th/detail/srettha-lacks-evident-integrity,-says-constitutional-court/54329

Thailand Development Research Institute. (2012). *Pol dee pol sia khong karn chamnam khao took med* [Advantages and Disadvantages of Pledging Unlimited Amount of Rice]. Thailand Development Research Institute. Retrieved February 10, 2024, from https://tdri.or.th/2012/10/ar3/

Thaler, R. H., & Sunstein, C. R. (2008). *Nudge: Improving decisions about health, wealth, and happiness*. Yale University Press.

Transparency International. (2020). *Global corruption barometer—Asia 2020*. Retrieved from www.transparency.org/en/gcb/asia/asia-2020

Transparency International. (2023). *Thailand*. Retrieved from www.transparency.org/en/countries/thailand

Tuan Mansor, T. M., Ariff, A. M., Hashim, H. A., & Ngah, A. H. (2022), Whistleblowing intentions among external auditors: an application of the moderated multicomponent model of the theory of planned behaviour. *Meditari Accountancy Research, 30*(5), 1309–1333. https://doi.org/10.1108/MEDAR-07-2020-0948

Vadera, A. K., Aguilera, R. V., & Caza, B. B. (2009). Making sense of whistle-blowing's antecedents: Learning from research on identity and ethics programs. *Business Ethics Quarterly, 19*(4), 553–586. https://doi.org/10.5840/beq200919432

Warsta, M. (2004). *Corruption in Thailand*. Presentation at Swiss Federal Institute of Technology Zurich.

Yomnak, T., Chaiwat, T., Poopunpanich, S., & Ruckchart, S. (2024). A social network analysis of information diffusion for anti-corruption cooperation in Thailand. *Thailand and The World Economy, 42*(1), 66–90.

11 Political Leadership and Public Sector Ethics in Africa

A Comparative Study of Ghana and Rwanda

George Babington Amegavi and Zechariah Langnel

Introduction

The relevance of the public sector to socio-economic development in Africa cannot be underestimated. An effective and well-functioning public sector is critical for providing goods and services and the rules that allow businesses to thrive. Without it, sustainable development, both political and socio-economic, is impossible (Ayee, 2012). There is growing recognition and concern that internalising ethical culture in the public sector is vital for ensuring that the public sector provides goods and services to the public and promotes the public interest (Asencio, 2022; Amegavi & Mensah, 2020). This ever-increasing concern is due to the growing ethical infractions that have bedevilled the public sector in Africa (Stoecker, 2022; Amegavi et al., 2022). Ethics violations often undermine social stability, public service delivery, and a constitutional state. Public servants are also regarded as the custodians of the administrative state (Rosenbloom et al., 2003) and make decisions on behalf of citizens. In this regard, they are required to perform their custodian responsibilities with utmost integrity. They must ensure their actions align with democratic, professional, ethical, and human values (Asencio, 2022). Indeed, where the norms to guide the conduct of public officials are non-existent or where existing public sector ethics standards are disregarded, citizens' trust in the state institutions may be eroded, and citizens' overall happiness in the government is undermined (Hoekstra et al., 2023).

Public sector ethics have often been discussed in the context of two schools of thought. Reflecting the early debate in the public administration literature, perhaps between Carl Friedman and Herman Finer, a critical question arises regarding whether compliance- or integrity-based approaches should guide the advancement of ethics in the public sector (Cooper, 2012; Perlman et al., 2023). On the one hand, while a compliance-based approach can be considered well intended, at least in principle, it is important to point out that they are insufficient in ensuring ethical behaviour in the public sector. A compliance approach might motivate public servants to comply with laws but may not necessarily encourage

DOI: 10.4324/9781003416258-12

them to apply them appropriately when circumstances change. It also often fails to address the cultural environment within which corruption and other unethical behaviours are nurtured. On the other hand, an integrity-based approach emphasises internal self-control and sound reasoning by public servants (Perlman et al., 2023). It stresses the need to encourage good conduct instead of punishment for unethical actions and a focus on results instead of means in managing ethics in the public sector (Paine, 1994).

The value of compliance- and integrity-based approaches for sustaining ethical practices and combating corruption in the public sector, especially in Africa and other developing countries, does not register much of an impact in practice. Thus, implementing compliance- and integrity-based approaches has fallen short of producing demonstrable results in achieving an ethical public sector across many African countries. Given this, many have suggested that any successful attempt at implementing compliance- and integrity-based approaches to promoting an ethical public sector must involve a genuine effort to identify and understand its root causes. We agree with this line of argument and contend that political leadership is a decisive factor in determining the success or failure of compliance- and integrity-based approaches to controlling corruption and promoting an ethical public sector in Africa. Without demonstrable political leadership, strategies to promote ethics in the public sector become empty gestures (Johnston & Kpundeh, 2004).

Against this background, this chapter seeks to contribute to the search for an ethical public sector by comparing the experiences of Ghana and Rwanda. The two countries differ in population, geographical location in Africa, and gross domestic product (GDP) per capita. Ghana is in West Africa, and Rwanda is in Central Africa. In 2023, Ghana's population and GDP per capita were estimated at 34 million people and US\$ 2,066, respectively. Meanwhile, in 2023, Rwanda had an estimated population of 14 million and a GDP per capita of US\$ 994 (World Bank, 2023). While both countries are classified as developing countries, Ghana has a relatively higher GDP per capita than Rwanda. Therefore, the two countries represent important case studies for examining the drivers of ethical governance and drawing critical lessons for building enduring ethics infrastructure in Africa.

The rest of the chapter is organised as follows: section two outlines the key concepts underpinning the study, compliance and integrity, as approaches for managing ethics and section three explores the role of leadership in ethics management in the public sector. The fourth section provides a background of ethics management in Ghana and Rwanda to understand the current situation of unethical practices and corruption in both countries. The fifth section explores the role of leadership in combating corruption and promoting ethics in Ghana and Rwanda. The sixth section concludes the chapter by drawing some lessons for Ghana and other developing countries in their quest to build and sustain ethics in the public sector.

Concepts of Public Ethics Management: Compliance and Integrity

Ethics in the public sector has become a critical issue for scholars and practitioners. Despite its importance, ethics in public administration literature only started gaining traction in the 1970s (Svara, 2014). The impetus emanates from the increasing corruption and declining levels of public trust in government. Public sector ethics refers to the standards of conduct, norms, and principles that govern the behaviour of public officials (Treviño & Nelson, 2021). Two approaches, compliance and integrity, are at the core of ethics management in the public sector. A compliance-based approach to ethics rests on the design and conformity with organisational codes. It is based on defined norms that monitor and control behaviour, deviations from which are sanctioned. Such norms are often legal manifestations of an organisation's expectations of the ethical conduct of employees. The concept's foundational principle is to ensure that public servants comply with specific demands and norms on a reactive basis (Rasche & Esser, 2007).

Generally, compliance has two levels. The first level involves the leadership of the organisation using internal organisational structures to impose boundaries on public servants, such as through a code of conduct. Second, the boundaries and norms of action may be defined externally and imposed. The organisation ensures the appropriate implementation of rules and regulations by controlling and monitoring behaviour and punishing unlawful actions (Tremblay et al., 2017). This orientation requires strict adherence to standards and obedience to authority (Roberts, 2009), and ethical responsibility is placed in the hands of public servants who are recognised as the final decision-makers and moral authority (Andrews, 1989).

Critics of the compliance approach to ethics management have stressed that it hinders opportunities for ethical reflection because it generally fails to offer opportunities to question the underlying assumptions that define legal norms (Rasche & Esser, 2007) and does not help public servants when dealing with the often dynamic and full range of issues that confront them (Roberts, 2009). Defining rules and regulations is not a discursive exercise but is conducted by law setters, external consultants, or management (Rasche & Esser, 2007). This signals a distrust of employees and could generate a calculating and self-interested response to ethics programs by employees. Compliance-oriented approaches to ethics management also reflect the view that public servants have no obligation to citizens beyond complying with laws and regulations and doing the minimum necessary for citizens (Anechiarico & Segal, 2020). Hence, Paine (1994) argues that the legal approach fails to inspire human excellence or distinction. Brown (2009) also points out that "[e]thics is fundamentally about *ethos*, attitude, one's grounded stance or existential orientation, not the extrinsicism of concepts or formalism of rules" (p. 294). Considering the shortfalls of the compliance-based approaches, the integrity-based approach was introduced into the ethics management architecture.

The integrity approach to managing ethics stresses the need to encourage good conduct instead of punishment for unethical actions and a focus on results instead of means in managing ethics in the public sector (Paine, 1994). As identified in the Organisation for Economic Co-operation and Development report,

> Public sector integrity management—often called ethics management—has been high on the agenda . . . . Underlying this evolution is a growing understanding that integrity is a keystone of good governance, a condition for all other activities of government not only to be legitimate and trusted but also to be effective.
>
> (2009, p. 6)

The ideas of social exchange theory are fundamental to the integrity-based approach (Perlman et al., 2023). According to the theory, the support and commitment an organisation gives to the goals of employees determine the level of obligation on the part of employees to support the organisational goals. It is a reciprocal relationship guided by a sense of responsibility to act ethically. This follows that enabling responsible conduct can be characterised as a goal of an integrity approach (Tremblay et al., 2017). Responsibility in this context requires responsiveness, given that integrity assumes that decisions are not made only for public servants affected by the decisions but should be included in the value-definition process. This means that integrity is not a value imposition process on public servants but rather a collaborative value-definition process with all stakeholders. Hence, the integrity approach to ethics management shifts the modus of ethical management by espousing an orientation premised on shared values.

The preceding analysis leaves little doubt that when considered together, the compliance and integrity approaches offer significant promise to combating corruption and promoting an ethical public sector. However, it is essential to appreciate that the leadership context within which these strategies are pursued can either derail or enhance success. This indicates that leadership is the most crucial starting point for the sustainable implementation of compliance and integrity measures for advancing ethics in the public sector.

Leadership and an Ethical Public Sector

Leadership has long been considered necessary in building an ethical public sector. In leadership literature, ethics is often considered a normative principle that focuses on how leaders ought to act and behave. Highlighting the critical role of leaders in ethics management, Treviño et al. (2000) argued that there are two important elements to an ethical leader: being a moral person and a moral manager. First, an ethical leader is perceived as a moral person when the leader is trustworthy, has integrity, acts, and makes decisions based on ethical values and principles (Treviño et al., 2000). It signifies the character of the leader. Second, an ethical leader is viewed as a moral manager when that leader role-models ethical conduct, sets ethical standards for employees, and holds everyone accountable for their actions and behaviour (Treviño et al., 2000). In a recent empirical study, Asencio (2022) reported a positive relationship between ethical leadership and employee commitment to act ethically in government agencies in the USA. Bowman and Knox (2008) examined views towards ethics in society and integrity in public agencies. According to their findings, people believe it is the responsibility of leaders in the public sector to set examples for people to follow. This hints that ethical leaders can foster and build an ethical public sector.

It has been recognised that, without a strong leadership commitment, reforms to advance ethics in the public sector are bound to fail (World Bank, 2020b; Stevulak & Brown, 2011). Leadership commitment refers to the sincerity of a leader's pledge to promote ethics by words and deeds. While leadership is instrumental in managing ethics in the public sector, the onus lies in their commitment to create the necessary conditions and systems to make unethical conduct unappealing. Most reforms to manage ethics in Africa have failed due to a lack of leadership commitment (ECA, 2010; Abdulai, 2009). When leaders commit to promoting ethical behaviour in their organisation, they integrate ethical values into their actions, decision-making processes, and organisational practices. These leaders set ethical codes that help public servants decide what is fair, right, and wrong when encountering ethical dilemmas. The most comprehensive and well-designed ethics management strategies often fail if management is not committed to its implementation. Lack of leadership commitment in ethics management manifests in various ways, including a lack of clarity in decision-making processes, conflicting application of rules and regulations, and incongruence in the application of sanctions, which leads to inconsistencies in values that guide the attainment of public service goals (Dess et al., 2011). Indeed, leadership commitment provides the necessary conditions that allow the seeds of an ethical public sector to sprout, grow, and develop.

Ethics Management in Ghana and Rwanda

Ghanaian Case

Unethical conduct and corruption have been pervasive problems in Ghana for decades. The public service system that Ghana inherited after independence from the British colonial rulers was based on the Weberian bureaucratic model (Economic Commission for Africa, 2010). The model is inspired by a legal-rational authority based on laws and regulations. Considering its dogmatic focus on over-regulation and complying with rules rather than achieving established goals, the system partly turned most public servants into a group of self-interested people (Ayee, 2012), which created a culture of unethical practices, including the use of public sector for personal and political exigencies (Economic Commission for

Africa, 2010). As a result, Ghana experienced several coup d'états until the early 1980s. The underlying justification for the coups was the enormous corruption and unethical practices in government and the public sector. For instance, the second coup in 1981 by Flt Lt. Jerry John Rawlings was justified by the growing corruption in the public sector under the erstwhile People's National Party government.

The country returned to democratic constitutional rule in 1992. Realising the country's complex nature of corruption and unethical practices, several laws and regulations were passed. Chapter 24 of the 1992 constitution provided a framework for a code of conduct for public servants. The Serious Fraud Office (SFO) Act (Act 466) was passed, and the SFO was established in 1993 to augment existing institutions such as the Commission on Human Rights and Administrative Justice (CHRAJ) and the Auditor General's Department in tackling corruption and unethical practices in the public sector. CHRAJ's guidelines on Conflict of Interest (CoI) and Codes of Conduct for public officials provide an extra layer to Ghana's efforts to fight corruption. The SFO Act was repealed in 2010, and the Economic and Organised Crime Office (EOCO) Act, Act 804, was passed. Additionally, the National Anti-Corruption Action Plan (NACAP) was adopted in 2015 as a holistic tool to fight corruption and promote ethics in the public sector. With CHRAJ as the implementation agency, NACAP represents a comprehensive and well-articulated national anti-corruption and ethics strategic plan designed to promote high integrity and ethical systems and practices, professional standards, and effective enforcement of anti-corruption laws in Ghana. In 2017, the Office of the Special Prosecutor Act (Act 959) was passed. Following the passage of the law, the Office of the Special Prosecutor was established in 2018 as the primary enforcer of compliance and anti-corruption laws in Ghana. Other laws that have also been passed to fight corruption and promote public sector ethics in Ghana include the Internal Audit Agency Act of 2003, Public Office Holders Declaration of Assets and Disqualification Act (Act 550), and Whistleblowers Act, 2006 (Act 720).

Notwithstanding these measures to advance ethics and mitigate corruption, evidence suggests that unethical practices are still pervasive in Ghana's public sector. In 2022, financial irregularities, according to the Auditor-General, increased from GH¢13,493,590.33 in 2021 to GH¢19,985,108.17 (Auditor-General Report, 2022). The United Nations Office on Drugs and Crime (2022) reports that 60% of bribes are paid at the direct request of public officials. Thus, Ayee (2016) argue that "unethical practices have become a way of life in Ghana" (p. 65).

Rwandan Case

Like Ghana, after independence in 1962, corruption was a major problem in Rwanda. Popular discontent with the growing corruption led to the country's first coup d'état in 1973, led by Juvenal Habyarimana (Riak, 2013). The coup d'état did not lead to any change in corruption; instead, Habyarimana's leadership strengthened the roots of corruption in Rwanda and nepotism in the country's public sector—which caused the eventual breakdown of effective government and contributed to the 1994 genocide (Bolongaita, 2005). In 2000, Paul Kagame assumed office following President Pasteur Bizimungu's resignation. Bizimungu resigned after allegations of corruption and plummeting levels of public sector ethics (Riak, 2013).

The new government led by Paul Kagame had zero tolerance for corruption and initiated a comprehensive strategy to mitigate corruption and promote ethics in the public sector. One significant strategy was the Vision 2020 strategy, which aimed to reform institutional and legal structures to help fight corruption and promote an ethical public sector in Rwanda (Government of Rwanda, 2000). Following the strategy, various laws were passed, including the Information Disclosure Law 2003; the Law on Prevention, Suppression and Punishment of Corruption and Related Offences 2003; and the integration of asset declaration for politicians in Rwanda's Constitution. In 2009, the National Advisory Council to Fight Corruption and Injustice was created and mandated to review anti-corruption reforms and initiatives in the country. The council then submits its report to the Office of the Ombudsman, which acts as the implementing agency. The government has also ratified the African Union and United Nations conventions against corruption.

In recent years, Rwanda has been widely recognised and praised as one of Africa's leading countries for successfully mitigating corruption and enhancing public sector ethics (World Bank, 2020b). Despite the country's experience of genocide, Rwanda has emerged as a highly promising investment destination in Africa because of its strong commitment to economic development and good governance practices. Hence, it is characterised by streamlined processes, institutionalised good governance practices, and a dedication to innovation (Bawole & Langnel, 2023). Between 2018 and 2023, Rwanda has consistently been ranked among Africa's five least corrupt countries in Transparency International's Corruption Perception Index (CPI). The World Bank ranked Rwanda 38 out of 190 countries worldwide based on its ease of doing business, making Rwanda the second-best performing country in Africa (World Bank, 2020a). Rwanda's significant progress in advancing public sector ethics and reducing corruption puts it at par with few countries that have substantially reduced unethical practices in its public sector over the last three decades (World Bank, 2020b).

In sum, Ghana's level of corruption sharply contrasts with Rwanda's, whose achievements in promoting ethics and reducing corruption are well recognised (Figures 11.1 and 11.2). Rwanda has outperformed Ghana on the CPI score and World Governance Indicators (WGI) over the last decade (2013–2023). Therefore, the critical question arises regarding how Rwanda has advanced ethics and reduced corruption. At the same time, Ghana continues to struggle to promote an ethical public sector after implementing different anti-corruption laws and ethics reforms.

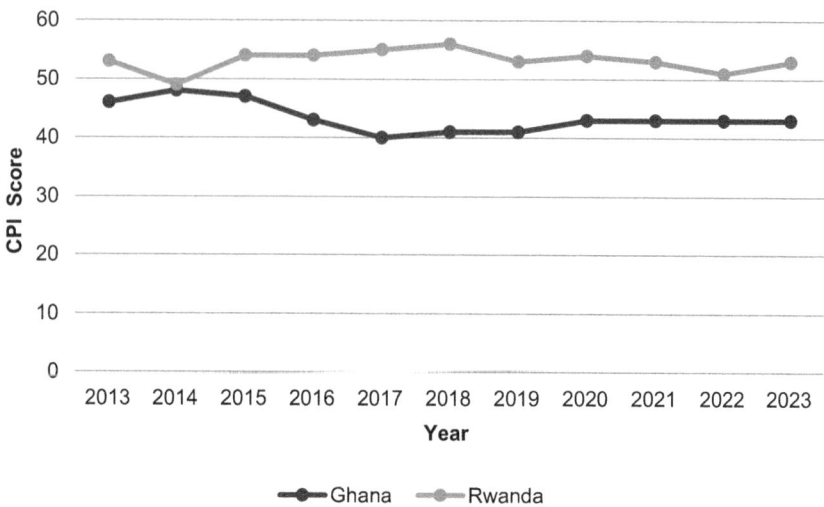

Figure 11.1 Corruption Perception Index for Ghana and Rwanda, 2013–2023.

Source: Transparency International (2024)

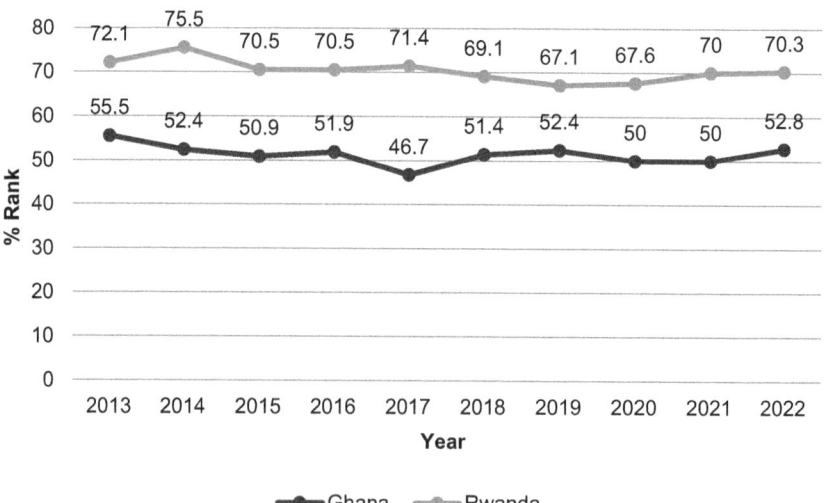

Figure 11.2 World Governance Indicators, Control of Corruption in Ghana and Rwanda.

Source: Word Bank (2023)

Explaining the Difference: Leadership an Enabling Factor

This section attempts to compare Rwanda's experience in mitigating corruption with that of Ghana, with the aim of ascertaining reasons why ethics and anti-corruption reforms and laws in Ghana remained largely ineffective. The analysis indicates that the most important factor explaining the differences in the effectiveness of ethical reforms and initiatives between Rwanda and Ghana is political leadership.

Leadership Integrity and Commitment

It is believed that leaders who have moral character and integrity are more likely to influence their people to act ethically. Few will disagree that leaders must have moral character and integrity and show commitment through their actions if unethical practices are to be effectively addressed in the public sector. In Rwanda, the willingness of public servants to act ethically is bolstered by President Kagame's integrity, validated by public perception that he has integrity and is not corrupt (Baez-Camargo et al., 2020). Political pressure and intimidation of officials of anti-corruption agencies have been drastically reduced, and any effort by a senior official to go to the president to protest investigations into ethical infractions is now perceived as a dangerous act with severe consequences (World Bank, 2020b). During the 2008–2009 anti-corruption campaign, Prosecutor Martin Ngoga asserted that the president urged him and his agency to follow corruption wherever it led, giving the agency enormous confidence in its investigations (Chemouni, 2017). Regardless of party affiliation, most government officials strongly maintain the president's zero-tolerance policy, and several high-ranking government officials involved in corruption have been either dismissed or prosecuted (Transparency International, 2021). From 2015 to 2017, an estimated 430 people were arrested and charged after trying to bribe a public officer (World Bank, 2020b). In 2007, the government dismissed 62 police officers for soliciting and taking bribes and 503 members of the judiciary for corruption and unethical conduct (Oyamada, 2017). The International Monetary Fund (2011) also reported that in 2008, 75% of the 159 corruption cases were processed by the state prosecutor, which exceeded the set target of 60% for the year. The 2021 Rwandan Bribery Index (RBI) showed that 72% of Rwandans believe that political leaders are committed to and are effectively fighting corruption in the country (Transparency International, 2021).

In assessing the integrity and commitment of political leaders in promoting an ethical public sector, one critical question that needs to be addressed is: Has the leader provided adequate resources to help fight corruption and build an ethical public sector? This question indicates that implementing compliance- and integrity-based approaches to advancing an ethical public sector requires financial and human resources. Under President Kagame's leadership, the Rwandan government has demonstrated a commitment to building an ethical public sector by providing adequate resources to ethics and anti-corruption agencies. The government has consistently provided the Office of the Ombudsman's entire budget allocation (Office of the Ombudsman, 2012). The government has also increased the agency's workforce from 68 in 2015 to 79 in 2016 (Oyamada, 2017). A recent World Bank (2020b) report on anti-corruption in Rwanda highlights the president's commitment and ownership of the ethics-building and anti-corruption agenda as a significant factor in empowering and ensuring the country's independence of ethics and anti-corruption agencies.

Contrary to the Rwandan experience, Ghanaians share a notion of a lack of leadership integrity and commitment to combating corruption. More than 80% of Ghanaians view key leadership positions, including the presidency, parliament, judges, and chief executives, as the most corrupt in Ghana (Afrobarometer, 2022). Since 1992, when Ghana returned to constitutional democracy, both the governments led by the National Democratic Congress (NDC) and the New Patriotic Party (NPP) have failed to prosecute their party officials who engaged in corruption while in government. Corruption is often accorded political characterisations. This has resulted in a situation where the claim of fighting corruption is seen only when they pursue opposition elements (Asomah, 2024). Most corrupt public officials are often not held accountable for their actions. The ruling governments have resorted to using the Committee of Enquiry to clear government officials of alleged wrongdoing or prevailed over anti-corruption institutions to drop charges against appointees (Stoecker, 2022). In 1995, a presidential advisor and two ministers of state were investigated for alleged corruption by CHRAJ and were found guilty of CoI and illegal acquisition of wealth. However, the erstwhile NDC government issued a White Paper on the Report by CHRAJ, effectively clearing the officials of wrongdoing. Again, in 2017, an internal audit of the Youth Employment Agency discovered payroll fraud estimated at GH¢ 50 million (US$ 11.1 million). However, the government did not hold anyone accountable. The absence of criminal prosecution in corruption cases deepens the public's moral disposition and suspicion of political leadership's commitment to promoting ethics in the public sector.

Furthermore, the government of Ghana has mostly failed to resource anti-corruption agencies adequately. In 2019, the government provided only 87.3% (GH¢27,803,365.50) of the budget of CHRAJ and 66.5% (GH¢13,545,850.41) in 2021 (CHRAJ, 2019, 2021, Annual Report). The Office of the Special Prosecutor is another anti-corruption and ethics agency that has consistently suffered acute budgetary constraints. The government of Ghana not only failed to meet the agency's request for increased budgetary allocations for 2020 but reduced it from the 2019 allocation. The Agency's budget was reduced from GH¢180,160,225.00 in 2019 to GH¢138,146,482.40 in 2020 (Government of Ghana, 2021). The lack of financial independence undermines the autonomy and effectiveness of these agencies. It may be argued that Ghana, as a developing country, may have other pressing development issues and cannot be expected to devote significant financial resources to anti-corruption agencies. However, increasing the available resources to anti-corruption agencies is entirely justified when compared with the costs of corruption to Ghana and the fact that Rwanda, with a relatively smaller economy and resources than Ghana, has effectively done so. Indeed, providing ethics and anti-corruption agencies with the resources to execute their mandate effectively will demonstrate political leaders' moral character and integrity (Treviño et al., 2000) and commitment to building an ethical public sector. Like Rwanda, if unethical practices in the public sector are to be mitigated and ethical norms advanced, Ghana's political leaders must lead by example and show more commitment.

Building an Ethical Climate and Responsibility

Building an ethical climate and responsibility is critical for fighting corruption and creating an ethical public sector. However, gaining the support of citizens and public officials and placing ethical responsibilities in their hands are essential to building an ethical public sector. Moral responsibility and support among citizens are most effective when citizens and public servants participate in anti-corruption and ethics-building initiatives (Abdulai, 2009; Bowman & Knox, 2008).

One of the consequences of the effectiveness of corruption prevention strategies in Rwanda has been the promotion of moral awareness and responsibility among public servants. The Rwandan government has adopted programs aimed, at least in part, at building and producing a more positive ethical climate in the public sector and gaining public support. Codes of conduct have been introduced for public servants. Senior government officials are required to comply, which in most cases includes a declaration of assets, liability, and income. Leading by example, President Kagame has consistently visited the Office of the Ombudsman to submit his asset declaration (World Bank, 2020b). Public officials who fail to declare their assets face sanctions, and their names and place of work are published in the annual report of the Office of the Ombudsman. This has created an ethical climate where senior government officials perceive asset declaration as a responsibility. Thus, in 2014, the Office of the Ombudsman reported that asset declaration among public officials increased by 96% (Oyamada, 2017).

Changing ethical climates towards a more value-inclined society must also involve attracting qualified people into the public sector. Meritocracy stresses recruitment based on principles of merit, not nepotism or political patronage. In Rwanda, upon assuming office, the president emphasised the need for transparent and merit-based recruitment to attract well-educated people with character into the public sector. Recruitment into the public sector of Rwanda is governed by a strict legal framework and supervised by the Public Service Commission (Chemouni, 2017). The process includes advertising job vacancies in the media, using digital application platforms, conducting recruitment exams, and publishing recruitment decisions at each stage to ensure transparency. Furthermore, the government audited the public sector, which identified 5,500 unqualified public servants who were fired (World Bank, 2020b). The government also shifted its training approach and focus. Rather than providing information and comprehensively explaining the rules and regulations for preventing corruption and other unethical practices and the consequences, the government started placing equal emphasis on the importance of core public sector values such as integrity, honesty, objectivity, and professionalism (World Bank, 2020b). These values have become a core approach to public education and training for public sector workers. By advancing these values, the government of Rwanda is building a shared notion that unethical practices are a significant moral failure.

As part of efforts to build a climate of integrity and responsibility among public servants, the political leadership led a campaign that promoted traditional Rwandan cultural values such as *ubunyangamugayo*—integrity (World Bank, 2020b), and the concept of "Rwandaness", that is, being Rwandan is about honesty and integrity (Baez-Camargo et al., 2020). These ideas and concepts were displayed on billboards and notices nationwide (Lamarque, 2017). Senior government officials also described and represented unethical practices or *Rushwa* as an antithesis to the country's development. Rwanda's Assistant Commissioner of Police described corruption as a "violation of human rights, a vice that fuels injustice, inequality, and deprives people of their right to certain services and slows down or affects service delivery" (World Bank, 2020b, p. 18). Furthermore, these initiatives emphasised *Ubudehe*—the practice of community support and collective action (Oyamada, 2017). Hence, public officials were encouraged to report suspected cases of unethical conduct for investigation and prosecution. Cyber cafes have been established across the country to encourage people to report instances of corruption (Oyamada, 2017). Consequently, *Rushwa* is significantly detested and stigmatised in Rwanda. Public officials convicted of unethical practices are named and shamed. The Ministry of Public Servants and Labour publishes a list of public servants involved in unethical practices such as embezzlement, bribery, and mismanagement. By raising awareness, naming and shaming people who engage in unethical practices, and promoting traditional Rwandan cultural values in the public sector, the government created an ethical climate and advanced public sector ethics as the responsibility of every public official.

By comparison, Ghana's political leaders have paid little attention and effort to building a climate of integrity and responsibility among public servants. Like the Rwandan case, codes of conduct have been introduced in Ghana's public sector, requiring senior government officials to comply by declaring their assets, liabilities, and income to the Auditor-General. Compared to the Rwanda experience, where public officials who fail to declare their assets face sanctions, in Ghana, senior public officials who fail to comply with the asset declaration are not sanctioned (Ashukem, 2022). Consequently, most senior government officials have failed to declare their assets. A year into his second term as president, only 19 out of the 120 ministers appointed by President Nana Akuffo Addo have declared their assets (The Fourth Estate, 2022). Similarly, the implementation of NACAP, the national anti-corruption and ethics strategic plan designed to promote integrity and ethical standards in the public sector, can best be described as marginal. Despite its promise, Rahman (2018) notes that it is "not all that rosy" for NACAP as political leadership across the political divide in Ghana seems uncommitted to the plan (p. 23).

While the political leadership in Rwanda is promoting and ensuring that recruitment into the public sector is based on merit, political leadership in Ghana has paid limited attention to the same. Recruitment into Ghana's public sector is often characterised by nepotism and political patronage. For many Ghanaians, recruitment into the public sector is practically impossible if you do not know any influential person. Unsurprisingly, the Senior Minister, Yaw Osarfo Marfo, speaking at a Ghana Economic Forum in August 2017, reiterated the government's freeze on public sector employment. However, in that same year, he was accused of using his position to secure appointments for his two sons in two different government organisations—the Social Security and National Insurance Trust (SSNIT) and the National Communications and Authority (NCA).[1] Undeniably, the political leaders from the NDC and NPP have interfered in the recruitment process for junior-level positions by recruiting party supporters into the public sector, most of whom are not well educated or without formal education (Brierley, 2021). A recent study by the United Nations Office on Drugs and Crime (2022) revealed that four out of every ten successful candidates who were recruited into the public sector admitted benefitting from nepotism. Political patronage and nepotism in recruitment practices produce flow-on-effects, including a weak commitment to developing ethical standards and prosecuting public servants who violate ethical standards, leaving the public sector bereft of an ethical climate. DeSouza et al. (2023) have rightly reported that Ghana has not been successful in promoting ethics in the public sector partly because the government has largely failed to address nepotism and political patronage in public sector recruitment practices, which are major facilitators of unethical practices in the public sector. The lack of merit in public sector recruitment practices creates an environment where professional competence fails to prevail, which impedes efforts to build an ethical climate and responsibility among public servants.

In Ghana, the active involvement of public officials and citizens in anti-corruption initiatives is almost non-existent, and strategies for promoting ethics and reporting corrupt practices in the public sector have mostly been ineffective. The Whistleblowers Act 2007 (Act 720) was passed as part of measures to promote the participation of public servants and citizens in promoting ethics in the public sector. However, political leaders have been poor in protecting public servants who blow the whistle to uncover corruption. For instance, in 2009, the

Minister of Youth and Sports was alleged to have misappropriated $20,000 on two separate occasions and used public resources to finance his girlfriend's trip to Germany. The Chief Director and the Chief Accountant of the Ministry of Youth and Sports revealed these ethical infractions. While the president asked the minister to resign without any sanctions, the two whistleblowers were asked to proceed on leave. The affected people went to court and were reinstated but faced intimidation and harassment after returning to work (Antwi-Boasiako, 2018). Hence, even with admissible evidence, most public servants in Ghana are unwilling to report unethical practices in their agency (Antwi-Boasiako, 2018). Furthermore, President Akuffo Addo's recent statement demanding that people who accuse government officials of ethical infractions produce evidence not only discourages people from reporting corruption in their organisation but also undermines efforts to build an ethical public sector.[2] It also raised critical questions about the president's genuineness when he declared his commitment to building an ethical public sector and asked for public support and participation during his inauguration in 2017.

Ultimately, in assessing the promotion of an ethical climate and responsibility compared to the Ghanaian experience, a shift in ethics and corruption disposition has occurred in Rwanda. There has been a change in attitude, with more interest and responsibility for ethical issues and promoting public interest. Thus, reporting acts of corruption has become a core concern for public servants in Rwanda.

Conclusion and Lessons

Governments and international development organisations have made concerted efforts over the last three decades to build ethics in Africa and other developing countries. A myriad of compliance- and integrity-based reforms have been tried to this end. The thesis of this chapter is that the effective implementation of compliance- and integrity-based systems for promoting and sustaining ethics in the public sector will require genuine and committed leadership from the top political elite. Indeed, without a strong and sustained leadership commitment, anti-corruption and ethics-building initiatives are bound to fail regardless of whether they are premised on compliance, integrity, or a combination of both approaches. Unsurprisingly, efforts to build an ethical public sector and combat corruption in Ghana lack strong and sustained political leadership and commitment. Despite enacting different anti-corruption laws and establishing agencies to promote ethics in the public sector, the evidence suggests that the commitment of political leadership to implementing these laws and strengthening ethics-building agencies remains perfunctory at best. On the contrary, Rwanda's efforts to combat corruption and build an ethical public sector have been largely effective, partly because of a strong and sustained political leadership commitment. Rwanda's anti-corruption and ethics-building measures are like a "hot stove" and "blind" to anyone. Anti-corruption and ethics-building agencies such as the Office of the

Ombudsman are autonomous and adequately resourced to execute their mandate effectively.

What lessons can Ghana and other developing countries learn from Rwanda's experience in mitigating corruption and their efforts to build an ethical public sector? From the comparative analysis made in this chapter, five important lessons can be deciphered for other countries aiming to build an ethical public sector.

First, for compliance and integrity measures to be effective and sustainable, political leadership must be genuinely committed to promoting ethical practices. Building an ethical public sector is a culturally conscious strategy that reflects the idiosyncrasies of leaders (Rasche & Esser, 2007). Leaders who attempt to set the tone and develop an ethical culture also risk being accused of double standards if subordinates perceive them as violating established standards and values (Paarlberg & Lavigna, 2010). This is likely to undermine any effort to build an ethical public sector. In this regard, political leaders must lead by example and model integrity, transparency, and character through words and deeds. Where government and political leadership also implement anti-corruption and ethics reforms for political expediency and other reasons, such as meeting the demands of international development organisations, such reforms are destined to fail.

Second, the autonomy and independence of anti-corruption and ethics agencies are necessary conditions for combating corruption and building an ethical public sector. Indeed, without leadership commitment to adequately resource anti-corruption and ethics agencies, these agencies are nothing more than "toothless dogs". As the case illustrated in this chapter suggests, with a strong leadership commitment to supporting and adequately resourcing anti-corruption and ethics agencies, Rwanda's Office of the Ombudsman have become more effective in executing its mandate of combating corruption and building an ethical public sector in Rwanda.

Third, employee self-reflection and responsibility for ethical norms and public sector values are critical for fostering integrity in the public sector. The need for ethical reflection becomes even more significant, given that public servants are motivated to the extent to which they perceive that their job affects the well-being of citizens (Paarlberg & Lavigna, 2010). It is, therefore, important to encourage public servants to feel that they are appreciated and are personally contributing to a public organisation that provides valuable services to society. Furthermore, people join the public sector for different reasons. Hence, it is essential to educate public servants about their call to public service, the significance of their roles, and their contributions to society. This can help them develop their motivation for public service (Amegavi & Mensah, 2020) and fulfil their custodian responsibilities (Rosenbloom et al., 2003).

Fourth, building an ethical public sector requires recruiting well-educated and professional people. Put differently, creating and sustaining an ethical public sector is highly challenging in an environment characterised by nepotism and political patronage. Therefore, to build an ethical public sector, recruitment into the public service must be based on meritocracy to ensure that the most qualified people are selected and employed.

The last important lesson is the need for broader stakeholder participation. Ethics reform initiatives must involve all stakeholders, citizens, civil society, and public and private organisations. Without broader stakeholder participation, it is unrealistic to assume that reforms to advance public sector ethics will succeed. It is vital to get the cooperation, support, and active involvement of citizens, the media, and civil society to play the watchdog role and report suspected cases of unethical practices for investigation. However, when citizens and civil society are required to provide evidence to substantiate their claims of suspected ethical infractions and corruption before investigations are conducted, they will feel reluctant to report and expose corruption.

In conclusion, the study has significant implications for future public sector ethics management research. Future studies could theoretically and empirically explore ways to build strong and committed leadership through comparative studies in developed and developing countries to help build and sustain ethics in the public sector. National elements such as culture and how it shapes leadership commitment to building and advancing ethics in the public sector could be considered. In calling for research into these issues, we conclude by agreeing with the view that integrating compliance and integrity approaches in all their forms, together with committed and moral leadership, can go a long way in advancing and sustaining ethics in the public sector and radically transforming the dysfunctional precepts of the public sector globally (Abdulai, 2009; Treviño et al., 2000).

Notes

1 www.peacefmonline.com/pages/politics/politics/201708/324054.php?page=1& storyid=100&
2 www.graphic.com.gh/news/general-news/we-need-evidence-to-prosecute-corrupt-officials-nana-addo.html

References

Abdulai, G. (2009). Political will in combating corruption in developing and transition economies: A comparative study of Singapore, Hong Kong and Ghana. *Journal of Financial Crime, 16*(4), 387–417.
Afrobarometer, (2022). *Summary of results. Afrobarometer Round 9 survey in Ghana, 2022*. Retrieved from www.afrobarometer.org/wp-content/uploads/2022/10/Summary-of-results-Ghana-Afrobarometer-R9-21oct2022-1.pdf
Amegavi, G. B., Quarshie, A., & Mensah, J. K. (2022). Mitigating corruption in sub-Saharan Africa: Does heterogeneity in corruption levels matter? *Public Integrity, 24*(2), 229–242.
Amegavi, G., & Mensah, J. (2020). Commitment to public interest and public service motivation development challenges: A qualitative inquiry. *Public Administration Issues, 6*, 67–83.

Andrews, K. (1989). Ethics in practice. *Harvard Business Review, 67*(5), 99–104.

Anechiarico, F., & Segal, L. (2020). Democratic governance as a function of ethics management strategies. *Public Integrity, 22*(3), 280–295.

Antwi-Boasiako, J. (2018). Why people refuse to blow the whistle in Ghana. *Public Policy and Administration Research, 8*(4), 1–7.

Asencio, H. (2022). Ethical leadership and commitment to behave ethically in government agencies. *International Journal of Public Administration, 45*(12), 907–916.

Ashukem, J. (2022). Assets declaration as a tool to combat corruption in Africa. In *Democratic governance, law, and development in Africa: Pragmatism, experiments, and prospects* (pp. 553–577). Springer International Publishing.

Asomah, J. (2024). Is democracy responsible for persistent corruption in some developing countries? The case of Ghana. *Crime, Law and Social Change, 82*(1), 45–67.

Auditor General Report. (2022). *Report and financial statements on the public accounts on the consolidated fund of the Republic of Ghana for the year ended December 31, 2022.* Retrieved from www.audit.gov.gh.

Ayee, J. (2016). The roots of corruption: The Ghanaian enquiry revisited. *Institute of Economic Affairs. Monograph,* 43, 1–82.

Ayee, R. (2012). Improving the effectiveness of the public sector in Africa through the quality of public administration. In *Rethinking development challenges for public policy: Insights from contemporary Africa* (pp. 83–116). Palgrave Macmillan.

Baez-Camargo, C., Bukuluki, P., Sambaiga, R., Gatwa, T., Kassa, S., & Stahl, C. (2020). Petty corruption in the public sector: A comparative study of three East African countries through a behavioural lens. *African Studies, 79*(2), 232–249.

Bawole, J., & Langnel, Z. (2023). Corruption-induced inhibitions to business: What business leaders have to say in Ghana. *Journal of African Business, 24*(1), 59–76.

Bolongaita, E. (2005). *Controlling corruption in post-conflict countries.* Kroc Institute, University of Notre Dame.

Bowman, J., & Knox, C. (2008). Ethics in government: No matter how long and dark the night. *Public Administration Review, 68*(4), 627–639.

Brierley, S. (2021). Combining patronage and merit in public sector recruitment. *The Journal of Politics, 83*(1), 182–197.

Brown, P. (2009). Ethics as self-transcendence: Legal education, faith, and an ethos of justice. *Seattle University Law Review, 32*(2), 293–310.

Chemouni, B. (2017). *The politics of core public sector reform in Rwanda.* (ESID Working paper 88/2017). University of Manchester, Effective States and Inclusive Development Research Centre. Retrieved from www.effective-states.org/working-paper-88/

Commission on Human Rights and Administrative Justice. (2019). *Twenty-sixth annual report, 2019.*

Commission on Human Rights and Administrative Justice. (2021). *Twenty-eight annual report, 2021.*

Cooper, T. (2012). *The responsible administrator: An approach to ethics for the administrative role.* John Wiley & Sons.

DeSouza, M., Swanzy, E., & Asumeng, M. (2023). Should I accept or refute? Understanding the socio-organizational factors influencing corruption in Ghana's public service. *Public Integrity,* 1–13.

Dess, G., Lumpkin, G., Eisener, A., & Peridis, T. (2011). *Strategic management: Creating competitive advantages* (3rd ed.). McGraw-Hill Ryerson.

Economic Commission for Africa. (2010). *Innovation and best practices in public sector reforms: The case of civil service in Ghana, Kenya, Nigeria and South Africa.* Retrieved from https://repository.uneca.org/bitstream/handle/10855/21041/Bib-19453.pdf? sequence=1

The Fourth Estate. (2022). *A project of the media foundation for Africa. The 19 akuffo addo ministers who fully complied with assets declaration law.* Retrieved from: https://thefourthestategh.com/2022/06/the-19-akufo-addo-ministers-who-fully-complied-with-assets-declaration-law/

Government of Ghana. (2021). *Medium-term expenditure framework for 2021–2024. office of the special prosecutor. Programme-based budget estimates for 2021.* Retrieved from https://mofep.gov.gh/sites/default/files/pbb-estimates/2021/2021-PBB-OSP.pdf

Government of Rwanda. (2000). *Vision 2020.* Ministry of Finance and Economic Planning. Retrieved from www.sida.se/globalassets/global/countries-and-regions/africa/rwanda/d402331a.pdf

Hoekstra, A., Huberts, L., & van Montfort, A. (2023). Content and design of integrity systems: Evaluating integrity systems in local government. *Public Integrity, 25*(2), 137–149.

International Monetary Fund. (2011). *Rwanda: Poverty reduction strategy paper.* (Progress Report, Report No. 11/154, 2011).

Johnston, M., & Kpundeh, S. (2004). *Building a clean machine: Anti-corruption coalitions and sustainable reform* (Vol. 3466). World Bank Publications.

Lamarque, H. (2017). *Insulating the borderlands: Policing and state reach in Rwanda.* (Doctoral dissertation, SOAS University of London, School of Oriental and African Studies).

Office of the Ombudsman. (2012). *Rwandan anti-corruption policy.* Kigali. Retrieved from www.ombudsman.gov.rw/

Organisation for Economic Co-operation and Development. (2009). *Towards a sound integrity framework: Instruments, processes, structures, and conditions for implementation.* Retrieved from https://one.oecd.org/document/GOV/PGC/GF(2009)1/en/pdf

Oyamada, E. (2017). Combating corruption in Rwanda: Lessons for policymakers. *Asian Education and Development Studies, 6*(3), 249–262. https://doi.org/10.1108/AEDS-03-2017-0028

Paarlberg, L., & Lavigna, B. (2010). Transformational leadership and public service motivation: Driving individual and organizational performance. *Public Administration Review, 70*(5), 710–718.

Paine, L. (1994). Managing for organizational integrity. *Harvard Business Review, 72*(2), 106–117.

Perlman, B., Reddick, C., & Demir, T. (2023). A compliance—integrity framework for ethics management: An empirical analysis of local government practice. *Public Administration Review, 83*(4), 823–837.

Rahman, K. (2018). Overview of corruption and anti-corruption in Ghana. U4 anti-corruption help desk. *Michelsen Institute.* Retrieved from https://knowledgehub.transparency.org/assets/uploads/helpdesk/overview-of-corruption-and-anti-corruption-in-ghana-2018.pdf

Rasche, A., & Esser, D. (2007). Managing for compliance and integrity in practice. In C. Carter (Ed.), *Business ethics as practice. Representation, reflexivity and performance* (pp. 107–127). Edward Elgar Publishing.

Riak, M. (2013). Reversing the trend of corruption in South Sudan: Is Rwanda a suitable model? *Journal of Developing Societies, 29*(4), 487–501.

Roberts, R. (2009). The rise of compliance-based ethics management: Implications for organizational ethics. *Public Integrity, 11*(3), 261–278.

Rosenbloom, D., Kravchuk, R., & Clerkin, R. (2003). *Public administration: Understanding management, politics, and law in the public sector* (6th ed.). McGraw Hill.

Stevulak, C., & Brown, M. (2011). Activating public sector ethics in transitional societies: The promise of integrity. *Public Integrity, 13*(2), 97–112.

Stoecker, A. (2022). Partisan alignment and political corruption: Evidence from a new democracy. *World Development, 152*, 105805.

Svara, J. H. (2014). Who are the keepers of the code? Articulating and upholding ethical standards in the field of public administration. *Public Administration Review, 74*(5), 561–569.

Transparency International. (2021). *Rwandan bribery index.* Retrieved from www.tirwanda.org/IMG/pdf/rwanda_bribery_index_rbi_2021.pdf

Transparency International. (2024). *Corruption perception index.* Retrieved from www.transparency.org/en/cpi/2023/index/

Tremblay, M., Martineau, J., & Pauchant, T. (2017). Managing organizational ethics in the public sector: A pluralist contingency approach as an alternative to the integrity management framework. *Public Integrity, 19*(3), 219–233.

Treviño, L. K., Hartman, L., & Brown, M. (2000). Moral person and moral manager: How executives develop a reputation for ethical leadership. *California Management Review, 42*(4), 128–142.

Treviño, L. K., & Nelson, K. A. (2021). *Managing business ethics: Straight talk about how to do it right.* John Wiley & Sons.

United Nations Office on Drugs and Crime. (2022). *Corruption in Ghana- people's experience and views.* Retrieved May 16, 2024, from www.unodc.org/documents/corruption/Publications/2022/GHANA-Corruption_survey_report_-_20.07.2022.pdf

World Bank. (2020a). Doing Business 2020. *Comparing business regulation in 190 economies. Economy Profile, Rwanda.* Retrieved from www.doingbusiness.org/content/dam/doingBusiness/country/r/rwanda/RWA.pdf

World Bank. (2020b). *Rwanda's anti-corruption experience: Actions, accomplishments, and lessons* (Report No. ACS29873). Retrieved October 09, 2024, from https://documents1.worldbank.org/curated/en/371741600749484414/pdf/Rwanda-s-Anti-Corruption-Experience-Actions-Accomplishments-and-Lessons.pdf

World Bank. (2023). World Governance Indicators. Retrieved September 6, 2024, from https://databank.worldbank.org/source/worldwide-governance-indicators

Index

Note: **Boldface** page references indicate tables. *Italic* references indicate figures.

absolutists 57
accountability 4, 6, 22, 44, 49, 60, 66, 68,
    73–74, 87, 92–95, 99, 107, 111, 137,
    142, 187–188, 198–199, 202, 211
Acemoglu, D. 172
Adams, Eric 2
Adams, G. 139
Addo, Nana Akuffo 229–230
Adler, P. S. 96
Administrative Disciplinary System
    (SICOR) 148, 154
administrative evil 50, 55
administrative rules 43–44
Affordable Care Act (ACA) 51
African political leadership, comparative
    study of: compliance-based approach
    and 217–220; ethical climate and,
    building 227–230; ethical public sector
    and 220–221; ethics management and
    221–223; in Ghana 218, 221–222, *224*,
    226–231; integrity-based approach and
    218–220; leadership as an enabling
    factor and 225–230; lessons from
    230–232; National Advisory Council
    to Fight Corruption and Injustice and
    223; overview 11, 218; public sector
    ethics and 217–218; responsibility and,
    building 227–230; in Rwanda 218,
    222–223, *224*, 225–226, 228, 230–231
Aggarwal, P. 22
Aidt, T. 172
Aiken, Henry David 60
Amegavi, George Babington 11
American Bar Association 28

American with Disabilities Act (ADA)
    compliance 29, 35
American Evaluation Association (AEA)
    code of ethics 32
American Institute of Certified Planners
    (AICP) 30, 36
American Planners Association (APA) 36
American Society for Public
    Administration (ASPA) 30, 33,
    40–41, 59
Amos, E. A. 142
analysis, ethical 53–54
Anechiarico, F. 98
Anti-Corruption Organization of Thailand
    (ACT) 205
Aristotelian virtues 92
Asencio, H. 221
Ash, A. 37
Athenian Oath 29
Auditor General's Department 222
authentic leadership *113*, 114–115
authority conflicts 63–64
awareness, ethical 49–50, 53

Bailey, S. K. 59
Balfour, D. L. 55
Ball, G. A. 21
Bandura, A. 116
Barnard, C. I. 134
Barr, A. 23
Barry, B. 104
Bashir, M. 123
Bass, B. M. 112
Batohi, S. 179–180

Bazerman, M. H. 82
Beach, D. 147, 153
Beccaria, Cesare 16
Becker, G. S. 16, 172
Beeri, I. 23
behavioral research/science 82–83, 85–88
behavior/conduct *see* ethical behavior/
    conduct; unethical behavior/conduct
Belle, N. 21–22
Berlusconi, Silvio 181
Bertok, J. 97, 99, 103
Bizimungu, Pasteur 223
Blenkinsopp, J. 205
Borgatti, S. P. 204
Borsellino, Paulo 176
Borys, B. 96
Bourne, H. 129
Bowman, J. 85, 221
Brazilian public ethics management case
    study: Administrative Disciplinary
    System and 148, 154; background
    information 148–149; causal
    mechanisms "M" and 153; Code
    of Conduct of the High Federal
    Administration and 158; conflict of
    interest and 159–162; Decree of 26
    May 1999 and 157–158; Decree No.
    1,171 (June 1994) and 157; Decree No.
    5,480 (July 2005) and 159; design of
    research 153–156; ethics management
    and, emergence of 157–158, 162–163;
    Ethics Management System of the
    Executive Federal Branch and 146,
    148, 153–155, 158–163; Ministry of
    Administration and State Reform and
    157; Ministry of Planning, Budget, and
    Management and 157; Office of the
    Comptroller General and 155, 158–163;
    overview 10, 147–148, 163–164;
    process tracing and 156–162; Public
    Ethics Commission and 146, 155,
    158, 160–163; Public Integrity System
    and 148, 154; Public Transparency
    and Combating Corruption Council
    and 158–159; reform issues 148–152;
    Special Commission of Investigation
    and 157; theoretical proposal 152–153;
    theory-testing causal scheme and 147,
    152–154, 156
bribery 19–20, 76, 161, 174, 178, 181,
    187–189

British Behavioural Insights Team 83
British Cabinet Office 83
Brown, M. E. 5, 114
Brown, P. 219
Buckingham, M. 119
bureaucracy 2, 18, 54–55, 96, 136, 141,
    173, 189–190, 193–194, 198, 200
Burke, R. J. 179
Burnham, Dan 121

Calder, G. 33
Cantarelli, P. 21–22
Carr, Danny Nathaniel 9, 16
case study approach 203–204
Catch-22 60–61
Cavazza, F. L. 173
Chan-o-cha, Prayut 203
Cheng, J. 118
Chesterton, G. K. 61
Chesterton's Fence 61
Chiesa, Mario 175
choice theory 9, 14, 16–17, 22, 24
Chuenjitsiri, J. P. 203
civic commitments/engagement 84, 205, 212
Claunch, R. 51–52
Clean Hands (*Mani Pulite*) scandal/
    investigation 169–170, 175–176, 180
coaching 117, 120, 123
Code of Conduct of the High Federal
    Administration 158
Code of Federal Regulations (CFR) 76
Code of Professional Ethics of Civil
    Servants 146
codes of conduct 30, 78–80, 222
codes of ethics: accountability and 22,
    44; administrative rules/legislation/
    policy and 43–44; authority for 34–35;
    capacity issues and 43; challenges
    43–44; clarity of 34; codes of conduct
    versus 30; communication of moral
    standards and 21–22; conflicts 28–29,
    36; context of 33–34; criticisms of 23;
    definition of 29–30; discretion and
    33; effectiveness of 20–22; emerging
    issues 44–45; ethical behavior/conduct
    and, promoting 33–34; ethics programs
    and 38–39; examples of well-written
    39–43; function of 30; implementation
    of 36–39, 111; integrity in 7, 33;
    internalization of 33, 37; legal
    standards 28–29; overview 9, 45;

private interest and 44; of professional associations 30, 58–59; public interest and 31, 44; as reminder of moral standards 21; reviewers of 36; revising 39; sustainability of 36–37, 39; terminology, differentiation of 28–30; training and employee development and 37–38, 59; transparency and 44; in United States 29; values in 30–33, 39; writing 34–36; *see also specific name*
code of values 130
Coffman, C. 119
Cokins, G. 140
Commission on Human Rights and Administrative Justice (CHRAJ) 222
comparative method/study 7–8, 31, 78, 107, 210; *see also* African political leadership, comparative study of
compliance: adherence to rules and 193–194; Americans with Disabilities Act 29, 35; defined 14–15; ethics management and 7; levels of 219; low road approach to ethics and 33, 72–73, 86, 94, 101–107; programs 38; training and employee development and 68–69
compliance-based approach: African political leadership and 217–220; characteristics of 97, **97**; choice theory and 9, 14, 16–17; contrasting dual approaches and 93–94; criticism of 219; effectiveness of 20–23; in ethics management 15; focus of 72–73; future research on 24–25; integrity-based approach versus 9, 14, 99–101; legal context of 19; monitoring and 22–23; motivation in 7; overview 9, 14–15, 23–24; political/social context of 18–19; preference for, lack of strong 98–101; Principle-Agent-Client model and 17; punishment and 16, 19; scope of 19–20; Thai public integrity challenges and 193–195; theoretical foundations of 15–17; in United States, development of 18–19; *see also* dual approach to ethics management
Compliance-Integrity Framework 5–8
compliance theory 194
conduct codes 30, 78–80, 222
conflicts: of authority 63–64; of codes of ethics 28–29, 36; of interest 63, 159–162; role 63; of values 134

conscience, following 62, 100, 107, 118
contrasting dual approaches: bridging high and low roads approach to ethics management and 101–106; compliance-based approach and 93–94; integrity-based approach and 93–94; overview 10, 92–93, 106–107; public management distinctions and 94–101
Cooper, T. L. 56, 62
corruption: in Africa 228; in bureaucracy 2; Chuenjitsiri et al. case study of 203–204; concern about 2; definition of 170; in Ghana 223, *224*, 226; issues emerging from 146–147; monitoring in reducing 23; in Rwanda 223, *224*; syndromes of 189; in Trinidad and Tobago Police Service 16; in United States 2; *see also* Italian corruption and anti-corruption reform
Corruption Perceptions Index (CPI) 2, 169, 187, 223, *224*
cost-benefit comparison of ethical behavior/conduct 83–84
courage 59
Criminal Conflict of Interest Laws 76
Croca Caeiro, Joaquim Manuel 10, 165
cultural norms 180–181
culture of organization 118

Damasio, Antonio 52–53
Davis, Kim 134
decision-making 6, 9–10, 17, 29–30, 33, 49, 51–55, 57–58, 60–66, 68, 79–80, 82–83, 85, 95, 98–100, 106, 122–123, 146, 148, 150, 164, 194, 202, 204, 221; *see also* values
deep democracy approach 202–203
dehumanization 55–56
Del Monte, A. 171–172, 174–175
Demir, T. 5
Denhardt, J. V. 128, 137
Denhardt, R. B. 128, 137
Department of Justice (DOJ) 2
designated agency ethics officials (DAEOs) 76
DeSouza, M. 229
deterrence/deterrence theory 16–17, 21, 98, 179, 194
devil's advocate 64, 97
Dickson, M. W. 136
Di Liberto, A. 171

discretion 3, 6, 10, 33, 72, 83, 85, 88, 94, 104, 119, 129, 150, 177, 203
disincentives 83, 85–86
Di Tella, R. 23
diversity, equity, and inclusion (DEI) 31–32, 36, 43
Dobel, J. Patrick 38
Dockthaisong, B. 190
Dodd-Frank Act (2010) 19, 81
Dolan, S. L. 140
Dose, J. J. 128
Dowling, J. 139
Downe, J. 23, 79
Drake, E. 202
Drucker, P. 140
dual approaches to ethics management: ethical behavior/conduct and 82–86; incentives and 72–74; institutional level of sanctions/incentives and 74–77; organizational level of sanctions/incentives and 74, 77–82; overview 9–10, 86–88; sanctions and 72–74; *see also* contrasting dual approaches
dual role modeling 82
duty-oriented ethics 58–59

Economic and Organised Crime Office (EOCO) Act 222
embezzlement 2, 177, 187, 189, 228
emotions 9, 52–53, 67
equity 31–32, 36–37, 39–40, 43–44, 49, 60
Ertas, Nevbahar 9–10
ethical analysis 53–54
ethical awareness 49–50, 53
ethical behavior/conduct: codes of ethics promoting 33–34; complexity of 93; cost-benefit comparison of 83–84; dual approaches to ethics management and 82–86; eliciting 73; enforcing 73; high road and 33, 86; importance of in public sector 49; incentives and 82–86; leadership and 65, 115–119; low road and 33, 86; rewarding 81–82, 85–86; values and 131, **132–133**, 134
ethical leadership *see* leadership
ethical practice 50–53
ethical reflection 60
ethics: duty-oriented 58–59; high road approach to 33, 73, 86, 94, 101–107; low road approach to 33, 72–73, 86, 94, 101–107; as scholarly discipline 29;

values and 111; virtue 59; *see also* codes of ethics; *specific type*
Ethics in Government Act (1978) 18, 30, 76
ethics management: African political leadership and 221–223; complexity of 101–102; compliance and 7; compliance-based approach in 15; contrasting dual approaches and 101–106; defined 15; Friedrich-Finer debate and 4; integrity and 7; leadership and 111–112; in public organizations 4–5; purpose of 94–98; research on 5–6, 74, 107; traditional approaches to 4, 6; traditional literature on 3; training and employment development and 49; trends in, new 102–106; values and 7; *see also* Brazilian public ethics management case study; compliance-based approach; contrasting dual approaches; dual approaches to ethics management; integrity-based approach; public sector ethics
Ethics Management System of the Executive Federal Branch (SGEP) 146, 148, 153–155, 158–163
ethics programs 5, 38–39
Ethics Research Center 80
ethics training *see* training and employee development
executive-level leaders 119
Executive Measure Act on Anti-Corruption Commission 188
Executive Order 8802 42
Executive Order 12674 (1989) 76
external controls 94
extortion 178, 189
extrinsic motivation/rewards 14, 72–73, 84–86

fairness 31, 59
Falcone, Giovanni 176
Falleti, T. G. 147, 153
False Claims Act 81
Faragher v. City of Boca Raton (1998) 52
Feldman, Daniel L. 10, 174
Finer, Herman 4, 94, 99, 217
Floyd (George) death 32
Flynn, James 56
Fonseca, C. M. 147, 153
Foote, M. F. 105
Forde, T. 16

Ford Motor Company 55
Foreign Corrupt Practices Act (FCPA) (1977) 19
France 181
Franco, Itamar 157
Frederickson, H. G. 173
Frey, Bruno S. 84
Friedrich, Carl 4, 74, 94, 99, 217
Friedrich-Finer debate 4, 10, 72–73, 94, 98

Gawthorp, L. C. 3
Gelderman, C. J. 15
Ghana 218, 221–222, *224*, 226–231
Gilman, S. C. 37–39, 73
Gino, F. 82
Global Corruption Barometer-Asia (GCB) 187
Gneezy, U. 84
Golden Rule 66
Gooden, S. T. 31
good governance approach 198–200, **199**, 202, 210–211
Goodsell, C. 134
Government Finance Officers Association (GFOA) 31, 42–43
grassroots participation 104, 202
Graudbard, S. R. 173
group pressures 64, 64–66
groupthink 50
Grundstein-Amato, R. 34, 36, 40
Gullo, Antonino 177
Gunia, B. C. 65–66

Habyarimana, Juvenal 222–223
Hambrick, M. E. 204
Hartley, J. 141
Hassan, S. 123
Heady, F. 8
Heller, Joseph 60–61
Heres, L. 121
Herzog, R. 51–52
high road approach to ethics 33, 73, 86, 94, 101–107
Hijal-Moghrabi, I. 18–19, 24
Hobson's Choice 61
Hoekstra, Alain 10, 105
Homer, Jessica 9
Huang, L. 117–118
Hummel, Ralph 54–55
hypothetical, engaging 56

incentives: behavioral research/science and 82–83, 85–88; dual approaches to ethics management and 72–74; ethical behavior/conduct and 82–86; extrinsic rewards and 85–86; at institutional level 74–77; interconnectedness with sanctions, accountability, and responsibility 73–74; intrinsic rewards and 85–86; at organizational level 74, 77–82; prosocial motivation and 84; public sector ethics and 72–74; reinforcement and 80–82; unethical behavior/conduct and 83
Individual Freedom Act (2022) 36
Institutional Analysis and Development (IAD) 147, 152
integrity: in codes of ethics 7, 33; essence of 95; ethics management and 7; government, benchmarks for 75; high road approach to ethics and 33, 73, 86, 94, 101–107; impact of public 92; leadership and 121–122, 225–227; Paine's understanding of 96; personal 33; self-governance and 95; training and employee development and 68–69; usage of term 95; values and 111, 194; *see also* Thai public integrity challenges
integrity-based approach: African political leadership and 218–220; characteristics of 97, **97**; compliance-based approach versus 14, 95, 99–101; contrasting dual approaches and 93–94; focus of 73; motivation in 7; preference for, lack of strong 98–101; Thai public integrity challenges and 193–195; *see also* dual approach to ethics management
integrity management systems (IMSs) 102–106
interconnectedness 73–74, 102–105
Internal Agency Act 222
internal controls 94
International Association of Chiefs of Police (IACP) 30, 33
International City/County Management Association (ICMA) Code of Ethics 30, 32–33, 41–42
International Monetary Fund (IMF) 225
intrinsic motivation/rewards 10, 14–16, 73, 84–86, 98, 121
IRS Whistleblower law 81

Italian corruption and anti-corruption reform: administrative norms and 171–172; assassinations of Falcone and Borsellino and 176; challenges to anti-corruption reform and 176–178; Clean Hands scandal/investigation and 169–170, 175–176, 180; Decree 231/2001 and 177–178; definition/variation of *corruption* and 170–171; dynamics of corruption between World War II and 1991 and 173–175; engrained dynamics of corruption and 178–180; factors affecting corruption and 171–173; governance and 172–173; institutional arrangements and 172–173; Law No. 3/2019 (January 2019) and 169; Law No. 3/2019 and 177–178; Law No. 97/2001 and 177; Law No. 300/2000 and 176; legal advancements to anti-corruption reform and 176–178; Legislative Decree 231/2001 and 177; lessons from 180–181; overview 10, 170, 180–181; ranking on CPI and 169; social dynamics and 171–172

Jacobs, J. B. 98
Janis, Irving 64
Jenkins, M. 129
Jensen, T. 23
Johnston, Michael 189
Jordan, J. 116
Jørgensen, T. B. 32
Jung, J. 77

Kagame, Paul 22, 223, 227
Kant, I. 58
Kappes, H. B. 53
Kaptein, M. 19–20, 22, 78, 103
Karssing, Edgar K. 10
Kaufman, H. 128
Kennedy, John F. 30, 32
Khaltar, O. 15
King Prajadhipok Institute (KPI) 210
Kipnis, Kenneth 53–54, 57, 59
Klitgaard, Robert 203
Knox, C. 221
Kobayashi Maru Scenario 62
Kontogeorga, G. N. 21–22

Langnel, Zechariah 11
Lartey, F. M. 19, 99–100

LaSpina, A. 174
Lasthuizen, K. 121
leadership: authentic *113*, 114–115; collaboration and 120; commitment and 225–227; cultivating ethical 121–123; culture of organization and 118; ethical 112, *113*, 114–115, 121–123; ethical behavior/conduct and 65, 115–119; ethical public sector and 220–221; ethics management and 111–112; executive-level 119; goal-setting and 119; hiring employees and 121; integrity and 121–122, 225–227; mentoring and 117, 119–120, 122–123; moral 112, *113*, 114–115; moral disengagement and 118; morality and 121–122; multiple 119–120; overview 10, 112, 123; public sector ethics and 5, 112–115; public service motivation and 118; role ethicality and 118; sector differences in 120–121; servant *113*, 114–115; supervisory-level 119–120; training and employee development for 122; transformational 112; values and 127–128, 140–141; *see also* African political leadership, comparative study of
legal ethical standards 28–29
legislation 43–44; *see also specific name*
Lewis, C. W. 38–39, 73
Limsira, Patthara 10–11
low road approach to ethics 33, 72–73, 86, 94, 101–107
Lynch, J. F. 147, 153

Maesschalck, J. 97, 99, 100, 102–103
Maggio, P. 177–178
Maharutsakul, P. 190
Mahoney, J. 147, 153
Management by Instructions (MBI) 140
Management by Objectives (MBO) 140
management by values (MBV) 139–141
Marfo, Yaw Osarfo 229
Marini, F. 31
Martineau, J. T. 100–101
Mattarella, Bernardo Georgio 177
Mazar, N. 22
McCandless, S. 31
McKeown, C. 134–135, 142
mechanismic lens 147
mentoring 117, 119–120, 122–123
Menzel, D. C. 24

Messick, D. M. 79
Milan City Council 175
Ministry of Administration and State
    Reform (MARE) 157
Ministry-Level Operation Against
    Corruption (MOCAC) 190–191
Ministry of Planning, Budget, and
    Management (MPOG) 157
Model Rules of Professional
    Responsibility 28
Molina, A. D. 134–135, 142
monitoring 22–23
Moon, M. J. 15
moral competence 20
moral disengagement 118
Morales, J. 173
moral leadership 112, *113*, 114–115
moral qualities 59
moral reasoning 57
Morewedge, C. K. 53
Morgan, D. F. 33
Mosher, W. E. 31–32
motivated reasoning 83–84
Mugellini, G. 170
Murphy, J. E. 81–82

Nacchio, Joseph 2
National Administrative Studies Project
    (2015) 77
National Advisory Council to Fight
    Corruption and Injustice 223
National Anti-Corruption Action Plan
    (NACAP) 222
National Anti-Corruption Authority
    (ANAC) 177
National Anti-Corruption Commission
    (NACC) 191–192
National Association of Executive Fire
    Officers (NSEFO) 33
National Command Center for Combating
    Corruption (NCCCC) 191
National Conference of State Legislatures 77
National Democratic Congress (NDC) 226
National Economic and Social
    Development Plan (NESDP) 199
National Strategic Plan (2018-2037) 199
National Whistleblower Center 81
Neck, C. P. 140
Newman, M. E. J. 204
New Public Management (NPM) 4,
    18–19, 128, 137, 198

New Public Service (NPS) 4, 128, 137–139
Ngoga, Martin 225
norms-based approach 6; *see also*
    compliance-based approach
Nostrom, K. 116
nudges 82–83
Nudge Unit 83

Obamacare 51
Oberholzer-Gee, Felix 84
objective responsibility 62
obligation to duty 58–59
Occupational Safety and Health
    Administration (OSHA) 84
Odeh, Diane L. 9, 31, 32–34
OECD Public Integrity Handbook (2020)
    75–76
Office of the Civil Service Commission
    (OCSC) 193
Office of the Comptroller General (CGU)
    155, 158–163
Office of the Decentralization of the Local
    Government Organization Committee
    (DLGO) 200
Office of Government Ethics (OGE)
    76–77
Office of the Inspector General (OIG)
    80–81
Office of the Ombudsman 226
Office of Personnel Management (OPM) 81
Office of Public Sector Anti-Corruption
    Commission (PACC) 193–194
Office of the Public Sector Development
    Commission (OPDC) 199–200
Office of the Special Prosecutor 226
Office of the Special Prosecutor Act 222
Oliveira Júnior, Temístocles Murilo de 10,
    147, 153, 165
Olken, B. A. 22
online training and employee development
    52
Opoku, A. 190
optimism 59
Ordóñez, L. D. 22
Organic Act on Counter Corruptions
    (2018) 188
Organisation for Economic Cooperation and
    Development (OECD) 19, 35, 75–76, 80,
    150–151, 155, 176, 193, 220
organizational culture 118
organizational ethics *see* ethics

organizational values *see* values
Orozco, David 194
Ouchi, W. G. 141
Owusu, G. M. Y. 205

Paine, L. S. 7, 93–101, 103, 219
Palidauskaite, J. 21
Papagni, E. 171–172, 174–175
Pareto improvement 51, 56
Park, H. 205
Park, T. Y. 83, 85
Paterson, T. A. 117–118
Pattison, S. 21
Pedersen, R. B. 147, 153
peer pressures 64–66
Pericles 29
Perlman, B. J. 101, 122, 129
perspective, processual 103–104
Pfeffer, J. 139
plan, do, check, and adapt (PDCA) cycle 103
Plunkett, W. 140
pluralistic theory of ethics program
    orientations 101
policy 43–44
Pongpisit, Tass 10–11
Poocharoen, Ora-Orn 190
practice, ethical 50–53
principle-agent (P-A) theory 203
Principle-Agent-Client (PAC) model 14,
    17, 23–24
prismatic societies 195, 198
private interest 44
professional codes 58–59; *see also*
    specific name
prosocial motivation 84
protections, employee 79
Public Ethics Commission (CEP) 146,
    155, 158, 160–163
Public Integrity System (SITAI) 148, 154
public interest 31, 44
Public Office Holders Declaration of
    Assets and Disqualifications Act 222
public policy 8, 51, 83
Public Sector Anti-misconduct
    Commission (PACC) 188
public sector ethics: African political
    leadership and 217–218; commitment
    to 1; comparative method and 7–8;
    compliance-integrity framework for
    5–7, 217–218; government legitimacy
    and 2–3; importance of 1–3; incentives
    and 72–74; leadership and 5, 112–115;
    norms-based approach to 6; overview
    8–11; rise in topic of 146; sanctions and
    72–74; self-enrichment opportunities
    and 2; traditional approaches to 3–5;
    uniqueness of 6; values-based approach
    to 6; *see also* ethics management
Public Sector Management and
    Governance Act (1999) 199
public sector values *see* values
public service motivation (PSM) 86, 118,
    121
Public Service Research Group 38
Public Transparency and Combating
    Corruption Council (CTPCC)
    158–159
public trust, stewardship of 86–87
Puglisi, Pino 176
punishment 9, 16, 19; *see also* sanctions
Putnam, Robert 60, 171–172

Quattrocolo, S. 177

Rahman, K. 229
Rawlings, Jerry John 222
Rawls, John 31, 59–60
reciprocity test 66
reflection, ethical 60
regime values 32
relativists 57
requisite variety 103–104
resources, stewardship of 31
responsibility 62–64, 73–74, 227–230
Rest, James 57
reversibility test 66
Revised Codes of Washington (RCW) 35
Rhode Island's Title 520 35
Richley, B. A. 140
Riggs, Frank W. 8, 195, 198
Rittel, H. 58
Rivera, Jason D. 10
Roberts, R. 18, 24, 76
Rohr, John 3, 32, 94, 100
role conflicts 63
role ethicality 118
role modeling 82, 115–116, 119
role model test 66
Ronquillo, J. C. 31
Roosevelt, Franklin Delano 42
Ruggiero, V. 174
rule-of-thumb ethics tests 66

rules-based approach *see* compliance-based approach
Ruona, W. E. A. 105
Rustichini, A. 84
Rwanda 218, 222–223, *224*, 225–226, 228, 230–231
Rwandan Bribery Index (RBI) 225

Sabharwal, M. 18–19, 24
Samms Brown, Chevanese 10
sanctions: dual approaches to ethics management and 72–74; enforcement and 73, 79; at institutional level 74–77; interconnectedness with incentives, accountability, and responsibility 73–74; at organizational level 74, 77–82; public sector ethics and 72–74
Sandburg, Carl 195
Sarbanes-Oxley Act (2002) 19
Sarkozy, Nicholas 181
Schargrodsky, E. 23
Schwartz, M. S. 38
self-enrichment opportunities 2
self-governance 95
self-regulation 23
Serious Fraud Office (SFO) 222
servant leadership *113*, 114–115
Sharp, Brett S. 9
Shinawatra, Yingluck 203
Sideri, M. 171
Social and Behavioral Sciences Team (SBST) 83, 88n1
social capital 60, 172, 174
social equity 31–32, 40, 43
social exchange theory 115–116
socialization 73, 131, 181
social learning theory 115
social media's effect on whistleblowing intention 206, **207–208**, 209, *209, 210*
social network analysis (SNA) approach 204, 211
Socratic Method 97
Sophie's Choice 61
Sørensen, D. L. 32
Special Commission of Investigation (CEI) 157
Spicer, M. 134
Standard of Ethical Conduct for Employees of the Executive Branch 76–77
Stansbury, J. 104
stewardship 31, 86–87

Stigler, J. 172
Stimmler-Caesmann, D. 101
Stone, C. 179–180
Stuke, M. E. 19
Styron, William 61
subjective responsibility 62
Sun, Rusi 10
Sunstein, C. R. 83
supervisory-level leaders 119–120
Svara, J. H. 32
Sweeting, Karen D. 10
systems theory 194

Tamronglak, Amporn 10–11
Tenbrunsel, A. E. 79
Thai-Corrective Action Against Corruption (Thai CAC) 191
Thai public integrity challenges: administrative corruption prevention and 190–191; anti-corruption agencies and 190–192, **191**; Anti-Corruption Organization of Thailand and 205; anti-corruption theories and 195, **196–197**, 198–200, **201**, 202–206; Big Six strategies and 195, 200, **201**; bureaucracy and 198; case study approach and 203–204; causes of corruption and 189–190; compliance-based approach and 193–195; confidence in government and 187; Constitution of 2017 and 188, 211–212; Corruption Perception Index ranking and 187; cultural practices and 190; deep democracy approach and 202–203; Executive Measure Act on Anti-Corruption Commission and 188; Global Corruption Barometer-Asia ranking and 187; good governance approach and 198–200, **199**, 202, 210–211; integrity-based approach and 193–195; legal framework against corruption and 188; Ministry-Level Operation Center Against Corruption and 190–191; modeling social media's effect on whistleblowing intention and 206, **207–208**, 209, *209*; National Anti-Corruption Commission and 191–192; National Command Center for Combating Corruption and 191; National Economic and Social Development Plan and 199; National

Reform Plan and 193; National Strategic Plan and 199; OECD Integrity Review and 205; Office of the Civil Service Commission and 193; Office of the Decentralization of the Local Government Organization Committee and 200; Office of Public Sector Anti-Corruption Commission and 188, 193–194; Office of the Public Sector Development Commission and 199–200; Organic Act on Counter Corruptions and 188; overview 10–11, 187, 212–213; principal-agent theory and 203; Public Sector Management and Governance Act and 199; research prospects and 210–211; social media's effect on whistleblowing intention and 206, **207–208**, 209, *209, 210*; social network analysis approach and 204, 211; Thai-Corrective Action Against Corruption and 191; theory of planned behavior and 11, 205–206; types of corruption and 188–189; whistleblowing and 205

theory of planned behavior (TPB) 11, 205–206

theory-testing causal (TTC) scheme 147, 152–154, 156

time pressures 64–66

Timmermans, J. 100

Traditional Public Administration 128, 136–137

training and employee development: absolutists and 57; analysis and, ethical 53–54; approaches to 50–51; codes of ethics and 37–38, 59; compliance and 68–69; concepts/frameworks for 56–67; conflicts of authority 63–64; decision-making and, ethical 60–62; design, effective 67, **68**; duty-oriented ethics and 58–59; effectiveness of 55, 68; ethics management and 49; group pressures and 64–66; hypothetical and, engaging 56; importance of 68; integrity and 68–69; for leadership 122; moral reasoning and 57; online 52; overview 9, 49–50, 68–69; practice and, ethical 50–53; professional codes and 58–59; reflection and, ethical 60; relativists and 57; responsibility and 62–64; rule-of-thumb ethics tests and 66;

setting 54–56; social capital and 60; time pressures and 64–66; training versus education and 51; veil of ignorance and 59–60; virtue ethics and 59; whistleblowing and 66–67; wicked problem and 58

transformational leadership 112

transparency 9, 19, 22, 44, 49, 63, 66, 87, 92, 127, 138, 140, 151, 159, 161–162, 187–188, 190, 193, 198–199, 200, 202, 204–205, 211–212, 228

Transparency International (TI) 2, 178, 187, 223

Transparency International Index 2

Tremblay, M. 100

Treviño, L. K. 6, 21, 65, 101, 107, 220

Trinidad and Tobago Police Service 16

Tuan Mansor, T. M. 206

unethical behavior/conduct 83–86, 111; *see also* corruption

United Nations Convention against Corruption (UNCAC) 155, 193

United Nations Office on Drugs and Crime 229

United States 2, 18–19, 29, 76, 81; *see also specific agency and regulation*

United States Code (USC) 76

Universal Design 35

utilitarianism/utilitarian approach 51, 56, 137

values: change and, adapting to 141–142; clarity of, lack of 131; code of 130; in codes of ethics 30–33, 39; communicating in workplace 128–135, *130*; conflicting 134; conformity and 134; culture of individuals and 135; decision-making and 128–129, 131, 135–136, 138–142; embedding 39; employee behavior and 135–136; employee support for 129; ethical behavior/conduct and 131, **132–133**, 134; ethics and 111; ethics management and 7; in Ghana 228–229; integrity and 111, 194; leadership and 127–128, 140–141; management based on 139–141; New Public Management and 128, 137; New Public Service and 128, 137–139; organizational 127–131, **132–133**, 134–139; overview 128; practice of 135–139; prioritization of

134–135; for public organizations 3–4; purpose of 127, 129; in Rwanda 228; shifts in 128, 136–139, **138**; Traditional Public Administration and 128, 136–137; utilitarian 3; *see also specific type*
values-based approach 6; *see also* integrity-based approach
values-based management (VBM) 10, 139–141
Van Montfort, A. 103
Vannucci, A. 175–176, 179
Van Wart, M. 3, 128, 134
variety, requisite 103–104
veil of ignorance 59–60
Verdier, T. 172
viral test 66
virtue ethics 59
virtue, promoting 32–33

Wainwright, P. 21
Waldo, D. 141
Warsta, M. 202
Washington State Code of Ethics for municipal officers 34–35

Watergate Scandal 76
Weathington, B. L. 142
Weaver, G. R. 6, 101
Webber, M. 58
Webster, D. W. 140
Welsh, D. T. 22
Western bias 107
West, J. P. 85
Whistleblower Protection Act 66
Whistleblowers Act (2006) 222
Whistleblowers Act (2007) 229
whistleblowing 66–67, 106, 205
wicked problem 58
Wise, C. R. 53
Witesman, E. M. 53
Working Group on Bribery in International Business Transactions 75
World Bank 170, 202, 223, 226

Yomnak, T. 204
Youth Employment Agency 226–227

Zhang, Yahong 10
Zittoun, P. 153

For Product Safety Concerns and Information please contact our
EU representative GPSR@taylorandfrancis.com Taylor & Francis
Verlag GmbH, Kaufingerstraße 24, 80331 München, Germany